Sarbanes-Oxley
Internal Controls

Sarbanes-Oxley Internal Controls

Effective Auditing with AS5, CobiT, and ITIL

ROBERT R. MOELLER

WILEY

John Wiley & Sons, Inc.

Library of Congress Cataloging-in-Publication Data:

Moeller, Robert R.
    Sarbanes-Oxley internal controls : effective auditing with AS5, CobiT and ITIL / Robert R. Moeller.
        p. cm.
    Includes index.
    ISBN 978-0-470-17092-2 (cloth : acid-free paper)
    1. Corporations—Auditing—Law and legislation—United States. 2. Auditing, Internal—Law and legislation—United States. 3. Corporate governance—Law and legislation—United States. 4. United States. Sarbanes-Oxley Act of 2002. I. Title.
    KF1446.M64 2008
    346.73'0664—dc22

                                                                    2007048496

Printed in the United States of America

10 9 8 7 6 5 4 3 2 1

Dedicated to my best friend and wife, Lois Moeller. Lois is my companion and partner whether we are on our Lake Michigan sailboat, skiing in Utah, traveling to all sorts of interesting places in the world, gardening in the backyard and cooking the results, or doing all sorts of home projects.

Contents

Preface

The passage of the Sarbanes-Oxley Act (SOx) in 2002 almost seems like distant history today. That legislation became effective after a series of accounting scandals led to the failure of several then major corporations, such as Enron and WorldCom, the conviction and imprisonment of multiple key executives, and the failure of the major public accounting firm, Arthur Andersen. With a time-based registration schedule to become SOx compliant, enterprises worldwide have struggled to change their processes to become compliant with all aspects of these new SOx procedures, and there certainly have been many "bumps" on that road along the way.

Perhaps the largest impediment to SOx compliance was that many enterprises initially struggled with the new internal control documentation requirements and the auditing standards rules published by the newly established Public Company Accounting Oversight Board (PCAOB) regulator. Enterprise management and their internal auditors often did not have consistent and well-recognized approaches for reviewing and understanding internal accounting controls and for complying with their external auditor's attest requirements. As SOx compliance was being rolled out to a wider group of enterprises both at smaller entities in the United States and others worldwide, there has been a recognized need for some changes surrounding SOx compliance.

The overall objective of this book is to describe and discuss some of the changes to SOx-related rules and supporting procedures since the legislation became U.S. law in 2002. Although there have not been any formal revisions to the basic SOx legislation at present, complying with SOx means following the rules established by the PCAOB and the SEC. A major objective of this book is to take another look at the more important aspects of SOx and to consider some of the changes and evolving standards that may make compliance easier for auditors and enterprise management.

This book will highlight some of the important or evolving new changes or frameworks that will make compliance with SOx less difficult for all enterprises, whether a domestic or a non-U.S. registrant. These same changes are more control risk based and applicable to all enterprises, despite their relative size. This text will look at the current status of SOx from the perspectives of internal audit, IT, and enterprise management:

■ *Chapter 1, Introduction: Sarbanes-Oxley and Establishing Effective Internal Controls.* We set the stage for the background and objectives of this book.

■ *Chapter 2, Sarbanes-Oxley Act Today: Changing Perspectives.* While the basic SOx legislation has never changed, the SEC and PCAOB rules surrounding it have changed, and the emphases on some aspects of SOx have been mixed. This chapter will provide a high-level overview of the Act, emphasizing areas where compliance practices are changing, such as for Section 404 internal control reviews. In other instances, the legislation remains on the books, and there has been minimal attention given to some rules. For example, many predicted considerable activity surrounding the whistleblower rules in SOx. That just has not happened, and we will review the current status of these rules. In general, this chapter will look at the rules and caution signs that are important in SOx today for all levels of management as well as for internal audit. The chapter will focus on areas that an internal auditor should consider when reviewing the adequacy of SOx-related internal control procedures in place.

■ *Chapter 3, AS5 Standards for Auditing Internal Controls.* This chapter will provide an overview of PCAOB auditing standards, with an emphasis on the newly issued and very important AS5 on auditing internal controls. These risk-based standards primarily apply to the manner in which external auditors perform their reviews, and each of the major public accounting firms has developed its own standards and interpretations of AS5 rules. This chapter will not attempt to critique public accounting audit procedures, but will outline the key elements of these standards that are important for managers and internal auditors in an enterprise.

■ *Chapter 4, Establishing Internal Controls Through COSO.* The COSO framework for organizing and understanding internal controls in all aspects of an enterprise has become the de facto standard in the United States as well as, to a growing extent, worldwide. While the COSO internal control framework has been available for many years, this chapter will look at COSO from the perspective of establishing effective internal controls in a SOx environment, and will also include guidance to help review the adequacy of COSO internal controls.

■ *Chapter 5, Using CobiT Framework to Improve SOx Controls and Governance.* As introduced in previous chapters, the CobiT framework is a useful tool for organizing and assessing both business and IT internal control processes. This chapter will provide a fairly detailed overview of the most recent version 4.1 release of CobiT and outline approaches for using CobiT to better manage internal controls under SOx. This chapter will also link CobiT with the ITIL framework introduced in Chapter 8. Although CobiT was originally developed just for IT auditors, the chapter will focus on CobiT as a tool and standard for establishing Enterprise-wide SOx compliance.

- *Chapter 6, Performing Section 404 Reviews Under AS5: An Ongoing Process.* Most larger, U.S.-based enterprises have now gone through several annual cycles of Section 404 reviews, with varying levels of frustration and pain. This chapter will discuss how to establish self-assessment processes and internal control improvement programs to help provide more value in SOx Section 404 processes. For the smaller-capitalization enterprises that are just beginning to become SOx compliant, this chapter will look at the risk-based changes to these rules to lessen burdens. For registrant enterprises, Section 404 rules can be tedious, but SEC and PCAOB changes have made this process less onerous. The goal should be to try to achieve process improvements through this SOx compliance work.

- *Chapter 7, Other SOx Requirements: Sections 302, 409, and Others.* Many business managers think of SOx only in terms of its Section 404 internal control requirements. This chapter discusses several other areas of SOx that are important to both managers and auditors today, with an emphasis on Section 302, where management is responsible for *signing off* on reported results, as well as a series of requirements for audit committees. In addition, we will consider the implications of Section 409R that are pushing management to move to almost real-time reporting of financial results—the continuous close. We are not there yet, but the requirement may soon have major implications for financial and IT managers and their processes.

- *Chapter 8, Using ITIL to Align IT with Business Processes.* The introductory paragraphs of this chapter talk about the growing recognition and importance of the ITIL set of best practices. This chapter will provide a complete overview of the ITIL service support and service delivery frameworks. The emphasis will be on the newly released version 3 of ITIL and how these best practice guidelines can be tied to CobiT when establishing effective SOx internal control processes. In particular, we will consider how compliance with ITIL best practices can change control processes and how these can be better built into improved management and internal audit processes.

- *Chapter 9, Importance of Enterprise Risk Management.* The COSO ERM framework is separate from the COSO internal control model and was released after SOx. This chapter introduces COSO ERM and discusses why considerations of risks are important at all levels. In addition, we will also look at risks from the basis of the new AS5 internal control standard as well as the newer AICPA risk-based guidance materials. The message here is that there is a need for a greater management consideration of risks when assessing internal controls.

- *Chapter 10, International Standards: ISO, Quality Auditing, and SOx.* With the increasing emphasis on globalization, appropriate ISO standards become important. This chapter will introduce two of these standards: ISO 9001 on quality management and ISO 17799 on IT security controls best practices. We will also look at the overall ISO processes and their increasing importance. In addition, the chapter will map the ISO 9001 quality management standard to SOx requirements to help better introduce quality management principles to SOx processes. The chapter will discuss internal and quality audit procedures in ISO environments.

- *Chapter 11, Internal Audit in a Sarbanes-Oxley Environment.* When SOx first went into effect, internal auditors had an undefined role in many enterprises. The term *internal audit* does not even appear in the text of the SOx legislation, and internal audit's SOx roles have differed across enterprises. The chapter will suggest some internal audit best practices in today's world of SOx internal controls. We will also introduce the new internal audit Body of Knowledge, recently released by its professional organization, the IIA,[1] and examine how the skills outlined here will allow internal auditors to be more effective in today's SOx environment.

- *Chapter 12, Importance of Effective Corporate Governance.* The whole legislative rationale behind SOx, when it first became law, was to prevent further Enron-type events and improve corporate governance. This chapter will discuss the implementation of whistleblower programs to report SOx potential infractions as well as other stakeholder-concern issues. The chapter outlines the new role of the *chief compliance officer* in an enterprise and also discusses the importance of both ethics programs and codes of conduct. The point here is that effective corporate governance practices are a major factor in building SOx internal controls throughout the enterprise.

---

[1] The Institute of Internal Auditors, Altamonte Springs, FL, www.theiia.org.

We have moved a long way since SOx was first enacted in 2002. Although the legislation has not changed, the administrative rules covering SOx compliance have, and we are all being impacted by new and evolving compliance standards. This book should bring the reader up to date on SOx today and introduce some important new and evolving processes for internal auditors and management in general.

Robert Moeller
April 2008

Introduction: Sarbanes-Oxley and Establishing Effective Internal Controls

As highlighted in the Preface, Sarbanes-Oxley (SOx) became U.S. law in 2002 and was the most sweeping set of new U.S. financial regulations since legislation passed in the 1930s aftermath of the Great Depression. SOx was enacted following a stream of major financial scandals at that time, with the accounting misdeeds at what was known as Enron Corporation[1] at the head of the pack, and lots of public concerns about poor corporate governance and public accounting practices. SOx created a new regulatory authority to set public accounting auditing standards, the Public Company Accounting Oversight Board (PCAOB), which essentially replaced the American Institute of Certified Public Accountants' (AICPA's) self-regulated auditing rule-setting authority, the Auditing Standards Board (ASB). Perhaps most important, SOx changed many of the processes that public companies had used for their own governance and to report their financial results to the Securities and Exchange Commission (SEC) in the United States and to the investing public. These SOx-initiated changes touched boards of directors, senior management practices, and the adequacy of the internal controls used to support financial and other processes.

SOx has had a major impact on the activities and responsibilities of auditors, whether external auditors, who now review the adequacy of reported standards following the PCAOB's auditing standards; internal auditors, who provide support and assurance to management and the audit committee on the adequacy of internal controls; or quality auditors, who assess the adequacy of other supporting processes. Each of these audit groups follows somewhat different standards and often has different objectives. Nevertheless, SOx has impacted all three audit groups. These are impacts that were developed by professional organizations and enterprises when

SOx was first launched and have evolved into various sets of best practices. The new PCAOB risk-based auditing standards, called *AS5*, however, have identified the need for all levels of auditors to change or at least reassess some of their SOx-related audit procedures.

The chapters that follow provide and discuss both definitions and suggested process improvements for these financial and operational internal controls, as well as supporting audit procedures. While many auditors are comfortable with these definitions, it may be sufficient here to say that internal controls are the types of procedures that consistently help assure that the "debits equal the credits" in accounting and business processes. Separation-of-duties rules are an example of a very simple internal control. One person might have the authority to initiate some financial transaction, but a separate person should be required to review and approve that same transaction. There is far less chance of fraud or even improper actions if two independent persons are involved in such a transaction. Although many enterprises have had good internal control rules and standards in place for many years, they often became much more informal between financial managers and the external auditors who reviewed and attested to them. Investigations into the failed Enron Corporation found many instances where its internal control processes, including overall corporate governance procedures, had very much failed.

The resultant corrective action here was the enactment of SOx. The U.S. Congress approved this legislation to correct what were viewed as a wide range of corporate governance and internal control shortcomings. The legislation was organized in a series of separate numbered sections covering specific areas of rules, which will be summarized in Chapter 2. As an example, SOx Section 404 rules require that management must first document and test their own internal controls, followed by an external auditor review and attestation of this enterprise internal control evaluation work. These SOx rules apply to any enterprise that has securities registered with the SEC. This could mean most major U.S. corporations, non-U.S. entities with stocks traded on U.S. exchanges, and many smaller enterprises.

Depending on an enterprise's size and annual report dates, SOx first became effective for larger corporations as early as late 2003. The rules have been relaxed and registration deadlines extended and further re-extended for foreign and smaller enterprises, but larger U.S. corporations today have been through at least two cycles of compliance with SOx rules. During its first years, SOx rules imposed major costs on many major U.S. corporations. As a result, many corporate managers and other observers saw little evidence of the value of these SOx-mandated internal control reviews. Perhaps it sounds a little too radical, but Scott McNealy, former CEO of Sun Microsystems, commented that the SOx procedures are like "throwing buckets of sand in the gears of a market economy."[2] Similarly, a poll of IBM clients revealed that SOx compliance ranked as "the biggest ineffective and wasteful use of time for IT departments." There have been numerous other very unfavorable comments about SOx since it became law. A general industry and commentator consensus was that some changes to the SOx rules were necessary.

Changes Since SOx Was First Introduced

SOx is a large piece of legislation covering a wide range of corporate governance issues. For example, there are rules that a chief executive officer (CEO) cannot give out what were sometimes lavish "consulting" contracts to nonemployee members of the board, that investment analysts covering public companies must follow a code of conduct, and that external auditors cannot take over the responsibility for a client's internal auditors through outsourcing. Nonemployee director "consulting" fees were allegedly being used by some CEOs to buy off members of their board, and some analysts were telling outside investors to invest in a stock while they told their own investment bankers that the same stock was "junk." Similarly, the internal auditor outsourcing prohibition was designed to improve independence between internal and external auditors. Perhaps the most important sections of SOx for general and financial management, the board, internal audit, and other key members of the management team are:

- Section 404: Management Assessment of Internal Controls
- Section 302: Corporate Responsibility for Financial Report
- Section 409: Real Time Issuer Disclosures

An introduction and recommendations for an effective implementation of each of these sections and others will be provided in greater detail in later chapters. While many portions of SOx may require changes and adjustments, the Section 404 rules on internal controls have caused management and internal auditors the greatest level of pain and suffering. Strictly interpreted, the legislation laid out some very tight internal control compliance rules. Initially, the PCAOB mandated that the existing ASB-issued auditing standards should be used. The promise was that the PCAOB would soon issue its own internal control auditing standards.

As any auditor or financial manager involved in the first two years of the SOx Section 404 reviews knows, this process was really a scramble at many affected U.S. corporations. The former "Big Five" public accounting firms had been reduced to four with the fall of Arthur Andersen after the failure of Enron, and those remaining firms seemed to take extra steps to comply with every letter of the new and very detail-oriented PCAOB issued SOx financial statement auditing rules, called *auditing standard number 2* (AS2). In addition, with Andersen gone, many corporations suddenly had a new external auditor.

An example of this complying-with-the-letter-of-the-law approach is the manner in which the issue of *materiality* was treated. Historically and before SOx, external auditors effectively ignored many smaller errors and omissions in their audits if they were not considered to be "material." Each of the major public accounting firms had their own measures here, but the idea was that if an error of misstatement was considered to be not material to the financial reporting results, the auditors would simply document the matter and move on. They considered errors that would not alter earnings per share by any more than some fraction of a cent not material. This concept is similar to speed limits on highways. If a road is posted for a speed limit of 65 miles per hour (mph), a driver faces little risk of being stopped for driving at 68 to 70 mph, under normal conditions. A driver speeding violation of 3 to 5 miles over the posted limit is just not considered to be material. Driving at more than 75 mph in a 65 mph zone may be another story.

Prior to SOx and its initial AS2 standards, these public accounting firm materiality measures seemed a little loose to outside observers. This author recalls one of his internal audit teams discovering an accounting error that involved tens of millions of dollars, only to have the external auditors tell the internal audit team that the error was not "material" for their purposes and to move on. The audit director—myself—and the audit team "bit their lips" on this matter. SOx rules have changed this. AS2 initially said that materiality should not be considered in reviews of internal controls. In effect, a $1 error was to be treated the same as a $1 million error—both were to be recorded as errors. Going back to our highway speeding example, this would say that a driver could be stopped and ticketed for speeding when driving 66 mph. Most drivers would view this as some level of lunacy.

While there were many other issues, the materiality consideration requirement was perhaps one of the issues raising the most complaints by corporate business executives in the United States. This attention to almost-trivial small problems took management's time and very much raised the costs of external audits. In its 2004 Audit Firm Performance Study, J.D. Power and Associates assessed SOx auditor performance through interviews with 1,007 audit committee chairs and 944 chief financial officers (CFOs). Nearly 90% of the CFOs involved in this study reported that the costs of compliance with SOx Section 404 requirements were greater than the resulting benefits. In addition, the study also showed that the accounting profession has experienced a decline in its performance ratings, with only 44% of the CFOs interviewed saying they had a high level of confidence in external auditors.[3]

These types of negative survey results, the throwing-sand-in-the-gearbox-type comments as mentioned above, and other negative comments encouraged some changed thinking in SOx rules by the PCAOB and the SEC. In addition, while SOx was originally enacted to cover all SEC registrants, including non-U.S. companies with securities traded through U.S. exchanges and very-low-capitalization smaller companies, many expressed concerns about the difficulty of establishing SOx compliance. To give non-U.S. and smaller corporations more time, the PCAOB extended the SOx compliance due dates for these two groups. Deadlines were extended and then extended again. At about the same time, the PCAOB announced in late 2006 that some of the more troublesome SOx compliance and enforcement rules would be changing.

The PCAOB has recently replaced its troublesome AS2 standard on auditing internal controls with an updated and more risk-based internal control auditing standard, AS5. Chapter 3 will introduce this new internal control auditing standard and will discuss how it impacts both internal and external auditors, as well as financial management. Some other PCAOB audit standards revisions are in process as this book goes to press, and the following section outlines some of these higher-level SOx changes. They will also be discussed more fully in Chapter 3.

PCAOB Internal Control Auditing Standards

As mentioned previously, auditing standards prior to SOx were developed and issued by the ASB, an appointed and very senior group of AICPA professionals. By auditing standards we are referring to the standards that external audit firms use to assess the accuracy and internal controls of the areas they are reviewing. They were published as numbered Statements of Auditing Standards (SASs). For example, SAS No. 99 describes the auditors' responsibility to identify fraud when performing reviews of financial statements. All AICPA external auditors are expected to follow this SAS No. 99 standard in any of their financial statement audits. For internal auditors, the Standards for the Professional Practice of Internal Auditing is a separate set of standards maintained by the Institute of Internal Auditors[4] (IIA) that applies to IIA members.

Developing and issuing SASs was a slow, ponderous process. Years ago, this author chaired a subcommittee of the ASB and was involved with developing and writing the then–SAS No. 55 on auditing IT general controls. It was not unusual to attend a subcommittee meeting to review an SAS draft where much discussion covered whether a section of the draft standard should say "the auditor *should*" or "the auditor *shall*." This is an important point, but such matters take lots of time.

After SOx became the law, the PCAOB stated that the existing SASs would be applicable until new replacements were issued. The PCAOB audit standards process here is different from the old days of the ASB. In the past, after the slow process of developing new SASs, the draft document was sent out for review and comment to a fairly wide group of auditing professionals. Their review comments would be used to modify the draft standard before developing the final SAS. This review process could take up to a year, followed by a long period prior to allow for actual implementation.

Although not that many standards have been issued to date, the PCAOB with SEC approval issues its auditing standards with a very limited time period for draft version review. For example, to initially aid external auditors in their reviews of internal controls, the PCAOB released its initial auditing standard on internal controls, called *AS2*,[5] quite quickly with limited time allowed for any draft version review and comment. That standard also was a good example of many of the common criticisms of governmental rules and regulations. AS2 contained over 150 pages of detailed requirements concerning the scope and reporting of an accounting firm's audit of a public company's internal controls over financial statements. This level of detail has often forced public accounting firms to audit internal controls too conservatively. Facing the risk of litigation for missing some small point, the public accounting firms under AS2 had a tendency to cover every point. Those original PCAOB-issued standards also gave no guidance to the enterprises on how to establish their internal controls.

AS2 caused a large amount of clamor and criticism, before the PCAOB announced its new internal control standard, AS5, in mid-2007. This more risk-based internal control auditing standard, described in Chapter 3, is a major change covering compliance with SOx Section 404 rules and should make the task less burdensome and onerous. In addition to Chapter 3 on AS5 and other PCAOB auditing standards, Chapter 9 talks about the importance of considering risks when establishing and evaluating internal controls, as well as the COSO Enterprise Risk Management (COSO ERM) framework.

Easing the Rules: Section 404 for Smaller Companies

When SOx was first launched, the SEC initially said it applied to any enterprise that had SEC-registered securities. While this seemed fair at first because a rule is a rule, this level of thinking meant that a relatively small, single business unit that has financed itself through a SEC-registered bond offering would be required to go through all of the same SOx procedures as a General Motors or a Microsoft Corporation. The PCAOB has given smaller enterprises more time to become compliant and has extended these due dates several times since. However, most reasonable persons would feel that a regional chain of mortuaries, with a single small SEC-registered bond issue, should not have to go through the same SOx procedures as a General Motors.

Beyond just extending due dates, the PCAOB has made things a bit easier for the smaller enterprise. The new AS5 rationalizes SOx requirements somewhat and calls for consideration to be given to risks when assessing internal controls. In addition, the PCAOB has chastised the major public accounting firms for being almost too dogmatic in the internal control review work. The rules are easing a little, and we are beginning to see more rational and hopefully less costly approaches here going forward.

Foreign Registrant Rules

The initial set of SOx rules applied to any and all non-U.S. corporations that had securities registered with the SEC. There are numerous companies around the world that want access to U.S. capital markets through listings on one of the U.S. exchanges. However, these SOx rules initially implied that the SEC was proposing to regulate all non-U.S. markets as well. This raised an initial clamor on a whole series of levels and non-U.S. company rules have been somewhat softened. Also, similar to smaller domestic company rules, filing deadlines have been extended multiple times here.

Despite somewhat relaxed foreign registrant rules, some corporations are seeking to de-list and move to places like the London Stock Exchange, but this de-listing process is difficult. Even worse, many newer or expanding non-U.S. corporations are really thinking twice about going through the rigors of compliance with SOx rules.

CONVERGING TRENDS: ITIL, COBIT, AND OTHERS

When SOx became effective in the United States, it established a require-ment for all SEC-registered enterprises to establish processes to better build, control, and monitor their internal controls. Almost concurrently with SOx, a raft of other U.S. regulations became law with often unpronounceable acronym names such as HIPAA, GLB, and FFIEC. In addition, with our increasing globalization of many areas of commerce, the International Orga-nization for Standards (ISO)[6] has released standards with long numerical names such as ISO 9000:2000 as the international standard for defining the characteristics of quality management systems. The manager in a SOx environment trying to tie all these controls together needs often some better guidance to sort out these standards and to achieve more effective SOx compliance. Although managers and auditors in the very first years of SOx

Section 404 used a variety of home-bred, ad-hoc procedures to better manage their internal controls, three important frameworks go under the names of CobiT, ITIL and relevant ISO standards. This chapter will provide some highlights, and each are discussed in chapters following.

CobiT: Control Objectives for IT

CobiT is a control framework that was introduced many years ago by a professional organization then known as the EDP[7] Auditors Association (EDPAA), and has evolved and been enhanced over the years. Discussed in more detail in Chapter 5, the Control Objectives for IT (CobiT) is a worldwide-recognized framework or model for managing controls—particularly IT controls—in the enterprise. We have all but forgotten the meaning of the acronym *EDP*, and the EDPAA professional organization first evolved into the Information Systems Audit and Control Association (ISACA) and then to the very timely named IT Governance Institute.[8]

The more traditional, finance-background manager might back away from anything with IT in its name as something for the techies in the enterprise, but because IT processes are so essential and pervasive in the enterprise, the CobiT framework is an excellent tool for managing and understanding all levels of internal controls. CobiT supports SOx internal controls through setting a model and standards for IT governance with the concepts that an enterprise's IT resources should be aligned with the business, that they are resources that should be used responsibly, and that IT-related risks should be managed appropriately.

An earlier version of the CobiT framework was used by some enterprises during their first cycle of SOx 404 internal control assessments. The framework has since been upgraded and is now better linked to concepts such as Information Technology Infrastructure Library (ITIL) as well as to SOx. CobiT in its newest version 4.1 is a useful framework for documenting and understanding internal controls at all levels.

ITIL for IT Service Management

We have described CobiT as a framework that evolved from the IT audit profession—once called *computer auditors*—into an excellent framework for managing SOx corporate governance processes and overall IT governance. Discussed and introduced more fully in Chapter 8, ITIL is a set of published best practices that was first primarily used in essentially IT areas, but today is valuable for better managing SOx internal controls. ITIL got its start as a set of published books put together by the British government Central Computer and Telecommunications Agency, now the Office of Government Commerce (OGC). ITIL evolved into a series of primarily IT-oriented best practices that first became widely used in the European Union (EU), and then gravitated to Australia, New Zealand, and finally Canada. Today, it is becoming widely recognized in the United States as well, with many enterprises embracing ITIL best practices. Names change over time, and many IT organizations are beginning to refer to this set of best practices as IT Service Management or ITIL Service Management. We will generally refer to this set of best practices as just ITIL.

In a somewhat different perspective than CobiT, ITIL is a tool to better align IT processes with overall business operations and is important for better understanding IT-related SOx internal controls in the enterprise. ITIL best practices are particularly valuable for matching or mapping IT operations and both CobiT and SOx internal accounting control points with what ITIL characterizes as customer relationship management. ITIL suggests that any non-IT business process has strategic, tactical, and operational elements. IT general and service-level management as well as change management processes should be in place to handle the supply-and-demand issues between these customer and IT organizations or entities. Exhibit 1.1 shows this relationship, and linkages at various levels. For example, service levels are defined and connected between business budget holders who contract for services and IT who manages this service level delivery. Chapter 8 will describe this relationship in greater detail.

ITIL represents an important set of best practices that will help an enterprise to better manage some and improve their internal controls. For example, IT and application system change management are important

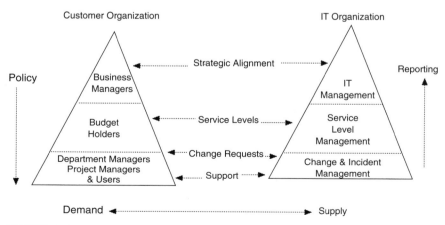

EXHIBIT 1.1 ITIL Customer Relationship Management

internal control processes for the entire enterprise. There should be a robust set of IT applications covering essentially all of its applications. However, internal controls break down if there are no strong processes in place to make certain that all such changes are properly authorized, tested, and otherwise approved before being placed into production.

ITIL best practices, as outlined in Chapter 8, provide some useful guidance for helping an enterprise to achieve SOx Section 404 compliance. In addition, this relationship with ITIL will help an enterprise to be compliant with both evolving IT best practices and SOx internal control requirements. ITIL provides an important set of tools to help improve the quality of an enterprise's IT operations.

ISO and Standards Convergence

As SOx takes on more and more of a worldwide focus and as all of our business operations become more global, the international standards known as ISO[9] are becoming important to U.S. enterprises. Although ISO standards have not historically directly impacted that many SOx activities, compliance with ISO standards is taking on an increasingly high level of importance, particularly as we become more of a global economy. Although these standards cover a wide variety of common processes and products (such as standards for the thread dimensions in an automobile bolt), the ISO standards covering quality management are important for maintaining effective internal controls.

ISO standards always have a number associated with them. For example, there is a series of ISO 9000 international standard standards for defining quality systems. Our goal is not to provide more than an overview of ISO standards, but Chapter 10 provides an description of several of the more important standards for internal controls improvement purposes. Enterprises worldwide use these standards, and their compliance is attested through a separate audit process.

Just as SOx or similar governance "SOx-like" guidance become rules on a worldwide basis, applicable ISO standards take an increasingly important role. Business professionals, and particularly internal and quality auditors, need to have an understanding of applicable standards such as ISO 9001 on effective quality management systems and how they map to SOx internal controls.

Whether it be SOx, CobiT, ITIL or others, a strong message throughout the following chapters of this book is that there is a growing convergence between these various governance standards and best practices. Internal audit standards are developed by their IIA professional organization, but quality management standards are issued by the Quality Audit Division of the American Society for Quality.[10] Although these two internal audit disciplines have operated in very separate camps over the years, their practices are growing closer as time goes on.

We may soon see a growing level of convergence between the skills and practices of IIA-based internal auditors and those of quality auditors going forward. As discussed in Chapter 11, this an area of growing standards convergence. They will become important as all levels in the enterprise realize the growing significance of standards such as ITIL. There is always lots of new material to learn and master; subsequent chapters will attempt to introduce some of these very important areas.

ENDNOTES

1. For more information on Enron, a good read is Kurt Eichenwald, *A Conspiracy of Fools: A True Story*, Broadway, 2005.
2. *The Behind Business Line*, February 9, 2006, //www.thehindubusinessline.com/ 2006/02/09/stories/2006020900241100.1.
3. *Fraud* magazine, March/April 2005.
4. The Institute of Internal Auditors, Altamonte Springs, FL, www.theiia.org.
5. Auditing Standard No. 2: "An Audit of Internal Control Over Financial Reporting Performed in Conjunction with an Audit of Financial Statements," www.pcaobus.org.
6. A French-language, Geneva, Switzerland–based organization; the correct acronym is ISO, www.iso.org.
7. EDP is an early-days computer system acronym that stands for *electronic data processing*.
8. IT Governance Institute, Rolling Meadows, IL, www.itgi.org.
9. The Geneva, Switzerland–based International Organization for Standards at www.iso.org, issues numbered ISO standards covering a wide variety of processes.
10. American Society for Quality, www.asq.org.

CHAPTER **2**

Sarbanes-Oxley Act Today:
Changing Perspectives

As a response to the accounting misdeed–related failures of such then-major corporations as Enron and WorldCom, the Sarbanes-Oxley Act (SOx) was passed in 2002 with its Securities and Exchange Commission (SEC)–defined administrative rules ready early in 2003. A major component of SOx was the Public Company Accounting Oversight Board (PCAOB), an independent entity to set auditing standards and to govern and regulate the public accounting industry. These were major changes that have impacted corporate governance, financial accounting, and auditing processes, first in the United States and now worldwide. SOx is a wide-ranging set of new requirements that has redefined how we both govern public enterprises and attest that their reported financial results are fairly stated.

Most of the attention on SOx requirements since its enactment has been on the internal control attestation rules, which are part of Section 404 of the Act and will be discussed in Chapter 6, as well as what are called the Section 302 rules, discussed in Chapter 7, making management responsible for its reported financial statements. Both of these areas attracted a major degree of effort and concerns as major corporations began to establish compliance with SOx in its first years starting after 2002. Other portions of the legislation just have not received that much attention or have not caused major compliance concerns. An example is a SOx requirement that audit committees establish what are called *whistleblower programs* to report fraudulent accounting anonymously. Although this first appeared to be a significant requirement, it has not received that much attention or activity to date.

This chapter will provide an overview of the SOx legislation, with an emphasis on the areas that are most important to corporations today as well as their managers and auditors. Much of the impact of the legislation depends on the detailed rules that are released by the PCAOB to interpret the SOx legislation. Perhaps the most significant of these are the newly released AS5 auditing standards discussed in Chapter 3. However, this chapter also will highlight other important SOx rules and how SOx is evolving into a worldwide global standard. The SOx legislation was drafted in a one-size-fits-all manner, suggesting that the SOx and related SEC rules applied to any entity, despite its home country or size. They applied to any security registered with the SEC. The general words used in legislation, however, are defined through formal rules established by a regulatory authority. For SOx, general guidance is established by the SEC with specific rules drafted by the PCAOB. Although such rules are subject to revision, this chapter will focus on the evolving rules that help to make SOx a worldwide global governance and internal control standard.

SARBANES-OXLEY ACT: KEY ELEMENTS

The official name for this U.S. federal law to regulate the accounting and auditing practices of publicly traded companies is the "Public Accounting Reform and Investor Protection Act." It became law in August 2002, with most of the final detailed rules and regulations released by the end of the following year. That title being a bit long, business professionals generally refer to it as the Sarbanes-Oxley Act from the names of its principal congressional sponsors. Still too long of a name, some refer to it as *SOx* and others as *Sarbox*, among many other variations.

SOx has introduced a totally changed process of issuing external auditing standards, reviewing external auditor performance, and giving new governance responsibilities to senior executives and board members. The PCAOB rule-setting authority issues financial auditing standards and monitors external auditor professional ethics and performance. As happens with all comprehensive federal laws, an extensive set of specific regulations and administrative rules has been developed by the SEC from the broad guidelines in the SOx text.

U.S. federal laws are organized and issued as separate sections of legislation called *titles* with numbered sections and subsections under each. Much of the actual SOx text only mandates rules to be issued by the responsible SOx agencies, the SEC and the PCAOB. Some of these specific SOx rules to be developed may not be that significant to internal or external auditors and business professionals. For example, Section 602 (d) of Title I states that the SEC "shall establish" minimum professional conduct standards or rules for SEC practicing attorneys. While perhaps good to know, many also will typically not be that concerned about these specific to-be-promulgated rules. Other to-be-issued SOx rule requirements were of great interest as industry waited for the final rules were issued. For example, Section 407 of Title I stated that the SEC will set rules requiring that at least one audit committee member be a "financial expert." While the definition of a *financial expert* went through multiple debates and revisions before it was settled, this particular rule is important for a chief audit executive (CAE) who will be dealing with both members of the audit committee and senior management. That financial expert should have some understanding of an effective internal control review process as well as audit committee and internal audit interactions.

Exhibit 2.1 summarizes the major components or sections of the SOx legislation, and the sections following describe the SOx legislation on a title-by-title basis. Most of the attention in this book is given to those areas that are more significant to internal auditors and business professionals. Our intent is not to reproduce the full text of this legislation—it can be found on the Web[1]—but to highlight portions of the law that are significant to both audit and business professionals today. Of interest, although an enterprise's internal control processes very much rely on both their external and internal auditors, the original SOx legislation makes almost no direct references to the important roles and responsibilities of internal auditors. The importance of internal audit in the overall SOx internal control review process has been highlighted in the new AS5 rules discussed in Chapter 3. In addition, Chapter 11 discusses the overall role of internal audit in today's SOx environment.

Title I: Public Company Accounting Oversight Board

The legislation starts with new regulatory rules for external auditors. Prior to SOx, the American Institute of Certified Public Accountants (AICPA) had guidance-setting responsibility for all external audit, public accounting firms through its administration of the Certified Public Accountant (CPA) test and its restriction of AICPA membership to CPAs. State Boards of Accountancy actually licensed CPAs, but the AICPA had overall responsibility for the profession. Auditing standards were set by the AICPA's Auditing Standards Board (ASB) and new or revised standards were set through a process that involved member task forces developing proposed changes, extensive review of draft versions, and then their eventual issuance as external audit standards. Although some basic auditing standards (generally accepted auditing standards (GAAS)) have been in place over the years, newer standards were released as a series of specific, numbered auditing standards called Statements of Auditing Standards (SAS). Much of GAAS was just good auditing practices such as the understanding that certain transactions must be backed by appropriate documentation. The SASs covered more

Section	Subject	Rule or Requirement
101	Establishment of PCAOB	Overall rule for the establishment of PCAOB including membership requirements.
104	Accounting Firm Inspections	Schedule for registered firm inspections.
108	Auditing Standards	The PCAOB will accept current but will issue new standards.
201	Out of Scope Practices	Outlines prohibited practices such as internal audit outsourcing, bookkeeping, and financial systems design.
203	Audit Partner Rotations	The audit partner and the reviewing partner must rotate off an assignment every 5 years.
301	Audit Committee Independence	All audit committee members must be independent directors.
302	Corp. Responsibility for Financial Reports	The CEO and CFO must certify the periodic financial reports.
305	Officer and Director Bars	If received as part of fraudulent/illegal accounting, the officer or director is required to personally reimburse funds received.
404	Internal Control Reports	Management is responsible for an annual assessment of internal controls.
407	Financial Expert	One audit committee director must be a designated financial expert.
408	Enhanced Review of Financial Disclosures	The SEC may schedule extended reviews of reported information based on certain specified factors.
409	Real-Time Disclosure	Financial reports must be distributed in a rapid and current manner.
1105	Officer or Director Prohibitions	The SEC may prohibit an officer or director from serving in another public company if guilty of a violation.

EXHIBIT 2.1   Sarbanes-Oxley Act Key Provisions Summary
Source: COSO Enterprise Risk Management: Understanding the New Integrated ERM Framework, Robert R. Moeller, page 183. Copyright © 2007 John Wiley & Sons. Reprinted with permission of John Wiley & Sons, Inc.

specific areas requiring better definition. SAS No. 79, for example, defined internal control standards and SAS No. 99 was titled "Consideration of Fraud in a Financial Statement Audit." The AICPA's code of professional conduct stated that CPAs were required to follow and comply with those auditing standards when applicable.

The AICPA's GAAS and numbered SAS standards were accepted by the SEC in the past and set the foundation for what constituted the reviews and tests necessary for a certified audited financial statement. Much has now changed since the passage of SOx! The accounting scandals that led to the passage of SOx signaled that the process of establishing auditing standards was broken, and SOx has taken this audit standard-setting process out of the major public accounting firm–dominated AICPA and given this responsibility to the PCAOB, a nonfederal, nonprofit corporation with the responsibility to oversee all audits of corporations subject to the SEC.

The PCAOB does not replace the AICPA but assumes responsibility for many functions that were formally managed by AICPA members for themselves. The AICPA continues to administer the CPA examination, with its certificates awarded on a state-by-state basis. It also sets auditing standards for private, non-SEC organizations. The PCAOB is defined in Title I of SOx and is a regulatory entity only for external and not internal auditors. However, because of the changes in the audit process and corporate governance, PCAOB rules will impact the manner in which internal auditors coordinate their work with external auditors as well as the overall process of corporate governance.

The PCAOB releases administrative rules to support, better define, and enforce the SOx legislation. As this book goes to press, there have been five standards through the very important AS5 (see www.pcaobus.org) discussed in Chapter 3.

PCAOB Administration and Public Accounting Firm Registration   The PCAOB is administered through five Board members appointed by the SEC with three of them *required* to be public, non-CPA members. SOx is insistent that the PCAOB not be dominated by CPA and public accounting firm interests. A Board member can be considered as one of the two CPA representatives even if that member was only *formerly* a practicing CPA. In addition, the PCAOB chairperson must not have been a practicing CPA for at least five years. These are strong rules with an objective to keep the PCAOB from being dominated by CPAs and public accounting firms. When the SOx legislation was being drafted, the AICPA mounted a major lobbying effort to keep the PCAOB under CPA control. Ongoing accounting scandals beyond Enron, however, made its case worse, and the AICPA has lost much of its authority and responsibility for self-regulation. The PCAOB is responsible for overseeing and regulating all public accounting firms that practice before the SEC, and its responsibilities include:

- **Register the public accounting firms that perform audits of corporations.** This registration is much more detailed than just filling out an application form and beginning business. The registering external audit firm must disclose the fees collected from the corporations it has audited, provide data on its audit and quality standards, provide detailed information regarding the CPAs who will be performing its audits, and disclose any pending criminal, civil, or administrative actions. A firm can be denied the right to register due to any PCAOB questions regarding its background.
- **Establish auditing standards.** These standards include auditing, quality control, ethics, independence, and other key audit areas. Although many of these PCAOB standards continue to follow earlier standards issued by the AICPA's Auditing Standards Board (ASB), new PCAOB standards will be gradually released as required. Perhaps the most significant have been AS2 and its AS5 successor (discussed in Chapter 3). As there are continuing demands for more continuous auditing and health and safety sustainability reporting audits, we can probably expect a whole different dimension of these standards in the future.
- **Conduct inspections of registered public accounting firms.** The PCAOB has responsibility for quality-related reviews of registered firms. In the past, this was the AICPA's peer-review process, but the major firms often found little to say in criticism of their peers. Activities are continuing here, and the PCAOB continues to perform reviews at the major firms as well as at many smaller practitioners.
- **Conduct investigations and disciplinary procedures.** These procedures apply to an entire registered firm or just to individuals within those firms. Wrongdoing discovered in formal investigations can result in sanctions that would prohibit a firm or an individual auditor from performing PCAOB audits.
- **Perform other standards and quality functions as the Board determines.** The PCAOB has indicated that it may get into other areas to protect investors and the public interest. There has been little activity here, but as the need for auditing services evolves, these standards may change and evolve.
- **Enforce SOx compliance.** The paragraphs that follow outline many of the SOx rules. The PCAOB is responsible for enforcing compliance to SEC auditing rules beyond the SOx overall legislation. This results in a variety of administrative law actions or other procedures as appropriate.

There is a required annual registration process for public accounting firms practicing before the Board. This registration application data will become public record, as will litigation matters and other traditionally somewhat confidential data about those firms.

This registration process and the available published data may be of particular value for an organization that is not using one of the Big Four accounting firms (once called the Big 8 and eventually the Big Five, now sometimes called the *Final Four*). There are many medium-sized and smaller but very highly credible public accounting firms that will provide an enterprise with excellent, high-quality services. However, if an organization is using one of these smaller public accounting firms, it would be very prudent for the entity's financial management to check these PCAOB registration records.

Auditing, Quality Control, and Independence Standards   SOx's Title I, Section 103 gives PCAOB the authority to establish auditing and related attestation standards, quality control standards, and ethics standards for registered public accounting firms to use for their financial audits. As discussed, this authority had been built over many years by the AICPA's Auditing Standards Board. Using impartial language, the SOx text recognizes that new PCAOB auditing standards may be based on "proposals from one or more professional groups of accountants or advisory groups." For example, the original SOx legislation only referred to an internal control standard, but PCAOB rules subsequently mandated use of the Committee of Sponsoring Organizations (COSO) internal control framework, as is discussed in Chapter 4. As we move to a greater global economy and as SOx becomes more of a worldwide standard, we can expect to see the international accounting standards discussed in Chapter 10 having an increasing influence.

The Institute of Internal Auditors' (IIA's) Standards for the Professional Practice of Internal Auditing, discussed in Chapter 11, fall into this class of standards and other professional-groups categories as well. They cover the work of internal auditors that may be used to support an external auditor's formal work in some areas, such as internal controls. IIA standards are designed to support all internal auditor review work but are not for an external auditor's audit and attest work. When an internal auditor has been working in support of the external audit counterparts on some review task, the work should follow PCAOB audit guidelines.

Although formal rules are still not in place in some areas, SOx legislation mandates that the PCAOB develop standards with the following minimum requirements:

- **Audit workpapers retention.**   Although this standard covers many areas, workpaper retention is defined in AS3, Audit Documentation.

Audit workpapers and other materials to support the auditor's report must be maintained for a period of not less than seven years. This requirement is certainly in response to an infamous event just prior to the fall of Enron and the subsequent end of its auditor, Arthur Andersen. While Enron was still in operation but under some financial threats, the SEC announced that it was going to conduct an onsite investigation at Enron. Enron's external auditor, then Arthur Andersen, used an internal firm policy to justify destruction of all but their most current documentation pertaining to its audit work at Enron. This was a motivating factor that led to SOx and to this retention rule.

■ **Concurring partner approval.** External audit standards now require a concurring or second-party approval for each audit report issued. This can be done by another member of the same public accounting firm or an independent reviewer. The major public accounting firms have all had independent review processes for their issued reports and workpapers, but these were often done more for an after-the-fact quality control review. Under SOx rules, a second external audit partner must "sign on the dotted line" and personally and professionally commit to the findings and conclusions in any audit.

The *concurring opinion* here refers to the external auditor's formal opinion, in the conclusion of an audit, stating the client's financial reports are "fairly stated" in accordance with generally accepted accounting principles (GAAP). Because of different interpretations of various GAAP rules in some audit situations, SOx has mandated those second, concurring opinions. The opinions expressed in internal audit reports typically do not require that same level of gravity. For example, an audit report on the internal auditor's observation of a physical inventory would not need a concurring opinion if the report covered primarily compliance observation findings, such as the failure to distribute documented counting instructions. However, if, in the internal auditor's opinion, the inventory taking was so lacking in internal controls that the final results might be suspect, a second concurring or review auditor opinion might be helpful.

■ **Scope of internal control testing.** PCAOB rules require the external auditor to describe the scope of testing processes as well as the findings from that testing. The result of this was much more detailed descriptions of testing procedures and led to extensive testing procedures under the AS2 rules. Prior to SOx, external auditors had sometimes used increasingly strained theories to justify the most minimal of test sizes. External auditors were frequently faced with very large test populations and then tested only a very small number of items. If no problems were found, they expressed an opinion for the entire population based on the results of this very limited sample. They now must pay greater attention to the scope and reasonableness of their testing procedures. There are no formal rules here; the new AS5 rules allow for the consideration of risk, but documentation must clearly describe the scope and extent of testing activities.

■ **Evaluation of internal control structure and procedures.** This is an area where we have seen considerable changes. The initial guidance was that ASB auditing standards were to be followed, and this included SAS No. 78 with its mandate to use the COSO model of internal control. The PCAOB then released the very detailed rule-based AS2 standards followed by our current risk-based AS5 procedures for the review and evaluation of internal controls. SOx rules further specify that an external auditor's evaluation contain a description of material weaknesses in such internal controls as well as any material noncompliance found on the basis of the auditor's testing.

Internal control reviews are areas where internal auditors can very much assist the enterprise and senior management through their focused reviews. If an internal audit function is emphasizing the COSO model as the basis for its current internal control review, the staff performing those reviews should take strong steps to get up to speed in developing a good understanding of the COSO model. For internal auditors, the bar has really been raised. They are required to document and update the effectiveness of internal controls, and an absence of this documentation, per SOx, should be considered a weakness of internal controls. This really puts a different spin on many internal auditor reviews that have been performed over the years. Internal auditors have frequently reviewed systems, found them to have adequate internal controls, but then only reported an audit finding that documentation for the system reviewed was out of date or otherwise deficient. Such matters were reported, but no one cared that much. AS2 put these small-matter internal control exceptions under the spotlight, but AS5 now says the same bright spotlight does not have to be used for the more minor, less-risky weaknesses.

■ **Audit quality control standards.** In the past, the AICPA's quality standards were fairly high level and limited to its peer review processes for large firms, but the AICPA is now registered under ISO 9000 quality standards. The growing importance of these ISO standards is discussed in Chapter 10. ISO is a worldwide standards process, and all auditors should gain a general understanding of the ISO process and how it fits into their organization. In addition, IIA standards, discussed in Chapter 11, require that internal audit departments have a quality improvement and assessment program. This guidance should help the internal auditors better comply with ISO 9000 and SOx quality standards.

While the PCAOB has not issued its own specific quality standards, the SOx legislation states that every registered public accounting firm will be required to have standards related to:

- Monitoring of professional ethics and independence
- Procedures for resolving accounting and auditing issues within firm
- Supervision of audit work
- Hiring, professional development, and advancement of personnel
- Standards for acceptance and continuation of engagements
- Internal quality inspections
- Other quality standards to be prescribed by the PCAOB

These are general quality standards, and we can expect that over time the PCAOB or some other body will release a specific set of quality standards that can be applied to all registered public accounting firms, if not to all firms. In a similar sense, the IIA or some other body may establish a set of quality standards that will be applicable to all internal audit departments.

Some business professionals or even internal auditors might ask, What does all of this PCAOB standards stuff have to do with me? For example, some internal auditors may claim they have their IIA Standards for the Professional Practice of Internal Auditing, and there is little need to become concerned here. However, PCAOB auditing standards impact business professionals and internal auditors as well as external audit. SOx rules for corporate governance very much increase the role and responsibility of the audit committee for many, and the internal audit function will become even more closely aligned with the audit committee. PCAOB standards cause significant changes in the manner in which internal audits are planned, performed, and reported. An organization's external auditors will be working under the SOx rules, and the audit committee will expect its external and internal auditors to operate in a consistent manner. Whether it is quality standards, effective internal control testing, or the abovementioned concurrent approvals, an internal audit department should begin to modify its procedures to comply with the PCAOB standards, with an emphasis on the AS5 standards discussed in Chapter 3.

Inspections, Investigations, and Disciplinary Procedures   The PCAOB is empowered to conduct a continuing program of registered accounting firm inspections to assess their compliance with SOx rules, SEC rules, and professional standards. These quality inspections were initially scheduled to be performed annually at the larger public accounting firms and once every three years if a registered firm conducts less than 100 financial statement audits. This was a fairly aggressive schedule, and the PCAOB initially got off to a slow start in initiating these reviews after SOx became law. The review process now is up to speed and external audit firms in the United States can expect regular PCAOB reviews. The inspections cover audits completed during the prior period and focus on selected offices and individual auditors. The reviews evaluate the quality control system of the firm reviewed as well as documentation and communication standards. The inspections are documented in a formal inspection report that is to be reported to the SEC and state Boards of Accountancy. When appropriate, the PCAOB will initiate disciplinary procedures.

Title I, Section 105 of SOx covers public accounting firm investigations and disciplinary procedures in some detail. The PCAOB is authorized to compel testimony, to require the production of audit work, and to conduct disciplinary proceedings. The latter may range from temporary suspension of an individual or firm, to substantial fines, or even to being barred from the profession. The enforcement process follows the same general rules as for any federal administrative legal actions, whether violation of an SEC securities rule or a pollution complaint under the Environmental Protection Agency (EPA).

Section 106 consists of one brief paragraph on foreign public accounting firms that has resulted in much controversy. It says that if any foreign public accounting firm prepares an audit report for an SEC-registered corporation, that foreign public accounting firm is subject to the rules of the PCAOB and related SEC rules. In addition, the Board can require those foreign firms to register under SOx rules, with their audit workpapers and the like subject to inspection.

Our multinational world is filled with many non-U.S. public accounting firms. These foreign public accounting firms are governed by their own national public accounting standards, some of which are modeled on GAAP but others of which follow the International Accounting Standards discussed in Chapter 10. No matter what standards they had followed, SOx says that they will be subject to these SOx rules if one of their clients has its securities listed on an SEC-regulated stock exchange, such as the New York Stock Exchange or NASDAQ. This has resulted in some firms no longer wanting to be listed on a U.S. stock exchange. Their argument is that the reach of U.S. law is too long and broad. The SEC and the PCAOB have somewhat delayed requirements here, and we will be seeing changes going forward with a greater reliance on International Accounting Standards.

Accounting Standards   Title I concludes with one section that affirms that the SEC has authority over the PCAOB, including final approval of rules, the ability to modify PCAOB actions, and the removal of Board members. While the PCAOB is an independent entity responsible for regulating the public accounting industry, the SEC is really the final authority. SOx recognizes the U.S. accounting standards–setting body, the Financial Accounting Standards Board (FASB), by saying that the SEC may recognize "generally accepted" accounting standards set by "a private entity" that meets certain criteria. The Act then goes on to outline the general criteria that the FASB has used for setting accounting standards.

There is and always has been a major difference between accounting and auditing standards. The former define some very precise accounting rules, such as saying a certain type of asset can be written off or depreciated over no more than X years. These are the principles called *GAAP*. Auditing standards are much more conceptual, highlighting areas that an auditor *should consider* when evaluating controls in some area. These auditing standards became increasingly loosely interpreted as we went into the 1990s, as management was frequently under pressure to continually report short-term earnings growth, and the external auditors often refused to say "no." The result was the financial scandals of Enron and others as well as Andersen's audit document destruction when it received news that the SEC was coming. SOx and the PCAOB now oversee public accounting companies.

Title II: Auditor Independence

Internal and external auditors have historically been separate and independent resources. External auditors were responsible for assessing the fairness of an enterprise's internal control systems and the resultant published financial reports, while internal auditors served management in a wide variety of other areas. In the early 1990s, this separation began to change with external audit firms taking overall responsibility for some internal audit functions as well. This started when larger enterprises began to *outsource* some of their non-core functions such as their employee cafeteria or a plant janitorial function. The thinking was that since employees who worked in these specialized areas were not really part of core enterprise operations, and an enterprise's janitorial function or other non-core functions might benefit all parties if they were outsourced to another company that specialized in areas such as janitorial services for many other enterprises. The previous in-house janitors would be transferred to the janitorial services company and, in theory, everyone would benefit. The enterprise that initiated the outsourcing would experience lower costs by giving a non-core function, janitorial services, to a company that better understood it. The outsourced janitors, in this example, also might have both better career possibilities and better supervision.

Internal audit outsourcing started in the late 1980s. External audit firms went to their client firms' management and offered to outsource or take over their existing internal audit functions. The idea appeared to make sense to senior management and audit committees on many levels. Senior management often did not really understand the distinctions between the two audit functions and were often more comfortable with their external auditors. In addition, senior management and audit committee members were often enticed by the promised lower costs of internal audit outsourcing. Although the IIA initially fought against the concept, internal audit outsourcing continued to grow through the 1990s. Although a few independent firms made efforts to get into this market, internal auditor outsourcing continued to be the realm of the major public accounting firms.

Internal audit outsourcing became very much of an issue with the Enron scandal, where its internal audit function had been almost totally outsourced to its external audit firm, Arthur Andersen. Both officially Andersen employees with different reporting relationships, the two audit groups worked side by side in Enron's offices. After Enron's fall, many raised after-the-fact questions about how that outsourced internal audit department could have been independent of Andersen. It would have been very difficult in this environment for internal audit to raise some concern to the audit committee about the quality of their external auditors. This potential conflict became a reform issue for SOx.

Limitations on External Auditor Services   SOx Section 201 has made it illegal for a registered public accounting firm to contemporaneously perform both audit and non-audit services for a client. The prohibitions include internal auditing, many areas of consulting, and senior officer financial planning. For the internal audit professional, the most significant element here is that it is illegal for a registered public accounting firm to provide internal audit outsourcing services if it is also doing the financial statement external audit work. This means that the major public accounting firms are now essentially out of the internal audit outsourcing business. Other firms, including independent spinoffs from public accounting firms or specialized internal audit consulting firms such as Jefferson Wells, can still provide internal audit outsourcing, but the era when an internal audit professional became an employee of his or her public accounting firm is over.[']

In addition to the ban on providing outsourced internal audit services, SOx prohibits public accounting firms from providing other services, including:

- **Financial information systems design and implementations.**   Public accounting firms had been installing financial systems—often of their own design—for clients for many years. They often came back and reviewed the internal controls of the systems they had just installed—a significant conflict of interest. This is no longer allowed.

- **Bookkeeping and financial statement services.** Public accounting firms previously offered accounting services to their clients in addition to doing the audits. Even for major corporations, it was not unusual for the team responsible for the overall financial statement audit to also do much of the work necessary in building the final consolidated financial statements. Again a potential conflict of interest, this is no longer allowed.
- **Management and human resource functions.** Prior to SOx, external audit firms often identified professionals from their own firms and helped to move them to client management positions. The result was an environment where virtually all of the accounting managers in an enterprise often were alumni of their external auditors. This was sometimes frustrating for internal auditors or others who were not from that same public accounting firm. Avenues for promotion above certain levels seemed limited because of "old-boy" network connections with the external audit firm.
- **Other prohibited services.** Although not having that much impact on internal audit, SOx also specifically prohibits external audit firms from offering actuarial, investment advisor, and audit-related legal services. Tax services are not included here. Although a prohibition was in the initial drafts of SOx, there were massive protests from the public accounting firms and tax services are allowed.

The overall theme under SOx is that external auditors are authorized to audit the financial statements of their client enterprises and that is about all. SOx allows that beyond the above-prohibited activities, external auditors can engage in other non-audit services only if those services are approved in advance by the audit committee. With the increased scrutiny of audit committees under SOx, many are typically wary of approving anything that appears to be at all out of the ordinary.

These SOx external audit service prohibitions also have had a major impact on internal audit professionals for many enterprises. Because external audit firms are now *just the auditors*, internal audit professionals are finding increased levels of respect and responsibility for their role in assessing internal controls and promoting good corporate governance practices. Internal audit's relationships with audit committees also have been strengthened as they will seek increasing help for services that were sometimes assumed by their external audit firms. New groups of professional-service firms have been organized to help with installing financial systems, providing bookkeeping services, or installing IT systems.

Audit Committee Preapproval of Services   Section 202 of SOx's Title I specifies that the audit committee must approve all audit and non-audit services *in advance.* While audit committees have or should have been doing this all along, that approval was often little more than a formality prior to SOx. Audit committees in "the old days" often received little more than a brief written and/or verbal report from the external auditors that was approved in the same perfunctory manner that business meeting minutes are often approved. SOx changed all of this, and audit committee members can now expose themselves to criminal liabilities or stockholder litigation for allowing a prohibited action to take place.

Of course, there are many minor matters regarding external auditor activities that should not have to go through this formal audit committee in advance approval process. Using legal terminology, SOx sets *de minimis*[2] exception rules for these audit committee permission requirements. Per SOx, preapproval is not required for some non-audit services if:

- The aggregate dollar value of the service does not exceed 5% of the total external audit fees paid by the enterprise during the fiscal year when the services were provided.
- The services were not recognized as non-audit services by the enterprise at the time the overall audit engagement was initiated.
- These services are brought to the attention of the audit committee and approved by them prior to the completion of the audit.

These exceptions give the external auditors and the audit committee some flexibility. However, the nature and accumulated dollar value of these additional non-audit services must be carefully monitored throughout the course of a fiscal year to maintain a level of compliance. Internal audit should become involved in this process to help ascertain that all provided extra services continue in compliance with the SOx rules, including disclosure to investors through the annual proxy statement. SOx allows that the audit committee may delegate this non-audit services preapproval authority to one or more of the outside directors on the audit committee. This would relieve the strain of lengthy audit committee business matters, but put even more responsibility on a few audit committee members over and above the many new legal responsibilities mandated by SOx.

External Audit Partner Rotation   Another section of Title II makes it unlawful for a public accounting firm lead partner to head an engagement for over five years. This is a reform that the major public accounting firms had corrected well before SOx. Lead partners from the major firms had been rotated on a regular basis, although there may have been exceptions with smaller firms and engagements. While lead partner rotation had been common, SOx makes the *failure* of a firm to rotate a criminal act. However,

SOx does not really address the common practice in audit partner rotation where a given person will play the lead on an audit and then continue to serve in an advisory role after his or her term. That advisory role partner can often maintain the same level of responsibility as the designated lead partner and could become a potential violation of SOx rules. For many firms, full audit partner rotation has brought challenges to internal audit functions. Internal audit may have been working comfortably with a designated audit partner over extended periods, and will need to become accustomed to working with a new audit team from time to time and playing a stronger role in introducing that new team to the enterprise.

External Auditor Reports to Audit Committees   External auditors have always communicated regularly with their audit committees in the course of the audit engagement as well as for any other matters of concern. In the aftermath of Enron and the other corporate scandals, it was discovered that this communication was sometimes very limited. A member of management might negotiate a "pass" from the public accounting partner on a suggested accounting treatment change, but the matter was reported to the audit committee only in the most general of terms if at all.

SOx again has changed this. External auditors are required to report on a timely basis all accounting policies and practices used, alternative treatments of financial information discussed with management, the possible alternative treatments, and the approach preferred by the external auditor. The whole idea here is that external auditors must report to the audit committee any alternative accounting treatments, the approach preferred by the external auditors, and management's approach. This really says that if there are disputed accounting treatments, the audit committee should be made well aware of the actions taken. This requirement points to the need for good audit committee documentation.

Conflicts of Interest and Mandatory Rotations of External Audit Firms   As discussed previously, it had been common for members of an external audit firm team to get promotions at their client firms into senior financial positions. SOx Title II, Section 206 now prohibits external auditors from providing any audit services to a firm where the CEO, CFO, or chief accounting officer participated as a member of that external audit firm on the same audit within the last year. This really says that an audit partner cannot leave an audit engagement to begin working as a senior executive of that same firm that was just audited. There were some outrageous examples of this switching of roles that were part of the investigations after the fall of Enron.

The CAE is not included in this prohibition of past external audit firm relationships. Also, staff members and managers can still move from the public accounting firm team to various positions in the auditee enterprise. The prohibition is limited to public accounting partners. There continue to be valuable opportunities for some persons beginning their careers in public accounting and then moving to junior or mid-level management positions at enterprises where they were assigned as auditors.

In addition to required partner rotation, initial drafts of SOx proposed mandatory audit firm rotation. It was initially proposed that a corporation should be required to change its external auditors periodically. That was met with massive objections from the major public accounting firms and from many corporations. Today, many enterprises have retained their external audit firms for decades. Both sides feel that such long relationships foster a better understanding of the enterprise being audited. In addition, when an enterprise changed auditors under the auditing standards of the past, it often raised investor questions. The feeling of many audit partners as well as corporate executives was that continuous audit services to one enterprise built up a level of trust to promote more efficient and better audits. While enterprises did not change their auditors that regularly, the fall of Andersen saw past clients of that firm searching for a new external auditor.

In the final versions of SOx, mandatory auditor rotation was put on hold. The U.S. government's General Accounting Office (GAO) was mandated to perform a one-year review and study the potential effects of mandatory auditor rotation. The GAO subsequently reported that mandatory auditor rotation for SEC companies may not be efficient; loss of knowledge and additional costs outweigh benefits.[3]

SOx Title III: Corporate Responsibility

While SOx Title II sets up new rules for external auditor independence, Title III prescribes audit committee performance standards along with a large set of corporate governance rules. SOx's Title III regulations represent some major regulatory changes for audit committees that had not been all that regulated prior to SOx. This is an area where internal auditors should have a greater level of interest as well as a role. Although there had been a trend for all audit committees to be composed of independent directors, there were still many exceptions prior to SOx. However, there were few governance rules covering corporate boards and their audit committees. Once again, SOx changed all of that!

Public Company Audit Committee Governance Rules   Under SOx, *all* registered enterprises must have an audit committee composed of only independent directors. The corporation's external auditors are to report directly to the audit committee, which is responsible for their compensation, oversight of the audit work, and the resolution of any disagreements between external audit and management. While major corporations in the United States have had audit committees for many years, these rules have been tightened and very much changed. Many other companies with smaller boards of directors, often dominated by insiders, have had to make some major adjustments. Internal audit departments also have had a reporting relationship to their audit committees for many years, but that has been sometimes a weak link in the past. The CAE often had only a nominal direct-line reporting relationship to the audit committee with a very strong dotted line to the CFO. Internal audit reported to and met with the audit committee on a quarterly or monthly basis but with limited interim communications. SOx has made this reporting link much stronger and more active.

Each member of the board's audit committee must be a totally independent director. To be considered independent, the audit committee member must not accept any consulting or other advisory fees from the enterprise and cannot be affiliated with any subsidiary or related unit of the enterprise. Prior to SOx, some corporations lavished "consulting fees" on their outside directors as a means of compensation or reward. Since these cannot now be granted to outside directors who are on the audit committee, the total extent of these previously often-lavish corporate director rewards has gone away.

SOx's audit committee regulations require that at least one member of the audit committee be a "financial expert." These rules were introduced because, in the hearings that led up to the enactment of SOx, it was discovered that some of Enron's audit committee members did not appear to understand many of the financial transactions they were being asked to review and approve. The first sets of financial-expert rules were very stiff. Per those first-proposed rules, many existing knowledgeable audit committee board members did not qualify. After much preliminary protest, the rules were modified, and the current SEC regulations define a *financial expert* as a person who, through education and experience, has:

- An understanding of GAAP and financial statements
- Experience applying such GAAP in connection with the accounting for estimates, accruals, and reserves that are generally comparable to the estimates, accruals, and reserves, if any, used in the registrant's financial statements
- Experience preparing or auditing financial statements that present accounting issues that are generally comparable to those raised by the registrant's financial statements
- Experience with internal controls and procedures for financial reporting
- An understanding of audit committee functions

These rules do not require any professional certifications, academic backgrounds, or other specific qualifications. They just say that someone on an audit committee must present herself as having some level of knowledge on accounting, financial reporting, and internal control issues. In some respects, an audit committee member is being asked to put herself in the potential line of fire if the enterprise is ever questioned regarding some financial or internal control decision.

The SOx legislation also calls for audit committees to establish procedures to receive, retain, and treat complaints and handle whistleblower information regarding questionable accounting and auditing matters. This really says an audit committee must become, in effect, almost a separate ongoing entity rather than a subset of the traditional board that flies every quarter to some distant meeting location. A nice-sounding idea, but most audit committee functions do not have the supporting resources to handle an enterprise-level whistleblower function—something that is often the responsibility of an enterprise's corporate-level ethics function. Despite the words in the SOx legislation, audit committee–level whistleblower functions today are run on essentially an ad-hoc basis. While SOx allows the audit committee to hire independent counsel and other advisors, an enterprise's internal audit function should be a good resource to help establish these procedures. Internal audit is a truly independent resource within an enterprise and can be a major resource in helping the audit committee become SOx compliant.

The whistleblower function described in SOx covers reported information regarding questionable accounting and auditing matters. SOx was trying to address an issue reported during the Enron debacle where an accounting department employee tried to get the attention of the external auditors or an Enron financial officer to recognize some improper accounting transactions. The employee's concerns were rebuffed. An ethics whistleblower or hotline function could be a resource to respond to these types of issues. Today, ethics functions are often tied to human resources or are otherwise not viewed as independent of senior management. An internal audit function can act as a conduit for SOx accounting and auditing whistleblower reports. Whistleblower functions are discussed further in Chapter 12 on effective corporate governance.

Corporate Responsibility for Financial Reports   Prior to SOx, enterprises filed their financial statements with the SEC and published the results for investors, but the responsible corporate officers who "signed" or authored those reports were not really *personally* responsible. The bar has now been raised! The CEO, the principal financial officer, or other persons performing similar functions must certify each annual and quarterly report filed. The signing officer, as part of what is referred to as Section 302, must certify that:

- The signing officer has reviewed the report.
- Based on that signing officer's knowledge, the financial statements do not contain any materially untrue or misleading information.
- Again based on the signing officer's knowledge, the financial statements fairly represent the financial conditions and results of operations of the enterprise.
- The signing officer is responsible for:
  - Establishing and maintaining internal controls
  - Having designed these internal controls to ensure that material information about the enterprise and its subsidiaries was made known to the signing officer during the period when the reports were prepared
  - Having evaluated the enterprise's internal controls within 90 days prior to the release of the report
  - Having presented in these financial reports, the signing officer's evaluation of the effectiveness of these internal controls as of that report date
- The signing officer has disclosed to the auditors, audit committee, and other directors:
  - All significant deficiencies in the design and operation of internal controls that could affect the reliability of the reported financial data and has, further, disclosed these material control weaknesses to enterprise's auditors
  - Any fraud, whether or not material, that involves management or other employees who have a significant role in the enterprise's internal controls
- The signing officer has indicated in the report whether there were internal controls or other changes that could significantly impact those controls, including corrective actions, subsequent to the date of the internal control evaluation.

Given that SOx imposes potential criminal penalties of fines or jail time on individual violators of the Act, the above signer requirement places a heavy burden on responsible corporate officers, who must take all reasonable steps to make certain that they are in compliance. There is a provision here that these requirements still apply even if the enterprise has moved its headquarters outside the United States (e.g., in 2000 and 2001, numerous U.S. corporations moved corporate registration to offshore locations, such as Bermuda, for income tax purposes).

This personal signoff requirement has raised major concerns from corporation CEOs and CFOs. The requirement causes a major amount of additional work for the accounting and finance staffs preparing these reports as well as signing officers. The enterprise needs to set up detailed paper-trail procedures such that the signing officers are comfortable that effective processes have been used and the calculations to build the reports are all well documented. An enterprise may want to consider using an extended signoff process where staff members submitting the financial reports sign off on what they are submitting. Internal audit should be able to act as an internal consultant and help senior officers establish effective processes here. The audit workpaper model, with extensive cross-references, might be a good approach. Exhibit 2.2 provides an example of an Officer Disclosure Signoff type of statement that officers would be requested to sign. This exhibit is not an official PCAOB form, but is based on an SEC document, showing the types of things an officer will be asked to certify. We have marked a couple of phrases here in *italics*. Under SOx, the CEO or CFO is asked to personally assert to these types of representations and could be held criminally liable if incorrect. While the officer is at risk, the support staff—including internal audit—should take every step possible to make certain the package presented to the senior officer is correct.

Despite initial concerns about the impact of Section 302 on corporate officers, these provisions have not caused nearly the concerns and issues once contemplated. Chapter 7 discusses the current status of Section 302 as well as other important SOx requirements.

In an interesting twist of the legal language used, this Section makes references to the enterprise's "auditors" rather than Title II's term *registered public accounting firm*. While there have been no legal rulings to date and while this author cannot hold himself out as a legal expert on such matters, Title III of the Act would appear to refer to *auditors* in its broadest sense and certainly includes both internal and external auditors. A CAE should recognize this and take appropriate steps to work with corporate officers to expand and improve internal controls and the like. An internal audit function must place a strong emphasis on performing reviews surrounding significant internal control areas. This can be done through a detailed risk assessment of the internal control environments, discussions of these assessments with corporate officers, and then a detailed audit plan documenting how these internal control systems will be reviewed.

Internal auditors should take particular care, given SOx rules, on the nature and description of any findings encountered during the course of audits, on follow-up reporting regarding the status of corrective actions taken, and on the distributions of these audit reports. Many internal audits may identify significant weaknesses in areas of the enterprise that are not material to overall operations. A breakdown in the invoicing process at one regional sales office may be significant to the performance of that sales

---

Certificate of Employee Regarding Sarbanes-Oxley Compliance

Certification: Understanding that we intend to rely upon these statements, the undersigned hereby certifies, represents, and warrants to each of them and to the Company as follows:

1. I have read those portions of the accompanying draft of the covered filing that relate directly to the scope of my responsibilities as an employee of the Company (the "certified information").
2. Based on my knowledge, the certified information, as of the end of the period covered by such filing, did *not contain an untrue statement of a material fact* or omit to state a material fact necessary to make the statements therein, in light of the circumstances under which they were made, not misleading.
3. Based on my knowledge, to the extent of the scope of the certified information, the certified information fairly presents, in all material respects, the financial condition, results of operations, and cash flows of the Company as of the close of and for the period presented in the covered filing.
4. I am not aware of any deficiencies in the effectiveness of the Company's disclosure controls and procedures that could adversely affect the Company's ability to record, process, summarize, and report information required to be disclosed in the covered filing.
5. I *am not aware of any significant deficiencies or material weaknesses* in the design or operation of the Company's internal controls that could adversely affect the Company's ability to record, process, summarize, and report financial data.
6. I *am not aware of any fraud, whether or not material,* that involves the Company's management or other employees who have a significant role in the Company's internal controls.

Signature: _____

Dated this _____ day of _____, 200 _____

Print Name: _____

Title: _____

EXHIBIT 2.2   Sample Officer Disclosure and Signoff Form
Source: Sarbanes-Oxley and the New Internal Auditing Rules, Robert R. Moeller, page 38. Copyright © 2004 John Wiley & Sons. Reprinted with permission of John Wiley & Sons, Inc.

region for the corporation, but will not be a materially significant internal control weakness if the problem is local and does not reflect a wider, more pervasive problem, and if the problem was corrected after being discovered by internal audit. The CAE should establish good communications links with key financial officers in the enterprise such that they are aware of the internal audits performed, key findings, and the status of planned corrective actions. Internal audit should also provide some guidance as to whether reported audit findings are material to the enterprise's overall system of internal controls. Similar communication links should be established with members of the audit committee.

Improper Influence Over the Conduct of Audits   SOx further states that it is unlawful for an officer, director, or related subordinate person to take any action in contravention of an SEC rule, to "fraudulently influence, coerce, manipulate, or mislead" any external CPA auditor engaged in the audit for the purpose of rendering the financial statements materially misleading. These are strong words in an environment where there had once been a high level of discussion and compromise between the auditors and senior management when a significant problem was found during the course of an audit.

Prior to SOx, there often were many "friendly" discussions between management and their external auditors regarding a financial interpretation dispute or proposed adjustment. The result was often some level of compromise. This is not unlike an internal audit team in the field that circulates a draft audit report with local management before departing. After much discussion and sometimes follow-up work, that draft internal audit report might have been changed before its final issue. The same things often happened in external auditor draft reports covering quarterly or annual preliminary results; SOx has some very strong rules to prohibit such practices. The rules evolved during the congressional hearings leading up to the passage of SOx, where testimony included tales of strong CEOs essentially demanding that external auditors "accept" certain questionable accounting entries or lose the audit business. There can still be these friendly disputes and debates, but if an SEC ruling is explicit in some area and if the external auditors propose a financial statement adjustment because of that SEC rule, management *must* accept it without an additional fight.

There can be a fine line between management disagreeing with their external auditors over some estimate or interpretation and management trying to improperly influence its auditors. External audit may have done some limited testing in some area and then proposed an adjustment based on the results of that test. This type of scenario could result in management disagreeing with that adjustment and claiming the results of the test were "not representative." While the external auditors under SOx have the last word in such a dispute, internal audit can sometimes play a facilitating role here as well. Internal audit resources, for example, can be used to expand the population of some audit sampling test or to perform other extended observations and testing regarding the disputed area. Doing this, internal audit is not helping to improperly influence the conduct of an audit, but helping to resolve the matter. AS5, discussed in Chapter 3, very much encourages these practices.

Forfeitures, Bars, and Penalties   Title III concludes with a series of other detailed rules and penalties covering corporate governance. Their purpose is to tighten existing rules that were in place before SOx or to add new rules for what often seemed to be outrageous or at least very improper behavior prior to SOx. These new rules outlined below do not impact the audit committee or internal or external auditors directly, as they are focused at other areas of what was believed to be corporate governance excess:

- **Forfeiture of improper bonuses.** Section 304 requires that if an enterprise is required to restate its earnings due to some material violation of securities laws, the CEO and CFO *must reimburse* the company for any bonuses or incentives received on the basis of the original, incorrect statements issued during the past 12 months. The same applies for any profits received from the sale of enterprise securities during that same period. During the SOx hearings, multiple instances were cited where a company had issued an aggressive but unsupportable earnings statement, its key officers had benefited from bonuses or the sale of stock from that good news, and then the company soon had to restate its earnings due to some material noncompliance matter. There would not have been those CEO and CFO bonuses under the revised, correct interpretations. SOx places a personal penalty on senior corporate officers who have benefited from materially noncompliant financial statements.
- **Bars to officer or director service.** Section 305 is another example of how SOx has tightened the rules. Prior to SOx, federal courts were empowered to bar any person from serving as a corporate officer or director if that person's conduct demonstrates "substantial unfitness to serve as an officer or director." SOx changed the standard here by eliminating the word *substantial*, saying that the courts can bar someone from serving as a director or officer for *any* conduct violation.
- **Pension fund blackout periods.** A standard rule for 401(k) and similar retirement plans is that a fund administrator can establish a blackout period over a limited time period that prohibits plan participants from making investment adjustments to their personal plans. A plan participant with a substantial amount of his retirement funds in company

stock could, because of bad company news, transfer funds from that company stock to a cash-based money market fund or some other investment option. These blackout periods are usually instituted for purely legitimate reasons such as a change in plan administrators. An Enron-related complaint raised during the SOx hearings was that there was a blackout in place during those final weeks before bankruptcy, preventing employees from making changes to their plan. However, those same blackout rules did not apply to the corporate officers, who had their own separate plan and who, in some cases, got out of Enron before things totally collapsed. SOx rules now state that the same blackout periods must apply to everyone in the company, from staff to corporate officers.

■ **Attorney professional responsibility.** Section 307 covers revised rules for attorney professional conduct and was initially very controversial. An attorney is required to report evidence of a material violation of securities law or a similar company violation to the chief legal counsel or the CEO. If those parties do not respond, the attorney is required to report the evidence "up the ladder" to the audit committee of the board of directors. SOx's initial rules also allowed that if an attorney discovered such a securities law violation, the attorney should withdraw from the engagement, reporting the violation particulars, in what is called a "noisy withdrawal" approach.

   The controversy here was that SOx effectively required an attorney to violate the rules of what is called attorney–client privilege. Under traditional rules, if a subsidiary executive met with an attorney to discuss some matter that constituted a potential violation of SOx, the attorney and the subsidiary manager client would work out the issues. The initial concern was that an attorney was supposed to blow the whistle on such discussion and bring the matter potentially all the way to the audit committee. The final rules, however, softened things to narrow the scope of attorneys and otherwise limit the rules' impact.

■ **Fair funds for investors.** The final section of Title III states that if an individual or group is fined for a violation through administrative or legal action, the funds collected will go to a "disgorgement" fund for distribution to the investors who suffered because of the fraud or improper accounting actions. The same rule applies to funds collected through a settlement in advance of court proceedings. Properties and other assets seized will be sold and also go into that disgorgement fund. The whole idea here is that investors who lost because of individual corporate wrongdoing may be subject to some financial settlement from such a fund.

Title IV: Enhanced Financial Disclosures

This title of SOx is designed to correct financial reporting disclosure problems, to tighten conflict-of-interest rules for corporate officers and directors, to mandate a management assessment of internal controls, to require senior officer codes of conduct, and other matters. There is a lot of material here. Many unexpected bankruptcies and sudden earnings failures around the time of the Enron failure were attributed to extremely aggressive, if not questionable, financial reporting. With the approval of their external auditors, companies pushed to the limits and often used such tactics as issuing questionable pro forma earnings to report their results or moving the corporate headquarters offshore to minimize taxes. While these tactics were in accordance with GAAP and existing laws, SOx tightened many rules and made some improved financial disclosure tactics difficult or illegal.

A common tactic at the time, what are called *pro forma financial reports*, were frequently used to present an *as-if* picture of a firm's financial status by leaving out nonrecurring earnings expenses such as restructuring charges or merger-related costs. However, because there is no standard definition and no consistent format for reporting pro forma earnings, depending on the assumptions used, it was possible for an operating loss to become a profit under pro forma earnings reporting. For example, for its 2001 fiscal year, Cisco Systems Inc., the San Jose, California–based maker of computer networking systems, reported net income of $3.09 billion on a pro forma basis but simultaneously reported a net loss of $1.01 billion on a GAAP basis. Cisco's pro forma profit specifically excluded acquisition charges, payroll tax on the exercise of stock options, restructuring costs and other special charges, an excess inventory charge, and net gains on minority investments. Cisco certainly was not all alone here, as many companies had reported pro forma earnings showing ever-increasing growth while their true GAAP results were not so favorable. The problem with these two sets of numbers was that investors and the press frequently ignored the GAAP numbers, focusing on the more favorable pro forma results. SOx-mandated rules now require that pro forma published financial statements must not contain any materially untrue statements or omit any fact that makes the reports misleading. Further, the pro forma results also must reconcile to the financial conditions and results of operations under GAAP. A common reporting technique prior to SOx, they are not at all common today.

Perhaps the major issue that brought Enron down was a large number of off–balance sheet transactions that, if consolidated with regular financial reports, would have shown major financial problems. Once they were identified and included with Enron's other financial results, the disclosure pushed Enron toward bankruptcy. SOx now requires that quarterly and annual financial reports must disclose all such off–balance sheet transactions that may have a material effect on the current or future financial reports. These transactions may include contingent obligations, financial relationships with unconsolidated entities, or other items that could have material effects on operations. While many of the SOx financial disclosure rules are really the responsibility of external auditors, this is an area where internal auditors might be of help. It is often an internal auditor, on a visit to a distant unit of the company, who encounters these types of off–balance sheet arrangements in discussions with field personnel. If significant, internal audit should communicate the appropriate details to the audit committee. The final rules here, after passage of SOx, require an enterprise to provide an explanation of its off–balance sheet arrangements in a separately captioned subsection of the Management's Discussion and Analysis (MD&A) section of the annual Form 10K.

Expanded Conflict-of-Interest Provisions and Disclosures   The hearings that led to the passage of SOx often pictured corporate officers and directors as a rather greedy lot. In arrangements that frequently appeared to be conflicts of interest, large relocation allowances or corporate executive personal loans were granted and subsequently forgiven by corporate boards. A CEO, for example, who requests the board to grant his CFO a large personal "loan" with vague repayment terms and the right to either demand payment or forgive certainly creates a conflict-of-interest situation. Although a series of exceptions are allowed, SOx makes it unlawful for any corporation to directly or indirectly extend credit, in the form of a personal loan, to any officer or director.

Another section of Title IV requires that all disclosures under SOx, as discussed previously, must be filed electronically and posted "near real time" on the SEC's Internet site. This would make the filing of such information much more current. Internal audit should potentially consider evaluating their control systems in place to handle such SEC online reporting. This is an area where reporting was often hardcopy based in the past, and there could be a risk of improperly transmitted data or security leaks without proper internal control procedures.

Management's Assessment of Internal Controls: Section 404   SOx requires that each annual report filing contain an internal control report that states management's responsibility for establishing and maintaining an adequate system of internal controls as well as management's assessment, as of the fiscal-year-ending date, on the effectiveness of those installed internal control procedures. This is what has popularly been known as the Section 404 rules. Internal audit, outside consultants, or even the management team—but not the external auditors—have the responsibility to review and assess the effectiveness of these internal controls. The external auditors are to attest to and rely on the sufficiency of the internal control reviews made by management.

Section 404 reviews were initially supported by AS2 auditing standards, and then, after many complaints about the difficulty of complying with these standards, were replaced by the new, risk-based AS5. Chapter 3 provides an overview of AS5, Chapter 4 reviews the COSO internal control framework that is used as a basis for understanding these internal controls, and Chapter 6 discusses the process of performing Section 404 reviews. While we only mention Section 404 here in our summary and overview of SOx and its key components, the reader is encouraged to consult these other chapters for more background on the current status of performing these very important internal control assessments.

Financial Officer Codes of Ethics   SOx requires that corporations adopt a code of ethics for their senior financial officers, including the CEO and principal financial officers, and disclose compliance with this code as part of their annual financial reporting. While SOx has made this a requirement for senior officers, employee codes of ethics or conduct have been in place in some enterprises for many years. They evolved to more formal ethics functions in larger corporations in the early 1990s, but were often established for employees and supervisors rather than for corporate officers. These codes defined a set of rules or policies that were designed to apply for all employees. They covered such matters as policies on the protection of company records or on gifts and other benefit issues. Exhibit 2.3 shows a sample *enterprise code of conduct* table of contents. Such a code of conduct should be designed for all employees rather than just corporate officers. The topics and concerns will vary due to the enterprise's line of business or other factors.

SOx has brought enterprise codes of conduct to new levels. With a growing public concern about the needs for strong ethical practices, many enterprises have appointed an ethics officer to launch such an initiative with a code of conduct as a first step. However, while that code of conduct received senior officer endorsement, it was often directed at the overall population of employees, but not the senior officers. This author recalls leading an effort to launch an ethics function for a large enterprise where he secured the endorsement of all senior officers for the policy rules outlined in the code of conduct. However, when certain of those code rules ran contrary to the business practices of a few senior officers, there were requests for exceptions to the rules on the grounds that the particular situation was "different" for these senior officers and the violation

The following are topics found in a typical enterprise code of conduct:

I. INTRODUCTION

 A. Purpose of This Code of Conduct: A general statement about the background of this Code of Conduct.

 B. Our Commitment to Strong Ethical Standards: A restatement of the Mission Statement and a letter from the CEO.

 C. Where to Seek Guidance: A description of the ethics hotline process.

 D. Reporting Noncompliance: Guidance for Whistleblowers— how to report.

 E. Your Responsibility to Acknowledge the Code: A description of the code acknowledgment process.

II. FAIR DEALING

 A. Our Selling Practices: Guidance for dealing with customers.

 B. Our Buying Practices: Guidance and policies for dealing with vendors.

III. CONDUCT IN THE WORKPLACE

 A. Equal Employment Opportunity Standards: A strong commitment statement.

 B. Workplace and Sexual Harassment: An equally strong commitment statement.

 C. Alcohol and Substance Abuse: A policy statement in this area.

IV. CONFLICTS OF INTEREST

 A. Outside Employment: Limitations on accepting employment from competitors.

 B. Personal Investments: Rules regarding using company data to make personal investment decisions.

 C. Gifts and Other Benefits: Rules regarding receiving bribes and improper gifts.

 D. Former Employees: Rules prohibiting giving favors to ex-employees in business.

 E. Family Members: Rules about giving business to family members, creating potential conflicts of interest.

V. COMPANY PROPERTY AND RECORDS

 A. Company Assets: A strong statement on employees' responsibility to protect company assets.

 B. Computer Systems Resources: An expansion of the company assets statement to reflect all aspects of computer systems resources.

 C. Use of the Company's Name: A rule that the company name should be used only for normal business dealings.

 D. Company Records: A rule regarding employee responsibility for records integrity.

(*continued overleaf*)

EXHIBIT 2.3 Enterprise Code of Conduct Sample Table of Contents

    E. Confidential Information: Rules on the importance of keeping all company information confidential and not disclosing it to outsiders.

    F. Employee Privacy: A strong statement on the importance of keeping employee personal information confidential in regard to outsiders and even other employees.

    G. Company Benefits: Employees must not take company benefits where they are not entitled.

VI. COMPLYING WITH THE LAW

    A. Inside Information and Insider Trading: A strong rule prohibiting insider trading or otherwise benefiting from inside information.

    B. Financial Reporting Disclosures: All accounting records as well as reports produced from those records will be produced in accordance with applicable laws as well as generally accepted accounting principles.

    C. Political Contributions and Activities: A statement on political activity rules.

    D. Bribery and Kickbacks: A firm rule against using bribes or accepting kickbacks.

    E. Foreign Business Dealings: Rules regarding dealing with foreign agents in line with the Foreign Corrupt Practices Act.

    F. Workplace Safety: A statement on the company policy to comply with OSHA rules.

    G. Product Safety: A statement on the company commitment to product safety.

    H. Environmental Protection: A rule regarding the company's commitment to comply with applicable environmental laws.

VII. COMPLIANCE WITH THIS CODE

    A. All stakeholders are expected to comply with the letter and spirit of this code as well as applicable government rules and regulations.

    B. Compliance with this code is a condition of employment.

EXHIBIT 2.3 *(continued)*

Source: Brink's Modern Internal Auditing, Sixth Edition, Robert Moeller, page 200. Copyright © 2005 John Wiley & Sons. Reprinted with permission of John Wiley & Sons, Inc.

should be thus permissible. Although this example is in a different time frame and only one company, prior to SOx some corporate senior managers often felt their company code of conduct rules were good in general but did not always apply to them.

    SOx does not address the specific content of enterprise-wide codes of ethics, but focuses on the need for the same standards for senior officers as for all employees in the enterprise. SOx specifically requires that an enterprise's code of ethics or conduct for its senior officers must reasonably promote:

- Honest and ethical conduct, including the ethical handling of actual or apparent conflicts of interest between personal and professional relationships
- Full, fair, accurate, timely, and understandable disclosure in the enterprise financial reports
- Compliance with applicable governmental rules and regulations

Many larger enterprises today have established ethics-type functions, but smaller ones have not. If an ethics function is not in place, internal audit can play an important role in helping its enterprise achieve compliance with SOx ethical rules for officers and other stake holders.

If an enterprise has a code of conduct, management should assure that this code applies to all members of the enterprise, is consistent with SOx and that these ethical rules are communicated to all members of the enterprise, including the officers. The key issue here is making sure that the existing code of conduct covers the above SOx rules, that it has been communicated to senior management, and that these officers have formally agreed to comply with it. While SOx compliance processes must be established just for senior officers, this is the ideal time to launch an ethics function throughout the enterprise that applies to senior management and to all employees as well.

A strong ethics function should be promoted throughout the enterprise and not just as a SOx legal requirement. A strong set of ethical standards can get an enterprise through a crisis situation and help it move in the right directions. A motivation for SOx and its strong provisions in these areas was the perception that certain corporate officers were operating on the basis of personal gain with no consideration for strong ethical values, as evidenced by correct and accurate financial reporting. SOx's ethical requirements can help any enterprise to better set itself up for improved ethical business conduct practices.

Other Required Disclosures   Title IV concludes with three other sections that have ongoing impacts on organizational governance. Section 407 formally describes the previously discussed rule that at least one member of every corporate audit committee must be identified as a financial expert. We have discussed these requirements as part of the rules covering audit committees. Two other important rule areas are Section 408 on enhanced disclosures and Section 409 on real-time financial systems disclosures.

Section 408 on SEC-Enhanced Disclosure Reviews   All SEC-registered entities are required to file annual Form 10Ks as well as other SEC financial reports. While the issuing enterprises filing those reports would anticipate an SEC review in some detail, the hearings leading to SOx revealed that these SEC reviews were not always that timely or comprehensive. In particular, the detailed corporate disclosures and footnotes reported did not receive sufficiently detailed SEC attention. Just as an individual hopes that her federal income tax return will not be very often subject to a detailed audit, corporations and their external auditors have had the same hopes. Some of the massive corporate accounting and financial problems leading up to the passage of SOx might have been detected had there been more diligent SEC reviews.

Section 408 mandates the SEC to perform "enhanced reviews" of the disclosures included in *all* company filings on a regular and systematic basis and no less often than once every three years. The SEC can decide either to perform an enhanced review of disclosures as soon as possible or to wait to schedule the review through the three-year window. This enhanced review could be triggered by *any one* of the following situations:

- If the corporation has issued a material restatement of its financial results
- If there has been a significant volatility in stock prices compared to others
- If the corporation has a large market capitalization
- If this is an emerging company with significant disparities in its stock price-to-earnings ratio
- If corporation operations significantly affect material sectors of the national economy
- Any other factors the SEC may consider relevant

This really says that the SEC may more regularly schedule such an extended disclosure review for large Fortune 500–size companies, leaders in some sectors of the economy, or where stock prices are out of average ranges. Of course, with the "other factors" consideration, virtually any corporation could potentially move to the head of the list for such an extended review.

In general, these rules say that enterprises should be prepared for their public filings to be reviewed by the SEC more thoroughly and more frequently than in the past. However, there have been limited SEC rules published to date on the nature of these planned enhanced disclosure reviews. Financial statement disclosures that are part of published financial reports are included in the section called Management's Discussion &

Analysis (MD&A) in the SEC's 10K report. They cover a wide range of issues, including transactions with unaffiliated subsidiaries or derivative trading activities. Unusual or hard-to-classify transactions are disclosed and discussed here. Exhibit 2.4 lists a few, but certainly not all, of the types of financial statement disclosures that could be subject to an SEC enhanced disclosure review. When SOx first became the law, there was a concern that this SEC enhanced disclosure review could lead to a full audit of the financial statements for the period reviewed, putting the SEC in almost a financial audit role. If they were to find inconsistencies between the disclosures and reported financial statements, this could lead to financial statement restatements. However, at the time of this publication there has been little SEC activity and no new rules here, but Section 408 enhanced reviews could have some interesting implications.

Section 409 on Real-Time Financial Statement Disclosures   The last section under Title IV mandates that the reporting corporation disclose to the public "on a rapid and current basis" any additional information containing material financial statement issues. Formal SEC rules have not been established here, but corporations are allowed to include trend and quantitative approaches as well as graphics for those disclosures. This is a change from

---

The SEC may schedule an enhanced or extended review of an enterprise's financial information in its periodic 10K or 10Q reports if the filing enterprise meets any of the following conditions:

- Enterprises that have issued material restatements of financial results. That is, a swing from a major reported loss to a massive profit over several periods could attract attention.
- Enterprises that experience significant volatility in their stock price as compared to other, similar enterprises.
- Enterprises with the largest market capitalization. In other words, the SEC may look at a Fortune 50– size corporation just because of its major size.
- New or emerging companies with disparities in price-to-earnings ratios. When stock market valuations compared to stock prices seem "out of whack," an enhanced review could be considered.
- Enterprises whose operations significantly affect any material sector of the economy.
- Any other factors that the Commission may consider relevant. In other words, the SEC could select any enterprise for an enhanced review.

EXHIBIT 2.4   Section 408 SEC Enhanced Disclosure Potential Review Items

traditional SEC report formats that allowed only text with the exception of corporate logos. The concept is to get key data to investors as soon as possible and not through traditional slow paper-based reports. Section 409 points to the concept of a real-time financial close, which soon may become a reality for many enterprises. Chapter 7 contains an extended discussion on current and future prospects for SOx real-time reporting requirements.

Title V: Analyst Conflicts of Interest

This SOx title and other subsequent sections do not directly cover financial reporting, corporate governance, audit committees, or external or internal audit issues. They were drafted to correct other perceived abuses that were encountered during the SOx congressional hearings. The reader should be aware of them only from a general knowledge basis, as they generally do not directly impact internal control and financial reporting issues.

Title V is designed to rectify some securities analyst abuses. Investors have relied on the recommendations of securities analysts for years. These analysts were often tied to large brokerage houses and investment banks, and were analyzing and recommending securities to investors and the financial institution employers. When they looked at securities where their employer had an interest, there were supposed to be strong separations of responsibility between the people recommending a stock for investment and those selling it to investors. In the frenzy of the late 1990s investment "dot-com bubble," these traditional analyst controls and ethical practices broke down. In the aftermath of the market downturns, analysts sometimes recommended stocks seemingly only because their investment bank employer was managing the initial public offering (IPO). Also, investigators found analysts publicly recommending a stock to investors as a "great growth opportunity" while simultaneously telling their investment banking peers that the stock was a very poor investment or worse.

Abuses of this manner existed in many circumstances. While investment analysts once relied on their own strong self-governing professional standards, the SOx hearings revealed that many of these standards were ignored by strong and prominent securities analysts. Title V attempts to correct these securities analyst abuses. Rules of conduct have been established with legal punishments for violations. SOx has reformed and regulated the practices of securities analysts. The result should be better-informed investors.

Titles VI and VII: Commission Authority, Studies, and Reports

Two of the final SOx legislative titles cover a series of issues ranging from the funding authorization SEC appropriations to plans for future studies.

These sections of the legislation include new rules to tighten what had been viewed as regulatory loopholes in the past. Among these, the SEC can now ban persons from promoting or trading "penny stocks" because these promoters had been past SEC disciplinary actions. The rules here bar someone from practicing before the SEC because of improper professional conduct. The latter rule gives the SEC the authority to effectively ban a public accounting firm from acting as an external auditor for corporations.

The professional misconduct ban could represent a major penalty to any public accounting firm or individual CPA who was found, through SEC hearings, to have violated professional or ethical public accounting standards. Although SOx outlines a series of hearings before any action is taken, individual CPAs or entire firms could be banned temporarily or permanently. This takes this monitoring and policing process away from the AICPA's peer-review process of the past and gives the regulatory authority to the SEC. While an individual negligent CPA can still work in non-SEC practice areas such as small business accounting or, for that matter, internal audit, even a temporary ban can be a death knell for a public accounting firm. All concerned must be aware of and follow SEC rules and procedures, particularly this new set authorized by SOx.

Title VII authorizes the SEC to engage in a series of studies and reports with specified due dates for the delivery of those reports to appropriate congressional committees or federal agencies. There are an untold number of such legislatively authorized reports that are filed with Congress or government agencies, and some just disappear in some bureaucratic swamp. SOx authorized five studies and reports including one titled, "Consolidation of Public Accounting Firms." This GAO study (03-864) was released in July 2003, and found no real economic or quality impact due to the current environment of just four major external audit firms. The study also found that smaller firms faced a barrier to entry because of their limited resources when compared to the Big Four.

Other Sox-mandated studies included a review of Credit Rating Agencies, a study on Securities Professionals Violations and Violators, an Analysis of SEC Enforcement Actions, and a Study of Investment Banks. These reports were developed by the SEC or GAO and did not change the overall objectives and rules behind SOx. All too often, some of these reports just concluded with recommendations for further study! The ongoing impact, if any, of these mandated studies is yet to be determined.

Titles VIII, IX, and X: Fraud Accountability and White-Collar Crime

SOx Titles VIII and IX seem to be very much a reaction to the failure of Enron and the subsequent demise of Arthur Andersen. The introduction to this chapter discussed some of the events surrounding the failure of Enron, including the conviction of the then-major public accounting firm Arthur Andersen for its destruction of Enron's accounting records. At that time, even though Andersen seemed very culpable to outside observers because of its massive efforts to shred company accounting records, Andersen initially argued that it was just following its established procedures and had done no wrong. The courts eventually found Andersen innocent of criminal conspiracy, but it is no more. Now, Title VIII of SOx has established specific rules and penalties for the destruction of corporate audit records.

The words in the statute are much broader than just the Andersen matter and apply to all auditors and accountants, including internal auditors. The words here are particularly strong regarding the destruction, alteration, or falsification of records involved in federal investigations or bankruptcies: "Whoever knowingly alters, destroys, mutilates, conceals, covers up, falsifies or makes false entry in any record, document, or tangible object with the intent to impede, obstruct, or influence the investigation . . . shall be fined . . . [or] imprisoned not more than 20 years, or both." Taken directly from the statute, these are some strong words! This says that any enterprise should have a strong records retention policy. While records can be destroyed in the course of normal business cycles, any hint of a federal investigation or the filing of bankruptcy papers for some affiliated unit should trigger activation of that records retention policy.

A separate portion of this section establishes rules for corporate internal audit records. Although we tend to think of SOx primarily in terms of rules for external auditors, it very much applies to internal auditors as well. Workpapers and supporting review papers must be maintained for a period of five years from the end of the fiscal year of the audit. SOx clearly states that these rules apply to "any accountant who conducts an audit" of an SEC-registered corporation. While internal auditors have sometimes argued in the past that they only do operational audits that do not apply to the formal financial audit process, the prudent internal audit group should closely align its workpaper records retention rules to comply with this SOx five-year mandate.

Several of the sections of the legislation are designed to tighten things and to correct what were viewed by others as excesses. One of the reported excesses leading up to SOx was reported instances where corporate officers got large loans from their board of directors based on stock manipulation and performance that was later found to be improper. Boards of directors regularly forgave those loans after some period of time. Now, SOx states that these debts cannot be forgiven or discharged if they were incurred in violation of securities fraud laws. The executive—now probably ex-executive—who received the forgiven loan is now obligated to repay the corporation. Another section here extends the statute of limitations for securities law violations. Now, legal action may be brought no later than two years after discovery or five years after the actual violation. Since securities fraud can take some time to discover, this change gives prosecutors a bit more time.

The Organizational Sentencing Guidelines is a published list of corporate penalties for violations of certain federal laws. If an enterprise is found to be guilty, the punishment or sentencing could be reduced if there had been an ethics program in place that should normally reduce the possibility of such a violation. While the basic concepts of the Sentencing Guidelines are still in place, SOx modifies them to include the destruction or alteration of documents as offenses.

Section 806 adds whistleblower protection for employees of publicly traded enterprises who observe and detect some fraudulent action and then independently report it to the SEC or some other outside parties. By employees, we mean officers, contractors, or agents as well. Any person who observes an illegal act can "blow the whistle" and report the action with legal protection from retaliation. SOx adds whistleblower language for securities law violations. It does not however, include the type of words that are in federal contract whistleblower provisions where the person reporting something may be rewarded with some percentage of the savings reported.

Securities law violations and whistleblowing raises an issue for internal auditors. More than almost anyone in the enterprise, internal audit has access to virtually all enterprise records. Following the code of ethics, as defined by the IIA, any violations discovered here should be handled not by a report to the SEC but through a report to proper levels of senior management. If an internal auditor discovers a security law violation by a senior financial officer, the matter would normally be first reported to the CEO. However, if the CEO is involved in the action, internal audit should report the matter to the audit committee for resolution. While an employee at a different level in the enterprise may not feel comfortable reporting something to an audit committee member, internal audit certainly has that established level of communication. Internal audit standards, as they exist today, are discussed briefly in Chapter 11. Where a standard appears to be in conflict with a law, such as SOx, the law will take precedence over professional standards.

Title VIII concludes with a very brief Section 807 defining the criminal penalties for shareholders of publicly traded companies. Summarized here, it simply states that whoever executes or attempts to execute a scheme to defraud any persons in connection with a corporation's securities or fraudulently receives money or property from that sale shall be fined or imprisoned for no more than 25 years or both. That is a strong potential penalty for securities fraud! The regulations, rules, and penalties outlined in SOx have made following these rules extremely important.

Title IX contains a series of white-collar crime penalty enhancements. It goes through existing criminal law penalties and raises maximum punishments. For example, the maximum imprisonment for mail fraud has now grown from 5 years to 20 and the maximum fine for Employee Retirement Income Security Act (ERISA) retirement violations has gone from $100,000 to $500,000. These increased penalties coupled with the provisions of the Organizational Sentencing Guidelines create an environment where an increasing number of persons found guilty of white-collar crimes may have to spend time in prison.

Finally, Section 906 of SOx Title IX introduces a strong new requirement for corporate CEOs and CFOs. Both must sign a supplemental statement with their annual financial report that certifies that the information contained in the report "fairly represents, in all material respects, the financial condition and results of operations." These effectively personal certifications are coupled with penalties of fines up to $5 million and 10 years for anyone who certifies such statements while knowing they are false. Since these are personal penalties, the prudent CEO and CFO must take *extreme care* to make certain that all issues are resolved and that the annual financial statements are correct and fully representative of operations.

Title X is a "Sense of the Senate" comment that corporate income tax returns should be personally signed by the CEO. Again, responsibility is placed on the individual officer, not the anonymous corporate entity.

Title XI: Corporate Fraud Accountability

While prior sections focused on the individual responsibilities of the CEO, CFO, and others, the last SOx title defines overall corporate responsibility for fraudulent financial reporting. Various sections focus on other existing statutes, such as the Organization Sentencing Guidelines, and reaffirm the rules for corporations and increase penalties. The SEC is also given authority to impose a temporary freeze on the transfer of corporate funds to officers and others in a corporation that is subject to an SEC investigation. This was done to correct some reported abuses where some corporations were being investigated for financial fraud while they simultaneously dispensed huge cash payments to individuals. A corporation in trouble should retain some funds until the matter is resolved.

Section 1105 also gives the SEC the authority to prohibit persons from serving as corporate officers and directors. This applies to persons who have violated the SOx rules outlined above. While this will not be an automatic ban, the SEC has the authority to impose this ban where it feels appropriate.

The idea is to punish the corporate wrongdoer who has been found culpable of securities law violations at one corporation, only to leave that troubled corporation to serve at another.

IMPACT OF THE SARBANES-OXLEY ACT

The previous sections have provided a general overview of the Sarbanes-Oxley Act. While this discussion did not cover all sections or details of SOx, the intent is to give internal auditors and other professionals an overall understanding of key sections that will have an impact on the annual audit of an enterprise and its audit committee. Whether a large, Fortune 100–sized U.S.-based corporation, a smaller company not even traded on NASDAQ, or a private company with a bond issue registered through the SEC, all will now or later come under SOx and its public accounting regulatory body, the PCAOB. Internal auditors will first see these changes in their dealings with their external auditors.

SOx has caused multiple changes to enterprises, particularly in the United States but now worldwide. The roles and responsibilities of both external and internal auditors have changed, and enterprises certainly look at the internal controls and business ethics from a much different perspective. The remaining chapters focus on the major or more significant areas of the SOx legislation, but as this summary of the law may explain, there are minefields throughout SOx where an enterprise can find itself in violation of one or another regulation if not closely monitoring this legislation.

ENDNOTES

1. The full text of the legislation can be found at http://fl1.findlaw.com/news .findlaw.com/hdocs/docs/gwbush/sarbanesoxley072302.pdf.
2. A principle of law: Even if a technical violation of a law appears to exist according to the letter of the law, if the effect is too small to be of consequence, the violation of the law will not be considered as a sufficient cause of action, whether in civil or criminal proceedings.
3. U.S. General Accounting Office, //www.gao.gov/highlights/d04216high.pdf.

CHAPTER 3

AS5 Standards for Auditing Internal Controls

The Sarbanes-Oxley Act (SOx) brought us the Public Company Accounting Oversight Board (PCAOB), an independent agency to regulate external audit firms and to establish auditing standards for external auditors. Prior to SOx, external auditors operated under peer-related governance rules established by the American Institute of Certified Public Accountants (AICPA) and auditing standards issued by the AICPA's Auditing Standards Board (ASB). No matter how well respected this AICPA-led process was in the past, the accounting scandals surrounding the fall of Enron indicated that the AICPA peer-review process was somewhat broken. The PCAOB initially assumed and recognized the existing ASB standards for audits of public corporations in the United States but indicated that it would be releasing its own auditing standards over time. An early release of these new PCAOB auditing standards was called Auditing Standard No. 2 (AS2), a very rule-based set of external auditing standards issued in May 2007.

Launched in SOx's first years with the PCAOB's early emphasis on large corporate early filers, AS2 rules encouraged external auditors to take overly conservative and detailed approaches in their audits of financial statements. As a result of this AS2-mandated "look at everything" detailed audit approach, enterprise external audit bills became much more expensive after AS2 took effect. While many larger enterprises gritted their teeth and put up with the new rules, there were frequent complaints by industry leaders, academics, and others loudly proclaiming that AS2 needed some revisions. The Securities and Exchange Commission (SEC) and the PCAOB agreed to revise these audit standards, with much of their focus on revisions to AS2 to make it more scalable for the 6,000 or more *nonaccelerated filers* that had yet to comply with SOx as of 2007. Those publicly traded enterprises with a public float of $75 million or less were soon to be required to have their Section 404 auditor attestation reports completed for fiscal years ending after December 15, 2008, and many felt they needed some relief from the AS2 audit rules.

In December 2006, the PCAOB and the SEC proposed a set of a top-down, risk-based-approach revisions to AS2, giving the public 70 days to comment on this draft. They each received nearly 200 comment letters on these proposed changes. After SEC approval and PCAOB detailed rules, Auditing Standard No. 5 (AS5) was issued in late May 2007. With the lengthy title, "An Audit of Internal Control Over Financial Reporting that Is Integrated with an Audit of Financial Statements,"[1] AS5 takes a much more risk-based approach to financial statement audits than its AS2 predecessor. This chapter will provide an overview of the new AS5 financial statement internal controls audit rules—a major change for public accounting audits of financial statements.

While AS5 is really a set of standards for external auditors who review and certify published financial statements, the new AS5 rules also are important for financial managers and internal auditors. AS5 introduces risk-based rules with an emphasis on the effectiveness of enterprise-level controls that are more oriented to enterprise facts and circumstances. In addition, the new auditing standard calls for external auditors to consider including reviews of appropriate internal audit reports in their financial statement audit reviews. AS5 allows external auditors to place more emphasis on management's ability to establish and document key internal controls, and both financial management and internal auditors need to understand these new risk-based and more scalable rules for the financial audits of their enterprises. This chapter will also consider how financial management and internal auditors can improve their internal controls using AS5 guidance.

AS5 OBJECTIVES

After some six months or more of review and public comment, the PCAOB released its new AS5 auditing standards in late May 2007. This new auditing standard is principles-based, unlike the previous AS2 rules-based standard, and it is designed to increase the likelihood that material weaknesses in internal controls will be found before they result in material misstatement of an enterprise's financial statements. One AS5 objective is, at the same time, to eliminate unnecessary financial statement auditing procedures and to emphasize activities necessary to perform high-quality audits that are tailored to an enterprise's facts and circumstances. Based on preliminary comments by the SEC, AS5 was launched to replace the earlier AS2 rules with four major objectives for financial statement audits:

1. **Focus internal control audits on the most important matters.** AS5 calls on external auditors to focus their reviews on areas that present the greatest risk that an internal control will fail to prevent or detect a material misstatement in the financial statements. This approach calls for incorporating certain best practices designed to focus the scope of an audit on identifying material weaknesses in internal controls, before they result in material misstatements of financial statements. AS5 also emphasizes the importance of auditing higher-risk areas, such as the financial statement period-end close process and controls designed to prevent fraud by management. At the same time, the new standard provides external auditors a range of alternatives for addressing lower-risk areas, such as by more clearly demonstrating how to calibrate the nature, timing, and extent of testing based on risk, as well as how to incorporate knowledge accumulated in previous years' audits into the auditors' assessment of risk. AS5 also allows the use of work performed by an enterprise's financial staff or internal auditors, when appropriate.

2. **Eliminate audit procedures that are unnecessary to achieve their intended benefits.** AS5 does not include the previous AS2 standard's detailed requirements to evaluate management's own evaluation process and clarifies that an internal control audit does not require an opinion on the adequacy of management's process. For example, AS5 focuses on the multi-location dimensions of risk in an enterprise rather than the AS2 requirement that auditors test a "large portion" of an enterprise's operations or financial positions. This should allow a reduction in financial audit work.

3. **Make the audit clearly scalable to fit the size and the complexity of any enterprise.** In order to provide guidance for audits of smaller, less complex companies, AS5 explains how to tailor internal control audits to fit the size and complexity of the enterprise being audited. The new standard does so by including notes throughout the standard on how to apply the principles in the standard to smaller, less complex companies, and by including a discussion of the relevant attributes of smaller, less complex companies as well as less complex units of larger companies.

4. **Simplify the text of the standard.** The new AS5 is shorter and easier to read than its AS2 predecessor. This is in part because it uses simpler terms to describe procedures and definitions. It is also because the standard has been streamlined and reorganized to begin with the audit itself, and to move definitions and other background information into appendixes. For example, AS5 eliminates the previous standard's rather lengthy discussion of materiality, clarifying that the auditor's evaluation

of materiality is based on the same long-standing principles applicable to financial statement audits. Also, AS5 conforms certain terms to the SEC's rules and guidance, such as the definition of *material weakness*, in order to use more consistent terminology.

The following sections provide an overview of each of the major elements of AS5 rules from integrating audits through evaluating identified deficiencies, wrapping up an audit, and reporting on internal controls. Given a new set of rules, the major external audit firms will be developing their own standards and interpretations based on AS5, and all are beginning to use it in their financial statement audits under SOx as this book goes to press. AS5 also contains numerous small changes to existing AU section financial accounting standards to make them consistent with these new financial statement auditing rules.

AS5 is a very new standard with limited applications of it to date. However, its new rules and guidance appear to meet many of the concerns that were raised as criticisms of its AS2 predecessor. Enterprise financial managers and their internal auditors should find AS5's risk-based approaches much more consistent with their own enterprise-based processes. Also, although AS5 is directed at independent external auditors, its rules on company-level controls and assessments of their risks should improve day-to-day business processes. The following sections represent a condensation of AS5 rules. We have tried to describe the AS5 financial statement auditing process from the perspective of financial managers and internal auditors who will be working with their external auditors to complete the financial statement auditing process.

Exhibit 3.1 contains an overview of the AS5 audit steps for a review of internal controls over financial reporting. This process is very similar to the financial reporting audit steps under AS2, and the guidance in the new AS5 rules is filled with comments to assess risks as auditors work through this process. The previous AS2 rules were filled with examples—not found in AS5—that imply an even greater level of detailed reviews and investigations. While the AS5 as well as the older AS2 rules are designed for external auditors who are releasing their audited financial statements, the rules impact an enterprise's financial management team, including internal auditors. With the prior AS2 rules, external auditors sometimes brought up almost trivial internal control concerns that caused management to figuratively roll their eyes and question the risks associated with them. AS5 now calls for a consideration of risk in the audit process and does not take a one-size-fits-all type of approach.

I. **Planning the Audit**
   A. Obtain knowledge of internal controls and other matters.
   B. Assess the role of risk assessment.
   C. Scale audit to size and complexity of the enterprise.
   D. Address the risk of fraud.
   E. Consider using work of others such as internal audit.
   F. Use same materiality considerations as in planning a financial statement audit.

II. **Developing Top-Down Audit Approach**
   A. Identify entity-level controls.
   B. Identify significant accounts, disclosures, and their relevant assertions.
   C. Understand likely sources of misstatement.
   D. Select controls to test.

III. **Testing Controls**
   A. Test design effectiveness.
   B. Test operating effectiveness.
   C. Relate risk to the obtained testing evidence.
   D. Consider subsequent year's audits.

IV. **Evaluating Identified Deficiencies**
   A. Evaluate the severity of control deficiencies.
   B. Understand material weaknesses.

V. **Wrapping Up the Audit**
   A. Form the audit opinion.
   B. Obtain written management representations.
   C. Communicate matters to management and the audit committee.

VI. **Reporting on Internal Control**
   A. Issue report with auditor's opinion.
   B. Report any material weaknesses.
   C. Review for subsequent events.

EXHIBIT 3.1   AS5 Internal Control Audit Steps

REVIEWING SECTION 404 INTERNAL CONTROLS UNDER AS5: INTRODUCTION

Beginning with a very brief introduction section, this and the following sections summarize AS5's published rules. As with any legal document, the official published rules are filled with references and footnotes. Our objective here is not to highlight all the external audit related references, but to summarize AS5 rules with an emphasis on their applicability and understandings by internal auditors and financial mangers. We generally are not quoting the precise words in AS5 here but are providing an overview of the rules. References to a concept such as *sufficient competent evidence* is important in auditing standards but has not been used in this summary of the AS5 rules (see www.pcaobus.org for the full text of the AS5 rules).

The AS5 introduction section sets the stage for an audit of internal controls over financial reporting. These are not the same standards that internal auditors would follow, but AS5 uses words and terminology that have been familiar to CPAs and students in financial accounting and auditing over the years. AS5 emphasizes that an auditor's objective is to express an opinion on the effectiveness of an enterprise's internal controls over financial reporting. Because these internal controls cannot be considered effective if one or more material weaknesses exist, the auditor must plan and perform an audit to obtain reasonable assurances about whether material weaknesses exist at the time of the audit.

An important paragraph in this AS5 introductory section sets the stage for the SOx Section 404 rules with the statement: "The auditor should use the same suitable, recognized control framework to perform his or her audit of internal control over financial reporting as management uses for its annual evaluation of the effectiveness of the company's internal control over financial reporting." This statement really outlines a key philosophy of this new auditing standard and corrects some problems of the past. There previously had been difficulties when an enterprise reviewed, documented, and tested its internal controls using something like the Control Objectives for IT (CobiT) framework discussed in Chapter 5, only to have its external auditors state after the fact that "no-no," they do not recognize CobiT and prefer their own firm's standards. CobiT, of course, represents a very viable framework for the evaluation of internal control effectiveness. However, this AS5 rule really says that there must be a level of planning between management and its external auditors on the internal control framework used and the overall Section 404 process. Management is responsible for reviewing their internal controls over financial reporting with the external auditor then attesting to that review work, but there always should be some advanced coordination and understanding before the process begins.

The AS5 introduction section concludes with several guidance statements on integrating financial reporting internal control audits. These are again rules to correct past problems. In the first days of SOx, it was not uncommon for external auditors to review and attest to management's Section 404 internal control assessments and then to have the same external auditors ignore that SOx 404 work. The result was that the external auditors would sometimes then proceed with a traditional financial statement audit that consisted of their own reviews of those same internal controls.

AS5 states that these audits of internal controls over financial reporting should be integrated with the audit of the financial statements. While the objectives of these audits are not identical, efforts should be made to plan and perform the work, including appropriate testing procedures, to achieve the objectives of both audits.

PLANNING THE SOx AS5 AUDIT

As every internal auditor should know, planning is a very important first step for any audit. In the early days of SOx, some external auditors went about things with an almost one-size-fits-all type of approach, performing audit procedures that were not always necessary or appropriate for some of their work. AS5 outlines 12 specific factors (summarized in Exhibit 3.2) that should be considered when planning an external audit. A variety of these considerations point to areas where the effectiveness internal audit procedures should influence the work of external auditors. For example, the Exhibit's Factor 1 is the external auditor's knowledge of financial reporting internal controls, and the relative complexity of operations is Factor 12. An effective internal audit function may raise many appropriate issues here through its regular work.

The emphasis with these 12 factors as well as supporting notes in the AS5 rules is that external auditors should consider the relative size and complexity of the enterprises they audit. The preface to this planning section also mentions that if there is an extensive involvement by senior management in the day-to-day activities, these factors should be considered when planning SOx-related audits. The AS5 rules for planning an audit have specific sections on risk assessments, scaling, fraud considerations, and using the work of others.

Included in the appendix to the published rule set, AS5 provides some high-level definitions that were also part of AS2 but were not outlined in a separate section. These can be useful to assure that management, auditors, and others are all talking the same language. For example, the basic AS5 supporting process, *internal controls over financial reporting*, is described as a process designed by, or under the supervision of, the enterprise's chief executive officer (CEO) and principal financial officers, and effected by both the enterprise's board of directors and management to provide reasonable assurance regarding the reliability and preparation of financial statements. This includes those policies and procedures that:

- Pertain to the maintenance of records that accurately and fairly reflect the transactions and dispositions of the enterprise assets.

These factors are part of the AS5 rules for planning financial statement audits of internal controls. An external auditor should evaluate whether any of these are important to an enterprise's financial statements and internal controls and should modify audit procedures as appropriate. Although the factors have a financial statement focus, many are also very appropriate for internal audit operational reviews as well:

1. Knowledge of the enterprise's internal control over financial reporting obtained during other engagements performed by the auditor
2. Matters affecting the industry in which the enterprise operates, such as financial reporting practices, economic conditions, laws and regulations, and technological changes
3. Matters relating to the enterprise's business, including its organization, operating characteristics, and capital structure
4. The extent of recent changes, if any, in the enterprise, its operations, or its internal control over financial reporting
5. The auditor's preliminary judgments about materiality, risk, and other factors relating to the determination of material weaknesses
6. Control deficiencies previously communicated to the audit committee or management
7. Legal or regulatory matters of which the enterprise is aware
8. The type and extent of available evidence related to the effectiveness of the enterprise's internal controls over financial reporting
9. Preliminary judgments about the effectiveness of internal controls over financial reporting
10. Public information about the enterprise relevant to the evaluation of the likelihood of material financial statement misstatements and the effectiveness of the enterprise's internal controls over financial reporting
11. Knowledge about risks related to the enterprise evaluated as part of the auditor's client acceptance and retention evaluation
12. The relative complexity of the enterprise's operations

EXHIBIT 3.2   Financial Statement and Internal Control Audit Planning Factors

- Provide reasonable assurance that supporting transactions permit preparation of financial statements in accordance with generally accepted accounting principles (GAAP), and that receipts and expenditures are made only in accordance with authorizations of management.
- Provide reasonable assurance regarding prevention or timely detection of unauthorized acquisition, use, or disposition of enterprise assets that could have a material effect on the financial statements.[2]

A note here emphasizes that external auditor procedures as part of either an audit of internal controls over financial reporting or an audit of the actual financial statements are not part of an enterprise's internal controls over financial reporting. The note further states that internal controls over financial reporting have inherent limitations because they involve human diligence, compliance, and lapses in judgment. AS5 recognizes that internal controls over financial reporting can also be circumvented by collusion or improper management override, and there is a risk that material misstatements may not be prevented or detected on a timely basis. Because these inherent limitations are known features of the financial reporting process, it is possible to design process safeguards to reduce, though not to eliminate, this risk.

Other definitions here cover such areas as *material weakness*, which is described as a deficiency in the internal controls over financial reporting such that there is a reasonable possibility that a material misstatement in the annual or interim financial statements will not be prevented or detected on a timely basis. A key theme through all of these definitions is the introduction of the concept of *risk*. Not stressed in the previous AS2 rules, risk is an important consideration that is pervasive in almost all of the new AS5 rules. A selection of these AS5 Appendix rules can be found in Exhibit 3.3.

Role of Risk Assessments

Committee of Sponsoring Organizations Enterprise Risk Management (COSO ERM), as discussed in Chapter 9, was released after SOx became effective. AS2 and other SOx guidance did not place that much emphasis on risk, perhaps because there was no firm and consistent definition of enterprise risk prior to the COSO ERM framework. The role of risk assessments is now part of the AS5 rules, which state:

> *Risk assessment underlies the entire audit process described by this standard, including the determination of **significant accounts and disclosures** and **relevant assertions**, the selection of controls to test, and the determination of the evidence necessary for a given control.*

The point here is that risk assessments should be a fundamental and underlying process when performing SOx-related audits. Auditors should recognize that a direct relationship exists between the degrees of risk that a material weakness could exist in a particular area of an enterprise's internal controls and the amount of audit attention that should be devoted to that

Control objective	A criterion for evaluating whether control procedures in a specific area provide reasonable assurance that a misstatement or omission in that relevant area is prevented or detected by controls on a timely basis.
Deficiency in internal controls	Exists when the design or operation of a control does not allow management or employees, in the normal course of performing their assigned functions, to prevent or detect misstatements on a timely basis.
Design deficiency	Exists when a control necessary to meet a control objective is missing or when an existing control is not properly designed so that, even if the control operates as designed, the control objective would not be met.
Detective controls	Controls that have the objective of detecting errors or fraud that have already occurred that could result in a misstatement of the financial statements.
Internal controls over financial reporting	A process designed by, or under the supervision of, the principal executive and financial officers and effected by the company's board of directors, to provide reasonable assurance regarding the reliability of financial reporting and the preparation of financial statements for external purposes in accordance with GAAP and other factors.
Material weakness	A deficiency, or a combination of deficiencies, in internal controls over financial reporting, such that there is a reasonable possibility that a material misstatement of the company's annual or interim financial statements will not be prevented or detected on a timely basis.
Operation deficiency	Exists when a properly designed control does not operate as designed, or when the person performing the control does not possess the necessary authority or competence to perform the control effectively.
Preventive controls	Controls that have the objective of preventing errors or fraud that could result in a misstatement of the financial statements from occurring.
Significant deficiency	A deficiency, or a combination of deficiencies, in internal controls over financial reporting that is less severe than a material weakness, yet important enough to merit attention by those responsible for oversight of the company's financial reporting.

EXHIBIT 3.3   Auditing Standards No. 5 Definitions

area. This comment again goes back to earlier criticisms when external SOx auditors spent extensive amounts of time and resources on less risky areas. The risk that an enterprise's company's internal controls over financial reporting will fail to prevent or detect misstatements caused by fraud usually is higher than the risk of failure to prevent or detect errors.

The complexity of the organization, business unit, or process has an important role in an auditor's risk assessment and determination of necessary audit procedures. AS5 states that auditors should focus more of their attention on the areas of highest risk. However, it is not necessary to test controls that, even if deficient, would not present a reasonable possibility of material misstatement to the financial statements. This type of guidance is a key element or change of concept that has come out of AS5. Whether it be the SOx-related financial statement audits discussed or the much broader area of internal audit rules, both external and internal auditors should always focus their work to areas of higher risk.

Scaling SOx Section 404 Audits

Scaling is one of those concepts or expressions that was not too common in the past but is frequently used in business today. Scaling means making the size of some process larger or smaller without losing its key attributes. A large enterprise may require a headquarters staff of 100 people to approve new customer accounts, following established internal controls procedures. That same account approval process can be *scaled down* to a small unit with a staff of two persons who would still be expected to follow the same general internal control procedures. Similarly, an IT application can be scaled up for processing on a large server processor or scaled down for operations on a small handheld device. In either case, that application would still have the same features and controls. The scaling of business processes can be difficult to control and manage. There is often a tendency to have too little or too much. This was often an expressed concern with the first round of SOx procedures when external auditors established review procedures that were appropriate for larger enterprises but sometimes failed to scale them down to smaller business units.

AS5 reminds external auditors that the size and complexity of an enterprise, its major processes, and business units may affect the way in which it achieves many of its control objectives. This enterprise size and complexity also might affect the risks of misstatement and the controls necessary to address those risks. Scaling considerations are a natural extension of risk-based approaches and should be applicable to all audits. A smaller, enterprise might achieve its control objectives differently than a larger more complex entity. Again, one-size-fits-all rules do not apply!

Considerations for Fraud

In the years prior to SOx, both external and internal auditor responsibilities for fraud investigation and detection had been rather ambiguous. Their arguments were along the lines that, "yes, fraud is wrong," but "I am an auditor and do not have the training and skills to detect and investigate fraud." The auditing profession was saying these things in the midst of a wide range of almost worldwide accounting scandals and potential fraudulent acts early in the twenty-first century. Of course, we have since had SOx with the PCAOB taking responsibility for financial auditing rules. However, just as the PCAOB was launched, the ASB issued its last old rules auditing standard, SAS 99,[3] which mandated external auditors to actively perform reviews to detect and correct financial statement fraud.

With the launch of SAS 99, the AICPA became very serious regarding an external auditor's responsibility to look for fraudulent activity in the course of their audits. The AICPA teamed up with the Association of Certified Fraud Examiners (ACFE) to provide training and fraud-related reference materials to help auditors better recognize and understand this important area. Although SAS 99 almost seemed to slip between the cracks when it became effective at about the same time as the then-new PCAOB-mandated AS2 rules, it directed external auditors to be more aware of the possibility of fraud in their reviews.

The risk of fraud has now come to the PCAOB rules as well. AS5 states that when planning and performing an audit of financial reporting internal controls, an auditor should perform an entity-level control fraud risk assessment, and then should evaluate whether the enterprise's controls are sufficient to address identified risks of material misstatement due to fraud as well as controls intended to address the risk of management override of other controls. AS5 specifies that controls are needed to address potential fraud-related risks including:

- Controls over significant, unusual transactions, and particularly those that result in late or unusual journal entries
- Controls over journal entries and adjustments made in the period-end financial reporting process
- Controls over related-party transactions
- Controls related to significant management estimates
- Controls that mitigate incentives for, and pressures on, management to falsify or inappropriately manage financial results

There are multiple areas where fraud can exist in the preparation of financial statements, and AS5 highlights some high-level warnings. Both internal and external auditors should be aware of the above types of potential "smoking gun" issues that can be warnings for fraudulent activities, recognizing that weak controls in each of the above may require some further investigation. When an auditor identifies deficiencies in controls designed to prevent or detect fraud during his or her audit, the auditor should take into account those deficiencies when developing responses to risks of material financial statement audit misstatements.

Using the Work of Others

For a whole series of reasons, external auditors may consider using the work of others to help perform their SOx financial statement internal control audits. This practice was not as well defined under previous SOx rules, but AS5 now explicitly allows this. AS5 states that an external auditor may use the work performed by, or receive direct assistance from, internal auditors, other company personnel, or third parties working under the direction of management or the audit committee, to provide evidence about the effectiveness of financial reporting internal controls. This is a major change for internal auditors. Chapter 11 highlights how internal auditors did not always have this role in the early days of SOx under AS2, but they now have a window of opportunity potential role.

Of course, the external auditors are signing off on or attesting to the audit results, and they must assess the competence and objectivity of the persons whose work they plan to use. The higher the degree of competence and objectivity of others, the greater use an auditor may make of their work. In particular, AS5 calls for an assessment of the competence and objectivity of internal auditors. *Competence* means the attainment and maintenance of a level of understanding and knowledge that enables persons to perform the tasks assigned to them, and *objectivity* means the ability to perform those tasks impartially and with intellectual honesty. To assess competence, an external auditor should evaluate the qualifications and ability of the internal auditors or others to perform the work the external auditor plans to use. To assess objectivity, AS5 calls for an external auditor evaluation of whether factors are present that either inhibit or promote a person's ability to perform with the necessary degree of objectivity the work the auditor plans to use.

AS5 goes on to state that external auditors should not use the work of persons who have "a low degree of objectivity, regardless of their level of competence," and also should not use the work of persons who have a low level of competence regardless of their degree of objectivity. Personnel serving as a testing or compliance authority at an enterprise, such as internal auditors, normally are expected to have greater competence and objectivity in performing this type of work and will be useful to the external auditors. This may be an area where enterprises may want to challenge their external auditors if they see no role for internal audit in the financial statement audit planning process.

Although AS5 talks about internal auditors in an almost generic fashion, the role of the professional IIA member internal auditor is important here. Based on the Standards for the Professional Practice of Internal Auditing, as summarized in Chapter 11, an Institute of Internal Auditors (IIA) internal auditor can be expected to have the competence and objectivity necessary to help in supporting an external auditor's review of Section 404 internal controls. While other persons, such as outside consultants, can be used to assist external auditors in their financial statement internal control reviews, internal auditors should have a major role, under AS5, in assisting their external auditors with Section 404 and AS5 compliance.

Internal audit's ongoing role here should be viewed with a level of caution. We have discussed how internal auditors can often be excellent resources to identify, document, and test key Section 404 processes. They could do this in a support role for the external auditor's attestation reviews. However, pure separation-of-duties independence rules say that they cannot perform these reviews as internal auditors within the enterprise and also then act as a third-party helpmate for the external auditors to help attest to that same work. This conflict of duties should be clearly understood by all parties, and care should be exercised by internal auditors and their management to prevent it.

AS5'S TOP-DOWN APPROACH

Both internal and external auditors have historically started on assessments of control risks at a fairly detailed level and then assembled their detailed reviews to develop and overall assessment and conclusion of the area audited. AS5 calls for external auditors to use a top-down approach that describes an auditor's sequential thought process in identifying risks and the controls to test, but not necessarily in the same order in which these auditing procedures will be performed. A top-down approach begins at the financial statement level and with the auditor's understanding of the overall risks to internal controls over financial reporting. Starting with the financial statement and internal control risks, the auditor would then focus on entity-level controls and work down to significant accounts and disclosures and their relevant assertions.

This financial statement auditing approach should direct an external auditor's attention to the accounts, disclosures, and assertions that could present a reasonable possibility of material financial statement misstatement. The external auditor should then verify his or her understanding of these risks in enterprise processes and select for testing those that sufficiently address any assessed risks of misstatement.

Identifying Entity-Level Controls

AS5 says an auditor should test important entity-level controls to assess whether there are effective internal controls over the enterprise's financial reporting. This evaluation of entity-level controls can result in increasing or decreasing the testing an auditor otherwise would have performed on other controls. Entity-level controls include:

- Controls related to the COSO control environment. This is part of the COSO internal control framework discussed in Chapter 4. AS5 focuses on this important area and highlights that the external auditor should assess:
  - Whether management's philosophy and operating style promote effective internal controls over financial reporting
  - Whether sound integrity and ethical values, particularly those of top management, are developed and understood
  - Whether the Board or audit committee understands and exercises oversight responsibility over financial reporting and internal controls
- Controls over management overrides. While controls here are important for all enterprises, they can be particularly important at smaller companies because of the frequent increased involvement of senior management in performing controls and in the period-end financial reporting process. For smaller companies, controls that address the risk of management override might be different from those at a larger enterprise. For example, a smaller enterprise might rely on more detailed oversight by the audit committee that focuses on the risk of management override.
- The enterprise's risk assessment process as discussed in Chapter 9 on COSO ERM.
- Centralized processing and controls, including shared service environments, as well as controls to monitor results of operations.
- Controls to monitor other controls, including internal audit activities and other self-assessment programs.
- Controls over the period-end financial reporting process.
- Policies that address significant business control and risk management practices.

- Period-end financial reporting processes. As part of its emphasis on entity-level controls, AS5 emphasizes that an external auditor must evaluate the period-end financial reporting process, including:
  - Procedures used to enter transaction totals into the general ledger
  - Procedures related to the selection and application of accounting policies
  - Procedures used to initiate, authorize, record, and process journal entries in the general ledger
  - Procedures used to record recurring and nonrecurring adjustments to the annual and quarterly financial statements
  - Procedures for preparing annual and quarterly financial statements and related disclosures

This section of the published PCAOB rules has an interesting note stating, "Because the annual period-end financial reporting process normally occurs after the 'as-of' date of management's assessment, those controls usually cannot be tested until after the as-of date." We comment that this is interesting as many of the review procedures outlined here should have been documented, evaluated, and tested as part of the Section 404 assessments discussed in Chapter 6. AS5 seems to be saying that it is necessary for the external auditors to return after the financial statement closing dates and then perform additional tests.

As part of evaluating this period-end financial reporting process, auditors should assess the overall process used to produce its annual and quarterly financial statements; the types of adjusting and consolidating entries; and the nature and extent of the oversight of the process by management, the board of directors, and the audit committee. In addition, this section of the rules calls for an assessment of the extent of IT involvement in the period-end financial reporting process. This says there must be some level of IT general and application control reviews as of the dates of the financial statement close periods.

While the AS5 review steps for an audit of internal controls over financial reporting, outlined in Exhibit 3.1, are very similar to the financial reporting audit steps under the old AS2, the guidance in the AS5 rules perhaps helps auditors better to assess risks as auditors work through this process. While AS5 rules are designed for external auditors who are releasing their audited financial statements, they also impact an enterprise's financial management team, including internal auditors. This new AS5 environment should lessen some of the sometimes almost trivial internal control concerns that, external auditors sometimes brought up under the prior AS2 rules. AS5 now calls for a consistent consideration of risk in the audit process and does not take a one-size-fits-all type of approach.

Identifying Significant Accounts, Disclosures, and Relevant Assertions

This section of AS5 introduces one of those terms that many CPA-trained financial auditors will understand but that may result in blank stares from many others—*internal controls financial statement assertions*. This concept is based on the word *assert*, where an individual may state that "I assert" or strongly believe some fact or condition to be true. AS5 calls for an auditor to identify significant accounts, disclosures, and their "relevant assertions." The underlying concept is that management and not the external auditors are responsible for the preparation of the financial statements. When management prepares those financial statements, they are asserting, among other matters, that the financial statement items, underlying account balances, and classes of transaction are complete and accurate. Auditing standards are based on five financial statement assertions as summarized in Exhibit 3.4. They are key concepts and underlying assumptions important in the overall financial statement audit process.

To identify significant accounts, disclosures, and their relevant assertions, AS5 calls for an external auditor to evaluate both the qualitative and quantitative risk factors related to the financial statement line items and disclosures. These risk factors include:

- Size and composition of each account
- Susceptibility to misstatement due to errors or fraud
- Volume of activity, complexity, and homogeneity of the individual transactions processed through the account or reflected in the disclosure

---

- **Existence or Occurrence:** Assets, liabilities, and owners' equity accounts reflected in the financial statements exist; the recorded transactions have occurred.
- **Completeness:** All transactions, assets, liabilities, and elements of owners' equity that should be presented in the financial statements are included.
- **Rights and Obligations:** The client has rights to assets and obligations to pay liabilities that are included in financial statements.
- **Valuation or Allocation:** Assets, liabilities, owners' equity, revenue, and expenses are presented at amounts that are determined in accordance with generally accepted accounting principles.
- **Presentation and Disclosure:** Accounts are described and classified in financial statements in accordance with generally accepted accounting principles, and all material disclosures are provided.

EXHIBIT 3.4 Financial Statement Audit Assertions

- Nature of the account as well as accounting and reporting complexities associated with it
- Exposure to losses in the account
- Possibility of significant contingent liabilities arising from the account activities reflected
- Existence of related-party transactions in the account
- Changes from the prior period in the account or its disclosure characteristics

As part of identifying significant accounts and disclosures and their relevant assertions, the new rules call for an external auditor to also determine the likely sources of potential misstatements by asking "what could go wrong?" types of questions within these significant accounts or disclosures. The auditor evaluation risk factors here are the same in audit of internal controls over financial reporting (SOx related) as in the traditional audit of the financial statements; significant accounts and disclosures and their relevant assertions are the same for both.

The rules recognize that the components of various significant accounts or disclosures might be subject to significantly differing risks, and if so, different controls might be necessary to adequately address those risks. Again, one-size-fits-all no longer applies! An appendix to the published AS5 rules provides some scoping decision guidance where there are multiple locations or business units.

Understanding Likely Sources of Misstatement

AS5 provides further guidance on selecting the controls to test. To further understand the risk that an undetected misstatement would cause financial statements to be materially misstated, an external auditor should:

- Understand the flow of transactions related to the relevant assertions, including how these transactions are initiated, authorized, processed, and recorded.
- Verify that the audit has identified the points within enterprise processes where a misstatement—including any due to fraud—could arise that, individually or in combination with other misstatements, would be material.
- Identify the controls that management has implemented to address these potential misstatements.
- Identify the controls that management has implemented over the prevention or timely detection of unauthorized acquisition, use, or disposition of company assets that could result in a material financial statement misstatement.

This same section on understanding likely sources of misstatement has a rule that the external auditor should also understand how IT affects the company's flow of transactions. There is a comment, however, that the identification of risks and controls within *IT is not a separate evaluation.* The italics here are our own to emphasize the importance of IT audit assessments under AS5. This understanding of IT should be an integral part of the top-down approach used to identify significant accounts and their relevant assertions, and the controls to test, as well as to assess risks and allocate audit effort as described by this standard.

The rules for understanding sources for misstatement end with a paragraph on performing walkthroughs. AS5 suggests that this process will frequently be the most effective way of understanding likely sources of misstatements. In performing a walkthrough, an auditor should follow a transaction from its origination through the related processes, including information systems, until it is reflected in the company's financial records. A common process used for documenting processes under SOx Section 404 work, walkthrough procedures usually include a combination of inquiry, observation, inspection of relevant documentation, and re-performance of controls.

In performing a walkthrough, at the points at which important processing procedures occur, the external auditor should question personnel about their understanding of what is required by the enterprise's prescribed procedures and controls. These probing questions, combined with the other walkthrough procedures, allow the auditor to gain a sufficient understanding of a process and to identify important points at which a necessary control is missing or not designed effectively. Additionally, probing questions that go beyond a narrow focus on the single transaction used as the basis for the walkthrough allow the auditor to gain an understanding of the different types of significant transactions handled by the process. These walkthrough procedures have frequently been performed by internal auditors as part of their normal internal control review work. The documentation gained through those internal audit procedures should help support an external audit team.

Selecting Controls to Test

Control testing should be performed to support an auditor's conclusion about whether enterprise controls sufficiently address the assessed risk of misstatement to each of the relevant assertions. For example, management may assert that the accounts covering some area are complete, but a financial auditor would then develop tests to determine whether those account processes are complete in that area. There might be more than one control that addresses the assessed risk of misstatement to a particular relevant assertion, and conversely, one control might address assessed risks for more than one relevant assertion. As an important AS5 rules change from AS2, it is not necessary to test all controls related to a relevant assertion nor necessary to test redundant controls, unless redundancy is itself a control objective.

The decision as to whether a control should be selected for testing depends on which controls, individually or in combination, sufficiently address the assessed risk of misstatement to a given relevant assertion rather than on how the control is labeled. That is, if there is an entity-level control, transaction-level control, and control activity, it is not necessary to test each of these areas. All too often under the old AS2 rules, there was a tendency for external auditors to insist on a test of each of these associated controls. AS5's more risk-based approach changes this perspective. While an enterprise's external auditors have the right to call the shots here, when an external auditor seems to have an old-rules mindset, management and the internal auditors should ask some hard questions about the risk assessment approach used for selecting controls to test.

TESTING INTERNAL CONTROLS

External and internal auditing processes both involve the detailed preparation of supporting documentation but sometimes lack a sufficient level of testing to support that documentation. Existing external audit standards call for external auditors to test both the design and operating effectiveness of key internal controls processes. These tests call for an auditor to determine if internal controls are operated, as prescribed, by persons possessing the necessary authority and competence to perform the controls effectively. In addition, testing here should assess whether the enterprise's control objectives can effectively prevent or detect errors or fraud that could result in material misstatements in the financial statements. Tests of design effectiveness also include a mix of appropriate personnel inquiries, observations of operations, and inspections of relevant documentation. AS5 also suggests that walk-through evaluations are ordinarily sufficient to evaluate design effectiveness. In addition, an auditor should test the operating effectiveness of a control by determining whether the control is operating as designed and whether persons performing the control possess the necessary authority and competence to perform the control effectively. If an enterprise uses a third party to provide assistance with its financial reporting functions, the external auditor should take into account the combined competence of enterprise personnel and other parties that assist with functions related to financial reporting.

To test operating effectiveness, AS5 calls for a mix of procedures including inquiries with appropriate personnel, observations of operations, inspection of relevant documentation, and re-performance of controls. For each control selected for testing, the level of evidence necessary to determine whether that the control is effective depends on the risk associated with the control. This is the risk that the control might not be effective and, if not effective, the further risk that a material weakness would result. As the risk associated with the control being tested increases, the evidence that the auditor should obtain also increases. Some factors that an auditor should consider include:

- The nature and materiality of misstatements that the control is intended to prevent or detect
- Whether there have been changes in the volume or nature of transactions that might adversely affect control design or operating effectiveness
- Whether the account has a history of errors
- The nature of the control and the frequency with which it operates
- The degree to which the control relies on the effectiveness of other controls, such as the control environment or IT general controls
- The competence of the personnel who perform the control or monitor its performance and whether there have been changes in the key personnel who perform or monitor the control
- Whether the control relies on manual procedures or is automated, because an IT-based control would generally be expected to be lower risk if relevant IT general controls are effective
- The complexity of the control and the significance of the judgments that must be made in connection with its operation

AS5 states that less evidence is needed when an auditor finds that a control is not operating effectively than is necessary to support a conclusion that a control is operating effectively. When an audit identifies deviations from the enterprise's controls, the auditor should determine their effect on an assessment of the risks associated with the control being tested as well as on the operating effectiveness of the control.

The evidence provided by these tests of the effectiveness of controls depends on the mix of the nature, timing, and extent of the auditor's procedures. For an individual control, different combinations of the nature, timing, and extent of testing can provide sufficient evidence in relation to the risk associated with the control. AS5 highlights that walkthroughs—typically consisting of a combination of inquiries, observations of operations, inspection of relevant documentation, and re-performance of controls—can provide evidence of operating effectiveness, depending on the risk associated with the control being tested, the specific procedures performed as part of the walkthrough, and the results of those procedures.

Some types of tests, by their nature, produce greater evidence of control effectiveness than others. AS5 ranks tests that an auditor might perform in order of the evidence that they ordinarily would produce, from *least* to *most*: inquiry, observation, inspection of relevant documentation, and re-performance of a control. In a side note, AS5 reminds us that "Inquiry alone does not provide sufficient evidence to support a conclusion about the effectiveness of a control." The nature of these tests of effectiveness depends, to a large degree, on the type of control to be tested, including whether the operation of the control results in documentary evidence of its operation.

Documentary evidence of the operation of some controls, such as management's philosophy and operating style, might not exist. In addition, a smaller, less complex enterprise might have less formal control documentation. In those situations, testing controls through inquiry combined with other procedures, such as observation of activities, inspection of less formal documentation, or re-performance of certain controls, might provide sufficient evidence about whether the control is effective.

Testing controls over a greater period of time provides more evidence of the effectiveness of controls than testing over a shorter period. Further, testing performed closer to the date of management's Section 404 assessment provides more evidence than testing performed earlier in the year. An external auditor should balance performing the tests of controls closer to the as-of date coupled with the need to test controls over a sufficient period of time to obtain evidence of operating effectiveness. As part of their SOx control assessment work, management often implements changes to their controls to make them more effective and efficient or to address control deficiencies. If an external auditor determines that the new controls achieve their related objectives and have been in effect for a sufficient period to permit an assessment of their design and operating effectiveness, the auditor will not need to test the design and operating effectiveness of the recently implemented controls for purposes of expressing an opinion on internal controls over financial reporting. However, the more extensively a control is tested, the greater the evidence obtained from that test.

When an auditor reports on the effectiveness of controls as of a specific date and obtains evidence about the operating effectiveness of controls at an interim date, he or she should determine what additional evidence concerning the operation of the controls for the remaining period is necessary. The additional evidence necessary to update the results of testing from an interim date to the enterprise's year-end depends on the specific controls tested prior to the as-of date, the nature and results of those tests, the sufficiency of the evidence of effectiveness obtained at the interim date, the length of the remaining period, and the possibility that there have been any significant changes in internal controls subsequent to that interim date.

In subsequent years' audits, an auditor should incorporate knowledge obtained from past audits of financial reporting internal controls into a process for determining the nature, timing, and extent of testing necessary. This decision-making process should include the extent of procedures performed in previous audits, the results of the previous years' testing, and whether there have been control or process changes since the previous audit. A prior year's audit with no significant control weaknesses identified might permit an auditor to reduce testing in subsequent years.

In addition, an auditor should vary the nature, timing, and extent of testing of controls from year to year to introduce unpredictability into the testing and respond to changes in circumstances. For this reason, each year an auditor might consider testing controls at a different interim period, increase or reduce the number and types of tests performed, or change the combination of procedures used.

EVALUATING IDENTIFIED AUDIT DEFICIENCIES

As a final step, an external auditor should evaluate the severity of each identified control deficiency to determine whether these deficiencies, individually or in combination, are material weaknesses as of the date of management's assessment. In planning and performing the audit, however, the auditor is not required to search for deficiencies that, individually or in combination, are less severe than a material weakness. The severity of an AS5 deficiency depends on whether there is a reasonable possibility that the enterprise's controls will fail to prevent or detect a misstatement of an account balance or disclosure as well as the magnitude of the potential misstatement resulting from the deficiency. The severity of a control deficiency does not depend on whether a misstatement actually has occurred but rather on whether there is a reasonable possibility that the enterprise's controls will fail to prevent or detect a misstatement.

Risk factors affect whether there is a reasonable possibility that a single deficiency or combination of deficiencies will result in a misstatement of an account balance or disclosure. These factors include, but are not limited to:

- The nature of the financial statement accounts, disclosures, and assertions
- The susceptibility of the related asset or liability to a loss or fraud
- The subjectivity, complexity, or extent of judgment required to determine the amounts involved
- The interaction or relationship of internal controls, including whether they are interdependent or redundant

- The interaction of identified deficiencies
- The possible future consequences of those deficiencies

Factors that affect the magnitude of the misstatement that might result from an internal control deficiency include the financial statement amounts or total of transactions exposed to the deficiency; and the volume of activity in the account balance or class of transactions exposed to the deficiency that has occurred in the current period or is expected in future periods.

Auditors should evaluate the effect of compensating controls when determining whether a control deficiency or combination of deficiencies is a material weakness. This was a major area of controversy under the old AS2 rules when external auditors sometimes classified fairly minor matters as material weaknesses. Under AS5 rules, indicators of material weaknesses in internal controls over financial reporting have been defined as:

- Any identification of senior management fraud, whether or not material
- Restatements of previously issued financial statements to reflect the correction of a material misstatement
- Auditor identification of a material misstatement of financial statements in the current period in circumstances that indicate that the misstatement would not have been detected by the enterprise's internal controls over financial reporting
- Ineffective oversight of the enterprise's external financial reporting and internal controls over financial reporting by the enterprise's audit committee

When evaluating the severity of a deficiency or combination of deficiencies, an auditor should also determine the level of detail and degree of assurance that would satisfy prudent senior management officials in the conduct of their own affairs and business operations. AS5 sums this up by declaring that if an external auditor determines that a deficiency or combination of deficiencies might prevent prudent officials, in the conduct of their own affairs, from concluding that they have reasonable assurance that their transactions are recorded as necessary to permit the preparation of financial statements in conformity with generally accepted accounting principles, then the auditor should treat the deficiency or combination of deficiencies as an indicator of a material weakness.

WRAPPING UP THE AS5 AUDIT

The purpose of AS5 is to provide guidelines for external auditors to form an opinion on the effectiveness of the internal controls over an enterprise's financial reporting. This process starts with enterprise management documenting and assessing their key internal controls through the SOx Section 404 process. The external auditors then must review and attest to this Section 404 work and form their own audit opinion following these AS5 rules. External auditors evaluate evidence obtained from all sources, including their own testing of controls, misstatements detected during the financial statement audit, and any identified control deficiencies. AS5 again emphasizes that as part of this evaluation, an external auditor should review reports issued during the year by internal audit that address controls related to internal controls over financial reporting and evaluate control deficiencies identified in those reports.

After forming an opinion on the effectiveness of an enterprise's financial reporting internal controls, the external auditor should evaluate management-prepared annual reports—the SEC Form 10K–mandated financial reports—in order to express an audited opinion on these reports. As part of this process, external auditors must obtain written representations from enterprise management acknowledging their overall responsibility for internal controls and these financial reports. The rules stating that management are responsible for their financial reports have been part of the external auditing process for some time, but they really became loose over the years prior to SOx. It was not unusual then for an external audit firm to do much of the financial statement accounting close work and then hand it to enterprise financial management. SOx Section 302, discussed in Chapter 7, requires management representation letters here give full responsibility to enterprise financial management.

As a final step, the external auditor must communicate to management and the audit committee all material weaknesses identified during the audit. If an external auditor concludes that the audit committee's oversight of financial reporting and internal controls is ineffective, the auditor must specifically communicate that conclusion to the board of directors. That is, external auditors are also reviewing the performance of the audit committee as part of their process. More important, an external auditor should also consider whether any deficiencies or combinations of deficiencies that have been identified during the audit are significant deficiencies, and must communicate them to the audit committee. The point of significant deficiencies is also highlighted in bold in the published AS5 rules. External auditors should also communicate to management and inform the audit committee of all lesser magnitude internal control deficiencies. When making this communication, it is not necessary for the auditor to repeat previously issued communications about deficiencies, whether they were made by the auditor, internal auditors, or others within the organization.

These rule changes represent a major simplification in SOx processes! Under the old rules, the bar for external auditor–identified deficiencies was much lower, and audit committees and management found themselves discussing external auditor–introduced deficiencies that were often low risk and really not that significant in the big picture of things. When an exasperated management previously asked their external auditors why they were spending so much time on such low-risk non-issues, the response then often was that these were the "SOx rules." Now, AS5 says that external auditors are only required to bring significant deficiencies to their audit committees, with the less significant matters only communicated to management. Although time and experience will tell here, these new AS5 rules simplify things to a great extent.

REPORTING ON AS5 AUDIT INTERNAL CONTROLS

AS5 concludes with a section on the external auditors' reports on internal controls. In many respects, not too much has changed regarding auditor's report guidance from the pre-SOx AICPA guidance or the rules under AS2. These rules outline specific requirements for the independent auditor's report—such as the requirement for a statement that management is responsible for maintaining effective internal controls over financial reporting and a statement that the audit was conducted in accordance with PCAOB standards.

A key portion of this AS5 section is the external auditor's opinion on whether the enterprise has maintained, in all material respects, effective internal controls over financial reporting as of the report date. In addition, there is guidance for separate or combined reports, where an auditor may choose to issue a combined report containing an opinion both on the financial statements and on internal controls over financial reporting or separate reports on the company's financial statements and on internal controls over financial reporting. AS5 has suggested words on the format of such opinion letters.

For an enterprise, an objective of this process is to have strong internal controls over financial reporting in place such that an external auditor will issue a favorable auditor's opinion. To cover such issues, AS5 also includes guidance and report formats for unfavorable or adverse opinion letters. Any of these are generally a damning indictment for an enterprise, but the AS5 rules provide reporting formats for each of these conditions.

In addition to outlining the rules of auditor opinion letters and reporting on material weaknesses, this section of the AS5 rules also provides guidance for handling subsequent events—matters that occurred after the formal audit has been completed but before the audit report is issued. These are changes in internal controls over financial reporting or other factors that might significantly affect internal controls subsequent to audit date but before the date of the audit report. External auditors should obtain written management representations if there were any such changes and also should examine such matters as internal audit reports issued during the subsequent period or any appropriate regulatory agency reports on the company's financial reporting internal controls. This guidance along with other sections of AS5 tightens ties between external and internal auditors for reviews of financial reporting internal controls.

IMPROVING INTERNAL CONTROLS USING AS5 GUIDANCE

AS5 does not require management to make any changes in their operations or internal control processes. Rather, AS5 sets the rules that their external auditors will use to audit those financial accounting controls. These new rules provide an opportunity for management and internal auditors to improve the efficiency and effectiveness of their evaluation processes. This may require a revisit of some of the internal controls that were documented and tested in previous Section 404 reviews to determine if there is a reasonable possibility that a material misstatement in the financial statements would not be prevented or detected. Risk is a key concept introduced in these new rules, and management should gather and analyze evidence about the operation of the controls being evaluated based on assessments of the risks associated with those controls.

Enterprise risk management is discussed in Chapter 9, but a robust program of risk evaluations and assessments will allow management and internal audit to work with their external auditors to highlight some and eliminate other areas because of their relative risks. Internal audit can play a key role here in including strong risk assessments in their financial statement internal control reviews. A key point is to use these evaluation techniques consistently throughout reviews in the enterprise, and the COSO enterprise risk framework, discussed in Chapter 9, should be a useful tool here.

While enterprise concerns regarding risks can cover many dimensions, the focus with AS5 should be on identifying those risks that may result in financial report material misstatements. The approach should be top down in its focus with concentration first on higher-level areas such as overall segregation of duties issues or IT general controls before focusing on more detail-level areas. However, for a larger, multilevel enterprise, there should be an emphasis on process-level key controls that are designed to address specific financial reporting risks.

In addition to AS5's emphasis on risk, another key change in the new rules are the frequent references to the work of internal audit and reliance on their published internal audit reports. While an effective internal audit function may be designing its own plan of reviews based on input from senior management and the audit committee, there may be an internal audit need for a greater emphasis on reviews of internal controls over various higher-risk financial statement elements. In the past, some internal audit functions have essentially let their external auditors perform financial statement reviews while internal audit focused more on operational-level controls. Now, there can be a greater shared approach here as long as there is strong communication and coordination. AS5 does not at all call for external auditors to treat their internal auditors as the outsourced internal auditors from those pre-SOx, pre-Enron days. Internal auditors are an independent entity performing important internal control reviews under the guise of their audit committees, but some level of coordination is important.

GOING FORWARD: POTENTIAL RISKS AND REWARDS

With its rules just published around June 1, 2007, AS5 is still very new. However, the AS5 top-down approach and emphasis on risk should ease some of the pain that the previous AS2 SOx rules imposed on the financial audit process in many enterprises. The challenge is that each of the major public accounting firms as well as even the engagement teams associated with each client audit may approach these new rules somewhat differently. Some may look at things using a "business as usual" approach with no significant changes to their audit procedures, while others may go almost too high level in their interpretations. At the start of each financial statement audit, it would be a good idea for enterprise financial management to meet with their external auditors, to understand how their financial statement audit approaches will differ from prior periods, given the new AS5 rules.

The focus of this book is directed much more at management, its internal auditors, and the audit committee rather than at the external auditors. The latter generally come from the major public accounting firms, each of which has its own firm-developed audit procedures. However, the management team working with their external auditors should have at least a general understanding of the PCAOB rules that govern those financial statement audit activities. This chapter has attempted to provide such a high-level description of these new financial statement auditing rules under AS5.

ENDNOTES

1. A public document, the full text of AS5 can be found on the PCAOB Web site: http://www.pcaobus.org/Rules/Docket_021/2007-05-24_Release_No_2007-005.pdf.

2. This definition of AS5 internal controls and all others in this chapter is a close approximation but not the AS5 word-for-word text. For example, the reference here to "principal financial officers" has an additional phrase in the actual rules: "or other persons performing similar functions." For purposes of space, our text descriptions have been carefully edited. The reader is encouraged to reference the Web site, www.pacaobus.org.

3. "Consideration of Fraud in a Financial Statement Audit," Statement on Auditing Standards No. 99, AICPA.

CHAPTER 4

Establishing Internal Controls Through COSO

A system of strong internal controls has been and continues to be the basis for effective operational and accounting business processes. Over the years in the United States, the term *internal controls*, although frequently referenced by auditors and business managers, did not have a consistent definition or use. However, a series of events in the United States in the 1970s led to the development and release of the Committee of Sponsoring Organizations (COSO) internal control framework. First recognized as a standard for assessing internal controls by U.S. internal and external auditors, the COSO internal control framework has received worldwide recognition and become the Sarbanes-Oxley Act's (SOx's) standard for building and measuring internal controls.

This chapter briefly discusses "how we got there"—the activities by auditors, regulators, and other professionals over recent years to develop a consistent approach to defining and understanding internal controls. The chapter will then introduce the COSO internal control framework and why its application is essential for establishing compliance with SOx internal accounting control requirements. It should be noted that there are two different COSO frameworks. The first COSO framework and the emphasis of this chapter provides a consistent definition for internal controls, and it is still often called just the COSO framework. However, after SOx became effective in 2004, COSO released an enterprise risk management framework as well (COSO ERM, introduced in Chapter 9). Although COSO ERM sometimes looks similar, it describes different areas and objectives. Throughout this book, we will reference the two as COSO ERM and the COSO internal control framework discussed in this chapter.

IMPORTANCE OF EFFECTIVE INTERNAL CONTROLS

Internal controls is one of the most important and fundamental concepts that business professionals at all levels and both external and internal auditors must understand. The business professional builds and uses internal controls while auditors review both operational and financial areas of the enterprise with an objective of evaluating those internal controls. Internal and external auditors have many different objectives, and most of our references to auditors in this chapter apply to internal auditors, whose activities with respect to SOx are discussed in Chapter 11 and whose general responsibilities are discussed in our overall guide to internal auditing.[1] Although there have been many interpretations in the past, a good textbook definition of *internal control* follows:

> *Internal control comprises the plan of enterprise and all of the coordinate methods adopted within a business to safeguard its assets, check the accuracy and reliability of its accounting data, promote operational efficiency, and encourage adherence to prescribed managerial policies. This definition recognizes that a system of internal control extends beyond those matters which relate directly to the functions of the accounting and financial departments.*

This long and rather academic-sounding definition says that a system or process has good internal controls if it (1) accomplishes its stated mission, (2) produces accurate and reliable data, (3) complies with applicable laws and enterprise policies, (4) provides for economical and efficient uses of resources, and (5) provides for appropriate safeguarding of assets. All members of an enterprise are responsible for the internal controls in their area of operation and for operating them effectively.

Despite or perhaps because of the above lengthy definition, many business professionals in the past had problems with this concept. Looking at the definition a bit differently, the concept of a control process and its internal controls goes back to basic mechanical and paperwork procedures that once frequently existed throughout one's everyday life. Control processes are necessary for activities inside and outside today's enterprise, and many basic concepts and principles are the same no matter where the control is encountered. An automobile provides some control examples. When the accelerator—a speed control—is pressed, the automobile goes faster. When the brake—another control—is pressed, the automobile slows or stops. When the steering wheel is turned, the vehicle turns. The driver *controls* the automobile, and all three of these represent an internal control system. If the driver does not use the accelerator, brake, or steering wheel properly, the automobile will operate *out of control*.

Expanding this concept just a bit, a stop sign, traffic direction sign, or gate crossing barriers all represent external controls to the auto and its driver. The driver is the operator of the automobile-based internal control process or system, but has little decision authority over the message delivered from a traffic light external control.

From an internal control perspective, an enterprise can be compared to our automobile example as well. There are many enterprise systems and processes at work, such as accounting operations, sales processes, and information technology (IT) systems. If management does not operate or direct these processes properly, the enterprise may operate out of control. All members of an enterprise should develop an understanding of appropriate control systems and then determine if they are properly connected to manage the enterprise. These are referred to as the enterprise's *internal control* systems.

A major component of SOx Section 404 calls for an independent management definition and documentation of enterprise internal control systems and processes. This was a major challenge for many enterprises as they began their first rounds of these required SOx reviews. Many had poorly documented internal control processes, and teams—often populated with outside consultants—were brought in to do this documentation work. For many this was an expensive and painful process. In almost the same situation, other enterprises previously relied on their external auditors to document these internal controls. SOx rules have banned this external audit role, even though external auditors can still provide help for non-audit clients.

In the first days of SOx Section 404 reviews, internal auditors had a sometimes ambiguous role. Internal audit standards said that they could not prepare the actual internal control documentation because of the risk of losing their audit independence. The Institute of Internal Auditors' (IIA's) standards have since been clarified such that internal auditors can separately operate as auditors and as consultants, provided these individual responsibilities have been disclosed and documented. This area will be discussed in Chapter 11. The role of internal auditors and others in the enterprise is increasingly involved with internal control reviews as outlined with the newer AS5 auditing standards and discussed in Chapters 2 and 3.

Internal auditors are often called on to describe an enterprise's control systems to management as part of their normal internal audit work. An internal auditor must be a spokesperson for the importance of internal controls, but to be effective, must have a good understanding of basic internal control objectives and components. The following sections will briefly discuss the long and often slow process to develop this consistent and now worldwide recognized framework to describe and define internal controls.

INTERNAL CONTROL STANDARDS: BACKGROUND

Although our concept and definition of internal controls is fairly well understood today through the COSO internal control framework, this was not true in the not-too-distant past. Although it has been an important concept, there had been no consistent agreement among many interested persons of what was meant by "good internal controls." Early definitions first came from the American Institute of Certified Public Accountants (AICPA) and were used by the U.S. Securities and Exchange Commission (SEC) for Securities Exchange Act of 1934 regulations to provide a good starting point. Although there have been changes over the years, the AICPA's first codified standards, called the Statement on Auditing Standards (SAS No. 1[2]), covered the practice of financial statement auditing in the United States for many years with the following definition for *internal control*:

> *Internal control comprises the plan of enterprise and all of the coordinate methods and measures adopted with a business to safeguard its assets, check the accuracy and reliability of its accounting data, promote operational efficiency, and encourage adherence to prescribed managerial policies.*

That original AICPA SAS No. 1 was further modified to add administrative controls and accounting controls to the basic internal control definition. Administrative control

> *includes, but is not limited to, the plan of enterprise and the procedures and records that are concerned with the decision processes leading to management's authorization of transactions. Such authorization is a management function directly associated with the responsibility for achieving the objectives of the enterprise and is the starting point for establishing accounting control of transactions.*

Accounting control

> *comprises the plan of enterprise and the procedures and records that are concerned with the safeguarding of assets and the reliability of financial records and consequently are designed to provide reasonable assurance that:*
>
> *a. Transactions are executed in accordance with management's general or specific authorization.*

b. *Transactions are recorded as necessary (1) to permit preparation of financial statements in conformity with generally accepted accounting principles or any other criteria applicable to such statement and (2) to maintain accountability for assets.*

c. *Access to assets is permitted only in accordance with management's authorization.*

d. *The recorded accountability for assets is compared with the existing assets at reasonable intervals and appropriate action is taken with respect to any differences.*

The overlapping relationships of these two types of internal controls was then further clarified in these pre-1988 AICPA standards:

The foregoing definitions are not necessarily mutually exclusive because some of the procedures and records comprehended in accounting control may also be involved in administrative control. For example, sales and cost records classified by products may be used for accounting control purposes and also in making management decisions concerning unit prices or other aspects of operations. Such multiple uses of procedures or records, however, are not critical for the purposes of this section because it is concerned primarily with clarifying the outer boundary of accounting control. Examples of records used solely for administrative control are those pertaining to customers contacted by salesmen and to defective work by production employees maintained only for evaluation personnel per performance.

Our point here is that the definition of internal control, as originally defined by the AICPA, was subject to changes and reinterpretations over the years. However, those earlier AICPA standards stressed that the system of internal controls extends beyond just matters relating directly to the accounting and financial statements. Over this period through the 1970s, there were many internal control definitions released by the SEC and AICPA as well as voluminous interpretations and guidelines developed by major external auditing firms.

Internal Control Definitions: Foreign Corrupt Practices Act of 1977

Just as the accounting scandals of Enron and others brought us SOx, the United States had experienced a similar situation some 30 years earlier. Although long ago, the period of 1974 through 1977 was a time of extreme social and political turmoil in the United States. The 1972 presidential election was surrounded by a series of illegal acts, including a burglary of the Democratic party headquarters in a building complex known as Watergate, which eventually led to the President's resignation. Related investigations found other questionable practices had occurred that were not covered by legislation. Similar to how the failure of Enron brought us SOx, the result then was the 1977 Foreign Corrupt Practices Act (FCPA).

The FCPA prohibited bribes to foreign—non-U.S.—officials and contained provisions requiring the maintenance of both accurate books and records and systems of internal accounting controls. With provisions that apply to virtually all U.S. companies with SEC-registered securities, the FCPA internal control rules that particularly impacted both internal and external auditors. Using terminology taken directly from the FCPA, the law stated that SEC-regulated enterprises must:

- Make and keep books, records, and accounts, which, in reasonable detail, accurately and fairly reflect the transactions and dispositions of the assets of the issuers.
- Devise and maintain a system of internal accounting controls sufficient to provide reasonable assurances that:
  - Transactions are executed in accordance with management's general or specific authorization.
  - Transactions are recorded as necessary both to permit the preparation of financial statements in conformity with generally accepted accounting principles or any other criteria applicable to such statements, and also to maintain accountability for assets.
- Ensure access to assets is permitted only in accordance with management's general or specific authorization.
- Ensure the recorded accountability for assets is compared with the existing assets at reasonable intervals, and appropriate action is taken with respect to any differences.

The FCPA was significant because, for the first time, management was made responsible for an adequate system of internal accounting controls. The Act required enterprises to "make and keep books, records, and accounts, which in reasonable detail, accurately and fairly reflect the transactions and dispositions of the assets of the issuer." Similar to today's SOx, the FCPA recordkeeping requirements applied to all public corporations registered with the SEC.

In addition, the FCPA required that enterprises keep records that accurately reflect their transactions "in reasonable detail." While there was no specific definition here, the intent of the rule was that records should reflect transactions in conformity with accepted methods of recording economic events, preventing off-the-books "slush funds" and payments of bribes. The FCPA required that companies maintain a system of internal accounting controls, sufficient to provide reasonable assurances that transactions are authorized and recorded to permit preparation of financial statements in conformity with generally accepted accounting principles. Also account-ability is to be maintained for an enterprise's assets, and access to them permitted only as authorized with periodic physical inventories. Passed over 30 years ago, the FCPA was a strong set of corporate governance rules, and because of the FCPA, many boards of directors and their audit committees began to take an active part in directing reviews of internal controls.

FCPA Aftermath: What Happened?

When enacted, the FCPA resulted in a flurry of activity among major U.S. corporations, including efforts to assess and document systems of inter-nal controls. Enterprises that had never formally documented procedures, despite a long chain of internal audit reports pointing out that weakness, now embarked on major documentation efforts. This FCPA documentation responsibility was often given to internal audit departments, who used their best efforts to comply with the FCPA's internal control provisions. Recall that this was in the late 1970s and very early 1980s, when most automated systems were based on mainframe batch-oriented devices, and available documentation tools were little more than plastic flowchart templates and #2 pencils. Similar to the first days of SOx Section 404, considerable efforts were expended in these early FCPA compliance efforts. Even though sys-tems and processes change relatively often, many large enterprises developed extensive sets of paper-based systems documentation with no provisions, once they had been completed, to regularly update them.

Many anticipated a wave of additional regulations or legal initiatives following the enactment of the FCPA. However, this did not occur. Legal actions were essentially nonexistent, no one came to inspect the files of assembled documentation that are part of the FCPA legislation, and today the FCPA has dropped off of the list of current hot management topics, replaced by others such as SOx. The FCPA is still very much in force, but today as more of an anticorruption, anti-bribery law. An FCPA-related search on the Web today will yield few if any references to the Act's internal control provisions. The law was amended in the early 1990s, but only to strengthen and improve its anticorruption provisions.

It is interesting to compare the first years of FCPA compliance activities in the late 1970s and our first efforts at SOx Section 404 compliance. In both cases, there were massive efforts to achieve compliance that were backed by huge amounts of almost unsupportable documentation. Today, however, we have the automated tools to update this documentation as well as requirements, tied to periodic financial reporting, to keep this internal control documentation current.

When enacted in 1977, the FCPA emphasized the importance of effective internal controls. Although there was no consistent definition at the time, the FCPA heightened the importance of internal controls, and its anti-bribery provisions continue to be important. The FCPA was an important first step for helping enterprises to think about the need for effective internal controls. A shortcoming, however, was that there were no guidelines or standards over these systems documentation requirements. Nevertheless, if there had been more attempts at FCPA internal control compliance documentation, we might never have had SOx.

EVENTS LEADING TO THE TREADWAY COMMISSION

Despite the FCPA requirements for documenting internal controls, it soon became obvious to many that we did not have a clear and consistent understanding of what was meant by *internal controls*. In the late 1970s, external auditors only reported that an enterprise's financial statements were "fairly presented," but there was no mention of the adequacy of internal control procedures supporting those audited financial statements. The FCPA had put a requirement on the reporting enterprises to document their internal controls but did not ask external auditors to attest to whether an enterprise was in compliance with these internal control reporting requirements. The SEC then began a study on internal control adequacy and issued a series of reports over about a 10-year period to better define both the meaning of internal controls and the external auditor's responsibility for reporting on those controls.

The AICPA formed a high-level Commission on Auditor's Responsibilities in 1974. This group, better known then as the Cohen Commission, recommended in 1978 that a statement on the condition of an enterprise's internal controls be required along with the financial statements. These Cohen Commission initiatives were taking place concurrently with the development and initial publication of the FCPA.

In the United States, the Cohen Commission's report initially ran into a torrent of criticism. In particular, the report's recommendations were not precise on what was meant by "reporting on internal controls," and external auditors strongly expressed concerns about their roles in this process. Many were concerned about potential liabilities if reports on internal controls gave inconsistent signals due to a lack of understanding over what were internal control standards. Although auditors were accustomed to attesting to the fairness of financial statements, the Cohen Commission report suggested that they should express an audit opinion on the fairness of the management control assertions in the proposed financial statement internal control letter. The issue was again raised that management did not have a consistent definition of internal controls. Different enterprises might use the same terms regarding the quality of their internal controls, with each meaning something a little different. If an enterprise reported that its controls were "adequate" and if its auditors "blessed" their assertions in that control report, the external auditor could later be criticized or even suffer potential litigation if some significant control problem appeared later.

The Financial Executives International[3] (FEI) professional organization then got involved in this internal control reporting controversy. Just as the IIA is the professional enterprise for internal auditors and the AICPA represents public accountants in the United States, FEI represents senior financial officers in enterprises. In the late 1970s, the FEI endorsed the Cohen Commission's recommendations on internal controls and suggested that corporations should report on the status of their internal accounting controls. As a result, many began to discuss the adequacy of internal controls as part of their annual report management letters. These internal control letters were an entirely voluntary initiative and did not follow any standard format. They typically included comments stating that management, through their internal auditors, periodically assessed the quality of their internal controls. They often included "negative assurance" comments indicating that nothing was found to indicate that there might be any internal control problem in operations.

The term *negative assurance* will return again in our discussions of internal controls. Because an external auditor cannot detect all problems as well as the risk of potential litigation, pre-SOx auditor reports were often stated in terms of a negative assurance. That is, rather than saying that they "found no problems" in an area under review, the auditors' report would state that they did not find anything that would lead them to believe that there was a problem. This is a subtle but important difference.

Using both the Cohen Commission's and FEI's recommendations, the SEC subsequently issued proposed rules calling for mandatory management reports on an entity's internal accounting control system. The SEC stated that information on the effectiveness of an entity's internal control system was necessary to allow investors to better evaluate both management's performance and the integrity of published financial reports. This SEC proposal again raised a storm of controversy as many chief executive officers (CEOs) and chief financial officers (CFOs) felt that this was too onerous on top of the then newly released FCPA regulations.

Questions came from many directions regarding the definition of internal accounting controls. While corporations might agree to voluntary reporting, they did not want to subject themselves—in those pre-SOx days—to the penalties associated with a violation of SEC regulations. The SEC soon dropped this 1979 proposed separate management report on internal accounting controls as part of the annual report to shareholders, but promised to rerelease the regulations at a later date.

Earlier AICPA Standards: SAS No. 55

Prior to SOx, the AICPA was responsible for releasing external audit standards through Statements on Auditing Standards (SASs). As discussed previously for SAS No. 1, these standards formed the basis of the external auditor's review of the adequacy and fairness of published financial statements. Although there were a few changes to them over the years, the AICPA was frequently criticized in the 1970s and 1980s that its audit standards were not providing adequate guidance to either external auditors or the users of their reports. This problem was called the "expectations gap," because public accounting standards did not meet the expectations of investors.

To answer this criticism, the AICPA released a series of new SASs on internal control audit standards during the period 1980 to 1985. These included SAS 30, "Reporting on Internal Accounting Control," which provided guidance for the terminology to be used in internal accounting control reports. That SAS did not provide much help, however, on defining the underlying concepts of internal controls and was viewed by critics of the public accounting profession as too little too late. SAS No. 55, "Consideration of the Internal Control Structure in a Financial Statement Audit," was another of these new standards. It defines internal controls in terms of three key elements:

1. Control environment
2. Accounting system
3. Control procedures

SAS No. 55 presented a different approach to understanding internal controls than had been used by the AICPA in the past, and it forms the thinking of much of our ongoing understanding of internal controls. Prior to SAS No. 55, an enterprise's internal control structure policies and procedures that were not directly relevant to the financial statement audit were often not formally considered by the external auditors. Examples of these internal control processes include policies and procedures concerning the effectiveness, economy, and efficiency of certain management decision-making processes or procedures covering research and development activities. Although certainly important to the enterprise, any related internal control concerns did not ordinarily relate to the external auditor's financial statement audit.

SAS No. 55 defined internal control in much broader scope than had been traditionally taken by external auditors and provided a basis for the COSO report's definition of internal control. SAS No. 55 became effective in 1990 and represented a major stride toward providing external auditors with an appropriate definition of internal control.

Treadway Committee Report

The late 1970s and early 1980s were a period of many major enterprise failures in the United States due to factors such as high inflation and the resultant high interest rates. There were multiple occurrences where enterprises reported adequate earnings in their audited financial reports, only to have the enterprise suffer a financial collapse shortly after the release of those favorable audited reports. Some of these failures were caused by fraudulent financial reporting, although many others were due to high inflation or other enterprise instability issues. Nevertheless, several U.S. members of Congress proposed legislation to correct these potential business and audit failures. Bills were drafted, congressional hearings held, but no legislation was passed.

Also in response to these concerns and the lack of legislative action, the National Commission on Fraudulent Financial Reporting was formed. It consisted of five professional organizations: the IIA, the AICPA, and the FEI, all mentioned previously, as well as the American Accounting Association (AAA) and the Institute of Management Accountants (IMA). The AAA is a professional organization for academic accountants, and the IMA is a professional organization for managerial or cost accountants.

This National Commission on Fraudulent Financial Reporting came to be called the Treadway Commission after the name of its chairperson. Its major objectives were to identify the causal factors that allowed fraudulent financial reporting and to make recommendations to reduce their incidence. The Treadway Commission's final report was issued in 1987[4] and included recommendations to management, boards of directors, the public accounting profession, and others. It again called for management reports on the effectiveness of their internal control systems and emphasized key elements in what it felt should be a system of internal controls, including a strong control environment, codes of conduct, a competent and involved audit committee, and a strong internal audit function. The Treadway Commission report again pointed out the lack of a consistent definition of internal control, suggesting further work was needed. The same Committee of Sponsoring Organizations (COSO) that managed the Treadway report subsequently contracted with outside specialists and embarked on a new project to define internal control. Although it issued no standards, the Treadway report was important as it raised the level of concern and attention regarding reporting on internal controls.

The internal control–reporting efforts discussed here are presented as if they were a series of sequential events. In reality, many of these internal control–related efforts took place in almost a parallel fashion. This 20-year effort redefined internal control as a basic methodology and standard terminology for business professionals and auditors. The result has been the COSO internal control framework, discussed in the following sections and referenced throughout this book.

COSO INTERNAL CONTROL FRAMEWORK

As mentioned, COSO refers to the five professional auditing and accounting organizations that formed a committee to develop this internal control report; its official title is *Integrated Control—Integrated Framework*. Throughout this book, it is referred to as the COSO internal control report or framework. These sponsoring organizations contracted with a public accounting firm and used a large number of volunteers to develop the report, and then released a draft in 1990 for public exposure and comment. More than 40,000 copies of the COSO internal control draft version were sent to corporate officers, internal and external auditors, legislators, academics, and other interested parties. Formal comments were requested and the internal control review procedures portion of the study, discussed later, was field-tested by five public accounting firms.

The final COSO internal control report was released in September 1992.[5] Although not a mandatory standard then, the report proposed a common framework for the definition of internal control, as well as procedures to evaluate those controls. In a very short number of years, the COSO internal control framework has become the recognized standard for understanding and establishing effective internal controls in virtually all business systems. This section will provide a fairly detailed description of the COSO internal control framework and its use for SOx Section 404 evaluations.

Virtually every public corporation has a complex control procedures structure. Following the description of a classic enterprise chart, there are levels of senior and middle management in its multiple operating units or within different activities. In addition, control procedures may be somewhat different at each of these levels and components. For example, one operating unit may operate in a regulated business environment where its control processes are very structured, while another unit may be an entrepreneurial startup operation with a less formal structure. Different levels of management in these enterprises will have different control concern perspectives. The question, "How do you describe your system of internal controls?" might receive different answers from persons in different levels or units in each of these enterprise components.

COSO provides an excellent description of this multidimensional concept of internal controls. It defines internal control as follows:

> *Internal control is a process, affected by an entity's board of directors, management, and other personnel, designed to provide reasonable assurance regarding the achievement of objectives in the following categories:*
>
> - *Effectiveness and efficiency of operations*
> - *Reliability of financial reporting*
> - *Compliance with applicable laws and regulations*[6]

Using this very general definition of internal control, COSO uses a three-dimensional model to describe an internal control system in an enterprise. Exhibit 4.1 defines the COSO model of internal controls as a pyramid with five layers or interconnected components comprising the overall internal control system. These are shown with a component called the Control Environment serving as the foundation for the entire structure. Four of these internal components are described as horizontal layers, and another

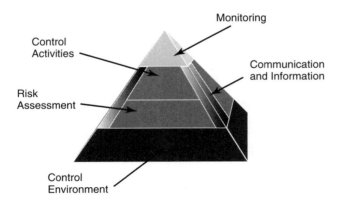

EXHIBIT 4.1 COSO Framework of Internal Control
Source: Brink's Modern Internal Auditing, Sixth Edition, Robert Moeller, page 85. Copyright © 2005 John Wiley & Sons. Reprinted with permission of John Wiley & Sons, Inc.

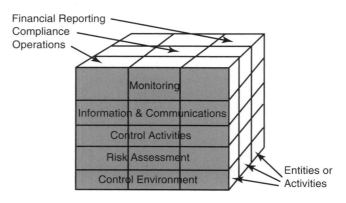

Relationship between Control Components,
Objectives, and Organization Entities

EXHIBIT 4.2   COSO Internal Control Model
Source: Brink's Modern Internal Auditing, Sixth Edition,
Robert Moeller, page 85. Copyright © 2005 John Wiley &
Sons. Reprinted with permission of John Wiley & Sons, Inc.

component of internal control, called Communication and Information, acts
as an interface channel for the other four layers. Each of these components
is described in greater detail in the following sections. Exhibit 4.2 shows
this same COSO model from a slightly different perspective. Here, the
three major components of internal control—effectiveness and efficiency
of operations, reliability of financial reporting, and compliance with applicable laws and regulations—give three dimensions to this model. Just as
the previous pyramid structure showed the internal control structure as the
environment for all internal control processes, this view adds equal weight
to each of these three components.

Auditors and managers should look at internal controls in a multilevel
and three-dimensional manner. While this is true for all internal audit work,
the concept is particularly valuable when assessing and evaluating internal
controls using the COSO framework. The following paragraphs describe
this COSO framework in greater detail.

COSO Internal Control Elements: The Control Environment

The foundation of any internal control structure is what COSO calls the
internal control environment. COSO emphasizes that this element of the
internal control environment foundation has a pervasive influence on how

activities are structured and risks are assessed. The control environment serves as a foundation for all other components of internal control and has an influence on each of the three objectives and all activities. The control environment reflects the overall attitude, awareness, and actions by the board of directors, management, and others concerning the importance of internal controls in the enterprise.

Enterprise history and culture often play a major role in forming this control environment. When an enterprise historically has had a strong management emphasis on producing error-free products, when senior management continues to emphasize the importance of high-quality products, and when this message is communicated to all levels, this becomes a strong enterprise control environment factor. These messages from the CEO or other very senior managers are known as the "tone at the top"—management's messages to all stakeholders. However, if senior management has had a reputation of looking the other way regarding policy violations, this same type of negative message will be similarly communicated to other levels in the enterprise. A positive tone at the top by senior management will establish the control environment for the enterprise.

The following sections outline some of the major elements of the COSO control environment component of internal controls. The management team helping to establish SOx compliance should always try to understand and evaluate this overall control environment when performing these reviews. In some instances, they may want to focus on specific reviews of some or all of these control environment factors covering the overall enterprise. In smaller enterprises, the control environment factors will be more informal, but the focus still should be on appropriate control environment factors throughout the entity, as essential components of internal controls.

Integrity and Ethical Values   The collective integrity and ethical values of an enterprise are essential control environment elements. These are often defined by the tone-at-the-top messages communicated by senior management. If the enterprise has developed a strong code of conduct that emphasizes integrity and ethical values, and if all stakeholders appear to follow that code, these stakeholders will have assurances that the enterprise has a good set of values.

A code of ethics or conduct is an important component of organizational governance. However, even though an enterprise may have a strong code of conduct, its principles can often be violated through ignorance rather than by deliberate employee malfeasance. In many instances, employees may not know that they are doing something wrong or may erroneously believe that their actions are in the enterprise's best interests. This ignorance is often caused by poor moral guidance by senior management rather than by any employee intent to deceive. An enterprise's policies and values must be communicated to all levels of the enterprise. While there can always be" bad apples" in any enterprise, a strong moral message will encourage everyone to act correctly. The objective should always be to transmit appropriate messages or signals throughout the enterprise.

All stakeholders, and certainly internal auditors, should have a good understanding of their enterprise's code of conduct and how it is applied. If the existing code is out of date, if it does not appear to address important ethical issues facing an enterprise, or if management does not appear to be communicating the code to all stakeholders on a recurring basis, management needs to wake up and correct this deficiency. If the enterprise does not have a formal ethics office function, the initiation of such a function may help in the dissemination of the enterprise's code of conduct.

While the code of conduct describes the rules for ethical behavior and while senior management should transmit a proper ethical message throughout the enterprise, other incentives and temptations can erode this overall control environment. Individuals may be tempted to engage in dishonest, illegal, or unethical acts if their enterprise gives them strong incentives or temptations to do so. For example, an enterprise may establish very high, unrealistic performance targets for sales or production quotas. If there are strong rewards for the achievement of these performance goals—or worse, strong threats for missed targets—employees may be encouraged to engage in fraudulent or questionable practices to achieve those goals. The kinds of temptations that encourage stakeholders to engage in improper accounting or similar acts include:

- Nonexistent or ineffective controls, such as poor segregation of duties in sensitive areas, that offer temptations to steal or to conceal poor performance
- High decentralization that leaves top management unaware of actions taken at lower enterprise levels and thereby reduces the chances of getting caught
- A weak internal audit function that has neither the ability nor the authority to detect and report improper behavior
- Penalties for improper behavior that are insignificant or unpublicized and thus lose their value as deterrents

In order to build integrity and ethical values, a strong internal audit function should be a major component of this COSO control environment. If internal audit finds that management is placing constraints on their internal audit function, they emphasize to the audit committee internal audit's importance as part of the enterprise's overall internal control structure.

Commitment to Competence   An enterprise's control environment can be seriously eroded if a significant number of positions are filled with persons lacking required job skills. Internal auditors, in particular, will encounter this situation from time to time when a person has been assigned to a particular job but does not seem to have the appropriate skills, training, or even intelligence to perform that job. Because everyone has different levels of skills and abilities, adequate supervision and training should be available to help each person until proper skills are acquired.

An enterprise needs to specify the required competence levels for its various job tasks and to translate those requirements into necessary levels of knowledge and skill. By placing the proper people in appropriate jobs and giving adequate training when required, an enterprise is satisfying this important COSO internal control environment component.

While an important portion of the control environment, an assessment of staff competence can be difficult. How does the SOx assessor or internal auditor determine that the staff is *competent* with regard to their assigned work duties? A strong Human Resources function, with adequate assessment procedures, is important. The objective here is to avoid one of those once-common rating schemes where everyone is rated "above average" with no further analysis or differentiation.

Board of Directors and Audit Committee   The control environment is very much influenced by the actions of an enterprise's board of directors and its audit committee. In years prior to SOx, boards and their audit committees often were dominated by senior management inside directors, often with a limited representation from outside, minority board members. This created situations where the boards were not totally independent of management. Company officers sat on the board and were, in effect, managing themselves, often with less concern for the outside investors. SOx has changed this, requiring audit committees in particular to be truly independent. An active and independent board is an essential component of the COSO control environment. By setting high-level policies and by reviewing overall enterprise conduct, the board and its audit committee have the ultimate responsibility for setting this tone at the top.

Management's Philosophy and Operating Style   The philosophy and operating style of top management has a considerable influence over an enterprise's control environment. Some top-level managers frequently take significant enterprise-level risks in their new business or product ventures while others are very cautious or conservative. Some managers seem to operate by the seat of their pants while others insist that everything must be properly approved and documented. Still others take very aggressive approaches in their interpretations of tax and financial-reporting rules while others go by the book. These comments do not necessarily mean that one approach is always good and another one bad. A small, entrepreneurial enterprise may be forced to take certain business risks to remain competitive while one in a highly regulated industry would be risk averse.

These management philosophy and operational style considerations are all part of the control environment for an enterprise. Internal auditors and others responsible for assessing internal controls should understand these factors and take them into consideration when evaluating the effectiveness of internal controls. While no one set of styles and philosophies is always best for all enterprises, these factors are important when considering the other components of internal controls in an enterprise.

Organizational Structure   The organization structure component provides a framework for planning, executing, controlling, and monitoring activities to achieve overall objectives. This control environment factor relates to how functions are managed and organized, following a classic organization chart. Some enterprises are highly centralized while others are decentralized by product, geography, or other factors. Still others are organized in a matrix manner with no single direct line of reporting. Organizational structure is an important aspect of the enterprise's control environment, but no one structure provides any preferred environment for internal controls.

The organization structure is the manner or approach for individual work efforts to be both assigned and integrated for the achievement of overall goals. While this concept could be applied to the manner in which a single individual organizes efforts, it is more applicable to a unit or group effort. For a larger modern corporation, a strong plan of organization is an important component of the system of internal controls. Individuals and subgroups must have an understanding of the total goals and objectives of the group or entity of which they are a part. Without such an understanding, an environment is created for significant control weaknesses.

Every enterprise or entity—whether business, government, or philanthropic—needs an effective plan of organization. Often, a weakness in organization controls can have a pervasive effect throughout the total control environment. Despite clear lines of authority, enterprises sometimes have built-in inefficiencies that can become greater as they expand over time, causing control procedures to break down.

Assignment of Authority and Responsibility   This COSO-defined aspect of the control environment is similar to the enterprise structure area previously discussed. An enterprise's structure defines the assignment and integration of the total work effort. The assignment of authority is essentially the way responsibilities are defined in terms of job descriptions and structured in terms of organization charts. Although job assignments can never fully escape some overlapping or joint responsibilities, the more precisely these responsibilities can be stated, the better. The failure to clearly define authority and workplace responsibility will often cause confusion and conflict between individual and group work efforts.

Many enterprises of all types and sizes today have streamlined their operations and pushed their decision-making authority downward and closer to the frontline personnel. A strong control environment says that frontline employees should have the knowledge and power to make appropriate decisions in their own area of operations rather than be required to pass an approval request for routine decisions up through enterprise channels. The critical challenge that goes with this delegation or empowerment is that although they can delegate some authority in order to achieve objectives, senior management is ultimately responsible for the decisions made by those subordinates. An enterprise can place itself at risk if too many decisions involving higher-level objectives are assigned at inappropriately lower levels without adequate management review. In addition, each person in the enterprise must have a good understanding of the enterprise's overall objectives as well as how individual actions interrelate to achieve those objectives. The framework section of the actual COSO report describes this very important area of the control environment as follows:

> *The control environment is greatly influenced by the extent to which individuals recognize they will be held accountable. This holds true all the way to the chief executive, who has ultimate responsibility for all activities within an entity, including internal control system.*

Human Resources Policies and Practices   Human resources practices cover such areas as hiring, orientation, training, evaluating, counseling, promoting, compensating, and taking appropriate remedial actions. While the human resources function should have adequate published policies in these areas, their actual practice areas send strong messages to employees regarding their expected levels of ethical behavior and competence. The higher-level employee who openly abuses a human resources policy, such as a plant smoking ban, quickly sends a message to other levels in the enterprise. The message grows even louder when a lower-level employee is disciplined for violating that same smoking ban while everyone looks the other way at the higher-level violator.

Areas where these human resources policies and practices are particularly important include:

- **Recruitment and hiring.** The enterprise should take steps to hire the best, most qualified candidates. Potential employee backgrounds should be checked to verify backgrounds, and interviews should be well organized and in-depth. They should also transmit a message to the prospective candidate about the enterprise's values, culture, and operating style.

- **New employee orientation.** A clear signal should be given to new employees regarding the enterprise's value system and the consequences of not complying with those values. This is often occurs when new employees are introduced to the code of conduct and asked to formally acknowledge their acceptance of that code. Without these messages, new employees may join the enterprise lacking an appropriate understanding of its values.
- **Evaluation, promotion, and compensation.** There should be a fair performance-evaluation program in place. Because issues such as evaluation and compensation can violate employee confidentiality, the overall system should be established in a manner that appears to be fair to all stakeholders in the enterprise.
- **Disciplinary actions.** Consistent and well-understood policies for disciplinary actions should be in place. Employees at all levels should know that if they violate certain rules, they will be subject to a progression of disciplinary actions leading up to dismissal. The enterprise should take care to ensure that no double standard exists for disciplinary actions—or, if any such double standard does exist, that higher-level employees are subject to even more severe disciplinary actions.

Effective human resources policies and procedures are a critical component in the overall control environment. Messages from the top of strong enterprise structures will accomplish little if the enterprise does not have strong human resources policies and procedures in place. Internal audit should always consider this element of the control environment when performing reviews of other elements of the internal control framework.

COSO Control Environment in Perspective   Exhibit 4.1 shows the components of COSO internal controls as a pyramid, with the control environment as its foundation. This COSO concept is important. Just as a strong foundation is necessary for a multistory building, the control environment provides the foundation for the other components of internal controls. An enterprise that is building a strong internal control structure should give special attention to placing solid foundation bricks in this control environment foundation.

Evaluating the control environment from a SOx internal control perspective does not result in a series of "do the debits equal the credits?" types of rules or measures, but points to the need for strong overall policies that might be different in many enterprises. For example, there is no set of rules for defining what is meant by *tone at the top*, and each senior executive's message may be different. However, the CEO and other key employees should adequately communicate these important enterprise messages.

COSO Internal Control Elements: Risk Assessment

Exhibit 4.2 shows the three-dimensional view of the COSO internal control framework with the next level or layer above the Control Foundation as Risk Assessment. The concept is that an enterprise's ability to achieve its objectives can be at risk due to a variety of internal and external factors. An understanding and management of the risk environment is a basic element of the internal control foundation, and an enterprise should have a process in place to evaluate the potential risks that may impact attainment of its various objectives. This risk assessment component has its focus on internal controls within an enterprise and has a much narrower SOx-related focus than the COSO ERM enterprise risk management framework discussed in Chapter 9.

The COSO internal control risk assessment component should be a forward-looking process that is performed at all levels and for virtually all activities within the enterprise. COSO describes *risk assessment* as a three-step process:

Step 1. Estimate the significance of the risk.
Step 2. Assess the likelihood or frequency of the risk occurring.
Step 3. Consider how the risk should be managed and assess what actions must be taken.

This COSO risk assessment process places a responsibility on management to assess whether a risk is significant and, if so, to take appropriate actions. COSO also emphasizes that risk analysis is not a theoretical process, but often can be critical to an entity's overall success. As part of its overall assessment of internal controls, management should take steps to assess the risks that may impact the overall enterprise as well as the risks over various enterprise activities or entities. A variety of risks, caused by internal or external sources, may affect the overall enterprise. COSO suggests that risks should be considered from three perspectives:

1. **Enterprise risks due to external factors.** These risks include technological developments that can affect the nature and timing of new product research and development or lead to changes in procurement processes. Other external factor risks include changing customer needs or expectations, pricing, warranties, or service activities. New legislation or

regulations can force changes in operating policies or strategies, and catastrophes, such as the World Trade Center 9/11 terrorist attack, can lead to changes in operations and highlight the need for contingency planning.

2. **Enterprise risks due to internal factors.** A disruption in an enterprise's information systems processing facility can adversely affect overall operations. Also, the quality of personnel hired, as well as their training or motivation, can influence the level of control consciousness within the entity. In addition, the extent of employee accessibility to assets can contribute to misappropriation of resources. Although now better remedied by SOx, the COSO internal control report also cited the risk of an unassertive or ineffective board or audit committee that could provide opportunities for indiscretions.

3. **Specific activity-level risks.** In addition to enterprise-wide risks, risks should also be considered at each significant business unit and key activity, such as marketing or information systems. These activity-level concerns contribute to the enterprise-wide risks and should be identified on an ongoing basis and built into various planning processes through-out the enterprise. Where no such risk-assessment process exists, they should be part of the overall SOx internal control assessment.

All too often, management may have a process in place giving the appearance of risk assessments but lacking substance. For example, a new-product authorization approval form may include a selection box for the requester to describe the risks associated with the proposed product. Local management may consistently describe them as "low," with no further analysis until there is some type of massive failure. When performing reviews in these areas, SOx or internal audit reviewers should review this analysis and discuss the reasoning behind these types of low-risk assessments.

The risk assessment element of COSO internal controls is an area where there has been much misunderstanding and confusion because of the more recent similarly named COSO ERM framework. The risk assessment component of the COSO internal control framework includes risk assessments for within an individual enterprise. The COSO ERM framework covers the entire entity and beyond. These are really two separate issues and one is not a replacement for the other.

COSO Internal Control Elements: Control Activities

The next layer up in the COSO internal control framework is called Control Activities. These are the policies and procedures that help ensure that actions identified to address risks are carried out, including a wide range of processes. Control activities exist at all levels and in many cases may overlap one another. The concepts of control activities are essential elements to building and then establishing effective internal controls in an enterprise. The COSO internal control framework identifies a series of these activities by their type of process. Together, they should be helpful in building effective SOx internal controls.

Types of Control Activities   There are different classifications of controls, including manual, IT, or management controls, and they are frequently expressed in terms of being preventive, corrective, and detective control activities. While no one set of control definitions is correct for all situations, COSO suggests a way to classify these control activities in an enterprise. While certainly not an all-inclusive list, the following represent some of these COSO-recommended control activities for an enterprise:

- **Top-level reviews.** Management at various levels should review the results of their performance, contrasting those results with budgets, competitive statistics, and other benchmark measurements. Management actions to follow up on the results of these top-level reviews and to take corrective action represent a control activity.
- **Direct functional or activity management.** Managers at various levels should review the operational reports from their control systems and take corrective action as appropriate. Many management systems have been built to produce exception reports covering such control activities. For example, an IT security system will have a mechanism to report unauthorized access attempts. The control activity here is the management process of following up on these reported events and taking appropriate corrective action.
- **Information processing.** IT systems contain many controls where systems check for compliance in areas and then report any exceptions. Those reported exception items should receive corrective action by systems automated procedures, by operational personnel, or by management. Other control activities include controls over the development of new systems or over access to data and program files.
- **Physical controls.** An enterprise should have appropriate control over its physical assets, including fixtures, inventories, and negotiable securities. An active program of periodic physical inventories represents a major control activity.
- **Performance indicators.** Management should relate sets of data, both operational and financial, to one another and take appropriate analytical, investigative, or corrective actions. This process represents an important enterprise control activity that can also satisfy financial- and operational-reporting requirements.

- **Segregation of duties.** Duties should be divided or segregated among different people to reduce the risk of error or inappropriate actions. This is a basic and important internal control procedure.

The above, included in the COSO internal control report, represents only a small number of the many control activities performed in the normal course of business. These and others keep an enterprise on track toward achieving its many objectives. Control activities usually involve both a policy establishing what should be done and procedures to effect those policies. While these control activities may sometimes only be communicated orally, COSO points out that no matter how communicated, the matter should be implemented "thoughtfully, conscientiously, and consistently." This is a strong message for the SOx team reviewing control activities. Even through an enterprise may have a published policy covering a given area there should be an established control procedure to support the policy. Procedures are of little use unless there is a sharp focus on the condition to which the policy is directed. All too often, an enterprise may establish an exception report as part of an automated system that receives little more than a cursory review by its recipients. However, depending on the types of conditions reported, those reported exceptions should receive appropriate follow-up actions, which may vary depending on the size of the enterprise and the activity reported in the exception report.

Integration of Control Activities with Risk Assessment   Control activities should be closely related to the identified risks from the COSO internal control risk assessment component. Internal control is a process, and appropriate control activities should be installed to address identified risks. Control activities should not be installed just because they seem to be the right thing to do even if there are no significant risks in the area where the control activity would be installed. Sometimes, there may be control activities in place that perhaps once served some control-risk concern, although those concerns have largely gone away. A control activity or procedure should not be discarded because there have not been control violation incidents in recent years, but management needs periodically to reevaluate the relative risks. All control activities should contribute to the overall control structure.

Controls Over Information Systems   The COSO internal control framework emphasizes that control procedures are needed over all significant information systems—financial, operational, and compliance related. COSO breaks down information systems controls into the well-recognized general and application controls. General controls apply to much of the information systems function to help ensure adequate control procedures over all applications. A physical security lock on the door to the IT server center is such a control that acts as a general control for all applications running in that facility.

Application controls refer to specific information systems processes. A control in a weekly payroll program that prevents any employee from being paid for over 80 hours in a given week is an example of an application reasonableness control. People may work extra hours, but it is doubtful many will record over 80 hours in a week. COSO highlights a series of information systems control areas for evaluating the overall adequacy of internal controls. General controls include all centralized data operations or computer systems controls, including job scheduling, storage management, and disaster-recovery planning. These controls typically are the responsibility of specialists in centralized computer or server centers. However, with newer, more modern systems connected to one another through internet links, these controls can be distributed across a network of server-based systems.

The COSO internal control framework document concludes with a discussion on the need to consider evolving technologies whose impact should always be considered when evaluating information systems control activities. Due to the rapid introduction of new technologies, what is new today will soon be replaced by something else. COSO has not introduced anything new with regard to information systems controls, but has highlighted their importance in the overall internal control environment.

COSO Internal Control Elements: Communications and Information   The Exhibit 4.1 pyramid model of the COSO internal control framework describes most components as layers, one on top of another starting with the control environment as the foundation. The Information and Communication component, however, is not a horizontal layer but spans across all of the other components. As important portions of the internal control framework, information and communications are related but distinct internal control components. Appropriate information, supported by IT systems, must be communicated up and down the enterprise in a manner and time frame that allows people to carry out their responsibilities. In addition to formal and informal communication systems, enterprises must have effective procedures in place to communicate with internal and external parties. As part of any evaluation of SOx internal controls, there is a need to understand the information and communication flows or processes in the enterprise.

Relationship of Information and Internal Control   Information at all levels is needed by an enterprise to achieve its operational, financial, and compliance objectives. For example, the enterprise needs information to prepare financial reports that are communicated to outside investors, as well as internal cost and external market preference information to make correct marketing decisions. This information must flow both from the top levels of the enterprise on down to lower levels and from the lower to the upper levels. COSO takes a broad approach to the concept of an information system, recognizing that information systems can be manual, automated, or conceptual, as well as either formal or informal. Regular conversations with customers or suppliers can be highly important sources of information and are an informal type of an information system. The effective enterprise should have information systems in place to listen to customer requests or complaints and to forward that customer-initiated information to appropriate personnel.

The COSO internal control framework also emphasizes the importance of keeping information and supporting systems consistent with overall enterprise needs. Information systems adapt to support changes on many levels. Internal auditors, for example, often encounter cases where an IT application was implemented years ago to support different needs. Although its controls may be good, the system may not support the enterprise's current needs. The COSO internal control framework also takes a broad view of systems and points to the need to understand both manual processes and automated technologies.

Strategic and Integrated Systems   Accounting and financial processes were the first automated systems in enterprises, starting with the unit record or IBM card accounting machines in the 1950s and then moving to the earliest computer systems. Most enterprises have upgraded their automated systems many times, but their basic mix of supporting automated processes may not have changed significantly. Some enterprises will have core general ledger, payroll, inventory, accounts receivable, accounts payable, and related core information systems, without too much else. COSO internal controls suggests that the effective enterprise should go a step beyond these core applications to implement strategic and integrated information systems.

By a strategic system, the COSO report suggests that management should consider the planning, design, and implementation of its information systems as part of its overall enterprise strategy. These strategic systems then support the enterprise's business and help it to carry out its overall business missions. There have been many examples of companies that developed strategic information systems to support their business strategies—systems that allowed enterprises to respond better to changes in their marketplaces and control environments.

COSO internal controls also emphasizes the importance of integrating automated information systems with other operations. Examples would be a fully automated manufacturing system that controls both production machines and equipment inventories or a highly automated distribution system that controls inventory and schedules shipments. COSO internal controls makes the point, however, that it is a mistake to assume that just because a system is new it will provide better controls. Older applications have presumably been tried and tested through use while the new system can have unknown or untested control weaknesses.

Quality of Information   The COSO internal control report has a brief section on the importance of the quality of information. Poor-quality information systems, filled with errors and omissions, affect management's ability to make appropriate decisions. Reports should contain enough data and information to support effective control activities. The quality of information includes ascertaining whether:

- The content of reported information is appropriate.
- The information is timely and available when required.
- The information is current or at least the latest available.
- The data and information are correct.
- The information is accessible to appropriate parties.

These points all circle back to SOx Section 404 requirements. While the COSO framework holds up these quality-of-information points as objectives, SOx effectively makes them requirements. Going beyond classic audit and control concerns, attention should be on the quality of the information produced by all manual and automated systems.

Communications Aspect of Internal Controls   Communications is defined as a separate internal control element in this component of COSO's internal control framework. Communication channels allow individuals to carry out their financial reporting, operational, and compliance responsibilities. The COSO internal control framework emphasizes that communication must take place in a broader sense in dealing with individuals or groups and their expectations. Appropriate channels of communication are an important element in the overall framework of internal controls, and an enterprise needs to establish them throughout its various enterprise levels and activities, as well as with interested outsiders. Although communication channels can have many dimensions, COSO highlights the separate components of internal and external communications. Internal auditors have always focused on the importance of formal channels of communication such as procedure manuals or published documentation. While that documentation is a very important element of communication, COSO takes an expanded view when considering internal controls.

Communications: Internal Components   According to COSO internal controls, perhaps the most important component of communication is that stakeholders should receive messages from senior management reminding them of their internal control responsibilities. The clarity of this message is important to ensure that the enterprise will follow effective internal control principles. This message is part of the tone at the top, discussed as part of the control environment. In addition to these overall messages, all stakeholders need to understand how their specific duties and actions fit into the total internal control system. If this understanding is not present, some may make risky or even bad decisions thinking no one cares.

All stakeholders need to know limits and boundaries and when their actions may be unethical, illegal, or otherwise improper. People also need to know how to respond to errors or other unexpected events in the course of performing their duties, and they typically require messages from management, procedure documentation, and adequate training. Internal auditors often encounter these issues in the course of their reviews. While auditors may have historically commented about a lack of documentation, sometimes treating this as a fairly minor point, both COSO and SOx emphasize that a lack of documentation may mean poor internal control communication channels.

Communication must flow in two directions, and the COSO internal control framework emphasizes that stakeholders must also have a mechanism to report upward throughout the enterprise. This upward communication has two components: communication through normal and through special, confidential reporting channels. Normal reporting refers to the process in which stakeholders are expected to report on status, errors, or problems up through their supervisors. This communication should be freely encouraged, and the enterprise should avoid "shooting the messenger" when bad news is reported. Otherwise, it will be understood that employees should report only good news, and managers may not become aware of significant problems. Because personnel may sometimes be reluctant to report matters to their immediate supervisors, the whistleblower programs discussed in Chapter 12 are essential. These are mechanisms where persons can anonymously report concerns to a higher level in the enterprise for resolution. This is the SOx requirement that the audit committee should establish a whistleblower program to allow the reporting of internal control errors or improper acts. The SOx whistleblower requirement was initially estimated to become a major component of SOx, even though this has not received much attention at present. The current status of SOx whistleblower rules is discussed in Chapter 12.

This section of the COSO internal control framework concludes with a discussion on the importance of communication channels between top management and the board of directors. Although the COSO internal control framework has been in place for about 30 years, the guidelines that management should inform the board of major developments, risks, and occurrences did not receive sufficient attention until they became the law through SOx.

External Communications   Enterprises need to establish communication channels with outside parties including customers, suppliers, shareholders, bankers, regulators, and others. This communication should go beyond the public relations type of function that large enterprises often establish to talk about themselves. Similar to internal communication channels, external information must flow in two directions. The information provided to outside parties should be relevant to the needs of outside parties, building a better understanding of an enterprise and the challenges it faces. Sending out highly optimistic reports to outsiders when many inside the enterprise realize there are problems is also giving an inappropriate internal message.

External communications can also be a very important way to identify potential control problems. Customer complaints regarding service, billings, or product quality often can point out significant operating and internal control problems. There should be independent mechanisms established to receive these messages and act on them, including corrective action taken when necessary. Open and frank two-way communications may alert the enterprise to potential communication problems or allow it to discuss and solve any problems in advance of adverse publicity.

Means and Methods of Communication   There is no one correct means of communicating internal control information within the enterprise. The modern enterprise can communicate its messages through bulletin board announcements, procedure manuals, webcasts, videotaped presentation, or speeches by members of management. However, actions taken either before or after the message will give a stronger signal to communication recipients. The COSO internal control framework summarizes this internal control element as follows:

An entity with a long and rich history of operating with integrity, and whose culture is well understood by people through the enterprise, will likely find little difficulty in communicating its message. An entity without such a tradition will likely need to put more into the way the messages are communicated.

COSO Internal Control Elements: Monitoring

Monitoring is the capstone of the pyramid of internal control COSO components. While internal control systems will work effectively with proper support from management, control procedures, and both information and communication linkages, a process must be in place to monitor these activities. Monitoring has long been the role of internal auditors, who perform reviews to assess compliance with established procedures; however, the COSO internal control framework now takes a broader view of monitoring as well. COSO recognizes that control procedures and other systems change over time. Controls that appeared to be effective when first installed may not be that effective in the future due to changing conditions, new procedures, or other factors.

A monitoring process should be in place to assess the effectiveness of established internal control components and to take corrective action when appropriate. While this certainly points to the role of internal audit, this internal control component cannot be relegated just to the internal auditors while management remains somewhat oblivious to potential control problems. An enterprise needs to establish a variety of monitoring activities to measure the effectiveness of its internal controls. This can be accomplished through separate evaluations as well as with ongoing activities to monitor performance and take corrective action when required.

Ongoing Monitoring Activities   Many routine business functions can be characterized as monitoring activities. Although internal auditors do not always think of these in that sense, COSO internal controls gives the following examples of this ongoing monitoring component:

- **Operating management normal functions.** Normal management reviews over operations and financial reports constitute an important ongoing monitoring activity. However, special attention should be given to reported exceptions and potential internal control deviations. Internal control is enhanced if reports are reviewed on a regular basis and corrective action initiated for any reported exceptions.
- **Communications from external parties.** This element of monitoring is closely related to the component of communications from external parties discussed earlier. External communication monitors, such as a customer complaint telephone number, are important; however, the enterprise needs to monitor closely these calls and then initiate corrective action when appropriate.
- **Enterprise structure and supervisory activities.** While senior management should always review summary reports and take corrective actions, the first level of supervision and the related enterprise structure often

play an even more significant role in monitoring. Direct supervision of clerical activities, for example, should routinely review and correct lower-level errors and assure improved clerical employee performance. This is also an area in which the importance of an adequate separation of duties is emphasized by COSO. Dividing duties between employees allows them to serve as a monitoring check on one another.

- **Physical inventories and asset reconciliation.** Periodic physical inventories, whether of storeroom stock or negotiable securities, are an important monitoring activity. An annual inventory in a retail store, for example, may indicate a significant merchandise loss. A possible reason for this loss could be theft, pointing to the need for better security controls.

These are examples from a longer list in the COSO report. They illustrate procedures that are often in place in many enterprises but are not thought of as ongoing monitoring activities. Any function or process that reviews enterprise activities on a regular basis and then suggests potential corrective actions can be thought of as a monitoring activity.

Separate Internal Control Evaluation   While COSO points out the importance of ongoing monitoring activities to support the internal control framework, it also suggests that "it may be useful to take a fresh look from time to time" at the effectiveness of internal controls through separate evaluations. The frequency and nature of these separate reviews or evaluations will greatly depend on the nature of the enterprise and the significance of the risks it must control. While management may want to periodically initiate an evaluation of its entire internal controls, most should be initiated to assess specific control areas. These reviews are often initiated when there has been an acquisition, a change in business, or some other significant activity.

COSO also emphasizes that these evaluations may be performed by direct line management through self-assessment reviews. Internal audit is not required to perform these reviews unless requested, and considerable time may pass before internal audit may schedule a normal review in some area of operation. However, responsible management in that area should consider scheduling and performing their own self-assessments on a more regular basis. The internally generated review can point out potential control problems and cause operating management to implement corrective action activities. Because these self-assessment reviews will typically not be as comprehensive as a normal internal audit, a follow-up review by the SOx team or others can be launched in the same general area if potentially significant problems are encountered through a limited self-assessment review.

Internal Control Evaluation Process   The COSO internal control guidance materials outline an evaluation process for reviewing internal controls. The evaluator should first develop an understanding of the system design, next test key controls, and then develop conclusions based on the test results. This is really the internal audit process. COSO also mentions *benchmarking* as an alternative approach. Benchmarking is the process of comparing an enterprise's processes and control procedures with those of peer enterprises. Comparisons are made with similar enterprises or against published industry statistics. This approach is convenient for some measures but filled with dangers for others. For example, it is fairly easy to benchmark the size, staffing levels, and average compensations of a sales function against comparable enterprises in the same general industry; however, the evaluator may encounter difficulties in trying to compare other factors due to the many small differences that make all enterprises unique.

Evaluation Action Plans   COSO recognizes that many highly effective procedures are informal and undocumented. Many of these undocumented controls, however, can be tested and evaluated in the same manner as the documented ones. While an appropriate level of documentation makes any evaluation of internal controls more efficient and facilitates employees' understanding of how the process works, that documentation is not always essential. A SOx team reviewing an enterprise's internal financial control systems will certainly request to see some level of systems documentation as part of their review work. If an existing process is informal, undocumented but recognized as effective, the review team will need to prepare their own evaluation action documentation to explain how the process works and the nature of its internal controls.

Reporting Internal Control Deficiencies   Whether internal control deficiencies are identified through processes in the internal control system itself, through monitoring activities, or through other external events, they should be reported to appropriate levels of management in the enterprise. The key question for the SOx or internal audit evaluator is to determine what should be reported given the large body of details that may be encountered, and to whom the reports should be directed. COSO states that "all internal control deficiencies that can affect the entity's attaining its objectives should be reported to those who can take necessary action." This is the same type of guidance that has led to the potential SOx gaps discussed in Chapter 2. While this COSO statement initially makes sense, it is often difficult to implement. The modern enterprise, no matter how well organized, will be guilty of a variety of internal control errors or omissions. COSO internal controls suggests that all of these should be identified and reported, and that even the most minor of errors should be investigated to understand if they were caused by any overall control deficiencies. The COSO internal control report uses the example of an employee's taking a few dollars from the petty cash fund. This could be viewed as a minor matter due to the small amount of the theft, but it still should be viewed as a control breakdown on several levels.

While the monetary amount may not be significant, COSO urges that the matter be investigated rather than ignored, since "such apparent condoning personal use of the entity's money might send an unintended message to employees." Prior to SOx, external auditors regularly applied the concept of materiality when performing their reviews. That is, they often decided that some errors and irregularities were so small that they were not material to the external auditor's overall conclusion. In the first years of Section 404 assessments and the initial AS2 auditing standards, the message from many external auditors was that *materiality* should not be considered—an error is an error. This approach caused frustration with many managers, who wondered why their external auditors were raising issues with what they felt were minor matters. With the AS5 rules discussed in Chapter 3, materiality as well as relative risk should be considered when evaluating the efficiency and effectiveness of internal controls.

The COSO internal control guidance concludes by discussing to whom to report internal control deficiencies in the enterprise. In one paragraph, COSO provides guidance that is useful for evaluations:

Findings on internal control deficiencies usually should be reported not only to the individual responsible for the function or activity involved, who is in the position to take corrective action, but also to at least one level of management above the directly responsible person. This process enables that individual to provide needed support or oversight for taking corrective action, and to communicate with others in the enterprise whose activities may be affected. Where findings cut across organizational boundaries, the reporting should cross over as well and be directed to a sufficiently high level to ensure appropriate action.

Although now tempered by AS5 rules, SOx has tightened this COSO internal control reporting guidance. Matters that appear to be of a material nature become an almost immediate CFO and audit committee reporting issue. The enterprise should also develop reporting procedures such that all internal financial control deficiencies, whether encountered through a SOx Section 404 review or through internal audit reviews of ongoing operations, are reported to appropriate levels of the enterprise. Management reporting and monitoring is a highly important aspect of internal controls.

OTHER DIMENSIONS OF THE COSO INTERNAL CONTROL FRAMEWORK

We sometimes forget that the COSO internal control framework is a three-dimensional model, as shown in Exhibit 4.2. In addition to the front-facing dimension on the model covering control activities, the right-side dimension covers entities or activities while the top of the framework cube covers the three dimensions of all internal controls:

- Effectiveness and efficiency of operations
- Reliability of financial reporting
- Compliance with applicable laws and regulations

Each of the control areas just discussed—from the control environment to monitoring—should be considered with respect to those other two dimensions.

With consideration given to the right-side dimension, internal controls should be installed and evaluated across all units in the enterprise. This does not mean that a control activity, such as an expense approval process, must be identical in all organization units, whether at corporate headquarters or a sales office in a remote geographical location such as a West African state. However, there should be a consistent set of control processes throughout the enterprise with considerations given for the relative risks and scopes of operations. Internal controls should be consistent, but they should be applied appropriately in individual operating units.

The third or top dimension of the COSO internal control framework is even more significant. It says that internal control activities should be installed in all operating units but with respect to the three factors of internal controls: effectiveness, financial reporting reliability, and regulatory compliance. Looking at internal controls from this three-dimensional viewpoint, there may always be some variations, but under a basic and consistent internal control framework. Again using our West African state example, country expense approval procedures may be subject to local laws and other processes may be somewhat different due to communication distances or differences in local IT systems. However, those internal controls should still be implemented in a manner that ensures reliability in financial reporting

The important and very significant concept supporting COSO internal controls is that all such control considerations must be considered in terms of the COSO three-dimensional cube. That is, the control must be considered in terms of where it fits in the overall enterprise and its relationship to the three control objective areas just discussed. This concept provides a powerful way of looking at internal controls from a SOx perspective. Although there have been changes in the SOx approach to looking at internal controls, the COSO internal control framework continues to be an important standard and set of guidance materials for measuring and evaluating internal controls.

ENDNOTES

1. Robert Moeller, *Brink's Modern Internal Auditing*, Sixth Edition. (New York: John Wiley & Sons, 2006).
2. American Institute of Certified Public Accountants, "Statement on Auditing Standards No. 1" (New York: AICPA).
3. Financial Executives International was formally known as the Financial Executives Institute.
4. Report of the National Commission on Fraudulent Financial Reporting (National Commission on Fraudulent Financial Reporting, 1987).
5. Committee of Sponsoring Enterprises of the Treadway Committee (Jersey City, NJ: AICPA, 1992).
6. COSO internal control standards can be found at http://www.coso.org/publications/executive_summary_integrated_framework.htm

CHAPTER 5

Using CobiT Framework to Improve SOx Controls and Governance

O ur professional and business world is filled with acronyms or initials that have become words themselves. We say the word *IBM* today often not thinking that it stands for the corporation's original name, International Business Machines. *COSO* also has become such a word—we forget what COSO stands for, and to many professionals it has just become a descriptive word. (Chapter 3 provides a description of the COSO framework and related background information.) While not at the same level of recognition, CobiT is an acronym that is becoming another generic word among business and IT professionals. You will find it sometimes abbreviated as *COBIT* rather than its official abbreviation as CobiT. The acronym or word stands for Control *O*bjectives for *I*nformation and related *T*echnology. Because of this framework's emphasis on controls and technology, the first and last letters are capitalized. CobiT is an important internal control framework that can stand by itself but is an important support tool for documenting and understanding COSO and Sarbanes-Oxley (SOx) internal controls. Although CobiT's original emphasis was on information technology (IT), the framework has been broadened today and professionals in many levels of business will benefit from having an understanding of the CobiT framework and its use as a tool for documenting, reviewing, and understanding SOx internal controls.

The CobiT standards and framework documentation are issued and maintained by the IT Governance Institute (ITGI) and its closely affiliated professional organization, the Information Systems Audit and Control Association (ISACA).[1] ISACA is more involved with IT auditing guidance while ITGI's focus is on research and governance rules. ISACA also directs the

Certified Information Systems Auditor (CISA) examination and professional designation as well as its newer Certified Information Systems Manager (CISM) certification and examination. ISACA was originally known as the EDP Auditor's Association (EDPAA), a professional group that was started in 1967 by internal auditors who felt their professional organization, the Institute of Internal Auditors (IIA), was at that time not giving sufficient attention to the importance of computer systems and technology controls as part of internal audit activities. We have almost forgotten that *EDP* stands for *electronic data processing*, today an almost-archaic term for information systems. Over time, this professional organization broadened its focus and became ISACA, and the IIA has also long since embraced strong technology issues.

The EDPAA, originally an upstart IT audit professional organization, began to develop IT audit professional guidance shortly after its formation. Just as the EDPAA evolved into ISACA and now ITGI, its original IT audit standards became a very excellent set of IT-oriented internal control objectives that evolved into CobiT, now in its 2007 version 4.1 edition.[2] With virtually all enterprise processes today tied to IT-related matters, the overall area of IT governance is critical and, as shown in Exhibit 5.1, the CobiT framework covers five broad areas of internal controls, with an emphasis on IT governance:

1. **Strategic alignment.** Efforts should be in place to align IT operations and activities with all other enterprise operations. These include ensuring linkages between enterprise business and IT plans as well as defining, maintaining, and validating quality and value relationships.

- **Strategic alignment** focuses on ensuring the linkage of business and IT plans; defining, maintaining and validating the IT value proposition; and aligning IT operations with enterprise operations.

- **Value delivery** is about executing the value proposition throughout the delivery cycle, ensuring that IT delivers the promised benefits against the strategy, concentrationg on optimizing costs and proving the intrinsic value of IT.

- **Resource management** is about the optimal investment in, and the proper management of, critical IT resources: applications, information, infrastructure and people. Key issues relate to the optimization of knowledge and infrastructure.

- **Risk management** requires risk awareness by senior corporate officers, a clear understanding of the enterprise's appetite for risk, understanding of compliance requirements, transparency about the significant risks to the enterprise and embedding of risk management responsibilities into the organization.

- **Performance measurement** tracks and monitors strategy implementation, project completion, resource usage, process performance and service delivery, using, for example, balanced scorecards that translate strategy into action to achieve goals measurable beyond conventional accounting.

EXHIBIT 5.1 IT Governance Focus Areas

Source: CobiT 4.1. ©1996–2007 ITGI. All rights reserved. Used by permission.

2. **Value delivery.** Processes should be in place to ensure that IT and other operating units deliver promised benefits throughout a delivery cycle and against a strategy that optimizes costs, emphasizing the intrinsic values of IT and related activities.
3. **Resource management.** With an emphasis on IT, there should be an optimal investment in, and the proper management of, critical IT resources, applications, information, infrastructure, and people. Effective IT governance depends on the optimization of knowledge and infrastructure.
4. **Risk management.** Management, at all levels, should have a clear understanding of an enterprise's appetite for risk, compliance requirements, and the impact of significant risks. Both IT and other operations have their own and joint risk management responsibilities that may individually or jointly impact the entire enterprise.
5. **Performance measurement.** Processes should be in place to track and monitor strategy implementation, project completions, resource usage, process performance, and service delivery. IT governance mechanisms should translate implementation strategies into actions and measurements to achieve these goals.

These five CobiT internal control concerns point to a wide range of enterprise activities that are a broad set of focus areas that are elements in the CobiT framework and generally represent IT governance. Some enterprises first used the earlier versions of CobiT to help document and organize SOx Section 404 internal control requirements after that legislation first became law. The CobiT framework was and still is an effective tool for documenting IT and all other internal controls. However, this chapter looks at the newer and current-version CobiT framework in the broader perspective of using CobiT to assist in the management, organization, and auditing of IT governance processes.

The following sections provide an overall description of the CobiT framework, in its newest version 4.1 release, and its key elements that link business goals with IT goals through key controls and effective measurement metrics. In addition, the chapter will describe the mapping of CobiT standards with the COSO internal control framework, discussed in Chapter 3, the ITIL Service Management best practices introduced in Chapter 8, and for overall IT and corporate governance. Elements and key components of what we call IT governance today will be discussed as well. The CobiT framework is an effective mechanism for documenting and understanding internal controls at all levels. Although CobiT first started primarily as a set of "IT audit" guidance materials, it is a much more powerful tool today.

COBIT FRAMEWORK

IT processes and their supporting software applications and hardware devices are key activities in any modern enterprise today. Whether a small retail business, with a need to keep track of its inventory and pay employees, or a large enterprise, all need a wide set of interconnected and often complex IT processes that are closely tied to their business operations. Exhibit 5.2 shows this relationship at a high level, with business processes providing the requirements to build and construct IT processes and IT then providing the information necessary to operate those business processes. All business processes and their supporting IT resources work in that relationship. IT cannot and certainly should not tell business operations what types of IT processes and systems they should consider implementing. In the very early days of IT systems, technical managers sometimes felt they had lots of answers and promoted systems solutions to their businesses, sometimes with very counterproductive results. However, this relationship has changed today and IT and business operations generally should have a close mutual relationship of shared requirements and information.

Exhibit 5.2 shows that IT has responsibilities over a series of other related process areas. These subsidiary processes have names such as Maturity Models and Activity Goals that will be discussed later in this chapter. In addition, these processes are audited by or through established audit guidelines, they are measured by performance indicator measures, and activities

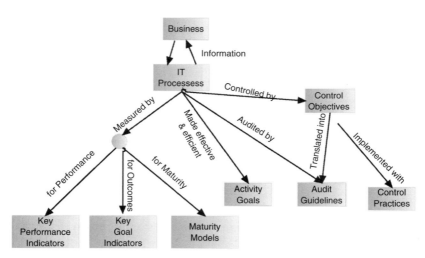

EXHIBIT 5.2 CobiT Component Interrelationships

are made effective through a series of activity goals. All of these become part of CobiT, a control framework including both IT and business processes.

Chapter 3 described the COSO internal control framework and its importance in defining SOx internal controls. One might ask, "I understand and use COSO internal controls—why another framework?" A major answer to this question is that CobiT provides an alternative approach to define and describe internal controls that has more of an IT emphasis than COSO internal controls. Information and supporting IT processes often are the most valuable resources for virtually all organizations today, and management has a major responsibility to safeguard their supporting IT assets, including automated systems. A combination of management, users of IT, and auditors all need to understand these information-related processes and the controls that support them. This combination is concerned about the effectiveness and efficiency of IT processes and overall business requirements, as shown in Exhibit 5.3. Basic CobiT principles call for business requirements driving the demand for IT resources and those resources initiating IT processes to develop enterprise information in a continuous circular manner. The idea is that each of these four groups has somewhat differing concerns regarding the business requirements of their IT systems, their supporting resources, as well as related IT processes. Management should be interested in the quality, cost, and appropriate delivery of their

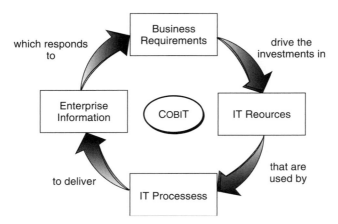

EXHIBIT 5.3 Basic CobiT Principles

Source: Control Objectives of Information and Related Technology (CobiT®), Third Edition. Copyright © 1996, 1998, 2000, the IT Governance Institute®, http://isaca.org and http://itgi.org, Rolling Meadows, IL 60008, USA. Reprinted by permission.

IT-related resources whose control components are the same three COSO internal control elements discussed in Chapter 3. The third leg of this framework is the IT processes that require appropriate levels of confidentiality, availability, and integrity controls. Internal controls over IT resources are very much based on the interdependencies of these four effectiveness and efficiency IT components.

IT governance is a key CobiT concept today that really did not exist as an element of CobiT prior to SOx. It is an important internal control concept today, with the IT Governance Institute playing a strong leadership role. CobiT has described its role in IT governance through the pentagon-shaped diagram, shown in Exhibit 5.1, illustrating CobiT's IT governance focus areas. Discussed later in this chapter, CobiT defines IT governance in a series of key areas ranging from keeping focus on strategic alignments to the importance of both risk and performance measurement when managing IT resources. We will see references to this IT governance focus areas pentagon as we navigate through the CobiT framework to better understand SOx-related internal controls.

In addition to these three interconnected process groups, CobiT looks at controls in three dimensions of IT: *resources*, *processes*, and *business requirements*. These three dimensions fit on what is called the *CobiT cube* (see Exhibit 5.4). Similar to the COSO framework cube discussed in Chapter 3 and Chapter 9's COSO enterprise risk framework, this CobiT model looks at IT controls from a three-dimensional perspective. However, its front-facing dimension, with its pictorial description of process flow diagrams, has perhaps scared off some non-IT people from considering the use of CobiT. The non-IT-savvy professional—and there are many—may look at the process diagrams on the face of the CobiT cube and decide this approach must be "too technical." This is not at all correct, and this chapter will better describe and explain the CobiT framework and why it can be valuable for understanding SOx internal controls and improving IT governance practices in the following sections.

IT Resources

Taking a closer look at the CobiT cube, the IT Resources side or dimension of this three-dimensional framework represents all of an organization's IT resources or assets, including its people, the application systems, installed technology, its facilities, and the value of data. This right-hand side of the framework cube represents the necessary concerns and considerations for all of the resources necessary for the control and administration of IT resources in an organization. These resources, either individually or in groups, should be considered when evaluating controls in an IT environment. CobiT resources are identified as follows:

Business Requirements

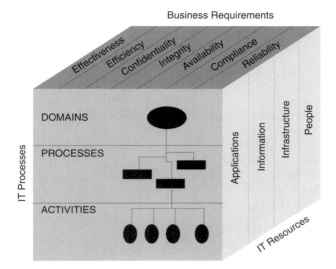

EXHIBIT 5.4 CobiT Cube

Source: CobiT 4.1. ©1996–2007 ITGI. All rights reserved.
Used by permission.

- Applications consisting of both automated user systems and manual procedures to process information
- Information, including the data input, output, and processed, for use by business processes
- Infrastructure components consisting of technology and facility components, including hardware, operating systems, databases, networks, and the environment that houses and supports them
- Key and specialized personnel to plan, organize, acquire, implement, support, monitor, and evaluate the information systems and services

We have started our CobiT description from the right-hand side of this three dimensional CobiT cube, but CobiT framework users should always try to think of control considerations in terms of how they relate to other components of the CobiT cube. There are interconnections and relationships for all processes and controls in this three-dimensional perspective.

IT Processes

The second and front-facing dimension of the CobiT framework references IT Processes and consists of three segments: domains, processes, and activities. Domains are groupings of IT processes that match to organizational areas of responsibility; there are four specific domain areas defined in CobiT:

1. **Planning and organization.** This domain area covers the strategy and tactics that allow IT to best contribute to and support the business objectives of the enterprise. This type of IT strategic vision message should be communicated throughout the enterprise—IT's mission and what it is trying to accomplish for all parties.
2. **Acquisition and implementation.** IT solutions need to be identified, developed, or acquired, and both implemented and integrated with business processes. This domain area covers changes and maintenance of existing systems.
3. **Delivery and support.** This domain area covers the actual delivery of required services, both application and infrastructure tools. The actual process of application data and controls is covered within this domain.
4. **Monitoring and evaluation.** This area includes control processes, including quality and compliance monitoring, as well as external and internal audit evaluation procedures.

Within an IT organization, the process to identify and build new applications—often called Systems Development Life Cycle (SDLC) procedures—could be viewed as part of the CobiT implementation domain and with quality assurance a part of the monitoring domain. CobiT descriptive materials describe each of these domain areas in greater detail. For the planning and organization domain, it suggests the following specific processes:

- Define a strategic IT plan.
- Define the information architecture.
- Determine technological direction.
- Define the IT organization and relationships.
- Manage the IT investment.
- Communicate management aims and direction.
- Manage human resources.
- Ensure compliance with external requirements.
- Assess risks.
- Manage projects.
- Manage quality.

Individual processes are the next level down. They are a series of joined activities with natural control breaks. Finally, activities are the actions needed to achieve measurable results. Activities have a life cycle, whereas tasks are discrete. For a life cycle, we can think of the SDLC process where a new application is designed, implemented, operated over time, and then revised or replaced with an improved process.

Business Requirements

The third dimension to the CobiT model or cube is described as Business Requirements, and has seven components:

1. Effectiveness
2. Efficiency
3. Confidentiality
4. Integrity
5. Availability
6. Compliance
7. Reliability

All IT overall systems or processes should be evaluated with consideration given to these seven criteria areas. Emphasis will vary depending on the type of process, but all IT processes should have these criteria in mind. Business functions will typically establish such requirements for general business needs and for IT as well. Each of these attributes is discussed in more detailed descriptions of CobiT in the following section as well as in Chapter 8 on using ITIL.

Similar to the COSO cube internal control model from Chapter 4 and the COSO enterprise risk model or framework discussed in Chapter 9, the CobiT cube presents an effective way to understand the relationships between business requirements, IT processes, and IT resources. The three-dimensional nature of the model emphasizes the cross relationships and interdependencies between business and IT processes. In our IT-dependent world, this is a useful way to look at and understand internal controls. CobiT is a rich—sometimes almost too rich—set of processes for focusing on business and IT goals, key controls, and identifying key measurement metrics. The sections following will discuss CobiT in some high-level detail, but the reader is encouraged to consult the previously referenced IT Governance Institute's CobiT materials.

USING COBIT TO ASSESS INTERNAL CONTROLS

In addition to Exhibit 5.4's CobiT cube, with its forward face showing process flow diagrams to emphasize relationships, the published CobiT guidance material[3] can look formidable to many business and even IT professionals. The basic CobiT reference material is published in a nearly

200-page manual filled primarily with an array of charts and tables. It is a useful set of materials but some study may be required to fully understand the concepts behind the CobiT framework, although the ITGI has recently published a good Web based Executive Summary document describing their newest version 4.1.[4] The following sections are designed to help navigate through the published CobiT framework, and more importantly use it to develop and assess enterprise internal controls.

Although any dimension of the CobiT cube can be used to understand control environments, the four previously discussed domains, starting with planning and organization, is an effective first step. Based on these three CobiT control cube dimensions, each IT process is evaluated through five navigation steps as follows:

I. The control of [*Process Name*]
II. Which satisfies [*list of business requirements*]
III. By focusing on [*list of important IT goals*]
IV. Is achieved by [*list of control statements*]
V. And is measured by [*list of key metrics*]

This five-step process can go from number I down or can start at the base level. In either case, the CobiT framework says that the control of any process should be satisfied by a list of supporting business requirements and that those business goals should focus on important IT goals. This only makes sense. A designated process would just be an idle name unless supported by specific business and IT requirements to drive and govern that process. Each of those requirements should be defined by one or more control statements with specific control practices. Finally, we cannot assess whether matters are operating effectively and key measurement metrics are necessary. Although CobiT's emphasis has historically been on IT, this type of analysis should be used for internal control, whether or not IT related.

Each major control objective in the published CobiT guidance material is based on the navigation framework shown in Exhibit 5.5. The upper-left corner of the exhibit shows business requirements. For each control, these may be marked with a *P* for a primary requirement, *S* for secondary, or just blank if not applicable to the control objective. The lower-right corner lists the IT resource areas. If any are applicable, they are noted with a checkmark. The lower-left corner shows the same pentagon diagram we saw in Exhibit 5.1. Here, sections are shaded or marked if they are of primary or secondary importance.

The center of each page has the "Control over the IT process of" series of statements completed for each control objective. We will show examples of completed statements as we review the CobiT domains in the

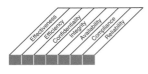

Control over the IT process of

process name

    that satisfies the business requirement for IT of

    summary of most important business goals

        by focusing on

        summary of most important IT goals

            is achieved by

            key controls

                and is measured by

                key metrics

■ Primary ■ Secondary

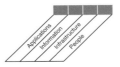

EXHIBIT 5.5 Navigating the CobiT Framework

Source: CobiT 4.1. ©1996–2007 ITGI. All rights reserved. Used by permission.

following sections. Even though the CobiT navigation and other supporting documentation is thorough and somewhat elegant, it can also scare away the first-time reader. The following sections look at CobiT navigation across various selected domains to give a feel for its organization. An enterprise's internal audit function, and particularly it's IT audit specialists, should have used and understand CobiT. The ITGI professional organization, at http://itgi.org/, also has a wide variety of offerings on the use of CobiT.

Planning and Organization

There should be a high-level group of processes that set the direction for the enterprise and its IT resources. For this domain, CobiT calls for 10 high-level *planning and organizing* (PO) control objectives:

PO1: Define a Strategic Plan
PO2: Define the Information Architecture

PO3: Determine Technological Direction
PO4: Define IT Process, Organization, and Relationships
PO5: Manage the IT Investment
PO6: Communicate Management Aims and Direction
PO7: Manage IT Human Resources
PO8: Manage Quality
PO9: Assess and Manage IT Risks
PO10: Manage Projects

These are all such very-high-level concepts that many managers might argue; "Of course!" when defending that, yes, they have a strategic plan, have defined their information architecture, or are in compliance with any of these high-level PO objectives. However, CobiT drills down into each of these control objective areas in greater detail. Using the PO1 on defining a strategic plan as an example, there are six more detailed objectives:

PO1.1: IT Value Management
PO1.2: Business-IT Alignment
PO1.3: Assessment of Current Performance
PO1.4: IT Strategic Plans
PO1.5: IT Tactical Plans
PO1.6: IT Portfolio Management

The numbering here is important as the CobiT guidance material references each of these and other objectives in terms of references to their inputs and outputs. The guidance material provides a high-level description for each of these objectives. For PO1.4 on strategic plans, the guidance material states:

> *Create a strategic plan that defines, in co-operation with the relevant stakeholders, how IT will contribute to the enterprise's strategic objectives (goals) and related costs and risks. It includes how IT will support IT-enabled investment programs and operational service delivery. It defines how the objectives will be met and measures and will receive formal sign-off from the stakeholders. The IT strategic plan should cover investment/operational budget, funding sources, sourcing strategy, acquisition strategy, and legal and regulatory requirements. The strategic plan should be sufficiently detailed to allow the definition of tactical IT plans.*

This paragraph is an example of one of the control objectives outlined throughout the CobiT guidance. It does not tell the professional *how* to write an IT strategic plan but provides excellent guidance to build such a plan, no matter the size or status of the enterprise. These general objectives are also good tools for internal auditors in their need to build review criteria in any of these areas. Those audit objectives can be developed by taking each sentence of such a control objective and developing audit review areas. The role of CobiT as an aid to internal auditors will be discussed in greater detail in Chapter 8 on the role of internal audit in today's SOx environment.

For each of the CobiT objectives, the guidance material contains a supporting RACI chart. A tool that evolved from quality initiatives in the 1960s, the RACI chart or model is good tool to identify roles and responsibilities. Using a spreadsheet format, activities are identified in a side column and with functions or position descriptions in cells across the top. Responsibilities for those activities are identified in intersecting cells through one or several of the RACI initials as follows:

R = **Responsible** = owns the problem or process
A = **Accountable** = must sign off on the activity before it is effective
C = **Consulted** = has the information and/or capability to complete the work
I = **Informed** = must be informed of the results but need not be consulted

This chart format can be useful in many areas to help identify responsibilities over multiple areas. Exhibit 5.6 is a RACI chart, adapted from CobiT materials, on the PO1 objective to define a strategic IT plan. Going down the column of responsibilities in this example, the Business Process Owner is **R**esponsible for analyzing program portfolios, is Informed on processes for building the strategic plan, and acts as a Consultant on other activities for this control objective. This type of RACI chart appears in the published guidance for each of the CobiT control objectives.

The CobiT material also concludes with a summary analysis of that control objective. For each, this is a metrics-based set of considerations that outlines the activity goals for a given control objective that are measured by a set of key performance indicators (KPI s) that, in turn, drive process goals that are measured by process-related key goal indicators. The latter drive IT goals that are measured by IT key goal indicators. This process and set of supporting CobiT documentation will be explained as we review the other CobiT control objectives.

For the PO major control objective, the guidance material discusses each of the control objectives here in the same manner and following the same approach. For each objective, CobiT outlines or suggests a high-level control review approach. Many items are suggested that may not be in place

Activities	CEO	CFO	Business Executives	CIO	Process Owner	Head Operations	HeadIT Admin	PMO	Compliance & Audit
Link Business Goals to IT Goals	C	I	A/R	R	C				
Identify Critical Dependencies and Current Performance	C	I	R	A/R	C	C	C		C
Build an IT Strategic Plan	A	C	C	R	I	C	C	I	C
Build IT Tactical Plans	C	I		A	C	C	C	C	I
Analyze Program Portfolios and Manage Service Portfolios	C	I	I	A	R	C	C	R	I

EXHIBIT 5.6 Defining a Strategic IT Plan RACI Chart

in all but larger IT organizations, but the CobiT guidance material has a range of approaches for each objective. For example, the objective PO3.5 on an IT architecture board calls for the need for such a function. Valuable guidance, here, but many smaller IT resources will not have the resources to establish such a formal function. Good guidance, but managers who use CobiT and auditors who evaluate compliance should always recall that this is a set of best practices guidance material but not standards or mandatory requirements.

Acquisition and Implementation

Each of the CobiT high-level control objectives discusses control procedures in the same general format. Whether it is in-house software development efforts or purchased IT components, the recommended high-level objectives here are:

AI1: Identify Automated Solutions
AI2: Acquire and Maintain Application Software
AI3: Acquire and Maintain Technology Infrastructure
AI4: Enable Operation and Use
AI5: Procure IT Resources
AI6: Manage Changes
AI7: Install and Accredit Solutions and Changes

Each of the detailed objectives in this domain covers control procedures over the implementation of new tools. While the emphasis is on software, the internal control concepts can be applied to the acquisition and implementation of many new enterprise tools.

While our space here does not allow complete coverage of each control objective, we will examine AI6 on managing change as an example of how CobiT uses its basic framework to outline the importance of this control area. For example, we had previously outlined CobiT's five-step process for evaluating control objectives. The outline for these steps appears in the center of the Exhibit 5.5 navigation page. AI6 on managing change is outlined as follows:

I. Control over the IT process of managing change
II. That satisfies the business requirement for IT of responding to business requirements in alignment with business strategy, while reducing solution and delivery defects and rework
III. By focusing on controlling impact assessment, authorization, and implementation of all changes to the IT infrastructure, applications, and technical solutions, minimizing errors due to incomplete request specifications and halting implementation of unauthorized changes
IV. Is achieved by
  • Defining and communicating change procedures, including emergency changes
  • Assessing, prioritizing, and authorizing changes
  • Tracking status and reporting on changes
V. And is measured by
  • Number of disruptions or data errors caused by inaccurate specifications or incomplete impact assessment
  • Application or infrastructure rework caused by inadequate change specifications
  • Percent of changes that follow internal change controls processes

This series of statements, taken from the CobiT guidance materials, describes the control requirements and measures for this specific AI6 control objective. The CobiT guidance material has a similar set of statements for each control objective. This is useful when attempting to better understand the characteristics of each control.

That same guidance material looks at how each control objective relates to the other two sides of the CobiT cube. For this AI6, Manage Changes, control objective it indicates that on the IT Resources side, all are important or have a checkmark in understanding this control objective. That is, the control object impacts Applications, Information, Infrastructure, and

People. Turning to the upper-left side of the navigation sheet's Business Requirements dimension, the guidance material indicates whether they are of Primary, Secondary, or of no significant importance. For this AI6 example control objective, the Business Requirements of Effectiveness, Efficiency, Integrity, and Availability are of Primary importance while Reliability is of Secondary importance. The remaining two, Confidentiality and Compliance, are not considered significant to this control objective.

For each control objective, the guidance material contains an image of the Exhibit 5.1 focus areas pentagon, showing that for this AI6 control objective, Value Delivery, is of Prime Importance with Resource Management secondary. The CobiT guidance material does not provide any detailed discussion of the reasons for that designation. Perhaps because there is so much guidance material in CobiT, the lack of an explanation here or for any of the control objectives is of no importance. The professional working with any of the CobiT control objectives can usually deduce why a given IT governance area has been designated as of primary or secondary significance.

Delivery and Support

Following the same general format, the third high-level CobiT control objective is called Deliver and Support (DS). This control objective largely covers Service Management issues and many of these objectives are related to the ITIL business process objectives discussed in Chapter 3. This really highlights some of the changes to our understandings of internal controls that have evolved since the enactment of SOx in 2002. Both CobiT and ITIL were with us at that time, but the SOx Section 404 emphasis on effective internal controls has brought things together. The CobiT DS control objectives are also similar to the ITIL internal controls to enhance business processes. Both cover the important area of what is known today as IT Service Management, the processes required to ensure efficient IT operations and to deliver these services.

In earlier days, concerns about IT internal controls focused on individual application-by-application controls. While much attention was given to the higher-level general controls such as perimeter security or disaster recovery planning, auditors and others often focused their reviews on computational and balancing controls in specific applications. However, no matter how well designed, all such IT applications must operate in an efficient, almost automated factory-like atmosphere. There will always be smaller problems, however, such as a legitimate systems user becoming locked out due to forgetting a password. There is a need for efficient service and problem management processes to report and resolve such matters. The CobiT DS control objectives cover many of these important areas:

DS1: Define and Manage Service Levels
DS2: Manage Third-Party Services
DS3: Manage Performance and Capacity
DS4: Ensure Continuous Service
DS5: Ensure Systems Security
DS6: Identify and Allocate Costs
DS7: Educate and Train Users
DS8: Manage Service Desk and Incidents
DS9: Manage the Configuration
DS10: Manage Problems
DS11: Manage Data
DS12: Manage the Physical Environment
DS13: Manage Operations

These control objectives represent important areas of IT operations that historically have not received sufficient attention by internal auditors or other members of management. The CobiT material looks at each of these in the same general format of summarizing how each control objective is achieved and measured as well as its relationships and interdependencies across all three sides of the CobiT cube.

Many of these control objective areas had not received sufficient attention in many internal control reviews prior to SOx Section 404. COSO objectives address internal controls at a high level but sometimes do not address more detailed service management–related internal control issues. The CobiT DS10 control objective for Problem Management is an example:

Effective problem management requires the identification and classification of problems, root cause analysis and resolution of problems. The problem management process also includes identification of recommendations for improvement, maintenance of problem records and review of the status of corrective actions. An effective problem management process improves service levels, reduces costs, and improves customer convenience and satisfaction.

IT users and internal auditors have had problems and frustrations for years with various systems and applications. Insensitive IT operations functions frequently have not done an appropriate job in efficiently resolving reported problems. All too often, if an application totally failed, there would be a strong effort to get it back in operation, but smaller, less critical problems would be brushed off in an almost cavalier manner as something to be "considered in the next update."

The published CobiT guidance material links this control objective to others that provide its inputs as well as outputs. For example, the objectives of AI6 on change authorization, DS8 for incident reporting, DS9 for IT configuration management, and DS13 on error logs all provide inputs to the DS10 control objective. Our purpose is not to reproduce the full contents of the published CobiT control objectives but to give the reader a feel for its approach. Here and for all of the domains and objectives, CobiT provides a powerful way to look at IT-related internal controls and their relationships.

We have discussed how each CobiT control has a series of detailed control objectives, has other control objective inputs and outputs, and has a RACI chart balancing functions and responsibilities for each control. In addition, the CobiT framework materials have a Goals and Metrics section for each control objective. Exhibit 5.7 shows this goals and metrics chart for the DS10 Problem Management control objective. Each CobiT control objective has a similar set of these very useful analyses. With this problem management example, there are three suggested goals or measurement metrics that should be considered. One of these is performing root-cause analyses of reported problems. An important goal that is sometimes missed, the related RACI chart highlights that the problem manager is responsible for this activity with others given a consulting role.

Under each activity goal is a table of key performance indicators that drive a set of process goals. Exhibit 5.7 is an example of a set of these process key goal indicators that drive the IT goals measured by IT key goal indicators. With different specific contents for each CobiT control, this type of analysis provides all parties with a good set of standards for measuring the performance of control areas and establishing metrics to assess achievement of these goals. This analysis for our selected control objective of Problem Management is a good example of the power of the published CobiT material. Many IT operations have some type of help-desk function to report and resolve problems. Here, we have some good suggestions for the types of measures and metrics that can be used to evaluate the achievement of this control objective.

Similar tables of goals and objectives as well as detailed control objectives exist for each control objective. These are standards or requirements similar to the SOx auditing standards under AS5, discussed in Chapter 3, or the internal audit professional practice standards, referenced in Chapter 11. However, CobiT provides excellent guidance material for establishing and then measuring effective internal controls.

Monitoring and Evaluation

The fourth CobiT domain is called Monitoring and Evaluation (ME), a set of control objectives that emphasize CobiT as a closed-loop process that never ends. CobiT calls for establishing baseline measures to allow an organization

Activity Goals and Metrics
Assigning sufficient authority to problem manager
Performing root-cause analysis of reported problems
Analyzing terms
Taking ownership of problems and problem resolution

are measured by Key Performance Indicators
Average duration between the logging of a problem and identification of root cause.
Percent of problems for which root-cause analysis was undertaken
The frequency of reports or updates to an ongoing problem based on its severity

drive Process Goals
Record and track operational problems through resolutions
Investigate the root cause of all significant problems
Define solutions for identified operations problems

are measured by Process Key Goal Indicators
Percent of problems recorded and tracked
Percent of problems that recur by time and severity
Percent of problems resolved with required time period
Number of open, new, and closed problems by severity
Average and standard deviation of time lag between problem identification and resolution
Average and standard deviation of time lag between problem resolution and closure

drive IT Goals
Ensure satisfaction of end users with service offerings and service levels
Reduce solution and service delivery defects and rework
Protect the achievement of IT objectives

are measured by IT Key Goal Indicators
Number of recurring problems with impact on business
Number of business disruptions caused by operational problems

EXHIBIT 5.7 DS10 Manage Problems Goals and Metrics

to measure how it is performing and to provide it with opportunities in future periods. This domain area covers quality assurance areas that are traditionally more common to manufacturing and other operations areas than they have been to IT. Although not discussed in the CobiT guidance material, the pioneering work of W. Edwards Deming provides a way of considering this CobiT domain area.

A consultant helping to rebuild Japan in the aftermath of World War II, Deming developed quality standards and approaches that helped Japan establish the quality practices that are now used worldwide today. Among other approaches, Deming developed a quality system approach that called for business processes to be analyzed and measured to identify the sources of variations that cause products to deviate from customer requirements. He proposed that each business process be placed in a continuous feedback loop so that managers could identify and change the parts of the process that needed improvement. This should be a continuous, never-ending cycle where we should always monitor current process performance and take actions to implement improvements to that process. Deming called this the *Plan, Do, Check, Act (PDCA) cycle*, as shown in Exhibit 5.8. The steps are:

Step 1. Plan: Business processes should be designed or revised to improve results.
Step 2. Do: Implement to plan and measure its performance.
Step 3. Check: Assess the measurements and report the results
Step 4. Act: Decide on needed changes to improve results.

Although Deming's focus was on industrial production, his concepts have been carried forward and are very appropriate for today's business environments including IT operations and SOx internal control monitoring. Chapter 2 discussed the status of SOx today and its continuing monitoring requirements, while this CobiT monitoring and evaluation component calls for such continuous monitoring processes.

Following the same format as the other CobiT domains, ME has four principle control objectives:

ME1: Monitor and Evaluate IT Performance
ME2: Monitor and Evaluate Internal Controls
ME3: Ensure Regulatory Compliance
ME4: Provide IT Governance

Following the same format as the other CobiT domains, this area should be of particular interest to auditors, internal control specialists, and members of the enterprise who may be outside of IT operations. The control

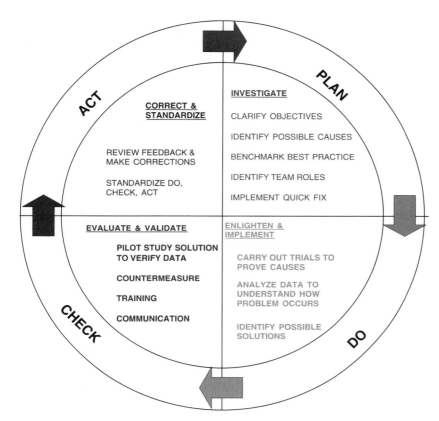

EXHIBIT 5.8 Deming's PDCA Cycle

material for ME2 on monitoring and evaluating internal controls is a good example of CobiT's strength. It states that the process of monitoring and evaluating internal controls is achieved by defining the system of IT controls embedded in the IT process framework, by monitoring and reporting on the effectiveness of these internal controls, and by reporting exceptions to management for corrective action. This is really the Deming PDCA process just discussed, and it should be measured by:

- Number of internal control breaches
- Number of control improvement initiatives
- Number and coverage of control self-assessments

As with most of the CobiT framework, the material here focuses on IT controls, but many of these concepts can be generalized to an overall internal control review process. The measure of control self-assessments refers to the process of ongoing internal reviews on the completeness and effectiveness of internal controls. Many internal audit functions are leading in these types of self-assessment processes today, as will be discussed in Chapter 11.

This Monitor and Evaluate Internal Controls objective has seven detailed supporting objectives. These detailed controls have been somewhat abbreviated for the CobiT guidance material but the following describe their essence:

ME2.1: *Monitoring of Internal Control Framework.* Continuously monitor the IT control environment and control framework. Assessment using industry best practices and benchmarking should be used to improve the IT control environment and framework.

ME2.2: *Supervisory Review.* Monitor and report the effectiveness of internal controls over IT through supervisory review, including, for example, compliance with policies and standards, information security, change controls, and controls established in service-level agreements.

ME2.3: *Control Exceptions.* Record information regarding all control exceptions and ensure that it leads to analysis of the underlying cause and to corrective action. Management should decide which exceptions should be communicated to the individual responsible for the function and which exceptions should be escalated. Management is also responsible to inform affected parties.

ME2.4: *Control Self-Assessment.* Evaluate the completeness and effectiveness of management's internal controls over IT processes, policies, and contracts through a continuing program of self-assessment.

ME2.5: *Assurance of Internal Control.* Obtain, as needed, further assurance of the completeness and effectiveness of internal controls through third-party reviews by the corporate compliance function, internal audit, outside consultants, or certification bodies.

ME2.6: *Internal Control at Third Parties.* Assess the status of each internal external provider's internal controls. Confirm that external service providers comply with legal and regulatory requirements and contractual obligations.

ME2.7: *Remedial Actions.* Identify and initiate remedial actions based on the control assessments and reporting. This includes follow-up of all assessments including: (1) review, negotiation, and establishment of management responses, (2) assignment of responsibility for remediation or risk acceptance, and (3) tracking the results of the actions taken.

These CobiT control objectives are described as "detailed" but provide openings for a wide range of even more detailed control procedures. For example, ME2.1 on monitoring the internal control framework requires internal auditors or other internal control specialists to develop detailed control procedures, often called *audit programs*. They typically will result in a program of many more tests or steps.

This control objective, as well as all of the others in the CobiT documentation, has a section on assessing the maturity of each internal control. The term maturity here refers to the Capability Maturity Model (CMM), a five-level assessment measure designed and developed by Carnegie Mellon University. The model has defined levels for when controls can be assessed, from a CMM level 1 of nonexistent, to level 2 of initial or ad-hoc controls, and all the way to level 5, called *optimized controls.*[5] The CobiT guidance material rates each of its controls against this CMM measure. For example, CobiT defines that an enterprise will be at level 3, defined process controls for ME2, Monitor and Evaluate Internal Controls, when management supports and has institutionalized internal control monitoring. The guidance goes on to say that policies and procedures should have been developed for processing and reporting internal control monitoring activities. To achieve this CMM level, an enterprise educational and monitoring program for internal control monitoring should have been defined and launched.

We have shown this limited extract for ME2, but the published CobiT material has a similar limited set of CMM maturity-level guidance materials for each of its internal controls. Although summarized at a very high level, these maturity model guidelines allow an organization to assess "how it is doing" with regard to each of CobiT's internal controls.

COBIT AND SARBANES-OXLEY

Chapter 2 discussed the current state of SOx Section 404 internal control assessment requirements and highlighted the more risk-based approaches that are now more frequently preferred for evaluating internal controls. CobiT is a powerful tool, particularly in an environment with a heavy concentration in IT processes and resources, to help management and internal auditors to perform these SOx Section 404 as well as Section 302 reviews. Discussed in Chapter 7, Section 302 is primarily concerned with the personal responsibilities of the CEO and CFO for financial reports and related disclosures. As part of this, SOx mandates that an organization's external auditors should perform limited quarterly reviews to determine whether there were any significant modifications to the internal control structure or changes in internal controls over financial reporting.

CobiT Objectives

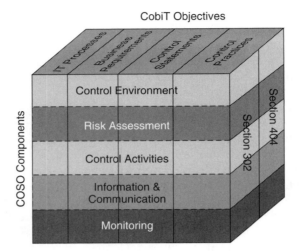

EXHIBIT 5.9 Relationship Between COSO
Components and CobiT Objectives
Source: Brink's Modern Internal Auditing, Sixth Edition, Robert Moeller, page 158. Copyright © 2005
John Wiley & Sons. Reprinted with permission of
John Wiley & Sons, Inc.

Both COSO internal controls and CobiT use three-dimensional cubical
frameworks to describe their internal control environments. They are similar, but with slight differences in classifications and terminology. Exhibit 5.9
shows how the CobiT framework maps to the COSO internal control model.
This shows that we can use CobiT's prime objectives, from Planning and
Organization to Monitoring and Evaluation, and use the control objectives
guidance for each to understand and evaluate internal controls through
COSO's five internal control components. The actual process, then, of performing the Section 404 compliance work is very similar to that outlined in
Chapter 6 on Section 404 assessments. Whether considering COSO internal
controls in general or using CobiT, the reviewer, such as an internal auditor, moves through a series a processes from planning to performing risk
assessments and on to identifying, documenting, and evaluating key internal
controls.

Because of CobiT's heritage of IT systems auditing, design, and processes, this documentation and guidance material relies very much on good
systems design and software engineering practices. For example, the documentation for each CobiT control objective describes how to assess that
control in terms of the previously referenced Capability Maturity Model

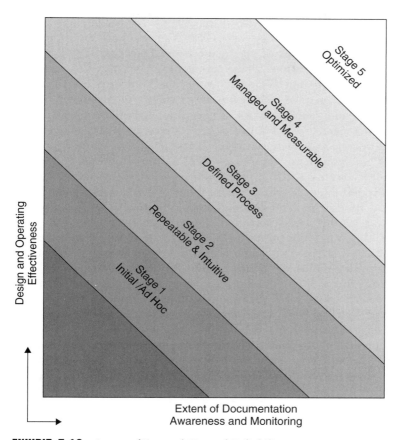

EXHIBIT 5.10 Stages of Internal Control Reliability
Source: Brink's Modern Internal Auditing, Sixth Edition, Robert Moeller, page 159. Copyright © 2005 John Wiley & Sons. Reprinted with permission of John Wiley & Sons, Inc.

(CMM), an approach for looking at IT organizations and processes in terms of relative maturity such as whether processes are ad hoc, defined and documented, or even better. Exhibit 5.10 shows this CMM control reliability framework in terms of the relative design of operating effectiveness and the extent of this documentation.

This control reliability framework provides a good way to assess internal controls over an individual CobiT control objective or over the entire organization. An internal control assessment, for example, might find a stage 0, nonexistent control environment. This implies a complete lack of a recognizable control process and an inability to be in compliance with Section 404 requirements at any level. This is an extreme situation, and if an internal auditor is part of an organization that appears to have the attributes of a stage 0 assessment, flags should have been raised or "whistles blown" if controls were that weak. Ideally, internal control assessors should hope to find *at least* a stage 2 and hopefully a stage 3 environment. Under stage 3, controls and related policies and procedures should be in place and adequately documented at a level sufficient for management to be able to assert to the adequacy of these controls.

With SOx, the increased emphasis on IT governance, and our recognition of the criticality of IT in most internal control situations, CobiT has gone through multiple editions until the previously referenced edition 4.1. CobiT's sponsoring IT Governance Association has been doing an excellent job releasing publications that map the CobiT framework to other standards and best practice frameworks. For example, there is an excellent and very detailed study[6] that maps the CobiT framework to SOx audit requirements. This published CobiT Section 404 review material, as well as that from earlier CobiT versions, does an excellent job of matching IT and CobiT control objectives with the five COSO components. Based on the published CobiT guidance, Exhibit 5.11 shows how the major CobiT control objective areas match or link with the major COSO components of internal control. This linkup ties together even better by going a level lower. For example, CobiT objective AI6 on Managing Changes under the Acquire and Implement control domain impacts the COSO components of Control Activities and Monitoring. The actual published CobiT detailed control objectives will tie to each of these COSO components. There is a close relationship between these CobiT and COSO control objectives and components.

The full set of CobiT control objectives will provide strong support for an internal auditor or others seeking to use CobiT to perform a SOx Section 404 internal control assessment review. While the concepts can be used in any internal control area, the emphasis is on IT applications and processes. For many organizations, an understanding and assessment of those IT-associated internal controls is a key area for achieving SOx compliance. CobiT has been around for some years now, but for too long, many had viewed it as just a specialized information systems audit tool and not a more general help for other internal audit work. Although its emphasis continues to be on IT, all internal auditors should explore and consider using the CobiT framework as an excellent tool for helping with current and evolving SOx compliance requirements.

COBIT Control Objectives	COSO Components				
	Control Environment	Risk Assessment	Control Activities	Information & Communication	Monitoring
Plan and Organize					
Define a strategic IT plan		X		X	X
Define the information architecture			X	X	
Determine technological direction					
Define the IT organization and relationships	X			X	
Manage the IT investment					
Communicate management aims and direction	X			X	X
Manage human resources	X			X	
Ensure compliance with external relationships			X	X	X
Assess risks		X			
Manage projects					
Manage quality	X		X	X	X
Acquire and Implement					
Identify automated solutions					
Acquire and maintain application software			X		
Acquire and maintain technology infrastructure			X		
Develop and maintain procedures			X	X	
Install and accredit			X		
Manage changes			X		X
Deliver and Support					
Define and manage service levels	X		X		X
Manage third-party services	X	X	X		X
Manage performance and capacity	X		X		
Ensure continuous service	X		X		X
Ensure systems security	X		X	X	X
Identify and allocate costs					

(continued overleaf)

EXHIBIT 5.11 COSO and CobiT Relationships

COBIT Control Objectives	COSO Components				
	Control Environment	Risk Assessment	Control Activities	Information & Communication	Monitoring
Educate and train users	X			X	
Assist and advise customers					
Manage the configuration	X		X	X	
Manage problems and incidents			X	X	X
Manage data			X	X	
Manage facilities			X		
Manage operations			X	X	
Monitor and Evaluate					
Monitor the processes				X	X
Assess internal control adequacy					X
Obtain independent assurance	X				X
Provide for independent audit					

EXHIBIT 5.11 (*continued*)
Source: *Control Objectives for Information and Related Technology (COBIT®)*, Third Edition, © Copyright 1996, 1998, 2000, the IT Governance Institute® (ITGI), http://isaca.org and http://itgi.org, Rolling Meadows, IL 60008 USA. Reprinted by permission.

ENDNOTES

1. IT Governance Institute, Rolling Meadows, IL, www.itgi.org.
2. *CobiT—Governance, Control and Audit for Information and Related Technology*, 4.1st ed. (Rolling Meadows, IL: IT Governance Institute, 2000).
3. CobiT 4.1, IT Governance Institute, Rolling Meadows, IL, 2005.

4. CobiT 4.1 Excerpt, http://www.stanford.edu/dept/Internal-Audit/infosec/docs/COBIT4.1-executive_summary-membership.pdf

5. A more detailed but still a summary review of CMM can be found in *Brink's Modern Internal Auditing*, Sixth Edition, by Robert R. Moeller (John Wiley & Sons, 2005).

6. *IT Control Objectives for Sarbanes-Oxley*, Second Edition (Rolling Meadows, IL: IT Governance Institute, September 2006).

Performing Section 404 Reviews Under AS5: An Ongoing Process

As discussed in other chapters as well, the Sarbanes-Oxley Act (SOx) is a large, complex piece of legislation covering many areas. While we still are following or complying with the text of the 2002 SOx legislation, SOx, like any U.S. federal act, is subject to detailed rules that define how we must comply with this legislation. Some significant governance rules changes have been introduced through the Act's Section 302, discussed in Chapter 7, but Section 404 of SOx covering reviews of internal accounting controls has received perhaps the most attention and compliance activity. Section 404 covers processes where a registrant enterprise is responsible for reviewing, documenting, and testing its own internal accounting controls. The results of that review work are passed on to the enterprise's external auditors, who are charged with reviewing and attesting to that internal controls review as part of their audit of the subject enterprise's reported financial statements and results. This area had been a major pain point for many enterprises because their external auditors were following a very detailed set of financial accounting audit procedures called Auditing Standard No. 2.

Despite some SOx concerns in other areas, Section 404 requirements have been a major concern and an area for ongoing criticisms and complaints regarding these reviews of internal accounting controls under AS2. During those first years after SOx became the law, Section 404 reviews have required massive amounts of time and attention as enterprises documented and then tested their internal controls. A major problem was that both enterprises and their external auditors were following these troublesome AS2 auditing standards that required very detailed reviews and did not give any benefit for small errors or omissions.

Most large U.S. enterprises have gone through at least their first, second, or more rounds of Section 404 internal control reviews, today and we now are using the newly implemented AS5 auditing standards discussed in

Chapter 3. While the basic SOx legislation has not changed, the Public Company Accounting Oversight Board (PCAOB) rules and overall approaches to maintaining compliance have changed. Whether previously exempt smaller enterprises, new registrants, or foreign companies that were given extra time before filing, there are still numerous enterprises that have not become SOx compliant and have not yet initiated these Section 404 compliance processes. This chapter provides an overall summary of SOx Section 404 rules and will discuss approaches for performing such reviews today, using AS5's more risk-based approach. Just as a point of clarification, we have used the term SOx registrants. When SOx became the law, the SEC established time-based rules when enterprises with SEC-registered securities had to be in compliancies. These rules were based on annual revenues and whether the company was U.S. or foreign. Once an enterprise met the criteria for Section 404 compliance, they are called or known as SOx registrants.

This chapter discusses steps and approaches to comply with SOx Section 404 and to keep the supporting documentation up to date. A SOx requirement, ongoing documentation update processes make the compliance task easier from year to year. SOx rules require that internal control documentation should be updated on an ongoing basis. This is a very important requirement that often slips between the cracks, but this chapter discusses approaches to keeping this documentation current.

AS5 as discussed in Chapter 3 AS5 has replaced the troublesome AS2 and made SOx Section 404 requirements a bit easier to implement and maintain, but the basic SOx legal or statutory requirements remain in place. Business professionals and internal auditors need to understand these Section 404 rules and to take appropriate steps to keep their enterprises in compliance. These rules impact both enterprises that have achieved SOx compliance in a previous period and those that are now coming under registration requirements.

SOx SECTION 404 ASSESSMENTS OF INTERNAL CONTROLS TODAY

Management has had an ongoing responsibility for designing and implementing internal controls over their enterprise's operations. Although the standards for what constituted good internal controls were not always that well defined in the past, they have remained a fundamental management concept. Chapter 5 discussed the steps that led to an effective definition of internal control as part of the initial Committee of Sponsoring Organizations (COSO) internal control framework. While external auditors have reviewed and tested an enterprise's internal control processes, detailed internal controls reviews have also been a fundamental internal audit task since their earliest days. Although the language and suggested audit approaches have changed, internal control reviews have been an audit responsibility going back decades.

External auditor internal control reviews came under major criticism during the period leading up to the enactment of SOx in 2002. The concern was that, prior to SOx, external auditors would themselves review and assess the internal controls surrounding a client's systems or processes and then would come back to perform audit procedures somewhat based on the results of their internal control review. Although external auditors were expected to perform these reviews following their American Institute of Certified Public Accountant (AICPA) standards, potential biases always existed in these processes. External auditors might not fully document or test some internal control procedure because they "understood it" due to their ongoing audit responsibilities. They might then go back and audit that same documented control, giving themselves the benefit of doubt regarding the strengths or weaknesses of that same internal control.

If an external auditor internal control review found no significant problems surrounding some process, the auditors would reduce their levels of testing—often to a minimum—and would rely on the controls identified from those same internal control reviews. The matter became even more dicey when consultants from that same external auditing firm built and installed the system first, and then members of the same audit firm would review these internal controls, followed by their auditing the process as well. This raised strong questions about the independence and objectivity of external auditor-led internal control reviews.

This whole issue changed with SOx Section 404 rules that essentially say that external auditors cannot review the internal controls of the same systems and processes that they are auditing. Another independent party—often from management—must perform the actual internal control reviews and the external auditors can then review and attest to the results of those independent internal control reviews. It is not enough to just document some process. The review should include some testing of each of the identified significant controls. Although there are a number of different methods here, the testing often employs one of the following procedures to test the effectiveness of a control:

- **Re-performance.** The reviewer here simply re-performs the operation of some control, such as a credit file analysis.
- **Examination.** The reviewer looks at the documentation supporting the operation of a control, such as a review of a bank reconciliation process for evidence of effective performance.

- **Observation.** The SOx 404 reviewer observes and documents the processing of a control, such as the processing of cash receipts. The auditor's documented observations provide evidence regarding the control. This type of test is only pertinent for the point in time when the observation is made.
- **Inquiry.** The reviewer asks a knowledgeable person about the operation of some control. This type of process usually does not provide sufficient evidence to support the operating effectiveness of some control.

The SOx review team should move through the identified internal controls and test them for operating effectiveness. The timing and extent of this testing will vary based on the nature of the control, its frequency of operation, its importance, and the quality of the control environment related to the specific internal control. Manual controls should generally be subject to more testing than automated control procedures, and more attention should be given to more important types of controls. Of course, all matters should be appropriately documented.

When Section 404 assessors find areas where there is a breakdown in some internal control, often caused by either the lack of some appropriate control process or the failure of a test of an established control, the matter should be identified as a weakness requiring corrective actions. The more significant of them are classified as *material weaknesses*—matters that will be forwarded to the audit committee for resolution and may prevent the issuance of audited financial reports. The AS5 auditing standard, as summarized in Chapter 3, has allowed a little more flexibility as to what must be classified as a material weakness, but the basic SOx rules have not changed. Even though the SOx legislation remains unchanged, the new PCAOB-mandated AS5 rules have been designed to drive more efficiency into this process by using more of a risk-based approach that focuses more on the key controls regarding the reliability of an enterprise's financial reporting.

SOx SECTION 404 REQUIREMENTS

SOx Section 404 requires the preparation of an annual internal control report for registered enterprises, as part of their Securities and Exchange Commission (SEC) financial reporting in what are 10K annual financial reports. In addition to the financial statements and other 10K disclosures, SOx Section 404 requirements call for each registrant to add the following two information elements to their 10Ks:

1. Formally state the responsibility of management for establishing and maintaining an adequate internal control structure and procedures for financial reporting.
2. Include an assessment, as of the end of the most recent fiscal year, of the effectiveness of the enterprise's internal control structure and procedures for financial reporting.

In addition, the public accounting firm that issued the supporting audit report is required to review and report on this process that led to management's assessment of its internal financial controls. Simply put, management is required to report on the quality of their internal controls, and their public accounting firm must audit or attest to that management-directed internal control report in addition to the external auditor's normal financial statement audit. Management has always been responsible for preparing their periodic financial reports, and the external auditors then audited those financial numbers and certified that they were fairly stated. With SOx Section 404, management is now responsible for documenting and testing their internal financial controls as well as to report on their effectiveness. External auditors then review the supporting materials leading up to that internal financial control report to assert that the report is an accurate description of the internal control environment.

To the non-auditor, this might appear to be an obscure or almost trivial requirement. Even some internal auditors that primarily specialize in more operational audits may wonder about the nuances in this process. However, audit reports on the status of internal controls have been an ongoing and simmering issue among the public accounting community, the SEC, and other interested parties going back to at least 1974. Much of the problem then was that there was no recognized definition for *internal controls*. The release of the COSO internal control framework in 1992 (discussed in Chapter 4) established an accepted standard for understanding internal controls. Under SOx Section 404, management is now required to report on the adequacy of their internal controls with public accounting firms attesting to the management-developed internal control reports. The more risk-based changes appearing in AS5 have not changed this basic process.

This process enforces a basic internal control on the importance of maintaining a separation of duties. That is, the person who develops some key transaction should not be the person who approves it. Under Section 404 procedures, the enterprise builds and documents its own internal control processes, then an independent party such as internal audit must review and test those internal controls for correctness, and finally the external auditors review and attest to the adequacy of this overall process. Their financial audit procedures will be based on these internal controls. This process corrects some pre-SOx shortcomings. In those per-SOx earlier days, external auditors frequently built, documented and then audited their own internal controls—a separation-of-duties shortcoming.

Launching the Section 404 Compliance Review: Identifying Key Processes

Every enterprise uses a series of processes to conduct its normal business activities. Some may be represented by automated systems, others are primarily manual procedures performed on a regular basis, while still others are a combination of automated and manual. These processes are normally considered in terms of basic accounting cycles and frequently include the:

- **Revenue cycle.** Processes dealing with sales or other revenue to the enterprise.
- **Direct expenditures cycle.** Covers expenditures of material or direct production costs.
- **Indirect expenditures cycle.** Operating costs that cannot be directly tied to production activities but are necessary for overall business operations.
- **Payroll cycle.** Covers all personnel compensation.
- **Inventory cycle.** Although inventory will eventually be applied to production as direct expenditures, special processes are needed due to the time-based-holding nature of inventory until it is applied to production.
- **Fixed assets cycle.** Property and equipment require separate accounting processes, such as periodic depreciation accounting over time.
- **General IT cycle.** This set of processes covers information technology (IT) controls that are general or applicable to all IT operations, such as software configuration management, continuity planning, help-desk operations, and a series of other IT service management processes.

Periodic financial reports, including a general ledger application, are an example of these cycle processes. For most, there are many manual financial adjustments in addition to the automated general ledger to complete the financial statement close. This can often be a major, periodic process for an enterprise.

The identification of the key or major processes here is an initial Section 404 compliance step. A term that is frequently used without too much thought of its meaning, a *process* is a particular course of action intended to achieve a result, such as an individual's process of obtaining a driver's license. It is a series of actions that have clearly defined starting points, consistent operational steps, and defined output points. The term *process* is used because this is a set of defined steps that can be repeated and followed consistently. The requirement to document, understand, and test "key processes" has been a major activity area for SOx Section 404 procedures since enactment. During the first years of SOx, some enterprises—often with the encouragement of their external auditors—attempted to define *every* process. They did not have guidelines for eliminating the less risky ones and often went through things to a high level of minutia. AS5 now has established a level of reasonableness here.

Internal audit often can be a major help to an enterprise in defining key processes. For many, internal audit may have already defined key processes through their annual audit planning and audit documentation. While it will depend very much on the nature and size of an enterprise, Exhibit 6.1 lists an example set of processes that might be found in a small-distribution enterprise. While such a list will be much larger and more extensive for a larger enterprise, the exhibit does list some—but certainly not all—of the basic processes that will support an enterprise. After discussions with management as well as with internal auditors who know the enterprise, such a process list should be developed to become a basis for launching a stream of internal control reviews for the enterprise.

Launching the Section 404 Compliance Review: Internal Audit's Role

With the exception of SOx specifically prohibiting external audit firms from performing internal audit services for their audit clients, there are few specific references to internal audit in the text of the SOx legislation. Despite being supported by a well-recognized professional group with strong internal control review standards, the Institute of Internal Auditors (ITA), these internal control specialists were not mentioned in the text of the original SOx legislation. However, even though SOx does not give any specific responsibility to internal audit, they have become an important resource in many enterprises for the completion of their Section 404 internal control assessments. Under SOx, a separate and independent function within the enterprise—often internal audit—reviews and documents the internal controls covering key processes, identifies key control points, and then tests those identified controls. External audit would then review that work and attest to its adequacy. For many corporations, internal audit now has a much greater set of responsibilities and importance in today's SOx world.

Internal audit has been referred to as a key resource for performing this work. Some internal audit functions originally distanced themselves from

1. **Purchase order management.** Processes must be in place to purchase or acquire the goods to be distributed.
2. **Inventory management.** Once goods have been purchased, there is a need for processes to manage them in inventory before distribution to customers.
3. **Warehouse management.** Processes must be in place to store product inventory in secure and well organized facilities, with sub-processes for the inspection and placement of goods.
4. **Demand planning.** An enterprise needs to know how customers will demand existing and new products. This may include marketing-based processes including customer surveys.
5. **Order processing.** Whether IT paper-based, processes should be in place to receive new orders, approve customer credit histories, and pick and pack the received orders.
6. **Shipping and receiving.** Process should be in place to ship to customers as well as to inspect and receive incoming ordered goods.
7. **Logistics management.** A distribution company is typically faced with requirements for special shipping arrangement, movement of goods between warehouse facilities, and other arrangements where logistics processes are needed.
8. **Billing and invoicing.** After orders are received and shipped, processes are needed to bill customers for payment and then to manage those accounts.
9. **Accounting systems.** Beyond accounts receivable, and enterprise needs accounting and financial processes for all of its accounting functions.
10. **Information systems.** Processes are needed for all aspects of IT operations, including IT service design, service operations, delivery of all aspects of IT services, and processes for continual IT improvements.
11. **Human resources.** Processes are needed to manage all people associated issues, including compensation, benefits, related taxes, and all human resource–based legislative legal requirements.
12. **Internal audit.** The enterprise needs an effective internal audit function.

EXHIBIT 6.1   Section 404 Compliance Review Work Breakdown Structure

this work because of their perceptions of internal auditor independence standards, but the more recent changes to internal audit standards discussed in Chapter 11, now allow them to act as consultants to help achieve this work. Another alternative for an enterprise is to bring in some other independent parties to perform the work, and AS5 rules now very much encourage internal audit's participation here. Internal audit's role in Section 404 reviews can take several different forms:

1. Internal audit can take the lead in actually performing the Section 404 reviews by identifying key processes, documenting their internal

controls, and performing appropriate tests of those controls. Internal audit would be following a documentation format consistent with their external auditors but will be doing this work separately and independently. The external auditors would then be responsible for reviewing these reviews as performed by internal audit.

2. An in-house function or outside consulting resources could be designated by the enterprise to perform their Section 404 reviews, and internal audit can act as a resource to support the external auditors in reviewing the results of the Section 404 work. This approach will reduce external audit resource costs provided there is some other resource available to actually perform effective Section 404 reviews. Of course, the matter must be approved by the independent external auditors.

3. Internal audit can work with and help other corporate resources—either internal or external—that are performing the Section 404 reviews without getting directly involved with those reviews, either as independent internal auditors or as agents for the external audit firm. This approach allows internal audit to devote more time and resources to other internal audit projects. This may also be the only alternative for a very small internal audit function.

The chief audit executive (CAE)—that is the executive in charge of internal audit, financial management, and the audit committee should work with the enterprise's external auditors to define responsibilities for these required Section 404 internal control reviews. In some cases, the decision will be that it is most efficient for resources, other than internal audit, to take the second approach described above. External audit might make arrangements with those internal auditors to review and assess the adequacy of that internal control review work. In this situation, internal audit would be working for external audit in reviewing and attesting to the results of those internal control reviews but would not be performing the actual reviews. As mentioned, this type of arrangement will save on overall external audit costs by giving internal audit an important role in helping external audit in achieving the Section 404 review objectives. The negative side of this arrangement is that the management team or affiliated consultants assigned may not have the time, resources, or process knowledge to perform these internal control assessments. This arrangement often works best when an enterprise has another internal audit–like function such as a strong quality assurance or risk assessment group. These are specialists that understand how to review, document, and test internal control processes.

In alternative 1, internal audit performs the review work for enterprise financial management for a subsequent but separate and independent assessment by the external auditors. The positive side of this arrangement is that internal audit is often the best and most qualified resource in the enterprise to perform these reviews. They understand internal controls as well as good documentation techniques and often have the skill to effectively review supporting information systems applications. Although this arrangement will involve more external audit resources, this may be an effective way to complete this Section 404 review requirement. All parties must realize their roles and responsibilities here.

SOx Section 404 reviews must be performed on an annual basis, and an enterprise and its internal audit function should change their review strategy over the years to comply with these Section 404 requirements. Documentation prepared and tested in the first year need only be updated and retested in future periods. There is no reason why the strategy selected might not be the same every year going forward as changes always introduce increased costs and added time spent relearning approaches. All parties should develop an approach that appears the most cost-effective to achieve these legally mandated SOx requirements. While we are now taking a more risk-based approach under AS5, the basic SOx Section 404 requirements have not changed.

Launching the Section 404 Compliance Review: Organizing the Project

Compliance with SOx Section 404 is a major challenge for SEC-registered enterprises. While prior to SOx, some previously took a hard look at their COSO internal control framework and evaluated the internal controls using that framework, others initially did not. Even enterprises that have evaluated their own controls in a COSO context almost certainly will have some work ahead. In getting started in documenting internal controls, they at least should have an understanding of their internal control environment. This documentation process has changed as a SOx registrant moves from its first few years of Section 404 compliance work up to the present. The external auditors who were going to be reviewing and attesting to those internal controls in SOx's early years frequently demanded massive amounts of documentation. Our more risk-based AS5 approach to SOx today is more constrained.

An effective internal audit function often can play a very major role in helping an enterprise get ready for its SOx Section 404 compliance. As discussed, there are also some very qualified consulting firms to help an enterprise to achieve SOx compliance, but the effective internal audit function should be in a key role to aid senior management here. Based on the IIA's internal audit standards discussed in Chapter 11, internal audit should not be directly responsible for implementing the internal financial control testing and documentation programs that they will be eventually requested to review. They should not assume the role as project manager here but only play an active participant role on the implementation team. Typically, internal auditors should recommend internal control improvements as the new processes are being developed, but they are not responsible for installing those new internal control processes. Thus, they can later review the Section 404 process documentation while maintaining their independence.

Whether performed by internal audit or some other independent parties, an initial Section 404 compliance review requires some formal, special project steps. While larger SOx-registered public enterprises have already gone through multiple rounds of their SOx compliance work, there are still many smaller or foreign entities that have not. The amount of effort required for new registrants would be based on the strength and sophistication of an enterprise's internal control processes, but should follow these steps:

Step 1. Organize the Section 404 compliance project approach. Assign a project team to lead the effort. A senior executive such as the chief financial officer (CFO) should act as the project sponsor with a team of both internal and external resources to participate in the effort. Roles, responsibilities, and resource requirements should be estimated as well. Internal audit can often assume major responsibilities here.

Step 2. Develop a project plan. The internal financial control compliance project should be well in process prior to the enterprise's financial year-end. While the existing plan can be updated in subsequent years, there will be a major challenge and time crunch for earlier years. The plan should focus on significant areas of enterprise operations with coverage over all significant business units. Although there can be many plan development variations here, Exhibit 6.2 shows some of the planning considerations for a Section 404 compliance review project. Although work steps described are at a fairly high level, the team should develop a detailed plan document to begin the SOx Section 404 internal financial control review.

Step 3. Select key processes for review. Every enterprise uses or depends on a wide range of financial and operational processes. A typical payroll system, for example, is a set of automated and manual routines that take time and attendance data and produces payroll checks or transfers in the employee checking accounts. The total payroll process is much larger and includes steps necessary to add employees, to process a pay increase, and to communicate

1. Determine status of review—Is this the first round of Section 404 reviews for the entity and a subsequent year follow-up?
2. If it is a new review, follow the work steps as outlined in Exhibit 6.1. Otherwise plan for a subsequent-period Section 404 review.
3. Review the detailed documentation covering prior 404 reviews, including process flowcharts, internal control gaps identified and remediated, as well as overall project-planning documentation for prior review.
4. Review any recently published PCAOB rules covering Section 404 reviews and related auditing changes, and adjust procedures to reflect those changes.
5. Meet with the external audit firm responsible for the current Section 404 attestations and determine if there are any changes in documentation and testing philosophy from the prior review.
6. Review any organizational changes since the last review, including acquisitions or major reorganizations, and develop plans to modify the review coverage, if necessary.
7. Through meetings with senior and IT management, identify if new systems or processes have been installed over the last period and if those new changes have been reflected in updated documentation.
8. Review any internal control weaknesses identified in the last review and assess whether internal control corrections reported as installed appear to be working.
9. Assess the status of existing Section 404 documentation and determine the extent of new documentation preparation necessary.
10. Assuming that the prior Section 404 review was done by internal audit, determine that appropriate, knowledgeable, trained resources are available to perform the upcoming review.
11. Interview all parties involved in the prior Section 404 review exercise to assess any lessons learned and develop plans for corrective actions in the upcoming review.
12. Based on discussions with external auditors and senior management, determine the scope of materiality parameters for the upcoming review.
13. Determine that the software, if any, used to document prior review is still current, and make any changes necessary to have adequate tools in place to perform the upcoming review.
14. Prepare a detailed project plan for the upcoming Section 404 review, with considerations given to coordination of review activities at business entity units and with external auditors.
15. Submit plan for approval by senior management.

EXHIBIT 6.2 Section 404 Project Planning Considerations
Source: Brink's Modern Internal Auditing, Sixth Edition, Robert Moeller, page 130. Copyright © 2005 John Wiley & Sons. Reprinted with permission of John Wiley & Sons, Inc.

with accounting and benefit systems. There can be numerous transaction flows in this overall process.

Internal audit and/or the Section 404 compliance team needs to review all enterprise processes and select the ones that are financially significant. This key process selection should focus on processes where there is a risk that a failure could cause a major financial or operational risk to the enterprise. These processes should then be ranked by the size of the assets controlled and other measures, with an overall consideration given to their risk of failure. Exhibit 6.3 contains some alternative factors to consider or guidelines for this key process selection. For example, in raising the question of whether the application software was purchased or built in-house, the enterprise might—and probably should—decide that purchased software often has a lower risk. Internal audit can assist in developing documented procedures to justify why one process is more worthy or significant for detailed review than another.

In the first years of Section 404 reviews when SOx became effective starting in 2003, there was a tendency toward overkill on this process selection. Registrants today have things a bit easier as there is no need to target lower-risk processes. However, the enterprise should develop some risk-based criteria for why they have or have not selected some process for review. The approach should be applied consistently. Also, it is a good idea to discuss such decisions with the external auditors and then to document decisions made.

Step 4. Document selected process transaction flows. The next important step is to prepare transaction flow documentation for the key processes selected. An easy step if there had been a previously prepared COSO internal control review by internal audit or others, existing documentation should be reviewed to determine if it is still accurate. Documentation can be much more of a challenge if this is the first SOx 404 review and the enterprise has never documented its processes. There are a variety of accepted documentation protocols, and the goal should be to select some notation that is easy to prepare, update, and is easily understood by all interested parties. The documentation should show key transaction flows and control points. A key need for any documentation is a supporting process to keep it updated. The once typically prepared three-ring notebooks full of process documentation will be of little value in the future if they have never been updated. Enterprises should

The following questions can help guide the selection of key processes to review as part of a SOx Section 404 review exercise. While there is no right or wrong answer to any, these should help in the selection of key enterprise processes for SOx Section 404 reviews:

I. Has the enterprise defined its key financial processes and are these processes linked to financial statement general ledger accounts?

II. Have each of these key processes been subject to a formal risk assessment to identify higher-risk areas?

III. Process or system status for higher-risk areas

    A. Has the process been documented and is that documentation current?

    B. Nature of the process or system to be reviewed:
- Is this a new system or process developed in-house?
- For IT supported applications, is this a newly purchased software package?
- Have there been major changes over the past period affecting functionality?
- Have past changes been described as only minor changes?
- Is there adequate current documentation supporting the process?

    C. Past history of process or system changes:
- Have there been significant changes over the past two years?
- Have changes been minor in the past two years?
- Have there been two years or more since the last change?
- Is this a new process or one with no recent changes?
- Is there an adequate document change control process in place?

    D. Process or system development team:
- Is the process managed by an outside contractor for its development or management?
- Is an in-house group responsible for process development and management?
- Is the process a purchased packaged solution with only minor local changes?

    E. Top management interest in process or project:
- Is this an enterprise-level process mandated by senior management?
- Does system or process responsibility reside at an operating-unit level?
- Is this a process initiated by middle management?
- Is the process an individual user or department responsibility?

(continued overleaf)

EXHIBIT 6.3   Section 404 Process Review Selection Guidelines

IV. Internal control and process failure significance
    A. Type of system or process:
        ○ Does the process support financial statement balances?
        ○ Does the process support major organizational operations?
        ○ Is the project primarily for logistical or administrative support?
        ○ Is this a less critical statistical or research application?
    B. Past SOx review history:
        ○ Has there been a prior SOx review including control improvement recommendations?
        ○ Have prior reviews concluded with only limited recommendations?
        ○ Have prior Section 404 test results found no significant internal control problems?
        ○ Were significant control weaknesses identified in a past review and have those weaknesses been corrected?
        ○ If control improvement recommendations have been made in prior reviews, do matters appear to have been corrected?
        ○ Does existing documentation appear to have past review corrective actions?
    C. System or process control procedures:
        ○ Are there process-to-process–generated internal controls and have these controls been documented?
        ○ Are there run-to-run controls with other systems or processes?
        ○ Is the process primarily operating with any significant batch mode or with manual controls, and have those manual procedures been documented and tested?
V. Impact of Process Failure
    A. Is there a high, medium or low risk of process failure?
    B. Impact of incorrect reported results. Would a process failure result in:
        ○ Potential legal liability?
        ○ Financial statement impact?
        ○ Potential for incorrect management decisions?
        ○ Limited decision support risks?
    C. Impact of application failure on personnel. Would a process failure result in:
        ○ Need for extra management analysis time?
        ○ Need for extra user clerical time?
        ○ Need for a wide range of specialized resources?
VI. Have external auditors reviewed process selection criteria and do they concur with these selections?

EXHIBIT 6.3   *(continued)*

Source: Brink's Modern Internal Auditing, Sixth Edition, Robert Moeller, page 130.
Copyright © 2005 John Wiley & Sons. Reprinted with permission of John Wiley & Sons, Inc.

establish procedures to ensure that all changes to previously documented systems are updated when required. The groups or functions that initially documented these SOx processes should be given the responsibility to maintain this documentation.

Documentation can be done through verbal descriptions, but it is usually best to use a flowcharting technique. The idea is to show the inputs, outputs, process steps, and key decision points for any process. Many different approaches can be used here, but Exhibit 6.4 shows a very simple flowchart describing a sales shipping and billing process. For a smaller enterprise without much activity, this may be too small of a process to even document in any detail, but the exhibit shows an example of the documentation process. This chart, for example, shows decision steps if the item is not currently in stock. The documentation should be prepared in a manner that can be easily understood by all interested parties, and, more importantly, can be easily updated in the event of process changes.

The term or expression *scalable* is an important IT concept that refers to how well a hardware or software system can adapt to increased demands. For example, a scalable IT network system would be one that can start with just a few connections but can easily expand to thousands. Scalability can be a very important internal control feature because it means that internal controls should be installed in a manner such that the enterprise will not outgrow them. When we build or document an internal control, its relative scalability should always be considered.

Step 5. **Assess selected process risks.** Once an enterprise has defined and documented its key processes, the next step is to assess risks

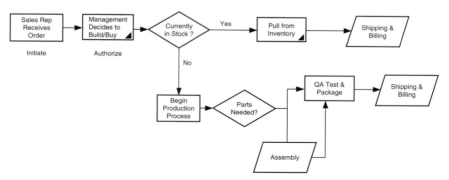

EXHIBIT 6.4   Process Documentation Flowchart Example

to determine what might go wrong. Here, the review team that first identified and documented key processes should go through a detailed "what could go wrong?" type of analysis. The idea is to ask questions about the potential risks surrounding each reviewed process. For example, in an accounts payable process, could someone gain access to the system and then arrange to cut an unauthorized check? Could system controls be sufficiently weak that multiple payments might be generated to the same authorized vendor? There could be numerous risks of this sort. Internal audit or the SOx review team should go through each of the selected processes and highlight potential risks in such an open-ended set of questions and then focus on the expected supporting controls. Based on their backgrounds, this is very much the type of analysis where internal audit can play a very valuable role. Exhibit 6.5 is an example of this type of review for an accounts payable (A/P) process and points to a review approach that should be developed for any key process. We have selected A/P as an example process as it is fairly easy to understand in most circumstances, but it includes the same type of what-if questions that should be raised for others as well.

Step 6. **Assess control effectiveness through appropriate test procedures.** System controls are of little value if they are not working effectively. Interviews and the initial documentation process can sometimes determine that appropriate controls do not appear to be in place or are ineffective. In that case, the conclusions from the assessment should be documented, discussed with the process owners, and an action plan developed to take corrective actions to improve the controls.

In most instances, the documented controls should be tested to determine that they are operating effectively. Called *audit testing*, this has been a common process over the years for both internal and external auditor reviews of controls. These audit tests were once extremely extensive and sometimes expensive with large sample transaction sizes. Evaluation of the results of these samples allowed internal or external auditors to draw conclusions regarding whether financial results were fairly stated or if the internal controls appeared to be working. Once a popular audit tool, statistically based audit sampling is less common today primarily because of audit efficiency pressures.

Whether there is a statistically based sample or not, the SOx process reviewer should use one or more sample transactions to test the process. While automated controls are expected to

1. Are Accounts Payable staff independent from purchasing and receiving functions?
2. Are debit memos, adjustments, and other noncash debits to Accounts Payable approved and regularly reviewed by supervisory personnel?
3. Are there defined cutoff procedures at month-end that are continually monitored by appropriate managers?
4. Are month-end accruals and other credit Accounts Payable estimates and adjustments reviewed and approved by appropriate managers?
5. Are all Accounts Payable vouchers and debit memos prenumbered through either manual or automated procedures?
6. Are all vendor invoices date and time stamped in sequential order with the sequence periodically reviewed for missing/duplicate items?
7. Are all unused forms and related documents controlled?
8. Are records maintained for all voided forms?
9. Is the Accounts Payable subledger maintenance separate from general ledger maintenance?
10. Are Accounts Payable balances and general ledger control accounts periodically reconciled and reviewed by appropriate managers?
11. Are approved reconciliations of monthly vendor account statements made against unmatched open purchase orders and receiving reports?
12. Is a receipt of vendor account statements performed by someone other than Accounts Payable accounting staff?
13. Are Accounts Payable risks reviewed regularly with corrective actions taken to limit those risks?
14. Have all control gaps from previous Section 404 reviews and internal audits been corrected?

EXHIBIT 6.5   Accounts Payable Process Review Procedures

be in place and working on a consistent basis, manual controls generally require larger sample sizes. Exhibit 6.6 outlines some manual control suggested sample sizes, based on the frequency of the control performance. The idea here is if a control covers many repetitive items, an item sample size to determine that it is operating effectively should be larger. The size of the sample can present a challenge for some processes, but if it is a largely paper-based process with many people-based approval steps, the SOx reviewer might borrow from other classic internal audit techniques and try a *walkthrough* type of test. The idea is to take a single transaction—such as a vendor invoice requiring approval—and individually walk that transaction through each of the processing steps prior to cutting the A/P check. Again, this

Frequency of Control Performance	Minimum Sample Size
• Multiple times per day	At least 30 items
• Daily	At least 25 items
• Weekly	At least 10 items
• Monthly	At least 5 items
• Quarterly	At least 2 items

EXHIBIT 6.6 Sample Size Guidelines for Manual Controls

is a test to assess internal controls over a process. If the results of the test are positive, the process reviewer could determine if the process appears to be working with adequate internal controls. This is an exercise that should be familiar to all internal auditors. The AS5 auditing standards highlights the use of walkthroughs, and they are discussed in Chapter 3.

Step 7. **Review compliance results with key stakeholders.** Senior financial and executive management are ultimately responsible for an enterprise's final Section 404 report. The project team should review their progress with senior management on a periodic basis, highlighting their review approaches and short-term corrective actions initiated. Similarly, since they must formally attest to the results of this financial internal controls review, the external auditors should be kept informed of progress and any outstanding issues in process of resolution.

Our reference to coordination with key stakeholders is important here. All too often in the first years of these Section 404 reviews, an assessment may have identified some potential internal control weakness at a local facility, documented it for that unit with little follow-up, and then raised it as a potentially significant weakness or gap back at the headquarters location. In many cases, the potential weakness had minimal impact to the overall enterprise and could have been resolved and corrected at a local level. Stakeholder communication at all levels is important here.

Step 8. **Complete report on the effectiveness of the internal control structure.** This is the final step in Section 404 compliance. Following SOx guidance, internal control reviews are not a one-time exercise, and all work should be documented for follow-up reviews. The documentation process here is similar to an auditors' financial audit process where results are documented in workpapers for ongoing periods. This is the report, along with the external auditor's attest work, that will be filed with the SEC as part of the enterprise's 10K annual report.

A first-time SOx Section 404 compliance review can be a major undertaking and certainly will require considerably more time and effort than is expressed in the limited number of work steps described above. However, the new AS5 rules have made this review process a bit easier. It is now not necessary to go back to ground zero in each review cycle year; one may rely on the work from prior periods. The old-timer SOx 404 reviewer, now experienced with multiple years of these reviews, might look at AS5 and say something like, "You should see how bad it was in the old days!" AS5 has simplified and rationalized these internal control review processes, but we still must keep the basic entity-level internal control review processes in place.

As has been discussed, Section 404 internal control reviews are a key area where internal audit can play a very significant but advisory role. The effort required will depend on the level of internal control work that has previously been performed in the enterprise. Many if not most larger U.S. major corporations have already gone through one or more cycles of their Section 404 reviews and are now in a maintenance mode. Often through the leadership of internal audit, these enterprises have reviewed, tested, and documented their internal controls following the COSO framework standard, and have the task of achieving Section 404 compliance on a continuing basis.

Also, if an automated system control was found to be effective in the first year and if there were no known changes to this process, it is no longer necessary to go back and re-document and retest that system in subsequent review periods. This is an example of exercising a more risk-based approach. As another major change, management now has the flexibility to exercise judgment to tailor review approaches to enterprise facts and circumstances. Section 404 reviews continue to be important, but AS5 rules offer more flexibility. We were often too detail oriented during SOx's first years, and the objective going forward should be to establish a more risk-based, reasoned approach to these assessments.

SECTION 404 FILING RULES: CHANGING DEADLINES FOR ELIGIBILITY

At the present time in these still-early days of SOx, there are still enterprises that have not been required to adopt SOx rules and become compliant with its procedures. As drafted, the legislation covers *any* entity that has securities registered with the SEC. This is a large population, including many very small, low-capitalization corporations with a limited number of shareholders, non-U.S. entities with some securities traded on SEC-regulated stock exchanges, and private companies that have SEC-registered debt instruments. Many enterprises, and especially smaller companies, did not have the size or sophistication necessary to comply with many SOx rules. Although the initial filing deadlines followed right after the major corporation rules, various pressures on the SEC caused them to be extended. Filing requirements have been tightened to favor larger entities, and the SEC has pushed filing deadlines out multiple times.

Many of these smaller SEC-registered entities that have not yet come onto the SOx radar screen face major SOx compliance challenges. Many of them have limited internal audit functions, and while they have performed some internal control reviews they have not otherwise embraced a COSO-like internal control framework. These are often enterprises where the internal audit function activities are focused on operational efficiency–related reviews or financial internal audit work in support of their external auditors. The PCAOB has eased up on smaller company filing rules as discussed in the next section.

Section 404 Small Company Registration Rules

SOx rules say that *all* SEC-registered enterprises must comply with these Section 404 rules. This includes many smaller enterprises whose stock trades on what were called "pink sheets," an old term going back to paper-based small company stock trading. In addition, there are numerous essentially private enterprises that only have some sometimes long ago bond offering registered with the SEC, making them subject to SOx. SOx Section 404 represents a major challenge for smaller U.S. corporations. They have the same SOx requirement to formally review and document their internal financial controls, to identify any weaknesses, and to take appropriate corrective actions. Such a review can be accomplished by the financial management team with help by an internal audit function, if it exists. Otherwise, the CFO and the financial teams would be expected to take on this responsibility, if there are sufficient time and other resources. The best solution here may be to contract for outside services. Many such smaller enterprises have little or no internal audit resources and often do not have the formally documented internal control processes normally found in more major enterprises.

"Horror stories" from larger enterprises about their experiences with Section 404 rules under the old AS2 caused trade associations and others to lobby the SEC to give smaller companies more and more time to file and to ease up on rules. The SEC has somewhat redefined the rules for these smaller companies, designated as *nonaccelerated filers*. This designation applies to the smaller enterprise that has a public stock market float less than $75 million, as computed on the last business day of the issuer's most recently completed second fiscal quarter.

The SEC has extended compliance deadlines several times for non-accelerated filers, and as this book goes to press, these smaller-enterprise nonaccelerated filers are not responsible for SOx 404 rules until fiscal years ending in 2008 or beyond. This says that a smaller enterprise with a December 31, 2008 year-end would not be required to become Section 404 compliant until 2009. Because SOx currently covers all enterprises with SEC-registered securities, and because there are many smaller entities here—many well below the $75 million limit—we can expect to see the rules or deadlines for smaller enterprises eased even more. While there is a strong legal argument that the same rules should apply to everyone, concerns about competitiveness and other factors are strongly pushing the SEC to ease up. Of course, another sometimes-discussed option to avoid SOx rules is for a corporation to buy back its stock and go private. While a frequent topic in the financial press, this is easier said than done with no real trends in this direction.

What does a smaller enterprise need to do to initially register for SOx under Section 404 rules? Chapter 3 discussed some of the steps a smaller enterprise needs to consider when getting ready for its first post-AS5 Section 404 internal control assessment work. Even with the AS5 risk-assessment approach, compliance can be a major task for a smaller, limited-resources enterprise. Many have been waiting for the SOx effective dates and restrictions to be extended and softened again and again. However, these rules are going to go away, and the prudent enterprise should begin to take the necessary steps to establish SOx and especially Section 404 compliance sooner rather than later!

Foreign Enterprise Section 404 Rules

When SOx became law in the United States, the legislation stated that *any* enterprise that had securities registered with the SEC was required to comply with SOx rules. While major U.S. corporations hunkered down and began their compliance efforts at once, the rules caused problems for both smaller enterprises, as discussed above, and non-U.S. foreign companies that had some securities listed on U.S. stock exchanges. A large number of international enterprises fell into this category. A German corporation, for example, might have its corporate headquarters in Frankfurt, Germany, and use that stock exchange as the major trading location for its stock. However, to expand international exposure and to gain access to U.S. capital markets, that same German enterprise would also have had its stock listed on the New York Stock Exchange (NYSE). The SOx foreign registrant rules have caused some serious problems in these environments.

Many non-U.S. corporations follow the international accounting standards (IAS), called International Financial Reporting Standards (IFRS), auditing and reporting rules rather than the slightly different U.S.-based Generally Accepted Accounting Principles (GAAP). Equally frustrating, accounting standards–setting authorities around the world have been working to establish a consistent set of rules and almost everyone but the United States has bought into the concept. However, the SEC initially said that *all* registrants, domestic or foreign, must follow the same GAAP rules. This was particularly irksome as the United States had participated in the development of IFRS but did not change to adopt these more worldwide rules.

Worse for foreign registrants, a major section of SOx mandates a set of new corporate governance board of directors rules. Many of these new SOx board of directors and audit committee rules really ran contrary to other national rules. For example, while SOx requires that audit committees must be composed of independent directors, some national rules were different. SOx required annual reports from the boards of SOx registrants, but some foreign corporations had different rules. There was much concern about the difficulty in complying with SOx rules for many non-U.S. enterprises, and a significant number took steps to terminate their U.S. exchange listings. In addition, a large number of newer non-U.S. enterprises seeking initial registration decided to not list their securities on a U.S. exchange but moved to London or elsewhere. The major reason given was the burden of SOx Section 404 compliance rules.

Even worse for some foreign corporations, many have had a small but limited presence on a U.S. exchange such as the NYSE. A French-based corporation may have had most of its stock traded in Paris but had been listed on the NYSE only to expand its international presence. Even though very few shares had been traded on the NYSE as compared to Paris, SOx rules require compliance due to that limited NYSE presence and a related SEC registration. The initial reaction of some international corporations was to just de-list their stocks from U.S. exchanges. However, SEC rules initially had made it very difficult to de-list these securities in the United States. SEC rules have since been issued making it easier to get off of an exchange and avoid SOx requirements. In addition, SOx filing deadlines have been extended for these foreign firms. Smaller foreign filers have more time, with current deadlines that still may be extended. This is a similar situation to the previously discussed deadline rules for smaller U.S. enterprises.

Convergence in Accounting Standards   An important development in cleaning up internal accounting and auditing rules is the growing movement toward a convergence of the IFRS international accounting standards and U.S. GAAP rules established by the Financial Accounting Standards Board (FASB). Starting with some very basic differences in the conceptual frameworks for accounting systems, there are strong accounting treatment differences in some of the following areas:

- Financial statement presentation
- Revenue and expense recognition
- Inventory methods and valuation
- Tangible and intangible assets
- Assets held for sale and discontinued operations
- Impairment testing
- Liabilities
- Employee benefits
- Equity items
- Financial instruments, derivatives, and hedging

Our objective here is not to explain these differences but to highlight some of them. For example, reported quarterly sales of $100 million for a U.S. corporation may not represent the same value for a European Union (EU)–based corporation because of differing accounting treatments. In the United States, we can record an item as a sale once the sale is recorded and it leaves the shipping dock. Elsewhere, accounting rules may require that the goods be received by the customer before recognizing it as a sale. These types of small accounting rules differences imply that quarterly reported sales of $100 million in India might not mean the same thing in the United States.

This problem of inconsistent accounting rules had a lot to do with the SEC initially requiring that U.S. GAAP accounting must be followed for SOx-related reporting. This matter is changing as we are gradually moving to one consistent accounting standard. The process of developing consistent international accounting standards is a long and slow one, but the IASB and the FASB have been working toward a convergence in their standards. The two Boards are now working together on several major projects, and they have essentially decided to coordinate agendas, so that any major project that one Board takes up will also be taken up by the other. In addition, the two Boards report to have been working on "short-term convergence" by not selecting one set of rules over the other but focusing on areas where both standards could be improved. This process involves incremental improvements rather than just looking at the two existing models and then picking what appears to be the better one.

We are currently seeing increasing announcements from the SEC and others about this trend toward convergence in auditing and accounting standards. This will almost certainly continue to be a long-term goal, easing the burden for foreign SOx registrants but increasing the global reach of accounting and financial standards. Although this will be a long, slow process, these accounting convergence changes will have impacts on many professionals. While we cannot predict how things will finally shake themselves out, we can pretty well expect a series of small accounting-related changes worldwide over perhaps the next decade or more as we reach accounting standards convergence.

GAPS AND COMPLIANCE COMMITTEES UNDER TODAY'S SOx RULES

SOx rules mandate that if any significant weaknesses—often called *gaps*—are found during a Section 404 review of internal controls, they must be documented along with corrective action plans initiated to correct them. After completion of a Section 404 review, the external auditors would then review this list of identified and still-open gaps and modify their internal controls and financial statement audit procedures as necessary. The more significant of these gaps should be categorized as *material weaknesses*. That is, they were sufficiently significant that the external auditors must modify their audit procedures or even could, in theory, give an unfavorable opinion on the enterprise's financial statements. More typically, they could delay their approval of the financial statements until these gaps are corrected. Either of these outcomes can become the kiss of death for the securities of an impacted enterprise. With no timely audited financial statements, investors often abandon the stock, loan covenants may be violated, and the whole matter can have dire consequences for the enterprise.

Perhaps a somewhat extreme example of what can happen here can be found in the highway truck and engine manufacturer Navistar, a company once known as the International Harvester Corporation, with a strong heritage going back to the last half of the nineteenth century. Although it had been an accepted practice over the years, several years ago Navistar's external auditors raised questions about the timing of their revenue recognition for sales contracts. As a result, Navistar did not receive an audited financial statement for several years. A further consequence of this is that it lost its

NYSE stock listing in January 2007 and the financial advantages that come with such a listing.[1] The NYSE has had a rule that listed corporations must have audited financial statements; the NYSE waived this rule for several years for Navistar, and then said no. Teams of consultants were brought in to research records and correct this gap, but the company lost a huge amount of prestige because of an open, unresolved internal control gap at that time.

On the positive side, this whole SOx process of identifying and correcting internal control gaps is an area that could be shown as an improvement due to SOx. In pre-SOx days, there was a tendency for external auditors to shrug off some of these issues without bringing the matter up to audit committees. SOx has changed this. Material weaknesses that were identified in the Section 404 internal control review process are brought up to the board audit committee, and enterprises are now establishing board-level *compliance committees* to disclose the control weaknesses and to take corrective actions.

Documenting SOx Gaps

SOx internal control gaps is the area that perhaps has caused the most criticism and published "bad press" regarding Section 404 internal control review processes. As discussed in Chapter 2 on SOx today, the PCAOB's original AS2 auditing standards were very detail oriented, and external auditors essentially directed their clients' Section 404 review teams to look at all internal control exceptions. In those first years of SOx, the concept of what had been called *materiality* was not considered. The guidance from the external audit firms attesting to the results of Section 404 internal control assessments generally was that an error was an error, no matter how large or small, and the PCAOB AS2 auditing standards dictated that approach. As a result, the SOx review teams frequently identified and documented internal control gaps that sometimes were just not that important in the big picture. An example might be an audit finding that a small parts-supply facility at a branch plant of a much larger corporation was not regularly requiring a second approving signature on purchase requisitions for local office supplies. The Section 404 reviewers at such a site—often internal auditors—might go through the following types of questions:

- Was this matter a violation of enterprise policy?—Yes.
- Is the part-supply facility significant in asset size to the enterprise?—No.
- Do other compensating controls there appear to have been violated? —No.
- Is there any other evidence of fraud at this small facility?—No.

Nevertheless, because the first question identified an enterprise policy violation, such an issue was then identified as a breakdown of internal controls at the supply facility. The problem that external auditors raised in the early days of SOx was that such matters were recorded and then passed up through channels without any level of review and screening. Yes, the lack of a second signature was a violation, but what is the risk? External auditors then frequently consolidated all of those internal control gaps, with no consideration to risk, and passed them up though senior management and the board audit committee. In the eyes of senior management in those first years of SOx, some of these identified gaps were just not that significant.

The risk-based AS5 auditing standards, discussed in Chapter 3, should resolve these matters. An enterprise needs to implement a risk management approach, based on COSO enterprise risk management (ERM) as discussed in Chapter 9, with a focus on the higher-risk gaps rather than on the earlier concerns that identified all internal control exceptions, no matter what the risk. Gaps should continue to be identified and documented at a unit level, and corrective action plans should then be developed. However, as Section 404 gaps are identified and move up through the channels of the enterprise hierarchy, the next senior level should have the authority to review these gaps and eliminate some of them as either not significant or of relatively lower risk.

This elimination process does not mean these concerns should just go away. If an enterprise has established a formal process to identify SOx internal control gaps through the review and testing of its internal controls, the matters should not become just memo items to be ignored. This was a weakness in the pre-SOx days when public accounting firms—sometimes almost without thinking or further analysis—said some internal control problem was not material and moved on. Pre-SOx internal audit standards called for them to follow up on such a matter, but many times it was taken off the table except for a workpaper entry in their files. Under today's SOx rules, if an internal control weakness has been identified as a gap, it should be documented and followed up on until resolved. Better SOx terminology for these gaps might be their formal designations as *significant* or *less-significant* internal control weakness or gaps. These are our suggested terms to get away from the problem-laden designations of *material* or *nonmaterial*.

The SOx review team should keep a log of all gaps identified during the review process. Exhibit 6.7 shows such a preliminary sample log of both significant and less-significant internal control gaps that might have been identified in an internal control review. Several important items on that gaps log are:

■ **Processing cycle.** SOx gaps should be identified by the major accounting control cycle, discussed previously, where they were encountered, such as Revenue, Expenditures, Payroll, or Inventory.

Business Unit	Department	Processing Cycle	Control #	Gap Description	Remediation Action Plan	Target Date	Responsibility	Criticality Status	Comments

EXHIBIT 6.7   Control Gaps Log Report

- **Control number.**   For control and tracking purposes, each gap should be assigned an identifying control number.
- **Gap description.**   A *gap* is the failure of either the control's design or its operating effectiveness. A brief description should be entered.
- **Remediation action plan.**   This area would include a brief description of plans for correction or remediation of the identified gap.
- **Target date.**   This is the planned date for implementation of the gap corrective action.
- **Criticality.**   While optional, it is always a good idea to arbitrarily designate each identified gap as High, Medium, or Low.

The log would normally be a database type of working document where matters are passed from level to level, with notations all along for their dispositions. Of course, this example is a hardcopy-format type of document, but its links should point to IT file references. The more significant—high criticality—gaps would be passed up to the Board Audit Committee.

Our introduction of this SOx 404 *gap summary report* is certainly not an official PCAOB SOx document for Section 404 reviews, but it represents the type of control document that may make it easier for enterprises to better manage their identified review gaps. The idea is to monitor them from period to period with a focus on closing open issues and clearing/monitoring those identified as significant.

SOx Disclosure Committee

The full SOx legislation is a long document with many rules and procedures. While every paragraph or page of that legislation is "the law," some areas certainly receive more attention than others. Section 404, discussed in this chapter, as well as Sections 302 and 409, covered in Chapter 7, are elements of SOx that have received major amounts of attention. Another large portion of the Act covers new rules on corporate governance, boards of directors, and their audit committees. Some of these board-related rules are summarized in Chapter 2, and a very key issue but sometimes ignored requirement is that a SOx registrant should establish a disclosure committee.

The SEC has recommended but not required that SOx-impacted enterprises create a disclosure committee to consider the materiality of information discovered, to identify relevant disclosure issues, and to ensure that material is disclosed to investors on a timely basis. In other words, someone should be responsible for reviewing all of the internal control review material presented, deciding what is important or *material*, and then determining when and if any matters are worthy of formal disclosure to investors. Typically, a disclosure committee reports to the CEO, CFO, or the audit committee, and its members may consist of senior managers from finance, legal, compliance, corporate communications, and investor relations. External legal counsel and the company's auditors are also often invited to attend the committee's meetings. It has responsibility for considering the materiality of information on a timely basis, determination of the disclosure, and treatment of material information.

A major task of a SOx disclosure committee is to consider the materiality of any exception information encountered. This disclosure committee should look over the data that will be presented to the external auditors for their review and report. We can almost certainly expect that there will be a tendency, at least in these early years of SOx, to err on the side of viewing too many matters as material. In the big picture of things in a large corporation, there may be many internal control weaknesses that individually or collectively are not all that material. This is a lot of the rationale behind the new AS5 rules.

The roles and responsibilities of a disclosure committee should not be confused with those of the audit committee or of any compliance committee. The audit committee of the board has been given high-level responsibility for SOx internal controls. Because of the many additional responsibilities that have been placed on board audit committees and the ongoing amount of new compliance and governance rules, the idea of a special compliance committee was suggested in the financial press when SOx first became the law. It appears to be an effective way to channel responsibility for the correction of material weaknesses and for improving the overall internal control environment. However, because an audit committee has some very specific internal control responsibilities, shifting matters to a separate committee may appear to reduce its overall significance.

The concept gets a little confusing because a few corporate boards have renamed their audit committees, calling them something like *board compliance committees*. They continue, however, to have all of the responsibilities of an audit committee. The concept of a separate compliance committee is not that common, and where they exist, these committees may be mandated for other special purposes. For example, a Web search will reference that the Microsoft Corporation board has a separate compliance committee, but that group[2] was mandated by the courts as part of an antitrust legal settlement. The issue here is specific court settlement compliance rather than SOx internal control compliance.

The audit committee receives reports on internal control strengths and weaknesses; it then takes action to correct those control weaknesses. If there are significant internal control problems as part of an annual review, they may be signaled by very-high-level comments for the external auditors as part of the audited financial reports or even through a delay in the issuance of those reports. In some respects, the role of the disclosure committee is to decide how much detail to give beyond an external auditor's high-level reference to a material weakness. The investing public wants as much information as possible, but many investors feel that there is no need to tell too much. A disclosure committee can be an important resource to help decide on how much to tell on high-level internal control decisions.

DOCUMENTING INTERNAL CONTROLS GOING FORWARD

SOx 404 internal control documentation—and any documentation for that matter—is of little value unless processes are in place to keep it up to date and current. This can be a major challenge for many enterprises that went through their first-year Section 404 documentation efforts, too often keeping their records in little more than folders on personal laptop computers, with few arrangements for good document management. Even worse, some enterprises have essentially placed their SOx 404 documentation in paper-format files. As years go by, there is a strong risk that documentation will become lost and forgotten.

In the early days of SOx 404 compliance and documentation efforts, this author observed an extreme example of *how not to* maintain such ongoing Section 404 documentation. Operating as part of a team to document internal controls at a large corporation within many small-town plant units, much of the local plant internal control process documentation work was described on local laptop computer system files, with some of the final documentation essentially printed and placed in three-ring-binders. After the completion of internal control walkthrough exercises using these notebooks, responsible plant controllers were instructed to place these SOx 404 binders in a bookcase on their desks for future reference.

However, that same enterprise experienced ongoing turnover of plant controllers, and there was no real provision for a handover when a new controller arrived. In addition, there were no provisions for ongoing maintenance. Section 404 year two would have caused a major rework. This consultant blew whistles and documented concerns about these practices. However, with not much heed given, the author's consulting engagement ended, and things were probably left as they were. We have referenced this as one potentially bad example, but there certainly have been many more. Documentation is of little value if it is not maintained in a secure manner and periodically updated.

All SOx-registered enterprises face a challenge in maintaining their compliance documentation and procedures for their Section 404 work. The SOx 404 legislation requires that supporting documentation be kept current and up to date. In theory, this says that whenever there are substantive process changes, the supporting documentation should be updated. The reality of this is that supporting documentation will not be updated on a real-time basis, but processes should be put in place to assure a regular update process. This process is easier if an enterprise is a new registrant and is going through its first cycle of reviews. It is more of a challenge if the enterprise was an earlier filer and now must update its existing internal control records.

Two important matters can impact this Section 404 documentation update process. First, the current status of any previously identified gaps should be documented. If the gap has been corrected, it is relatively easy to simply confirm that previously documented status. New gaps should receive the same level and extent of documentation that had been done previously. If a gap has been corrected, the existing and related internal control documentation will almost certainly need updating. The idea is to document that the previously identified matter has been corrected.

A second level of SOx documentation concern covers the rules' transition to more of a risk-based environment. When changes have been made to drop the documentation of testing some internal control, care should be taken in this documentation to describe any changes in approach due to the revision of PCAOB standards. As is the case with many compliance activities today, a complete set of documentation is very important. External auditors and potentially even outside reviewers will be expecting a complete set of supporting, descriptive documentation. Exhibit 6.8 lists some documentation considerations for SOx Section 404 compliance internal financial control reviews. As highlighted in the exhibit, an enterprise should implement some type of software tool for documenting its internal control processes. There are many commercial software tools on the market, and once an enterprise has launched one or another, it will probably be using the same product over the upcoming years. Some of the existing software tools are very—often too—complex but others are little more than simple spreadsheet templates. Any software tool installed should meet overall enterprise IT standards and should be acceptable to the external auditors. Exhibit 6.9 lists some of the software requirements that should be considered when acquiring a SOx Section 404 documentation software tool.

1. Does the enterprise have an established system in place for documenting other processes and is that system well understood by the SOx review team?
2. Are existing documentation processes compatible with the software tools that will be used for the Section 404 documentation effort?
3. Has a standard process flow approach been developed for all Section 404 documentation that identifies inputs, outputs, and other activities in a consistent manner?
4. Have consistent processes been established for documenting gaps?
5. Have appropriate staff members been trained in Section 404 documentation standards?
6. Have project planning/time tracking procedures been established to track the costs and time requirements of SOx documentation?
7. Have arrangements been made for providing ongoing documentation help as well as for approving documentation?
8. Have revision control standards been established for all documentation?
9. Is the SOx documentation located in a secure facility and included in continuity/disaster recovery processes?
10. Are formal checkout procedures in place for removing documentation for review and/or updates?
11. Have documentation approaches been reviewed with external auditors and are they comfortable with them.?
12. Is the documentation in a format such that senior members of management can readily access and understand the documentation approach?

EXHIBIT 6.8   SOx Section 404 Documentation Planning Considerations

CONTROL OBJECTIVES AND RISKS UNDER SECTION 404

Larger U.S.-based SEC-registered enterprises are now expected to comply with SOx requirements. Once an enterprise has completed its first round of Section 404 compliance reporting, it is easy to just say something along the lines of, "Wow, we're done with that. Now let's get back to business as usual." However, it will not be that easy. Once an enterprise has gotten itself through its first Section 404 review, it should establish processes for a continuous monitoring, evaluation, and improvement process.

Going forward, the enterprise needs to monitor its key systems, determine if there were any changes in subsequent periods, and design internal control procedures to correct any control weaknesses or otherwise fill control gaps. This an ongoing periodic exercise, and the team that first implemented the Section 404 compliance work will almost certainly have returned to

The following are considerations when acquiring SOx Section 404 documentation software:

- *Enterprise SOx maturity.* Is this the first year for establishing Section 404 compliance or will the software be used to support prior-period efforts?
- *Current software linkages.* If the software product is planned to improve on a prior-period effort, can documentation files be easily ported over to the new software product?
- *IT tools integration.* Does the proposed new software easily integrate with existing software tools and operating systems?
- *Section 404 activities scope.* Does the software have facilities for all aspects of the 404 assessment process, including process documentation, descriptions of control strengths and weaknesses, and transaction testing?
- *International operations.* If the SOx documentation is going to be developed on a worldwide basis, does the software support these requirements?
- *Summary reporting.* Does the software allow for 404 results reporting sufficient for external auditor and audit committee requirements?
- *Operating mode.* Can documentation activities be easily ported across multiple user laptops and then concatenated to a central source location?
- *Record safekeeping.* Does the software provide strong tools for the secure storage and retention of SOx documentation?
- *Audit trails.* Does the software contain tools to record all changes to approved 404 documentation and provide audit trail reporting?
- *Vendor training and support.* Does the software vendor have sufficient tools to train users on the product and is there an appropriate help and support function?
- *Software updates.* Does the software vendor promise to provide regular upgrades to the software due to PCAOB-mandated or other changes?
- *Benchmarking.* Will the vendor supply a list of contacts from other customers for independent software satisfaction reviews?

EXHIBIT 6.9 SOx Documentation Software Tool Requirements

normal job duties. This is the time to look at the Section 404 review work that was completed and make any necessary changes to improve the efficiency and value of these reviews. Given the time and resources expended in completing these reviews, an enterprise should use this material to improve its overall internal control environment. AS5 has made things easier, but there will still be ongoing changes in becoming compliant with these internal control auditing rules and standards.

An enterprise's Section 404 documentation standards and supporting materials need to be reviewed and updated on a regular basis. Systems and processes change and acquisitions or corporate reorganizations modify the environment. Section 404 and its internal control review processes are a very key element in achieving SOx compliance. Getting through matters after the first years makes things easier, and AS5 should have simplified the process, but this continues to be a very important area for achieving SOx compliance.

ENDNOTES

1. "Navistar to Be Delisted," *Chicago Tribune*, http://www.chicagotribune.com/business/chi-0612160041dec16,0,2163531.story?coll = chi-business-hed.
2. http://www.microsoft.com/about/companyinformation/corporategovernance/committees/antitrust.mspx.

CHAPTER 7

Other SOx Requirements: Sections 302, 409, and Others

The Sarbanes-Oxley (SOx) legislation is filled with a wide range of new rules, although many professionals such as internal auditors think of SOx rules primarily in terms of Section 404 on internal control assessments. As discussed in Chapter 6, Section 404 has been the major pain point for many larger corporations attempting to establish compliance in SOx's first years. In addition to complaints from major U.S. corporations, the anguish of smaller enterprises and the threat of foreign corporations to seek U.S. stock exchange de-listing to avoid SOx registration, caused the Securities and Exchange Commission (SEC) and Public Company Accounting Oversight Board (PCAOB) to release the AS5 risk-based auditing standards introduced in Chapter 3. These should make SOx compliance less painful going forward. However, we sometimes forget that SOx contains a large set of rules impacting enterprise financial management and governance beyond Section 404 internal controls. While there have been no new AS5-like rules changes in these other areas, this chapter will highlight several other areas of SOx that are important to financial management and internal auditors.

This chapter will revisit five other areas beyond the Section 404 internal control assessment rules under AS5:

1. Section 302 on management's responsibility for their financial reports
2. Section 401 setting the rules for enhanced financial reporting disclosures
3. Section 409 calling for the immediate disclosure of significant changes in financial conditions and operations
4. Section 802 on penalties for altering documents
5. Section 806 whistleblower rules

The above sections are perhaps the more important SOx requirement areas, beyond Section 404, that impact senior managers and internal auditors. Of course, there are important rules in other areas. The SOx legislation covering the board of directors and its audit committee has changed a large number of corporate governance rules and certainly has strengthened relationships between internal auditors and their audit committee. Other rules, however, do not have that much of a direct impact on most finance and internal audit professionals. For example, SOx includes a set of significant rules covering the financial analysts that make investment recommendations regarding enterprises. While these new requirements are important to individual investors, the rules do not really impact financial professionals and internal auditors working to improve overall governance and compliance within an enterprise. While SOx legislation has a wide variety of rules covering many aspects of governance, this chapter will focus on some other rules important to financial and internal audit management.

OTHER IMPORTANT SOx COMPLIANCE RULES

Going beyond Section 404 on internal control assessments, the following sections discuss some other SOx requirements that have important compliance and governance implications. Some of these compliance rules have not been that controversial, such as Section 302 requiring financial officers to be responsible for financial reports issued over their signatures. This is a rule that only seems logical. Prior to SOx, a chief financial officer (CFO) could deny any knowledge of the details—particularly questionable details—supporting a SEC-filed financial statement saying that his accounting or financial staff did the work. Section 302 said that because the CFO's name is on a financial statement, he or she is personally responsible for its contents.

Objections about Section 302 were raised at first, but financial managers now have usually established chain-of-command signoff processes with no substantive changes to the SOx rules here as originally drafted. This section will revisit Section 302 as well as some other important SOx provisions, where either final rules did not come out as severe as first anticipated or they remain as perhaps "sleeping giants" where the rule is on the books but with little current compliance or regulatory activity. An enterprise should be aware of these key SOx rules beyond Section 404 and take appropriate compliance actions.

SECTION 302: MANAGEMENT'S FINANCIAL REPORT RESPONSIBILITIES

Prior to SOx, the responsible corporate officers who signed the financial reports submitted to the SEC did not have to acknowledge *personal* responsibility for their contents. When questioned about the nature of some transaction, they could push the solution or problem down multiple levels, sometimes virtually to an accounting department staff level. It was easy for a senior financial executive to claim he or she was not aware of the details and thus had no direct responsibility for some financial or accounting misstatement. Although they should have detected matters through their own procedures, external auditors also could pass the buck for some matters, claiming that the CFO gave them some schedule that he did not fully investigate. SOx Section 302 has changed the rules here! The chief executive officer (CEO) and CFO must now personally certify that for each annual and quarterly financial SEC filed report:

- The signing officer has reviewed the report.
- Based on that signing officer's knowledge, the financial statements do not contain any materially untrue or misleading information.
- Again based on the signing officer's knowledge, the financial statements fairly represent the financial conditions and results of operations of the enterprise.
- By signing, the officer also acknowledges responsibility for:
  - Establishing and maintaining internal controls
  - Having designed these internal controls to ensure that material information about the enterprise and its subsidiaries was made known to the signing officer during the period when the reports were prepared
  - Attesting that the enterprise's internal controls have been evaluated within 90 days prior to the release of the report
  - Having presented in these financial reports the signing officer's evaluation of the effectiveness of these internal controls as of that report date
- The signing officer also has disclosed to the external auditors, the audit committee, and other directors:
  - All significant deficiencies in the design and operation of internal controls that could affect the reliability of the reported financial data and has, further, disclosed these material control weaknesses to enterprise's auditors
  - Any fraud, whether or not material, that involves management or other employees who have a significant role in the enterprise's internal controls
- The signing officer has indicated whether there were internal control or other changes that could significantly impact those controls, including corrective actions, subsequent to the date of the internal controls evaluation.

This is a strong personal attestation, not to be taken lightly. Given that SOx imposes the potential criminal penalties of fines and/or jail time on individual violators of the Act, these Section 302 signer requirements place a heavy burden on the officer signing a financial report. Corporate officers must take all reasonable steps to make certain that they are in compliance. There is also a provision here that these requirements still apply even if the enterprise has moved its headquarters outside the United States and is beyond the immediate reach of the SEC (e.g., in 2000 and 2001, numerous U.S. corporations moved their corporate registration to offshore locations, such as Bermuda, for income tax purposes).

This personal signoff requirement initially raised major concerns for CEOs and CFOs, and it caused a major amount of additional work for the accounting and finance staffs preparing these periodic financial reports. A CFO who once just relied on financial results from division controllers and their staffs, now has a strong personal responsibility to make certain this published financial data and the supporting internal controls do not present any misleading information. An enterprise needs to set up detailed chain-of-command paper-trail procedures such that the signing officers are comfortable that effective processes have been used and the calculations to build the reports are all well documented. The idea is that at each level in an organization, a responsible manager should certify the reported financial information and the adequacy of supporting internal controls before passing the material up to the next level in the organization chart. An enterprise should consider using an extended signoff process where staff members submitting the financial reports sign off on what they are submitting before passing it to the next level up. Internal audit should be able to act as an internal consultant and help senior officers establish effective processes here. The internal audit workpaper model, with extensive cross-references, might be a good approach.

SOx Section 302 rules should really have been nothing new. Using U.S. president Harry Truman's late-1940s dictum, "The buck stops here," a senior executive should always be responsible for the reports and actions of all persons within his or her span of control. Managers at each level should be responsible for the work of their subordinates. Good internal controls and strong ethical practices will encourage this. In addition, managers at each level should be directed to attest to and sign off on the work at their level. Chapter 2's Exhibit 2.2 is an example of an Officer Disclosure Signoff–type of statement that senior managers would be requested to sign. Officer subordinates, such as controller-level directors, should similarly be asked to acknowledge their understanding of the accuracy of their operating unit's submitted financial reports. While a series of Exhibit 2.2–type attestations down through lower organization levels is perhaps a bit of overkill, there will be value in at least asking senior- or director-level financial managers to acknowledge that they have reviewed and approved submitted financial reports before passing them on to the CFO level. Exhibit 7.1 is a senior management financial report acknowledgment document. The idea is not to require every level in an organization to submit such an attestation, but to pass some of this Section 302 responsibility down to major enterprise financial reporting units. The idea is to pass on the message that while the enterprise CEO and CFO are ultimately responsible for submitted financial reports, the signing Exhibit 7.1 manager has a shared responsibility for passing on correct and accurate financial information up through the enterprise organization ranks. Under SOx, the CEO or CFO is asked to personally assert to these types of representations and could be held criminally liable if materially incorrect. While the officer is at risk, the support staff—including internal audit—should take every step possible to make certain the package presented to the senior officer is correct.

Although the initial SOx rules caused some concerns that everything on a financial report would have to be balanced to almost a nickel-and-dime level, AS5 has added a degree of reality here. The same AS5 risk-based approaches discussed in Chapter 3 for Section 404 should apply here as

 Global Computer Products   Financial Report Acknowledgment

Operating Unit _____ Responsible Controller _____ Date ____
Activity Description _____ Asset Value _____ Cntl # ____

1. I have read and am submitting the attached _____ reports dated, _____ that relate directly to my responsibilities as an employee of the Company.

2. Based on my knowledge, as of the end of the period covered, this reported information does **not contain an untrue statement of a material fact** or omit to state a material fact.

3. Based on my knowledge, this reported information fairly presents, in all material respects, the results of _____ unit's operations and cash flows as of the close of and for the period presented.

4. I am not aware of any deficiencies in the effectiveness of this operating unit's controls and procedures, except as noted in an attached schedule, which could adversely affect the ability to record, process, summarize and report this attached financial information.

6. I **am not aware of any significant deficiencies or material weaknesses** in the design or operation of this unit's internal controls that could adversely affect the Company's ability to record, process, summarize and report financial data.

7. I **am not aware of any fraud, whether or not material**, that involves this operating unit's management or other employees who have a significant role in the Company's internal controls.

Unit Controller's Acknowledgment Signature _____

EXHIBIT 7.1   Senior Officer Financial Report Acknowledgment

well. The signing CEO and CFO should recognize the risks of violations in this area but must establish strong control and individual integrity requirements such that they can have a high level of confidence that their published financial reports meet Section 302 requirements.

In an interesting twist of the legal language used, this section of SOx makes reference to the enterprise "auditors" rather than employing the phrase "registered public accounting firm" used in SOx's Title II. While there have been no legal rulings to date and while this author cannot hold himself out as a legal expert on such matters, the Title III section of SOx would appear to refer to auditors in its broadest sense and certainly include both internal and external auditors. (Note: See Chapter 2 for an overview of the SOx legislation and its sections or Titles.) A chief audit executive (CAE) should recognize this and take appropriate steps to work with corporate officers to expand and improve internal controls and the like. An internal audit function must place strong emphasis on performing reviews surrounding significant internal control areas. This can be done through a detailed risk assessment of the internal control environments, discussions of these assessments with corporate officers, and then a detailed audit plan documenting how these internal control systems will be reviewed.

Internal auditors should take particular care, given SOx rules, in the nature and description of any findings encountered during the course of audits, in follow-up reporting regarding the status of corrective actions taken, and in the distributions of these audit reports. Many internal audits may identify significant weaknesses in areas of the enterprise that are not material to overall operations. A breakdown in the invoicing process at one regional sales office may be significant to the performance of that sales region for the corporation, but will not be a materially significant internal control weakness if the problem is local and does not reflect a wider, more pervasive problem, and if the problem was corrected after being discovered by internal audit. The CAE should establish good communications links with key financial officers in the enterprise such that they are all aware of audits performed, key findings, and corrective actions taken. Internal audit should also provide some guidance as to whether reported audit findings are material to the enterprise's overall system of internal control. Similar communication links should be established with members of the audit committee.

SECTION 401: OFF–BALANCE SHEET DISCLOSURES

Section 401 of SOx ties directly back to the Enron scandals that got SOx rules started. It says that an enterprise's published financial statements are required to be accurate and presented in a manner that does not contain incorrect statements or that fails to state material information. The financial statements should also include all material off–balance sheet liabilities, obligations, or related transactions. These disclosure failures were issues that were regularly and fraudulently practiced at Enron, that were essentially blessed by their Arthur Andersen external auditors, and that, once disclosed, brought Enron into bankruptcy. Generally accepted accounting principles (GAAP) allow that a variety of financial balances and transactions do not have to be reported on financial statements. These are typically situations where the corporation had a small, less than majority, interest in some entity. Such activities would not show up on published financial reports and also were not even disclosed in 10K report footnotes.

These types of not-reported transactions were really the crux of Enron's failure. Making matters worse, many there were side transactions between Enron and its CFO and other insiders. Under SOx, the SEC rules that require *enhanced disclosure* of these off–balance sheet arrangements and contractual obligations. These matters are to be discussed in a separate Management's Discussion and Analysis (MD&A) section on the enterprise's annual 10K reports. There was initially some discussion and concern about the scope of these transactions, but the final SEC Section 401 rules define such off–balance sheet matters as standby letters of credit, guarantees of stock prices, guarantees of the collection of scheduled contractual cash flows from individual financial assets, or a contingent interest in assets transferred to an unconsolidated entity or similar arrangement that serves as credit, liquidity, or market risk support to that entity for such assets.

SOx Section 401 rules require the disclosure of such off–balance sheet arrangements that "have or are reasonably likely to have" a current or future effect on the issuer's financial condition, changes in financial condition, revenues or expenses, results of operations, liquidity, capital expenditures, or capital resources that is material to investors. Our objective here is not to provide a tutorial on these and an extended set of the complete final rules, but to point out some of the many things that can trigger the need for Section 404 internal control-related disclosures. These are special transactions where an enterprise is required to disclose the information necessary for an understanding of the off–balance sheet arrangement and its effect, including, to the extent necessary:

- The nature and business purpose of its off–balance sheet arrangement
- The importance to the issuer of such off–balance sheet arrangements in respect of its liquidity, capital resources, market risk support, credit risk support, or other benefits provided by the arrangement to the issuer
- The amounts of revenues, expenses, and cash flows of the issuer arising from such arrangements

- The nature and amounts of any interests retained, securities issued, and other indebtedness incurred by the issuer in connection with such arrangements
- The nature and amount of any other obligations or liabilities arising from such arrangements that are or are reasonably likely to become material and the triggering events or circumstances that could cause them to arise
- Any known event, demand, commitment, trend, or uncertainty that will result in or is reasonably likely to result in the cancellation, or material reduction in availability, to the report issuer. Examples here are any material contractual provisions that result in the termination or material reduction of an off–balance sheet arrangement

Any such off–balance sheet arrangements must be disclosed and discussed in published financial reports. These are generally the kinds of often-complex transactions that may be exercised by CFO-level financial management with approval of the board.

Section 401 matters can cover a wide variety of financial transactions, and senior financial management should be aware of events and transactions that require Section 401 disclosures. Many if not all of these are normal business transactions that had been done as sort of sideline deals prior to SOx. Although perhaps buried as a footnote in a voluminous 10K report, they are now open to the investing public. Section 401 has not had the impact or caused the pain associated with some other SOx rules, but enterprises should not lose sight of it in their financial reporting.

SECTION 409: DISCLOSURES ON FINANCIAL CONDITIONS AND OPERATIONS

Again a simple-sounding rule, Section 409 requires SOx-registered enterprises to disclose to the public, on an *urgent basis*, information on material changes in their financial condition or operations. These disclosures are to be presented in terms that are easy to understand and supported by trend analyses, qualitative information, or graphic presentations as appropriate. Section 409 mandates that the reporting enterprise must disclose to the public "on a rapid and current basis" any additional information containing material financial statement issues. Although it has not received the same level of attention directed at SOx sections 302 or 404, this set of rules can have some major impacts on enterprise compliance efforts.

The reference to the use of trend analyses, qualitative information, or graphic presentations in corporate reporting is a change from traditional SEC report formats that had previously allowed, with the exception of corporate logos, only pure text and numerical presentations in SEC-format financial reports. For years, enterprise 10K, 10Q, and other SEC reports have looked to the reader, whether on the Web or as a printed document, as if they had been prepared on typewriters. SOx now allows and suggests more modern reporting techniques and hopefully more descriptive processes.

The "real-time" reporting words in Section 409 are even more significant. When the legislation was first drafted but before the final rules, there was massive speculation about what was meant by these real-time reporting requirements. At the extreme, the preliminary rules suggested the need for real-time reporting monitors to generate SEC reporting. However, rather than attempting to call for massive revisions to existing financial reporting systems, the SEC now requires enterprises to file Form 8K reports only for any of 12 events, including bankruptcy or receivership, changes in their certifying accountants, or resignations of their directors. A form 8K is a special-circumstances type of report is required only when some event occurs. These required 8K events are listed in Exhibit 7.2. While the SEC gave enterprises 14 days to file 8K reports under pre-SOx rules, Section 409 guidelines now require them to file their 8Ks in as little as 48 hours—a rapid response but certainly not real time.

While hardly real time from an IT perspective, enterprises need to be diligent in filing their 8Ks on what they define are *material* events. Most if

1. Changes in corporate underwriting agreements
2. Plans of purchase, sale, reorganization,arrangement, liquidation, or succession
3. Changes in Articles of Incorporation
4. Changes in Corporate Bylaws
5. Instruments defining the rights of security holders, including indentures
6. Correspondence from external auditors regarding nonreliance upon a previously issued audit report or completed interim review
7. Changes to the Corporate Code of Ethics
8. Letter or notice of a change in certifying external auditors
9. Letter or notice on the departure of a corporate director
10. Consents of experts and counsel
11. Filings of powers of attorney
12. Additional exhibits including other material events

EXHIBIT 7.2 Section 409 Section 8K Filing Events

not all of the events that the SEC has said must trigger 8K filings should not exactly come as a surprise to enterprise executives, and the increasingly popular *executive dashboard* type of corporate reporting should help to alert them to quickly evolving issues. A probable major motivation for Section 409 is that the SEC wants to make investors properly aware of these important matters very quickly after they have become known within an enterprise.

Section 409 rules have not turned out to be nearly as dramatic or as technology driven as was once expected. Aside from such major investor-related events such as a change in external auditors, the enterprise can decide when it considers an event to be sufficiently material to report as an 8K Section 409 event. The draft reports and discussions that led up to the final rules suggested such topics for material events as the loss of a major customer. However, just using this as an example, the definition and impact of what is a major customer can vary depending on the enterprise. The SEC dropped a long list of material and even qualifying conditions and left matters to the enterprise for its own resolution. Senior management and the board should develop some high-level guidelines on whether to report some occurrence as an 8K Section 409 event. Failing to report some matter of investor interest can lead to potential litigation problems for the enterprise, and a good strategy may be to file an 8K if there is some feeling it might be appropriate.

SECTION 802: PENALTIES FOR ALTERING DOCUMENTS

Past history or events often have a major impact on our current rules of law. However, time passes and we often forget that past triggering event. SOx Section 802 has these historical roots. In 2002, when Enron was imploding and the SEC had announced a scheduled investigatory visit to the corporation, the Enron's then–external auditors, Arthur Andersen, went through an exercise to clean up their audit workpapers and records. Andersen claimed they were following an established firm procedure, and they went through an intense, worldwide effort to shred and destroy a massive amount of paper-based documentation and to delete computer files covering their audit work at Enron. There was a high suspicion of wrongdoing at Enron at the time, and television and newspaper news clips of Andersen auditors shredding the documents led many to think of this as a classic case of the destruction of evidence.

Both Enron and Arthur Andersen are now gone, but this audit work-paper clean-up exercise, no doubt, was a major motivating factor for the SOx Section 802 rules outlining penalties for the destruction of documents. The rules require external auditors who audit or review an enterprise's financial statements to retain certain records relevant to that work, including workpapers and other documents that form the basis of the audit or review. These retention requirements include memoranda, correspondence, communications, other documents, and records, as well as related electronic records that are created, sent, or received in connection with the audit work and contain conclusions, opinions, analyses, or financial data related to the work. These records are to be retained for seven years after the auditor concludes the financial statements review. This rule was nothing new for many internal auditors as many audit functions have followed similar document retention rules based on U.S. tax document retention guidelines.

As any internal auditor knows, there are numerous types of documents that may be accumulated as part of an audit or review. The final rule here requires the retention of all records relevant to the audit, including workpapers and other documents that form the basis of the audited financial statements, as well as certain supporting documents. The guideline for document retention is that they must meet two criteria: (1) Documents are created, sent, or received in connection with the audit or review, and (2) the documents contain conclusions, opinions, analyses, or financial data related to the audit or review.

Because documents—particularly IT files and data resources—can amount to huge numbers, volumes and materials, subsequent rule clarifications have somewhat tempered this requirement. The final SEC rules here state, "We do not believe that Congress intended for accounting firms to duplicate and retain all of the issuer's financial information, records, databases, and reports that might be read, examined, or reviewed by the auditor." In keeping with the same AS5 rules discussed in Chapter 3, there must be a reasonableness approach to audit document retention.

These audit document retention rules refer to external audit records in support of their financial statements. Document retention rules for internal auditors are covered by their own standards, discussed in Chapter 11, and the enterprise's own retention procedures. All auditors should be aware of the document retention requirements and should establish processes to retain significant documents.

SECTION 806: WHISTLEBLOWER PROVISIONS

SOx Section 301 mandates that board-of-director audit committees establish procedures to "handle whistleblower information regarding questionable accounting or auditing matters." This whistleblower provision initially had been a little-noticed provision of SOx. It perhaps became part of the original legislation because many of the questionable accounting practices that originally gave rise to SOx came to light, at least in part, as a result of employees who blew the whistle. That is, one Enron internal auditor sent a confidential letter to then CEO, Ken Lay, expressing concerns about accounting malpractices.[1] She was granted an interview, the matter was brushed off by the CEO, and the matter became a matter of evidence in the criminal charges trial of Lay and others. However, even before the scandals at Enron, WorldCom, and others broke, whistleblower protections had been part of many federal laws as a means to help regulators ferret out violations and wrongdoing. The whistleblower provisions of SOx are patterned after similar federal statutory procedures for protecting workers in the airline and nuclear power industries.

Whistleblower laws allow an employee or stakeholder who sees some form of wrongdoing to independently and anonymously report that perceived wrongdoing with no fear of recrimination. The matter should be first reported to appropriate persons in the enterprise or alternatively to regulatory authorities. There should be no recrimination against the whistleblower employee and legal action sometimes can be initiated to recover damages. These whistleblower cases can inflict serious damage on an enterprise's reputation as well as on the careers of accused managers. While whistleblower programs have been around for some time to support federal contracting laws, health and safety regulations, and others, SOx moved these rules into enterprise business offices. While SOx requires the audit committee to establish whistleblower procedures, other functions, such as the ethics department, human resources, or internal audit, will typically set things up.

Whistleblower functions have been part of federal laws for stakeholders in a wide range of other activities, from federal contracts to employee health and safety. Any employee or stakeholder who observes some type of improper or illegal activity can blow the whistle and report the incident. The matter should then be investigated, and corrected if the allegations prove true, and the original whistleblower sometimes may receive a proportionate reward from the savings. An employee whistleblower, for example, may observe that a contract calls for some machine part, under a federal contract, to be constructed with a certain gauge of steel, but also discovers that the enterprise is using a cheaper gauge of material, violating contract terms, and potentially endangering the safety of the component. The employee has a right and indeed an obligation to blow the whistle on this practice by contacting the enterprise's contract compliance office, human resources, procurement or internal audit function. If no action is taken by the company, the employee can blow the whistle again to federal contract administration authorities. Once the matter has been reported, either internally or externally, the law allows for the whistleblower to be legally protected from any form of workplace recrimination.

The SOx-mandated whistleblower program adds accounting and auditing issues to topics for whistleblower complaints although it does not promise cash rewards beyond out-of-pocket expenses. This SOx whistleblower provision initially seemed to throw a new challenge to audit committees. As a body that meets monthly at most with no formal administrative staff, members of an audit committee would find it difficult to act as recipients of stakeholder whistleblower accusations. However, to date, there have not been many SOx whistleblowers and even fewer prosecution-related actions. SOx whistleblower rules may be a bit of a "sleeping giant" today, but enterprises and their audit committees should be aware of these rules and the requirements to establish such a facility.

Federal SOx Whistleblower Rules

The U.S. Department of Labor (DOL) administers and enforces more than 180 federal laws covering workplace activities for about 10 million employers and 125 million workers. Most labor and public safety laws and many environmental laws mandate whistleblower protections for employees who complain about violations of the law by their employers. SOx now adds federal whistleblower protection to all employees of SEC-registered enterprises, and public companies will need to pay special attention to these new protections for corporate whistleblowers. SOx Section 806 mandates whistleblower protection for stakeholders in SOx-registered enterprises. That provision provides that no public company or any officer, employee, contractor, or agent of such company "may discharge, demote, suspend, threaten, harass, or in any other manner discriminate against an employee in the terms and conditions of employment because of any lawful act done by the employee." Those lawful acts are when the employee provides information or otherwise assists in an investigation conducted by a federal regulatory or law enforcement agency, Congress, or company personnel regarding any conduct that the employee "reasonably believes" constitutes a violation of SEC rules and regulations or fraud statutes; or files, testifies, participates in, or otherwise assists in a proceeding—pending or about to be filed—relating to an alleged violation. In other words, the employee or stakeholder who perceives some financial wrongdoing and then reports the matter is legally protected during its investigation and resolution.

These SOx whistleblower provisions are primarily designed to protect employees who think they have discovered some accounting or internal control–related wrongdoing. Virtually any personnel action taken against a whistleblower employee, including a demotion or suspension, can potentially be subject to legal action under this provision. Although there have been limited SOx-related whistleblower actions up until the present time, an employee or stakeholder who registers a whistleblower complaint will be protected until the matter is resolved. SOx does seek to avoid frivolous complaints by requiring that the whistleblower must have a "reasonable" belief that the practice reported constitutes a violation.

SOx Section 1107 makes it a crime for anyone "knowingly, with the intent to retaliate," to interfere with the employment or livelihood of any person—a whistleblower—who provides a law enforcement officer any truthful information relating to the possible commission of a SOx violation offense. The law allows the stakeholders who believe they have been unlawfully discharged or discriminated against, due to their whistleblower action, to seek relief by filing a complaint, within 90 days after the date of the violation, with the DOL or initiating federal district court action. The aggrieved will typically need to secure legal help to seek relief, but the process can be time consuming and expensive for the accused corporation. The DOL procedural rules to prevail on a complaint require that the employee demonstrate that discriminatory reasons were a "contributing factor" in the unfavorable personnel action. Relief will be denied, however, if the employer demonstrates by "clear and convincing evidence" that it would have taken the same personnel action in the absence of protected activity.

An employee prevailing in such an action is entitled to full compensatory damages including reinstatement, back pay with interest, and compensation for the litigation costs and attorney fees. However, if the DOL does not issue a final decision within 180 days of the whistleblower's complaint filing, the matter may be moved to a the federal district court. Complicating matters further, the harmed whistleblower can take action on several fronts, seeking protection under federal and state laws as well as any applicable collective bargaining agreement. Employers are exposed to potential "double jeopardy" for whistleblower actions with liability under both SOx provisions and state or federal laws on wrongful discharge and similar causes of action. In addition, the aggrieved whistleblower can seek punitive damages through separate court actions. Based on administrative and judicial experiences in the nuclear energy and the airlines industries, SOx whistleblower protection laws could become a potential minefield for corporations. If an employee raises any sort of SOx accounting or auditing matter regarding an improper or illegal act, that whistleblower is totally protected until the matter is investigated and resolved.

The SOx whistleblower rules seem harsh-sounding for an enterprise, but there has been little legal action to date. Some commentators had speculated that SOx whistleblower laws and regulations might have as much effect on business practices, in the twenty-first century, as did civil rights laws in the twentieth. But the recent years' experience under SOx suggest that reality—at least so far—is falling well short of these predictions.

When it first became law, many administrative complaints were filed for administrative law review through the DOL. However, this has been a slow process with many complaints dismissed for procedural reasons.

Legal actions associated with SOx whistleblower complaints to date have been in the hundreds, not thousands. However, these actions even when resolved favorably can be very troublesome for an enterprise. A small matter involving BioSante Pharmaceuticals of Lincolnshire, IL, is an example.[2] In 2006, a former officer of the corporation filed a SOx-related whistleblower complaint against BioSante for wrongful termination. After a lengthy investigatory and legal process, the whistleblower, a former vice president of product development, received $780,000 plus $110,000 for legal fees in the settlement. However, in addition to the payment of nearly $1 million in damages to the whistleblower, the SEC subsequently announced in 2007 that its enforcement division was conducting "an investigation" into the matter.

BioSante Pharmaceuticals (BPA) is a relatively small enterprise. Whatever the issues on the matter, time spent resolving an SEC inquiry would only consume resources. Using BioSante as an example, the SOx whistleblower requirements could represent a significant concern to employers. If employees can claim that a job action arose in retaliation for an employee's supposed complaint about a violation of *any* rule or regulation (that is, not just disclosure of accounting fraud, and not even just disclosure of a violation of an SEC rule, but disclosure of a violation of any federal rule or regulation), whistleblower complaints could indeed become the threat that early commentators feared. Potential consequences include not only the whistleblower's civil damage remedies and attorneys' fees, but the threat of an investigation by a regulatory agency, adverse publicity, and even criminal sanctions.

SOx Whistleblower Rules Today

SOx was enacted because of the misdeeds discovered in a variety of corporate accounting scandals shortly after the turn of this century. Although some of the culprit corporations, such as Enron, had previously been viewed by the outside financial press as doing an outstanding job and reporting solid profits, whistleblowers within several of those same enterprises raised internal control concerns to their management. For example and as discussed, Sherron Watkins, an internal audit manager at Enron, blew the whistle regarding some of Enron's accounting misdeeds by sending a confidential note to then-CEO, Ken Lay. Watkins presented her concerns to Lay, who evidently was reported to have listened but took no direct actions.

Enron collapsed, as did another major accounting scandal–tainted corporation, WorldCom, whose corporate management also had an ignored internal corporate whistleblower, Cynthia Cooper. In recognition of these whistleblowers, who attempted to stem these accounting scandal problems, *Time* magazine in 2002 named Watkins and Cooper as well as Coleen Rowley, an FBI agent, as "Co-Persons of the Year." This was a major endorsement for the role for whistleblowers, and shortly after SOx became effective, many in industry predicted a tidal wave of SOx whistleblower complaints. Legal actions, to date, have been very limited and have moved at a very slow and deliberative pace.

SOx whistleblowers can normally proceed in one of three directions. First and hopefully the easiest, a stakeholder who observes an accounting-related fraud or improper act should anonymously report the concern through the internal chain of command or over a corporate hotline function. To make this type of process work, the enterprise must have communication processes in place to encourage the reporting of any observed or suspected improper accounting or internal control practices. Most important, the whistleblower should feel free to report these concerns with no fear of recrimination.

In many instances, however, whistleblower stakeholders do not trust their enterprise management team or feel that they must otherwise go through legal channels to report things. Depending on the nature of the whistleblower complaint, the first place to report matters may be to the DOL, which will normally assign the matter to OSHA. The reported concern should be turned over to an administrative law function to investigate the complaint and take action as appropriate. This is often a slow process, and the whistleblower's complaint will sometimes be rejected by OSHA with little explanation. However, if the reported concerns are either dismissed or not investigated within 180 days, the whistleblower can carry the matter to a federal court filing. This is usually a slower and even more expensive process both for the aggrieved whistleblower and the enterprise. In addition, final outcomes may be surprising for either of the parties.

SOx whistleblowers are often aggrieved persons who internally make some complaint, do not receive satisfaction, and often are then terminated. The result is usually an unexpected outcome for both parties. Although there are many cases on record, the legal skirmishes surrounding *Collins v. Beazer Homes USA* illustrate the danger SOx whistleblower cases continue to pose for employers. The following is a summary of the legal abstract from a SOx whistleblower case from around 2005 that shows the difficulties and uncertainties of the process for all concerned.

Whistleblower Example: *Collins v. Beazer Homes*[3]

The plaintiff or aggrieved person in this case, Collins, was a newly hired director of marketing who was terminated after complaining to her employer, Beazer Homes, about what she felt were various improper marketing and other decisions. After her initial hire, Collins began having conflicts with her manager, the division president, and the director of sales. Collins felt that these individuals were inappropriately favoring a particular advertising agency. While secretly taping her conversations, Collins complained to the vice president of sales and marketing that she was having problems implementing her marketing decisions and objected to the division president's management style. She raised concerns—pointing to improper activities—about how the company was paying its current advertising agency, and about how marketing costs were being categorized. Collins also secretly tape-recorded a meeting with the company's vice president of human resources and then sent an e-mail letter to Beazer's CEO, making further claims about the existence of a "cover-up/corruption," but she did not indicate any specifics. In another e-mail, Collins said that she suspected kickbacks in the company's business practices and that, in order to hide information, marketing costs were not being properly allocated.

Based on her allegations, Marty Shaffer, a vice president, met with Collins. Again tape-recording their conversation, Collins made a number of complaints, but did not specifically say that illegal activity was taking place. Shaffer told Collins that he would have to let her go, since the two individuals about whom she was complaining had been with the company for some time, and since it did not appear that the conflict was going to end. Collins then filed a SOx whistleblower complaint through the DOL to OSHA, and when OSHA failed to issue a final administrative decision within 180 days, she filed in federal court. Beazer's legal counsel then moved for a summary court judgment.

The court initially rejected Beazer's arguments in favor of summary judgment, and then Beazer argued that Collins failed to show an actual violation of the law. The court also noted that Collins "reasonably believed" that there was a violation of a law or regulation that was protected by SOx, and that the standard is one of a reasonable person, even if the employee is mistaken or misunderstands the requirements of law. The court also rejected Beazer's argument that because Collins never specifically alleged securities or accounting fraud, and because her complaints were "vague" and amounted only to "personality conflicts" and "differences in marketing strategies," she did not state a claim. Given the "broad remedial purposes" behind SOx, the court found that genuine issues of fact precluded a finding as a matter of law that the plaintiff did not engage in protected activity.

Beazer's claims that Collins's allegations were vague or not serious were contradicted, the court held, by the company's investigation of the matter by various senior executives, and the seriousness with which it treated these allegations. The court also rejected Beazer's additional argument that, because Shaffer was not fully ware of the nature of Collins's allegations, and since Shaffer was the "sole decision maker" in her discharge, the company was unaware of plaintiff's protected activity as a matter of law. Accepting this argument, the court said, would permit an employer to avoid SOx liability simply by bringing in a manager unaware of the employee's claims in order to fire her. Finally, the court held that the period between the time of plaintiff's complaints and her discharge was more than adequate to establish circumstances suggesting that this activity was a contributing factor in her termination. The court concluded that Beazer could not establish by clear and convincing evidence as a matter of law that it would have fired her even absent her protected activity.

Our point in this legal description is not to argue the pertinent legal issues but to highlight that SOx whistleblower cases can be lengthy, not straightforward, and time consuming for all parties. In many respects, few really win from such actions. The terminated employee making the allegations will have spent considerable time and resources making the case with little chance for major damage rewards. In addition, it can often be a challenge for that same protesting employee to subsequently find attractive employment opportunities elsewhere within his or her profession.

A search on the Web for "Sarbanes-Oxley whistleblowers" finds others such as this *Beazer Homes* matter. The issues are usually not the financially improper transactions matters that brought us these rules with the passage of SOx. Rather, employees or other stakeholders are often terminated and claim SOx whistleblower issues as a vehicle to press their claims. This certainly was not the type of issue first anticipated when whistleblower rules appeared in the SOx legislation. However, that is the reality of things, and enterprises should take steps to create an atmosphere in an enterprise to encourage employees and stakeholders to act in an ethical manner and to report whistleblower-like concerns in an anonymous manner.

Enterprises registered through SOx should advise their employees and stakeholders about SOx whistleblower provisions through policies, training sessions, and summary postings of these rights. Other good steps to create a better working atmosphere between the employer and potential employee whistleblowers include:

- Anti-retaliation provisions documented in manuals and employee hand-books. That is, the enterprise is formally saying the employee will be protected if whistleblower provisions are raised.
- Whenever a whistleblower complaint is received, the enterprise should draft a letter to acknowledge that the complaint has been received and will be investigated.

- Always evaluate the appropriateness of having the whistleblower remain in his or her position if the allegations flow directly to the supervisor.
- Conduct an unbiased investigation of complaints, preferably by an independent or even a qualified outside party.
- Limit all communication regarding the complaint, the investigation, and its conclusion only to those with a need to know.
- Always maintain a paper trail of all management deliberations and actions regarding the matter.
- When advising employees that a complaint has been received and an investigation will be undertaken, request that all impacted persons sign statements acknowledging that each has been advised that retaliatory conduct will not be tolerated.

Chapters 2 and 3 discussed some of the changing rules impacting SOx today. For example, the risk-based rules in AS5 have somewhat simplified the auditing process compared to those under AS2. The SOx whistleblower rules have become somewhat of a nonevent rather than characterized by many troubling legal actions. An enterprise can ensure against other impacts by installing or strengthening its ethics function and establishing a hotline function to encourage anonymous reporting.

KEEPING SOx RULES IN FOCUS

Whether SOx or other legislation, laws tend to contain a mixture of both specific statements of law and supporting rules issued by regulatory authorities. Enforcement activities will also vary over time depending on whether the rules cover a current "hot topic" or an area of little general interest. However, laws are often not revised or rescinded due to lack of applicability or current public concerns. Discussed in Chapter 4 on background events leading to the COSO internal controls framework, the Foreign Corrupt Practices Act of 1977, and amended several times since then, had strong but vague internal control provisions that required enterprises to build and maintain internal control documentation. Major U.S. corporations went through massive first-year documentation efforts in those days of limited automation and many manual systems, but there was little evidence of regulatory enforcement actions covering the internal control section of this law, and the provision today has been largely forgotten.

Our point here is that an enterprise does not necessarily need to go back through every clause and paragraph in legislation, such as SOx, and attempt to establish full 100% compliance. Rather, an enterprise should concentrate on the significant aspects of SOx and establish strong compliance procedures.

This statement begs the question of what is significant. It is not an easy one to answer, but under SOx an enterprise today should, of course, concentrate on Section 404 compliance under AS5 as well as Section 302. With tools to monitor activities on a real-time basis and with tightened SOx fining dates, more attention should be given to the Section 409 rules just discussed. Rules such as Section 401 are also best practices and an enterprise should achieve compliance through its other strong internal controls.

The situation is perhaps a bit different for the SOx whistleblower rules. Although when SOx first became law, there were predictions of a huge amount of legal and compliance activity here, there has been little activity or even news in this area. How do we predict what is going to become an important SOx issue? An enterprise's legal counsel can be of tremendous help, but little beats massive and ongoing news monitoring. The Web is a terrific source, and news of some enforcement action or even compliance initiative taking place elsewhere should encourage an enterprise to examine its own status regarding some rule and to take any actions as appropriate. In addition to the Section 404 review processes examined in Chapter 6, the SOx rules discussed in this chapter should stay in enterprise management's focus. Some sections, such as 302 and 401, have become regular business practices, while others, such as Section 409, have not commanded much of the spotlight today but certainly soon could.

ENDNOTES

1. "Sherron Watkins Had Whistle, But Blew It," *Forbes*, http://www.forbes.com/ 2002/02/14/0214watkins.html.
2. "BioSante Pharm: SEC Probing Whistleblower Complaint," Dow Jones Newswires, May 1, 2007.
3. This description is based on a legal abstract published by Nixon Peabody LLP, attorneys at law, http://www.nixonpeabody.com/linked_media/publications/ ELA_12282004.pdf. We have edited some of this material for ease of reading, and this description should not be considered an abstract for legal reference purposes.

CHAPTER 8

Using ITIL to Align IT with Business Processes

As previous chapters have demonstrated, the world of Sarbanes-Oxley (SOx) is filled with a stream of acronyms, such as AS5, CobiT (Control Objectives for Information Technology), COSO (Committee of Sponsoring Organizations), and the PCAOB (Public Company Accounting Oversight Board). They have all become sort of shorthand that allows professionals to identify and describe some of the key processes that support enterprise SOx compliance. ITIL (Information Technology Infrastructure Library), introduced in Chapter 1, is yet another acronym that soon should become much more familiar to enterprises seeking SOx internal control compliance over their information technology (IT) infrastructure operations. ITIL describes recommended best practices for IT service support and service delivery processes, such as how to investigate and solve reported problems called into the operations help desk. These are the best practices and processes that are necessary for IT to process its applications in an efficient and well-controlled environment.

ITIL best practices were first developed in the 1980s by the British government's Office of Government Commerce (OGC)—formerly called the Central Computer and Telecommunications Agency. ITIL is a vendor/supplier-independent collection of best practices that have become widely observed in the IT service industry, first in the United Kingdom, then in the European Union (EU), next in Canada and Australia, and now are increasingly recognized in the United States and worldwide. ITIL is a detailed framework or description of a number of significant IT practices, with comprehensive checklists, tasks, procedures, and responsibilities that are designed to be tailored to any IT organization. As an example of this best practices approach, ITIL suggests that any IT operation should have some form of *help desk* where users of IT can ask questions or resolve problems. Beyond this, ITIL suggests the kinds of call monitoring logs, problem resolution databases, and other best practices to strengthen such an IT help-desk facility. Dividing key processes between those covering IT service delivery and those for service support, ITIL has become the de facto standard for describing some fundamental processes in IT service management such as *problem management.*

This chapter will explore ITIL's major service delivery and service support components along with its security management components. All of these help to bridge gaps and smooth operations between the IT infrastructure, systems or applications management, and business or enterprise processes. Similar to the COSO internal control framework discussed in Chapter 4, ITIL is a set of suggested best practices designed to better organize and manage IT infrastructure processes. However, ITIL is not a prescriptive standard such as the AS5 internal control auditing standards discussed in Chapter 3. The use of ITIL best practices should help an enterprise to better manage and operate all aspects of its IT resources and ensure stronger SOx internal control compliance.

The use and understanding of ITIL best practices should be particularly important for internal auditors. ITIL presents a set of guidelines that internal auditors can use when reviewing and assessing many areas of an enterprise, whether within IT or the general business areas that use and rely on IT infrastructure operations. This chapter will look at ITIL infrastructure services and controls from an internal audit perspective and conclude with some audit checklists and guidelines for assessing this very important area of IT service management.

IMPORTANCE OF THE INFORMATION TECHNOLOGY INFRASTRUCTURE

Once called just "computer systems operations," professionals today are increasingly using the term *infrastructure* to describe all of the supporting processes that make an IT department or function work. An IT function has developers to install new applications and to manage existing production operations. It also needs hardware devices, such as servers and network controllers, as well as skilled operations staff functions to operate those systems. In addition to technology-driven areas, an IT infrastructure organization needs processes to support and deliver services to the users of IT—its customers. This very broad area includes a team to manage and maintain operating systems, communications networks, people to manage capacity and configurations, and even a support desk function to help IT's customers who may have questions or perhaps need password resets. This broad area is known as the *IT infrastructure,* a service-driven and service-support area where the focus is less on technology and more on customer satisfaction.

ITIL best practices are based on the widely recognized concept that information is the most important strategic resource that any enterprise must manage. The quality of an enterprise's IT systems and services is key to the collection, analysis, production, and distribution of this information on strategic and organizational levels. The enterprise must invest sufficient levels of resources into their support and delivery, but the emphasis is too often on just the more tangible resources such as hardware, communications facilities, or applications. However, some aspects of the IT infrastructure are often overlooked or only superficially addressed within many enterprises. These issues facing business and IT managers include implementing continuous improvement programs, improving project delivery status, or managing offshore operations. Exhibit 8.1 is a list of some of these issues. Our point is the need to think beyond just the conventional IT processes to improve overall service management.

This list is not all-inclusive, but illustrates many of the service and control issues facing an IT enterprise in partnership with overall business processes. Both must work in partnership to deliver high-quality IT services that reduce total costs and better manage changes. This requires a close alignment with (1) the people responsible for managing IT, (2) the key processes, (3) tools and technology partners, and (4) products including suppliers, vendors, and outsourcing organizations. Communication links

- IT and business strategic planning
- Using IT to gain competitive advantages
- Integrating and aligning IT and business goals
- Implementing continuous improvement initiatives
- Acquiring and retaining the right resources and skill sets
- Measuring and assessing IT organization efficiency and effectiveness
- Reducing costs and the *total cost of ownership* (TCO)
- Achieving and demonstrating *value for money* (VM) and *return on investment* (ROI)
- Demonstrating the business value of IT
- Developing business and IT partnerships and relationships
- Improving project delivery timing and processes
- Managing outsourcing and other alternative sourcing arrangements
- Establishing service- , performance- , and cost-level agreements with IT and with customers of IT services
- Implementing a strong program of IT governance

EXHIBIT 8.1 Key Issues Facing an IT Organization

should be developed among all four of these areas. In the pre-ITIL days of IT enterprises, these communication links often did not exist. In addition to these, IT enterprises often were isolated from business operations, and internal IT people, processes, products, and partners did not always operate in a coordinated manner.

One of the main objectives of ITIL[1] is to assist enterprises "to improve IT efficiency and effectiveness while improving the overall quality of service to the business within imposed cost constraints." These objectives create some strong goals for IT services, including:

- Develop and maintain good and responsive relationships between IT and business operations.
- Meet existing IT requirements of the business.
- Make effective and efficient use of all IT resources.
- Contribute to the improvement of the overall quality of IT services within imposed cost constraints.

A common strategic management-planning slogan of the 1990s was to "think outside of the box." That is, people were encouraged to go beyond their existing practices and conventions, designing strategies that went beyond those older, more organization chart boxed-in levels of thinking. ITIL encourages this type of thinking. In the past, there was far too much "us-versus-them" thinking between IT and business functions. ITIL encourages a much broader level of coordination and continuous quality improvements in this area.

ITIL FRAMEWORK

ITIL best practices are built around a core set of service delivery and service support practices that closely link these IT processes with business needs. Exhibit 8.2 illustrates the ITIL framework and these relationships. As discussed in the following sections, the ITIL model represents a series of best practices that link and support IT infrastructure management with business operations. The exhibit shows seven ITIL elements, as follows:

1. **Service delivery.** This core ITIL area covers processes required for the planning and delivery of quality IT services, with an emphasis on improving the quality of IT services delivered.
2. **Service support.** A second core ITIL area, concerns here are the day-to-day support and maintenance activities associated with the provisioning of IT services.

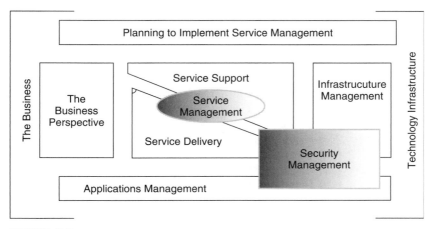

EXHIBIT 8.2 ITIL Framework

3. **IT infrastructure management.** This area covers all aspects of IT operations from the identification of business requirements through the testing, installation, deployment, and ongoing operation of IT components and services.
4. **Service management implementation planning.** Processes are necessary to plan, implement, and then improve the ITIL enterprise service management. This area includes the development of a vision and strategy as well as implementation methods.
5. **IT application management.** This area describes the management of IT applications from initial business needs through all stages of the application development life cycle up through retirement. The emphasis is that IT projects and strategies should be tightly aligned with the business, throughout their life cycles, to obtain best values for these investments.
6. **Business perspectives.** An essential component, business-related issue must provide advice and guidance to help IT personnel, at all levels, to better contribute to business objectives for improved alignment maximum benefits.
7. **Security management.** Best practices here include the process of planning and managing a defined level of security for IT services and the information managed, including all aspects associated with security incidents, the management of risks and vulnerabilities, and the implementation of cost-justified countermeasures.

The real message of ITIL is that management processes should be installed to link business needs and requirements with the IT infrastructure, including its operations, applications, and management. A strong set of ITIL processes will yield a wide range of improvements, including a better SOx internal control environment.

ITIL processes cover the IT infrastructure, the supporting processes that allow IT applications to function and deliver their results to systems users. All too often, internal auditors and others focus too much attention on the new application development side of IT and ignore important service delivery and service support processes. An enterprise may devote massive efforts, for example, to building and implementing a new budget forecasting system, but that budget application will be of little value unless there are good service processes in place, such as *problem* and *incident management*, to allow customers or the users of that budget application to report systems difficulties or to otherwise effectively achieve benefits from the application. Also needed are good IT infrastructure capacity and availability processes to allow the new application to run as expected. A well-designed and well-controlled application is of little value to the ultimate users or customers without strong service support and service delivery processes in place. ITIL provides a good general best practices model to follow, and all levels of internal auditors should learn to use ITIL in their reviews. The following sections will provide an overview of some ITIL processes, including such areas as *capacity* and *service level* as well as *configuration management*.

ITIL SERVICE DELIVERY BEST PRACTICES

The *ITIL service delivery module* describes best practices for the more customer-focused areas of IT operations. It starts with *service level management*, where requirements and standards are defined between the business and the IT providers of the service to be delivered. The other modules include *availability, capacity, financial,* and *financial management.* These service delivery processes cover areas more closely aligned with the smooth and efficient operation of the overall IT infrastructure. Some, such as the *continuity management* process have traditionally received the attention of internal control specialists and internal auditors. Others, such as *financial management* for IT services, also are very important but often do not receive the necessary level of attention. Service delivery processes, some of their major deliverables, and the connection between business leadership and performance results are described in Exhibit 8.3.

Service Delivery Service Level Management

Service level management is the process of planning, coordinating, drafting, agreeing, and monitoring activities between IT and the providers and

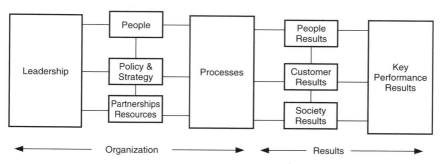

EXHIBIT 8.3 ITIL Service Delivery Processes

recipients of IT services. This is a two-sided process where users will make formal service requests to IT, such as their expected systems response times, and IT will negotiate and outline its requirements. Structured similar to a formal purchase order contract, these agreements are called *service-level agreements* (SLAs); they represent a formal agreement between IT and providers of services to IT as well as IT and its end-user customers.

When IT contracts for services with some outside provider, such as for disaster recovery backup services, these arrangements should be covered by a formal contract where the disaster recovery provider agrees to provide certain levels of service, following some response time–based schedule, and IT agrees to other terms. The governing contract here is an SLA between IT and providers of the disaster recovery services. Perhaps even more important, from an internal control perspective, are SLA agreements between IT and its own users or customers. We have used the term *customer* here for the older but still-common term *IT users*. There are many groups in an enterprise that are users or customers of IT services, all expecting certain levels of service and responsiveness. Their joint expectations should be defined through SLAs, a written agreement between IT and its customers defining the key service targets and responsibilities of both parties. The emphasis should be on agreement, and SLAs should not be used as a way of holding one side or the other for ransom. A true partnership should be developed between the IT provider and the customer for a mutually beneficial agreement; otherwise the SLA could quickly fall into disrepute and a culture of blame can prevent any ongoing service quality improvements from taking place.

An SLA should be a formal agreement where IT promises to deliver services per an agreed-on set of schedules and understands there will be penalties if service standards are not met. The goal here is to maintain and improve on service quality through a constant cycle of agreeing, monitoring, reporting, and improving the current levels of IT service. SLAs should be strategically focused on the business and maintaining the alignment between the business and IT. Exhibit 8.4 outlines general provisions in a typical SLA. This should not be the type of document that would be found in a major sale of goods or as part of a house mortgage closing. Rather, IT customers should negotiate the service requirements that they are seeking, such as an average response time "no more than___" or a "financial system close processing completed by___." To temper expectations and show what could be available, larger IT functions—as part of the service level management process—often describe their capabilities and options in a service offerings catalog. The customer requirements will be prepared per specifications and customer needs and, after some negotiation, formal SLAs will be established. Performance against SLAs should be monitored and reported on an ongoing basis. Failure to meet these SLA standards could result in additional negotiations and SLA adjustments.

SLAs and the service level management process provide the following joint benefits to the business and to IT:

- Because IT will be working to meet negotiated standards, IT services will tend to be of a higher quality, causing fewer interruptions and improvements in the productivity of the IT customers as well.
- IT staff resources will tend to be used more efficiently while IT provides services that better meet the expectations of its customers.
- Through the use of SLA's, services provided can be measured, and the perception of IT operations will generally improve.
- Services provided by the third parties are more manageable with the underpinning contracts in place.
- Monitoring overall IT services under SLAs makes it possible to identify weak spots that can be improved.

The SLA process should be an important component of IT operations. If an enterprise does not use formal SLAs, internal auditors reviewing IT operations internal controls should consider recommending using formal SLA processes. SLAs eliminate accusations and finger-pointing and can create a totally new environment within an IT enterprise. All parties will better understand their responsibilities and service obligations, and the SLA can become a basis for resolving many issues. Internal audit can use them as a basis for assessing internal controls in a variety of areas and for making strong control improvement recommendations.

Service Delivery Financial Management for IT Services

In its earlier days, the IT function in most enterprises was operated as a "free" support service with its expenses handled through central management

Introduction
- Parties to the agreement as well as signatories.
- Title and brief description of the agreement.
- Dates: start, end, and review.
- Scope of the agreement; what is covered and what is excluded.
- Responsibilities of both the **service** provider and the **customer**.
- Description of the **services** covered.

Service hours
- Hours that each service is normally required (e.g., 24×7, Monday to Friday 08:00–18:00)
- Arrangement for requesting service extensions, including required notice periods (e.g., request must be made to the **service** desk by 12 noon for an evening extension, by 12 noon on Thursday for a weekend extension).
- Special hours allowances (e.g., public holidays).
- Service calendar.

Availability
- Availability targets within agreed-on hours, normally expressed as percentages—measurement period and method should be stipulated. This may be expressed for the overall service, underpinning services, and critical components, or all three.

Reliability
- Usually expressed as the number of service breaks, or the mean time between failures (**MTBF**) or mean time between **system** incidents (**MTBSI**).

Support
- Support hours (where these are not the same as service hours).
- Arrangements for requesting support extensions, including required notice periods (e.g., request must be made to the service desk by 12 noon for an evening extension, by 12 noon on Thursday for a weekend extension).
- Special hours allowances (e.g., public holidays).
- Target time to respond to incidents, either physically or by other method (e.g., telephone contact, e-mail).
- Target time to resolve incidents, within each incident priority—targets vary, depending upon incident priorities.

Throughput
- Indication of likely traffic volumes and throughput activity (e.g., the number of transactions to be processed, number of concurrent users, amount of data to be transmitted over the network).

(continued overleaf)

EXHIBIT 8.4 Service-Level Agreement Sample Contents

Transaction response times
- Target times for average, or maximum, workstation response times (sometimes expressed as a percentile—e.g., 95% within 2 seconds).

Batch turnaround times
- Times for delivery of input and the time and place for delivery of output.

Changes
- Targets for approving, handling and implementing change requests, usually based upon the **category** or **urgency**/priority of the change.

IT Service continuity and security
- Brief mention of IT service continuity plans and how to invoke them, and coverage of any security issues, particularly any responsibilities of the customer (e.g., backup of free-standing Systems, password changes).
- Details of any diminished or amended service targets should a disaster situation occur (if no separate **SLA** exists for such a situation).

Charging
- Details of the charging formula and periods (if charges are being made). If the **SLA** covers an **outsourcing** relationship, charges should be detailed in an addendum because they are often covered by commercial confidentiality provisions.

Service reporting and reviewing
- The content, frequency, and distribution of service reports, and the frequency of service review meetings.

Performance incentives/penalties
- Details of any agreement regarding financial incentives or penalties based upon performance against service levels. These are more likely to be included if the services are being provided by a third-party organization.

EXHIBIT 8.4 (*continued*)
Source: Adapted from *Brink's Modern Internal Auditing*, Sixth Edition, Robert Moeller, page 571. Copyright © 2005 John Wiley & Sons. Reprinted with permission of John Wiley & Sons, Inc.

and with no costs allocated to benefiting customers. As a result, not much attention was given to the costs of IT. If a department wanted some new vendor-developed application, they would pressure IT management to purchase the package and add any additional necessary people to manage it. Over time, IT functions began to establish chargeback processes to cover

IT costs, but these were too often viewed as a series of "funny-money" transactions where no one paid too much attention to the actual costs and pricing of IT services.

Today, the costs and pricing of IT services are or should be a much more important consideration. The well-managed IT function should operate more as a business, and financial management is an important and key ITIL process to help manage the financial controls for that business. The objective of the ITIL *service delivery financial management* process is to suggest guidance for the cost-effective stewardship of the assets and resources used in providing IT services. IT should be able to fully account for its spending on IT services and to attribute these costs of the services delivered to the enterprise's customers. There are three separate subprocesses associated with ITIL financial management:

1. **IT budgeting** is the process of predicting and controlling the spending of IT related money within the enterprise. Budgeting consists of a periodic, usually annual, negotiation cycle to set budgets along with the ongoing day-to-day monitoring of current IT budgets. Budgeting ensures that there has been planning and funding for appropriate IT services and that IT operates within this budget during the period. Other business functions will have periodic negotiations with IT to establish expenditure plans and agreed investment programs; these ultimately set the budgets for IT.

2. **IT accounting** is the set of processes that enable IT to account fully for the way its money is spent by customer, service, and activity. Many IT functions historically have not always done a good job in this area. An IT organization has a wide variety of external costs including software, equipment lease agreements, telecommunications, and others. However, these costs are often not well managed or reported. They have enough data to pay the bills and evaluate some specific area costs, but IT functions often lack the level of detailed accounting that such as those found in a large manufacturing enterprise, for example. The manufacturing cost accounting or activity-based accounting model has applicability here. A major starting point is for an enterprise to define and identify its costs in terms of those that can be classified as direct and indirect. Direct costs can be specifically related to an IT service, such as rental on a specialized software or equipment, while indirect costs cover multiple activity areas.

3. **Charging** is the set of pricing and billing processes to charge customers for the services supplied. Rather than making them appear to be "free" to all customers, a charging process moves costs back to specific benefiting users. Charging for IT services requires sound IT accounting

but should be done in a simple, fair, and well-controlled manner. The IT charging process sometimes breaks down because billing reports of IT services are too complex or technical for many customers to understand. IT needs to produce clear understandable reports of the IT services used such that customers can verify details, understand enough to ask questions regarding service, and negotiate adjustments if necessary.

Financial management for IT services provides important information to the service level management process, discussed previously, about the IT costing, pricing, and charging strategies. While generally not operated as a profit center, the financial management process allows both IT and its customers to think of IT service operations in business terms. The financial management process may allow IT and overall management to make decisions about what, if any, functions should be retained in-house or outsourced to an external provider.

The financial management process should also allow accurate cost-benefit analyses of the IT services provided, allowing IT to set and meet financial targets. It should also provide timely reporting to the service level management process such that its customers can easily understand the charging and pricing methods used. Of all of the ITIL service support and delivery processes, financial management is one that frequently gets short shrift. IT people have a technical orientation and tend to think of financial management as an *accounting issue*, almost beneath them. On the other side of the coin, finance and accounting resources tend to look at IT financial issues as too technical beyond such simple transactions as equipment lease accounting or facility space charges. Internal auditors should use their financial skills as well as IT knowledge to review and assess financial management process internal controls.

Exhibit 8.5 provides some audit procedures for an internal audit review of the costs and pricing of IT processes and services. This is often not a common review area for internal audit, but given the large costs distributed to customers as well as the importance of an enterprise's IT resources, this should be an important audit area. IT financial management is important for managing costs and remaining competitive in the marketplace. Enterprises with good IT financial management processes should benefit because IT will be viewed more as a business asset and not just an expense.

Service Delivery Capacity Management

The *capacity management* process is designed to ensure that the capacity of the IT infrastructure is aligned to business needs and to maintain a required level of service delivery at an acceptable cost through appropriate levels

1. Develop and document a general understanding of the cost structure for IT operations, including costs of hardware and software leases, maintenance agreements, telecommunications, supplies, and salaries.
2. Review and understand costing philosophy for IT operations—is it an overhead function, cost recovery, or revenue generating?
3. Review processes for costing and pricing IT services:
   a. Are all IT costs covered? What are accounting processes for variances?
   b. Based on customer interviews does the costing and pricing system appear to be understandable?
   c. Is there a process in place to administer the process and to make adjustments if necessary?
4. Review the negotiation process with IT users to understand the pricing process—are expected costs included in SLAs?
5. Review and document the IT cost-monitoring process.
6. Select pricing reports during a period for several processes and check to determine the prices are included in SLAs.
7. Review appropriateness of adjustment process over a period to determine the corrections are investigated and applied when appropriate.
8. Review IT services billed for one accounting period and determine that they cover all actual IT costs. Investigate and report on any differences.
9. For a selected accounting period, trace IT pricing charges to appropriate accounting system entries.
10. Review processes in place for booking corrections and adjustments to IT service charges.

EXHIBIT 8.5   Review of IT Costs and Pricing Internal Audit Procedures
Source: Brink's Modern Internal Auditing, Sixth Edition, Robert Moeller, page 575. Copyright © 2005 John Wiley & Sons. Reprinted with permission of John Wiley & Sons, Inc.

of capacity. Through gathering business and technical capacity data, this process should result in a plan to deliver cost-justified capacity requirements for the enterprise. In addition to a prime objective to understand an enterprise's IT capacity requirements and deliver against them both in the present and in the future, capacity management is also responsible for understanding the potential advantages new technology could have and assessing its suitability for the enterprise.

The concept of capacity management goes back to the old days of mainframe computers when an enterprise would have concerns whether its centralized computer systems could handle application system demands. As the capabilities of these systems went up and their costs went way down, capacity management became a low concern for many IT professionals. However, ITIL capacity management processes still have some important

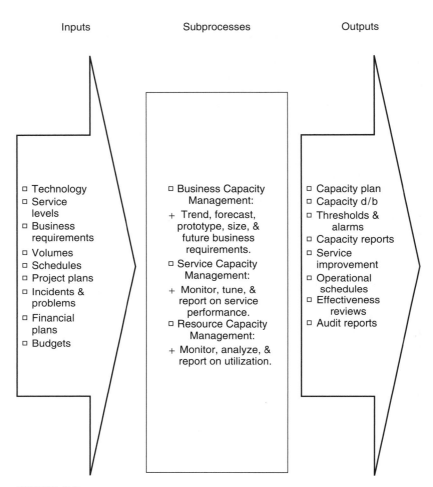

EXHIBIT 8.6 Capacity Management Activities

processes and concerns. Exhibit 8.6 lists capacity management activities in terms of their inputs, subprocesses, and outputs. An effective capacity management process requires ongoing monitoring and analysis to manage demands for IT resources.

Capacity management is generally considered in terms of three subprocesses that cover business, service, and resource capacity management. *Business capacity management* is a long-term process to ensure that the future requirements are taken into consideration and then planned and implemented as necessary. *Service capacity management* is responsible for ensuring that the performance of all current IT services falls within the parameters defined in existing SLAs. Finally, *resource capacity management* has more of a technical focus and is responsible for the management of the individual components within the infrastructure. The multiple inputs to these three capacity management subprocesses include:

- SLAs and SLA breaches
- Business plans and strategies
- Operational schedules as well as schedule changes
- Application development issues
- Technology constraints and acquisitions
- Incidents and problems
- Budgets and financial plans

As a result of the above multiple inputs, the capacity management process—often under a single designated capacity manager—should manage IT processes, develop and maintain a formal capacity plan, and make certain capacity records are up to date. In addition, the capacity manager must be involved in evaluating all changes to establish the effect on capacity and performance. This capacity evaluation should happen both when changes are proposed and after they are implemented. Capacity management must pay particular attention to the cumulative effect of changes over a period of time that may cause degraded response times, file storage problems, and excess demands for processing capacity. Other capacity management roles and responsibilities include some duties of network, application, and systems management in order to translate business requirements into the capacity needed to optimize IT performance.

An effective capacity management process offers IT the benefits of an actual overview of the current capacity in place and the ability to plan capacity in advance. Effective capacity management should be able to estimate the impact of new applications or modifications as well as provide cost savings that align with business requirements. Proper capacity planning can significantly reduce the overall cost of IT system ownership. Although formal capacity planning takes time, internal and external staff resources, and software and hardware tools, the potential losses incurred without capacity planning can be significant. Lost productivity of end users in critical business functions, overpaying for network equipment or services, and the costs of upgrading systems already in production can more than justify the cost of capacity planning. Capacity management is an important ITIL process.

Service Delivery Availability Management

Enterprises increasingly demand and business requires that their IT services be available on a 7-days-a-week/24-hours-a-day basis. When these IT services are unavailable, in many cases the business stops as well. It is therefore vital that IT manage and control the availability of its services. This can be accomplished by defining the requirements from the business regarding the availability of the IT services and then matching them with enterprise IT capabilities.

Availability management has multiple inputs that also must be able to function well. These include linkages among users of IT, the service providers, and both internal and external suppliers and maintainers. Exhibit 8.7 maps out the basic concepts of availability management.

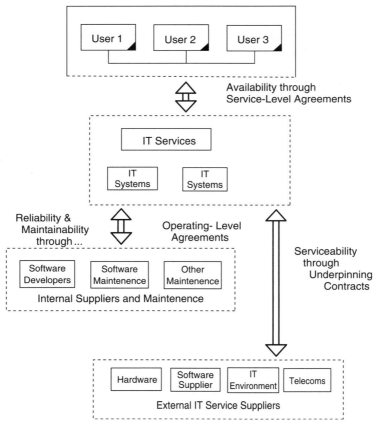

EXHIBIT 8.7   *Availability Management Basic Concepts*

Customers require IT systems and services that demand the reliability and maintainability of IT service suppliers. The exhibit references service-level and operating-level agreements (SLAs and OLAs). SLAs were discussed previously; OLAs are similar agreements between the IT service providers supplying application services and software and hardware suppliers. These are formal contracts between service providers and suppliers covering expected levels reliability, maintainability, recoverability, and serviceability.

The activities within the availability management process can be described as planning, improving, and measuring. Planning involves determining availability requirements to find out if and how the IT enterprise can meet them. The service level management process, discussed previously, maintains contact with the business and will be able to provide the availability expectations to the availability management process. Business units sometimes have unrealistic availability expectations and an incomplete understanding of what this means in real terms. For example, they may want 99.9% availability and yet not realize that this will cost about five times more than providing 98% availability. It is the responsibility of the service level and the availability management processes to manage these expectations.

An IT enterprise can design for either *availability* or *recovery*. When the business cannot afford a particular length of service downtime, the IT enterprise will need to build resilience into the infrastructure and ensure that preventative maintenance can be performed to keep services in operation. In many cases, building "extra availability" into the infrastructure is an expensive task that can be justified by business needs. Designing for availability is a proactive approach to avoiding downtime in IT services.

When the business can tolerate some downtime of services or a cost justification cannot be made for building additional resilience into the infrastructure, designing for recovery is the appropriate approach. Here, the infrastructure should be designed such that in the event of a service failure, recovery will be "as fast as possible." Designing for recovery is a more reactive management approach for availability. In any event, processes such as *incident management* need to be in place to recover as soon as possible in case of a service interruption.

The main benefit of availability management is that IT services are designed, implemented, and managed to meet agreed availability requirements. This requires a thorough understanding of IT business processes and customer requirements. Other benefits of effective availability management processes include:

- There is a single point of contact for managing the availability of IT products and services.
- Standards require that new products and services meet agreed-on availability standards.

- Availability standards are continuously monitored and improved where appropriate.
- Occurrences and durations of unavailability should be reduced.
- The emphasis should be shifted from remedying faults to improving service.
- It is easier for an IT organization to prove its added value.

An effective availability management process should reduce often-heard complaints that "The system is down!" Effective implementation of the best practices in this ITIL service delivery process should result in a higher availability of the IT services and increased customer satisfaction.

Service Delivery Continuity Management

As businesses are ever more dependent on IT, the impact of any unavailability of IT services has drastically increased. Every time the availability or performance of a service is reduced, IT customers cannot continue with their normal work. This need for a high dependency on IT support and services increasingly influences direct IT customers, managers, and decision makers. It is important that the impact of a total or even partial loss of IT services is estimated and *continuity plans* are established to ensure that the business, and its supporting IT infrastructure, will always be able to continue to operate.

Continuity management means much more than the previously common term, *IT disaster recovery planning*. There, the concern was to get IT hardware and software back in operation in the event of a major service failure due to an event such as a fire or flood. In those days, IT functions developed plans to back up files and restore services with little connection to their business impacts. The term *IT continuity planning* has been evolving over recent years, and ITIL really brings it back to its importance as a best practice.

ITIL continuity management calls for an appropriate strategy to be developed that contains an optimal balance of risk reduction and recovery options. The activities here include:

- Assessing the risk and impact of a disruption in IT services following a disaster event
- Identifying services critical to the business that require additional prevention and protection measures
- Defining periods within which services have to be restored
- Taking measures to prevent, detect, prepare for, and mitigate the effects of potential disasters
- Defining approaches to be used to restore services

■ Developing, testing, and maintaining a recovery plan with sufficient detail to survive a disaster event and to restore to normal services within a defined period

ITIL continuity management raises this very important component of IT service delivery to a higher, more business-oriented approach than has normally been found with classic disaster recovery planning. Aligned very much with some AS5 concepts, continuity management says an enterprise should work closely with its business continuity management resources to perform an impact analysis, do a risk assessment, and then develop a service continuity strategy. These should be followed by development of a plan, supporting procedures, and initial testing to strengthen processes. Once continuity processes have been implemented, processes should be installed for their regular and periodic audits and updates.

We have described ITIL best practices as a bridge between IT processes and business operations. Perhaps ITIL continuity management is the best or most important example of the values from that link. A disaster-level disruption in IT services will have severe impacts on all levels of business operations. ITIL outlines the types of processes necessary to minimize these risks, giving both IT and management some best practices to consider when developing effective continuity management processes.

ITIL SERVICE SUPPORT BEST PRACTICES

As shown in Exhibit 8.2, core ITIL *service management* processes are split between those covering service support and service delivery. *Service support* processes help make IT applications operate in an efficient and customer-satisfying manner. The *service delivery* processes, discussed previously, cover areas to improve the efficiency and performance of IT infrastructure elements such as improved availability. Service support is the other set of best practices modules. There are five ITIL service support best practice processes, as shown in Exhibit 8.8, ranging from *release management*, for placing a process into production, to *incident management*, for the orderly reporting of IT problems or events. ITIL service support processes cover good practices for any IT enterprise, whether a centralized operation using primarily centralized server systems as its IT central control point, or a highly distributed operation. Because of the many variations possible in the structure and enterprise of an IT operations function, ITIL does not prescribe the details of *how* to implement service support processes such as configuration or change management. Rather, it suggests good practices and ways to manage inputs and relationships among these processes. There is no order or precedence among each of these processes. Each can be

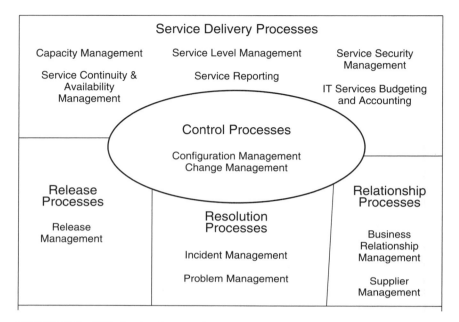

EXHIBIT 8.8   ITIL Service Support Processes

considered and managed separately but all are somewhat linked to one another.

There are five ITIL-defined service support processes that suggest preferred approaches for an IT operations function to organize and operate its productions systems in a manner that will promote efficient operation and will deliver quality services to the customers of these services. These are particularly useful for an internal auditor performing a review and making recommendations in an IT operations area. Many internal auditors have a good understanding of selected individual system controls as well as new application development controls and procedures. Those same internal auditors frequently do not give sufficient attention to these important supporting infrastructure ITIL best practices.

When observing and reviewing internal controls within an IT function, a very useful approach is to think in terms of separate processes. For example, the first process discussed here is *incident management*, or what has traditionally been called the "help desk," a facility where systems customers can call in with a question or problem. While these types of functions can be very useful, they are often a source of complaint when, for example, the same problem is called in repeatedly with no evident efforts by IT to analyze things and initiate a solution. Going beyond just a casual help desk and thinking of this as an overall process where matters are reported to other supporting processes will improve performance here and the overall quality of IT operations.

Service Support Incident Management

ITIL incident management covers the activities necessary for restoring an IT service following a disruption. By a disruption, we mean any type of problem that prevents some IT customer from receiving adequate services, whether an overall system failure, the user's inability to access the application for any of a variety of reasons, a password failure due to a "fat fingers" typing error, or any of a host of other problems. The reported problem is called an *incident*, some type of deviation from standard operations. Using another ITIL expression, the *service desk* is usually the owner for this process although all service support groups across the IT enterprise may have a role. Although many IT functions today have a help desk, a customer support group, or call it what you will, we will refer to this general function as the *service desk*.

The objective of incident management is to restore matters to normal operations as quickly as possible in a cost-effective manner with minimal impact on either the overall business or the user. How quickly is *quickly* should not be subject to interpretation. Restoration timeframe standards should have been defined in SLAs, discussed previously, between IT and the customer or user of IT services. Effective SLAs are an important component of the IT infrastructure and were discussed as one of the ITIL service delivery processes. The first component of the ITIL incident management process is the detection and documentation of the reported incident by the service desk, as a single point of contact. Incidents include such matters as a user calling in and informing the service desk of an application-processing problem.

Once received, the service desk should classify the incident in terms of its priority, impact, and urgency. The definition of a reported incident's priority is one of the more important aspects of managing IT incidents. Every person who calls in an incident tends to think that his or hers is the most important, and the incident management function has the difficult task of defining the relative priority of the reported incident, its importance and impact on the business. Exhibit 8.9 shows the life cycle of an incident from the initial call reporting the matter through resolution and closure. A formal SLA, as part of the service level management process, should define the priority with which incidents need to be resolved. The effort put into the resolution of and recovery from incidents depends on:

- The *impact or criticality* of the incident on the reporting entity or overall enterprise. Incident management should assess, for example, how many

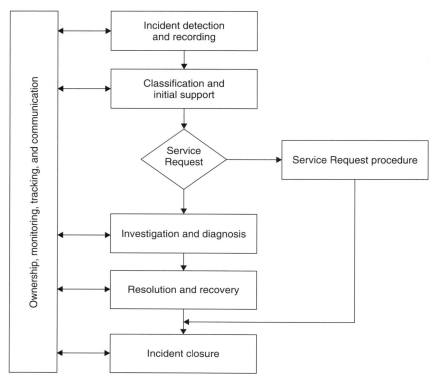

EXHIBIT 8.9 Incident Management Life Cycle

Source: Brink's Modern Internal Auditing, Sixth Edition, Robert Moeller, page 561. Copyright © 2005 John Wiley & Sons. Reprinted with permission of John Wiley & Sons, Inc.

users will suffer as a result of a reported technical failure of a hardware component. Similarly, a call regarding a problem with the month-end financial close process should be assigned a higher level of criticality than a problem with the system that generates purchase orders.

- The *urgency* of the reported incident. Urgency refers to the speed necessary to solve an incident of a certain impact. A high-impact incident does not, by default, always have to be solved immediately. An incident call that reports that some user group cannot work at all because of some service outage may often be of greater urgency than a senior manager calling to request a functionality change.

- The *size, scope, and complexity* of the incident. The incident management team should investigate the reported incident as soon as possible to determine its extent. A reported failure of some component may just mean that a device is out of service or might indicate a server is down. Those types of incidents often are not very complex and can be repaired relatively easily. A telecommunications failure that might impact multiple international units and thus might delay the monthly financial close can be much larger in size and scope.

Once an incident has been logged in, the process of investigation and diagnosis should begin. If the service desk cannot solve the incident, it should be assigned to other support levels for resolution. However, all parties that work on the incident should keep records of their actions by updating a common incident log file.

Some incidents can be resolved through a quick fix by the service desk, others by a more formal problem solution, or in the case of more significant problems, by a work-around to get things back in partial operation coupled with a formal request for change (RFC) to systems, to a vendor, or to whatever parties are needed to correct the problem. In any event, efforts should be marshaled to correct the problem with the incident management function retaining ownership of the matter until resolution. Solid documentation should be maintained to track the incident until its resolution. The incident can be formally closed once matters have been fixed, of if not easily solved, the incident should be passed to the *problem management* process function as discussed below.

All ITIL best practice processes are somewhat related to one another, but in many instances, incident management represents the first line between customers of IT services and IT itself, a reactive task get back to work as soon as possible. Properly organized, incident management should be much more than the help desks of an earlier time, when users called in with problems but often did not get much help beyond password resets. Incident management is a first point of contact between the customers—users—and the overall IT function. Incidents, caused by failures or errors within the IT infrastructure, result in actual or potential variations from the planned operation of services. Sometimes, the cause of these incidents may be apparent and can be addressed or fixed without the need for further investigation. In other situations, there may be a need for a hardware or software repair, a matter that often takes some time to implement. Short-run solutions may be a work-around, a quick fix to get back in operation, or a formal RFC to the *change management* process to remove the error. Examples of short-term work-arounds might be just instructing a customer to reboot a personal computer or resetting a communications line, without directly addressing the underlying cause of the incident.

EXHIBIT 8.10   Logical Flow of Problem Resolution from Incident Management

Where the underlying cause of the incident is not identifiable, it is often appropriate to raise a *problem record* for the unknown error within the infrastructure. Normally a problem record is raised only if investigation is warranted, and its actual and potential impact should be assessed. Problem management is the next line up and another service delivery process, as discussed in the following sections.

Successful processing of a problem record will result in the identification of the underlying error, and the record can then be converted into a *known error* once a work-around has been developed, and/or an RFC initiated. Exhibit 8.10 shows the relationship and logical flow among customers, incident management, problem management, work-arounds to correct known errors, and other ITIL processes to be discussed in the following sections.

Incident management is often the first line or connection between IT production process customers and the IT infrastructure. When everything works, there will be no problems with production operations. However, any type of reported problem will or should result in a reported incident. Processes should be in place to record or document the incident, to investigate or diagnose it, and to resolve it. That resolution may involve correction and documentation of the matter or passing it on to the level of problem management.

Service Support Problem Management

When incident management encounters a deviation of any sort with an unknown cause or reason, that incident should be passed on to *problem management* for resolution. The objective here is to minimize the problem's total impact through a formal process of detection and repair as well as taking actions to prevent any reoccurrence. Incident management often handles the quick fixes, but the problem management process is the next step in criticality and should be considered in terms of three subprocesses: *problem control, error control*, and *proactive problem management*. ITIL defines a *problem* as an unknown underlying cause resulting from one or more incidents, and a *known error* as a problem that has been successfully diagnosed and for which a work-around has been identified. The idea is not to necessarily create a second administrative function in an IT enterprise to take help-desk-reported incidents, but to identify when and how some help-desk-reported incidents should be passed on to another person or authority to better diagnose the reported matter and treat it as a problem. An effective problem management process can do much to improve overall IT customer service.

Inputs to the problem management process, as defined by ITIL, are:

- Capturing the incident details from the incident management process as discussed previously. Incident management is the first point of contact for reported IT problems. If the incident management resources cannot easily and efficiently diagnose and solve a problem, those details should be reported to a problem management function.
- An effective *configuration management database* (CMDB), as discussed below, should become a key tool to better understand the problem's background and environmental details, such as the software versions used, past problem history, and any other configuration details.
- Incident management often tries to fix a reported matter through an informal work-around procedure. When these do not solve things, the matter should be passed on to problem management, which should use this work-around data to help diagnose the problem.

In addition to solving any single incident that was bumped-up to the problem management process, IT should try to establish processes for better problem and error control, including maintaining data to help identify trends and suggesting improved procedures for the proactive prevention of problems. Data should be maintained on solutions and/or any available work-arounds for a resolved problem and closed problem records. In many instances, problem management may encounter a situation where it is necessary to go a step further and file a formal RFC either through the IT development function or through a hardware or software vendor.

An effective problem management process focuses on finding *patterns* among incidents, problems, and known errors. A detailed review of these patterns allows an analyst to solve the problem by considering the many possibilities and narrowing things down to a solution, which is called *root-cause analysis*. There are many good techniques for resolving and correcting problems, which are often caused by a combination of technical and nontechnical factors. The problem management process is a good area for internal audit to diagnose IT service delivery processes in order to better understand the overall health of IT operations. Areas where internal audit may ask some questions include:

- The number of RFCs raised and the impact of those RFCs on the availability and reliability of the overall IT services covered

- The amount of time worked on investigations and diagnoses for various types of problems by organizational unit or vendor
- The number and impact of incidents occurring before a root problem is solved or a known error is confirmed
- The plans for resolution of open problems with regard to people and other resource requirements as well as related costs and budgeted amounts

The ITIL service support problem management process is an important area for internal auditors to consider and understand when assessing the overall health of IT infrastructure operations. An efficient incident management process is necessary to receive customer calls and take immediate corrective actions, but an effective problem management process will go a step further to analyze and solve the problem, initiating RFCs where necessary and otherwise improving IT customer satisfaction.

Service Support Configuration Management

No matter their relative size, virtually all IT operations functions are complex with multiple types and versions of systems components that must work together in an orderly, well-managed manner. This is certainly true for a major corporation with classic mainframe systems, server farms, and a multitude of storage devices and communications gear, but smaller server-based systems operations can be complex as well. A formal *configuration management* function is an important service delivery process supporting the identification, recording, and reporting of IT components, their versions, constituent components, and relationships. Items that should be under the control of configuration management include hardware, software, and associated documentation. Configuration management here is not the same concept as the tax rules for an asset management depreciation accounting process, although the two are related. Asset management accounting systems maintain details on IT gear above a certain value, its business unit, and its location. Configuration management also maintains relationships between assets, which asset management usually does not. Asset management tracks the inventory of IT components while configuration management tracks versions on contents as well as how various IT assets relate to one another.

The basic activity of the configuration management process is to identify the various individual components in IT operations, called *configuration items* (CIs), and then to identify key supporting data for these CIs, including their owners, identifying data, version numbers, and systems interrelationships. This data should be captured, organized, and recorded in what is often known as a *configuration management database*, as shown at a very

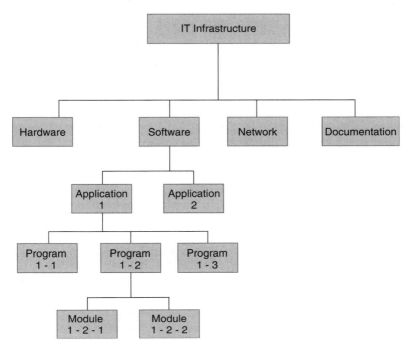

EXHIBIT 8.11   Configuration Management Database Structure Example

high level in Exhibit 8.11. The team responsible for configuration management should select and identify these configuration structures for all of the infrastructure's CIs, including establishing relationships between each CI and connected components in the overall IT infrastructure configuration. Going beyond just their entry on the CMDB, the process should ensure that only authorized CIs have been accepted and that no CI is added, modified, replaced, or removed without an appropriate change request and updated specification. CMDB software products are often implemented with what are called "auto-discovery" tools, software agents that constantly monitor the configuration environment and report on any changes or discontinuities.

An internal auditor can think of the importance of the configuration management process in terms of desktop applications in the audit department. Every internal auditor on the team will have a laptop computer, but unless each has consistent versions of software on their computers, there will be difficulties in their systems communicating with one another. This is where configuration management is particularly important. It is very important when attempting to have an understanding of the various versions or even types of software and equipment in a large IT operation.

The configuration management process also includes some control elements. For example, a series of reviews and audits should be implemented to verify the physical existence of CIs and check that they are correctly recorded in the configuration management system. Although we have used the word *audit* here, this is not an internal audit process but a task of the IT team responsible for the configuration management process. Configuration management should also maintain records for CI status accounting to track the status of a CI as it changes from one stage to another, for instance, from being under development, to being tested, to going live, and then to being withdrawn.

An enterprise can have some level of CMDB by just using spreadsheets, local databases, or even paper-based systems. However, there are multiple specialized CMDB products on the market to manage relationships. In addition, there may be a need to use physical and electronic libraries along with the CMDB to hold definitive copies of software and documentation. The CMDB should be founded on database technology that provides flexible and powerful interrogation facilities. It should hold the relationships among all system components, including incidents, problems, known errors, changes, and releases.

The existence of controls supporting a CMDB can be a good point for internal audit to understand an enterprise's configuration management process and its supporting controls. If the enterprise does not have an effective and adequately maintained CMDB, internal audit can anticipate seeing strong internal control problems throughout the IT infrastructure. Exhibit 8.12 outlines audit procedures for reviewing an enterprise's configuration management process.

The configuration management process interfaces directly with *systems development, testing, change management*, and *release management* to incorporate new and updated product deliverables. Control should be passed from the project or supplier to the service provider at the scheduled time with accurate configuration records. In addition, the CMDB can be used by the service level management process to hold details of services and to relate them to the underlying IT components. The CMDB can also be used to store inventory details of CIs, such as supplier, cost, purchase date, and renewal date for a license. An additional bonus is the use of the CMDB to cover the legal aspects associated with the maintenance of IT licenses and contracts.

Service Support Change Management

The problem management process, discussed previously, often results in the need for IT changes while many other changes can come from programs to increase business benefits such as through reducing costs or improving

1. Review and understand existing configuration management practices as well as their interfaces to the service management processes, procurement, and development.
2. Assess the knowledge and capability of existing IT functions and staff in terms of controls and processes for configuration, change, and release management processes.
3. Document and understand information process flows between configuration, release, and change management processes as well as the CMDB. Document and follow up on any potential internal control gaps.
4. Review extent and complexity of existing configuration data held in hardcopy form, in local spreadsheets, or in configuration management databases (CMDB), and develop an understanding of that database and its retrieval tools.
5. Determine the extent of any auto-discovery tools in place, as part of the CMDB tools, and assess adequacy of supporting procedures and documentation.
6. Using the CMDB reporting tool, define the inventory of configuration items (CIs) for one system and physically trace reported CIs to actual configuration components.
7. Determine processes are in place to link configuration management business processes and procedures with the CMDB tools
8. Test the CMDB and other support tool(s) to determine that key components, software, and documentation have been implemented and controlled on the CMDB.
9. Review adequacy of facilities to provide secure storage areas to manage CIs (e.g., cabinets, controlled libraries, and directories).
10. Assess adequacy of processes to communicate and train staff in the importance and use of configuration management.
11. Review problem management processes to determine the extent and appropriateness of their use of the CMDB for resolving problems.
12. Determine that appropriate access and update controls are in place to prevent unauthorized or inappropriate use of the CMDB.
13. Determine that the CMDB receives adequate security controls and backups, and that it is part of the continuity plan key resources backup and recovery procedures.

EXHIBIT 8.12 IT Configuration Management Audit Procedures

Source: Brink's Modern Internal Auditing, Sixth Edition, Robert Moeller, page 565. Copyright © 2005 John Wiley & Sons. Reprinted with permission of John Wiley & Sons, Inc.

services. The goal of the ITIL *change management* process is to utilize standardized methods and procedures for the efficient and prompt handling of all changes in order to minimize their impact on service quality and the day-to-day enterprise operations. A broad range of components should come under the change management process, including:

- IT hardware and system software
- Communications equipment and software
- All applications software
- All documentation and procedures associated with the running, support, and maintenance of live systems

The last point above is important both for maintaining SOx Section 404 documentation and for internal auditors. Chapter 10 discussed the importance of keeping internal control documentation current, but all too often IT hardware and software is upgraded or revised with little concern given to changing the supporting documentation. Changes to any IT components—for example, applications software, documentation or procedures—should be subject to a formal change management process.

Internal auditors often encounter IT functions where change management processes are haphazard at best. Examples are changes to applications without thinking through their implications for the overall IT infrastructure, incident management fixes that create other changes, or senior management requests for changes to solve short-term or immediate problems. A formal change management process that reviews and approves any proposed changes will almost always improve IT and enterprise internal control processes. The change management process should be tightly linked to configuration management, discussed previously, for ensuring that information regarding the possible implications of a proposed change is made available, and any possible impacts are detected and presented appropriately. Exhibit 8.13 shows change management typical activities, starting with receipt of RFC documentation through building and testing and ending with evaluation and closure.

Change management processes should have high visibility and open channels of communication in order to promote smooth transitions when changes take place. To improve this process, many IT functions have instituted a formal Change Advisory Board (CAB), made up of people from both IT and other functions within the enterprise, to review and approve changes. A CAB is a body that exists to approve changes and to assist in the assessment and prioritization of changes. It should be given the responsibility of ensuring that all changes are adequately assessed from both a business and a technical perspective. To achieve this mix, the CAB

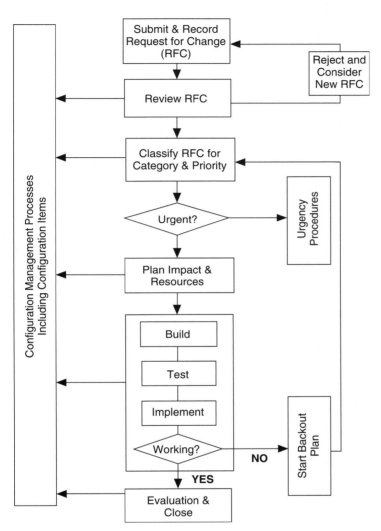

EXHIBIT 8.13 Change Management Activities

should consist of a team with a clear understanding of the customer business needs as well as the technical development and support functions. Chaired by a responsible enterprise manager, the CAB membership should include IT customers, applications developers, various experts/technical consultants as appropriate, and any contractor or third-party's representatives in an outsourcing situation.

The CAB should meet on a regular basis to review and schedule proposed changes. However, such a function should not act as an impediment to IT operations but should exist to provide an orderly scheduling and introduction of all types of IT infrastructure changes. When major problems arise, there may not be time to convene the full CAB, and there should be several responsible people with the authority to make emergency decisions.

Efficient overall service management processes require a capability to change things in an orderly way without making errors and taking wrong decisions. An effective change management process is indispensable for an effective IT infrastructure. When reviewing IT internal controls, internal auditors should look for well-controlled change management processes. The benefits of good change management include:

- Better alignment of IT services to business requirements
- Increased visibility and communication of changes to both business and service-support staff
- Improved risk assessments
- Reduced adverse impact of changes on the quality of services
- Better assessments of the costs of proposed changes before they are incurred
- Fewer changes that have to be backed-out, along with an increased ability to do this more easily when necessary
- Increased productivity of IT customers through less disruption and higher-quality services
- Greater ability of IT to absorb a large volume of changes

An effective change management process is an important component of IT infrastructure controls. The process must align tightly with other key processes in the IT infrastructure: change, configuration, capacity, and release management.

Service Support Release Management

IT customers and the IT function itself need effective processes to ensure that changes are introduced to all impacted parties in an orderly and well-controlled manner. The *release management* process covers the introduction of authorized changes to an IT service. A *release* will typically consist of a number of problem fixes and enhancements to the service, including new or changed software and hardware needed to implement the required approved changes. Releases follow one of three formats or levels:

1. **Full release.** All components in the release unit are built, tested, distributed, and implemented together. This eliminates the danger that obsolete versions of CIs (discussed in configuration management, above) will be incorrectly assumed to be unchanged and used within the release. With a full release, all components supporting some application area or system should be released as a single component.

   With all new and existing components bundled together, any problems are more likely to be detected and rectified before entry into the live environment. The disadvantage is that the amount of time, effort, and computing resources needed to build, test, distribute, and implement the full release will increase. Although in some circumstances the testing of a delta release, as discussed below, may need to be as extensive as that for an equivalent full release, the amount of building effort required to test a delta release is normally far less than for a full release.

   An example of a full release would be a new version of a major component of an enterprise resource planning (ERP) software package. The full release concept is applicable to both software and hardware, although the full release of IT hardware is normally limited to major components and not the total system. A full release is often difficult because it is easy to miss a systems interface when rolling out the new system. Strong configuration management processes are vital!

2. **Delta release.** A delta, or partial, release is one that includes only those CIs that have changed or are new since the last full or delta release. For example, if the release unit is the enterprise's set of manufacturing control systems, a delta release would contain only those modules that have changed, or are new, since the last full or delta release of the program of the modules. There may be occasions when release of a full unit cannot be justified, and in such cases, a delta release may be more appropriate. A decision should be made on the circumstances allowing delta releases. There is no single correct choice, and a decision to do a delta release should be taken case by case with the CAB making the recommendation. Items for considering whether to launch a full or delta release include the size of the release, its urgency, and the resources that are available for building, testing, distributing, and implementing the release.

3. **Package-level releases.** A package can contain an initial version of a new service, several new versions of batch programs, and a number of new and initial versions of individual modules, together with the release of a complete new desktop system (both hardware and software). Package releases can reduce the likelihood of old or incompatible software being wrongly kept in use and can help to ensure that all changes will be made concurrently.

There are normally dependencies between a particular version of software and the hardware required for it to operate. This will drive the packaging of software and hardware together to form a new release of the service, along with any related functional requirements. For example, a new version of an application software system may require an upgrade to the operating system, or some other hardware change may require a fix to some application. Changes of this sort should be bundled with other changes that could require a hardware change, such as a faster processor or more memory. The release management process is concerned with changes to define IT services. These can be implemented by rolling out a combination of the new applications software together with upgraded or new hardware, or simply changes to service support hours.

The controls and procedures surrounding new hardware and software releases can have a major impact on the overall IT infrastructure control environment. Strong processes should be in place to build the configuration per established requirements, to test it, and then to obtain user acceptance. Exhibit 8.14 summarizes key release management activities as a CI moves from development through testing to its distribution and installation. IT organizations are often relatively good at building and launching new applications through their use of systems development life cycle (SDLC) processes, but controls can break down when introducing other infrastructure releases. Strong processes and controls, following ITIL best practices, are essential, and internal auditors should consider this overall area as a component of their reviews in this area.

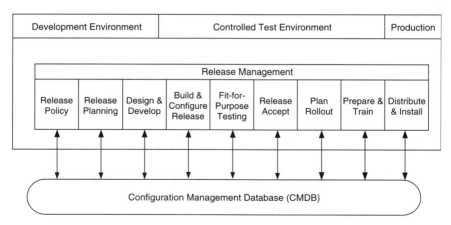

EXHIBIT 8.14 Release Management Activities

SECURITY MANAGEMENT

Security management is the set of best practices that influence and impact many other ITIL best practices. Exhibit 8.2 shows the security management process as overlaying elements of service support, service delivery, and application and IT infrastructure management processes. This is vital: The modern business can no longer operate without the supply of IT systems and information, but those resources need to be protected through confidentiality, integrity, and availability security-related processes. While IT professionals, internal auditors, and others often think of security in terms of access to an application or physical facility, ITIL security management focuses on appropriate arrangements though other ITIL processes.

SLAs, discussed previously and illustrated in Exhibit 8.4, are a key element to effective ITIL security processes within the IT infrastructure. End users or customers for IT services should be expected to define their security requirements through an SLA. It is then the responsibility of the IT service provider to implement, maintain, and control these security processes as illustrated in Exhibit 8.15. The concept can easily break down, however, if the customer does not understand security-related risks or even enterprise-wide security policies. As should be understood by the effective internal auditor, strong enterprise-wide security policies and standards are needed.

Beyond establishing security requirements through SLAs, security management should become the key issue in other ITIL processes including:

- **Configuration management.** Relevant security measures and procedures should be defined in the CMDB through specific configuration items. In addition, appropriate security controls, including backup and recovery procedures, should be established for the CMDB and its supporting software tools.
- **Incident management.** Processes should be in place to recognize and report on all security incidents. This should include security matters regarding specific SLAs or violations of overall standards.
- **Problem management.** This process should be responsible for identifying and solving structural security failings. In addition, care must be given that problem solutions or work-arounds do not introduce new security issues.
- **Change management.** This is often one of the most important ITIL security management–related processes as changes to the IT infrastructure can introduce new security measures and risks.
- **Release management.** The regular acceptance process to roll out new hardware, software, and communications infrastructure elements

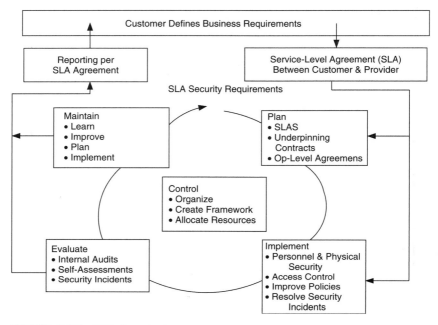

EXHIBIT 8.15 ITIL Security Management Process

should include testing and acceptance criteria to ensure compliance with security management processes.

- **Service level management.** As discussed, security requirements at a customer level should be defined through SLAs.
- **Availability management.** These processes address the technical service availability of IT components. Many security measures, such as continuity management, require the availability of IT components.
- **Capacity management.** Security is important here as this process can impact service level management.
- **Continuity management.** Security management processes are essential to almost all aspects of continuity management. Continuity processes and components must be managed and protected in a secure manner.

There are many security-related risks and concerns in the IT infrastructure. Adequate security processes are essential to ITIL, and the emphasis here is that good security processes should be built into and should overlap other ITIL best practices. There are numerous standards, frameworks, and certifications covering IT security, but the ISO 17799 international security-related standard is a good starting point. This international standard is introduced and discussed in Chapter 10.

LINKING ITIL WITH COBIT AND SOx INTERNAL CONTROLS

The major strength and feature of ITIL best practice processes is that they provide a link between the business users of IT services and the IT infrastructure. Exhibit 8.2 showed this environment with the IT infrastructure and its applications providing links with ITIL best practices. These ITIL best practices have been around since the 1980s, when the *L* in *ITIL* really stood for a published *library book* and the IT infrastructure was far simpler than it is today. ITIL has grown and has become much more process-oriented in its current version 3 when compared with its earlier incarnations. It has become the defacto standard for service management, although its origins date back to well before SOx.

CobiT, discussed in Chapter 5, has similar origins that also go back to well before SOx. Its origins trace to a day when IT-oriented internal auditors needed some control objective approaches for reviewing IT general and application controls. Starting out as a set of fairly specific and detailed control objectives, CobiT now is a series of some 30+ high-level IT governance objectives to help enterprises implement controls. Many CobiT control objectives are very closely aligned with ITIL. For example, CobiT AI16, Manage Changes, has nearly the same objectives as ITIL change management or CobiT DS9, Manage the Configuration, and has a similar theme as ITIL configuration management. The main difference is that in ITIL the emphasis is on efficient and effective processes. CobiT's focus is more on audit and control.

Given its audit and control emphasis, CobiT maps very closely to SOx Section 404 internal control requirements. Some of CobiT's control objectives are focused more on general operational internal controls, such as PO7, Manage Human Resources, while others are more IT application and infrastructure oriented. Given CobiT's breadth, these control objectives can be used to define, document, and evaluate Section 404 internal controls. With AS5, this link is even stronger.

All three of these framework processes—ITIL, CobiT, and SOx—have objectives to improve and strengthen internal controls in an enterprise. While their components are not one-to-one matches, each can assist in the overall evaluation of enterprise internal controls. While previous chapters have discussed SOx under AS5 as well as CobiT, this chapter has introduced ITIL service management best practices. By establishing best practices that have an emphasis on strong internal controls, the implementation of strong ITIL best practices can help an enterprise to achieve SOx Section 404 compliance. Based on our introduction here, internal auditors should learn more about ITIL best practices!

ENDNOTE

1. "An Introductory Overview of ITIL," IT Service Management Forum, www .itsmf.com.

CHAPTER 9

Importance of Enterprise Risk Management

R*isk* is a frequently used term found in internal control standards and procedures. The Committee of Sponsoring Organizations' (COSO's) internal control framework, discussed in Chapter 4, stressed the importance of understanding and recognizing risks when building and assessing internal controls; many other topics in this book, such as Chapter 5 on CobiT or Chapter 8 on ITIL, discuss the importance of considering risks in today's Sarbanes-Oxley (SOx) internal control environment. However, *risk* has too often in the past been one of those terms where many professionals have said, "Yes, we must consider risks!" even though their understandings and assessments of risk have not been that consistently well defined. One professional's concept and understanding of risk may be very different from someone else's, even though they are both working for the same enterprise and in similar areas. Among professionals working to improve SOx-related compliance, there has not been a consistent understanding of the concept of risk.

As our use and understanding of SOx rules and compliance matures, internal auditors and professionals need to have a better understanding of risk and how it impacts their processes and procedures for building and developing effective internal controls. Chapter 3 on AS5 introduced the newer risk-based considerations that are now part of this public corporation auditing standard. As discussed in that chapter, when the Public Company Accounting Oversight Board (PCAOB) first released its previous AS2 auditing standards, it placed a detailed and lengthy set of requirements on enterprises and on the external auditors reviewing and attesting to those internal accounting controls. This was somewhat of a reaction to those pre-SOx days when public accounting auditing standards allowed external auditors to ignore many errors and internal control problems by arguing that they were "not material." That is, if the error or problem would not impact earnings by more than some arbitrary measure, the external auditors frequently would only note it with little additional follow-up and move on with their financial attest audits. In the eyes of many prior to SOx, external auditors too often ignored major, potentially high-risk problems by using this not-material argument.

SOx and the PCAOB quickly changed things. Their initial AS2 guidance was that every error or exception found should be considered as a potential internal control weakness, and the very detailed AS2 public accounting auditing standards reflected this. The remaining major public accounting firms adopted these new rules with fervor, and in the first years after SOx became effective, many audit committees were asked to develop corrective action plans on internal control findings that just did not seem very significant to senior management. This early PCAOB guidance tended to look at things from the perspective that an error is an error—whether $1 or $1,000,000. After a massive amount of furor and public comments regarding the values and costs of SOx compliance due to these detailed nitpicking rules and audit findings, the PCAOB has released its risk-based AS5 auditing standards, as discussed in Chapter 3.

A major concept behind AS5 is that management and their external auditors should consider relative risks when implementing and assessing internal controls to achieve compliance with the SOx Section 404 internal control rules. In order to use these new AS5 auditing standards effectively, all parties should understand the risks surrounding their enterprise and be able to document and attest to when they did or did not raise an internal control exception issue, based on relative risks. This chapter will look at some basic risk-based approaches and considerations to help management and internal auditors perform more effective SOx-oriented audit procedures.

An ongoing problem in our use and understanding of the risk concept has been the lack of a consistent and accurate definition of *risk*. While the word has some origins in the insurance industry, *risk* has not been used consistently throughout the insurance industry, let alone by management, auditors, and business professionals. Many have talked about how they had "considered risk" when implementing a control or process, but there have been no consistent definitions here. The question of *what steps were followed* in such a risk consideration often produced a wide range of answers.

This all changed when COSO released its *enterprise risk methodology*, the COSO Enterprise Risk Management Integrated Format standards (COSO ERM).[1] This is a framework or approach to enable an enterprise to consider and assess its risks at all levels, whether in an individual area such as an information technology (IT) development project, or covering global risks regarding an international expansion. Released by the same COSO guidance-setting function that has developed and maintains the COSO internal control framework, COSO ERM sometimes looks like its internal control "brother," but it has a much different feel and approach.

This chapter will introduce the COSO ERM framework and its elements, but the emphasis will be on why COSO ERM can be an important tool to better design and evaluate the risks surrounding SOx-based internal controls at all levels. The chapter will describe major elements of the COSO ERM framework for building and installing effective SOx internal controls. We will also look at how internal audit functions, in particular, can better build COSO ERM principles into their audit processes as well as steps for auditing the effectiveness of an enterprise's risk management processes. Although the basic framework models are similar, COSO ERM is different from the COSO internal control framework discussed in Chapter 4.

IMPORTANCE OF RISK MANAGEMENT

Every enterprise, whether for-profit commercial, not-for-profit, or a governmental agency, exists to provide value for its stakeholders; these include the employees and stockholders for a commercial enterprise or voters for a governmental entity. That stakeholder value is created, preserved, or can be eroded through management decisions at all levels of the enterprise and in all activities, ranging from day-to-day regular operations to setting strategy for some future but uncertain endeavor. All of these activities are subject to uncertainties or risks. Whether it is the challenge caused by a new and aggressive competitor or the damage and even loss of life caused by a major weather disturbance, all face a wide range of risks. While it is essentially impossible to estimate the probability of a major weather event or a building fire, individuals and enterprises usually take some steps to shield themselves from these risks, such as by purchasing insurance, and to effectively accept other risks. This is frequently called a *risk versus risk-adjusted return trade-off process*, where we balance, for example, the cost of purchasing flood insurance for a home with the potential of incurring a flood. If a home is on high ground with no nearby waterways, we may decide there is not much risk of a flood. It then might not make sense to purchase flood insurance.

Enterprises generally have two problems with balancing the amount of risk they are willing to accept against the potential and adjusted returns or costs from accepting those risks. First, there has not been a good and consistently accepted definition of risk across overall enterprises, and second, we often do not think of risks in a total enterprise sense but only component by component. For example, we think of risks in terms of perhaps a security breach within an individual business unit or computer operation, but often do not think of the impact of those risks to the overall enterprise. This concern was emphasized by the comments of John Flaherty, the first and now past chairman of COSO: "Although a lot of people are talking about risk, there is no commonly accepted definition of *risk management* and no comprehensive framework outlining how the process should work, making risk communication among board members and management difficult and frustrating.[2]" These same types of concerns occurred in the early 1980s, when many professionals looked at the lack of a common definition and understanding of internal control. The result then was the COSO internal control framework.

A second risk-versus-return problem is that we often take a silo approach in our assessments of risks rather than considering them in terms of the total enterprise. *Silo approach* refers to the tall and narrow agricultural storage containers used on farms. Everything within a silo is secure and protected, but there is no interaction between one silo and another nearby. While this might be appropriate where each individual silo is used to store a separate commodity with no need for interaction, separate business or enterprise processes each stored in their own silos often need connections and interactions with other processes that may exist in other such silos. An enterprise may have a good risk management process for credit operations housed in the silo covering that area of operations as well as a good risk assessment process in the silo covering IT continuity planning, but there is often a need for these two processes to communicate and use some common approaches. Risks should be considered on a total enterprise level.

COSO ERM is framework that will help enterprises have a consistent definition of risk and to consider their risks across the entire enterprise in a consistent manner. It also is an important tool for understanding and improving SOx internal controls. COSO ERM was launched in manner similar to the development of the COSO internal control framework, as discussed in Chapter 4. An advisory council of members from the sponsoring enterprises was formed and PricewaterhouseCoopers (PwC) was contracted to develop and draft this risk framework description. A draft version of the ERM framework was released for comment in mid-2003 with the final version published after the SOx rules in September 2004. The remainder of this chapter summarizes COSO ERM in some detail.[3]

Just as the COSO internal control framework started by proposing a consistent definition of its subject, COSO ERM starts by defining enterprise risk management as follows:

> *Enterprise risk management is a process, effected by an entity's board of directors, management and other personnel, applied in a strategy setting and across the enterprise, designed to identify*

potential events that may affect the entity, and manage risk to be within its risk appetite, to provide reasonable assurance regarding the achievement of entity objectives.

Given this rather academic-sounding definition, professionals should consider the key points supporting this description of the COSO ERM framework, which include:

- **ERM is a process.** An often misused expression, the dictionary definition of *process* is a *set of actions designed to achieve a result.* However, this definition does not provide much help for many professionals. The idea is that a process is not a static procedure such as the use of an employee badge designed and built to allow only certain authorized persons to enter a locked facility. Such a badge procedure—like the key to a lock—only allows or does not allow someone entry to the facility. A process tends to be a more flexible arrangement. In a credit approval process, for example, acceptance rules are established with options to alter them given other considerations. An enterprise might bend the credit rules for an otherwise good credit customer that is experiencing a short-term problem. ERM is that type of a process. An enterprise often cannot define its risk management rules through a small, tightly organized rulebook. Rather there should be a series of documented steps to review and evaluate potential risks and to take action based on a wide range of factors across the entire enterprise.
- **The ERM process is implemented by people in the enterprise.** ERM will not be effective if it is only implemented through a set of rules sent into an operating unit from a distant corporate headquarters, where those corporate people who drafted the rules may have little understanding of the various decision factors surrounding them. The risk management process must be managed by people who are close enough to the risk situation to understand the various factors surrounding that risk, including its implications.
- **ERM is applied through the setting of strategies across the overall enterprise.** Every enterprise is constantly faced with alternative strategies regarding a vast range of potential future actions. Should the entity acquire another complementary business or just build internally? Should it adopt a new technology in its manufacturing processes or stick with the tried and true? An effective ERM set of processes should play a major role in helping to establish those alternative strategies. Since many enterprises are large with varied operating units, ERM should be applied across the entire enterprise using a portfolio type of approach that blends in a mix of high- and low-risk activities.

■ **The concept of risk appetite must be considered.** A new concept or term for many internal auditors, risk appetite is the amount of risk, on a broad level, that an enterprise and its individual managers are willing to accept in their pursuit of value. Risk appetite can be measured in a qualitative sense by looking at risks in such categories as high, medium, or low; alternatively, it can be defined in a qualitative manner. An understanding of risk appetite covers a wide variety of issues that will be discussed further in this chapter as part of implementing COSO ERM to strengthen an enterprise's SOx internal control environment. The basic idea is that every manager and, collectively, every enterprise has some level of appetite for risk. Some will accept a risky venture that promises high returns while others prefer more guaranteed-return low-risk ventures. One can think of this appetite-for-risk concept in terms of two investors. One may prefer very low-risk but typically low-return money market or index funds while another may invest in low-cap startup technology stocks. This latter investor can be described as having a high appetite for risk. As another example, on a street intersection with WALK or DON'T WALK crossing lights, the person who keeps crossing the intersection well after the light has begun to flash WALK, meaning it will soon change to DON'T, has a higher appetite for risk.

■ **ERM provides only reasonable, not positive, assurance on objective achievements.** The idea here is that an ERM process, no matter how well thought out or implemented, cannot provide management or others with any assured guarantee of outcomes. A well-controlled enterprise, with people at all levels consistently working toward understood and achievable goals, may achieve those objectives period after period—even over multiple years. However, an unintentional human error, an unexpected action by another, or even a natural disaster can occur. Despite an effective ERM process, an enterprise can experience a major and totally unexpected catastrophic event. Reasonable assurance does not provide absolute assurance.

■ **An ERM process is designed to help attain the achievement of objectives.** An enterprise, through its management, should work to establish high-level common objectives that can be shared by all stakeholders. Examples here, as cited in COSO ERM materials, include such matters as achieving and maintaining a positive reputation within an enterprise's business and consumer communities, providing reliable financial reporting to all stakeholders, and operating in compliance with laws and regulations. The overall ERM program for an enterprise should help it to achieve those objectives.

ERM-related goals and objectives are of little value unless they can be organized and modeled together in a manner where management can look at the various aspects of the task and understand (at least sort of) how they interact and relate in a multidimensional manner. This is the real strength of the COSO internal control framework model! It describes, for example, how an enterprise's compliance with laws and regulations impacts all levels of internal controls, from monitoring processes to the control environment, and how that compliance is important for all entities or units of the enterprise. The COSO ERM framework provides some common definitions of risk management and can help achieve SOx internal control objectives as well as better risk management processes throughout the enterprise.

COSO ERM FRAMEWORK

The COSO internal control framework, shown in Exhibit 4.2, has become a worldwide model for describing and defining internal controls, and has been the basis for establishing SOx Section 404 compliance. Perhaps because some of the same team members were involved with both COSO internal controls and ERM, the COSO ERM framework—at first observation—looks very similar to the COSO internal control framework. This COSO ERM framework is shown in Exhibit 9.1 as a three-dimensional cube with the components of:

- Four vertical columns representing the strategic objectives of enterprise risk.
- Eight horizontal rows or risk components.
- Multiple levels to describe any enterprise, from a "headquarters" entity level down to individual subsidiaries. Depending on organization size, there can be many "slices" of the model here.

This section will describe the horizontal components of COSO ERM, while later chapter sections will discuss its other two dimensions and how they all relate to one another. The concept behind the ERM framework is to provide a model for enterprises to consider and understand their risk-related activities at all levels as well as how these risk components impact one another. An objective of this chapter is to help professionals at all levels— from board members to staff auditors—to better understand COSO ERM and how it can help manage the SOx-related risks facing their enterprises.

The COSO ERM framework diagram looks very similar to the COSO internal control framework that has become familiar to many professionals over recent years and certainly after SOx. Some initially and incorrectly viewed COSO ERM as just a new update to their familiar COSO internal

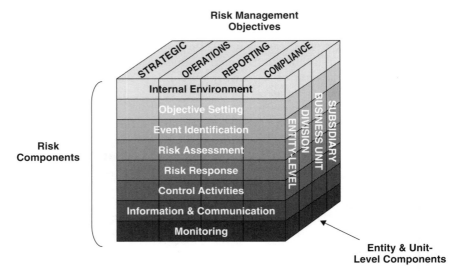

Risk Management Objectives

STRATEGIC OPERATIONS REPORTING COMPLIANCE

Internal Environment
Objective Setting
Event Identification
Risk Assessment
Risk Response
Control Activities
Information & Communication
Monitoring

ENTITY-LEVEL
DIVISION
BUSINESS UNIT
SUBSIDIARY

Risk Components

Entity & Unit-Level Components

EXHIBIT 9.1 COSO ERM Framework

Source: COSO Enterprise Risk Management: Understanding the New Integrated ERM Framework, Robert R. Moeller, page 53. Copyright © 2007 John Wiley & Sons. Reprinted with permission of John Wiley & Sons, Inc.

control framework. However, COSO ERM has different objectives and uses! *COSO ERM should not be considered just a new and improved or revised version of the COSO internal control framework!* It is much more. The following sections will outline this framework from a risk components perspective and with a focus on how ERM can improve SOx internal control processes.

COSO ERM Components

Internal Environment Looking at the front or face of this COSO ERM cube, there are eight levels or factors. The first, *internal environment*, is located at the top of the COSO ERM framework components. This is in contrast to the control environment factor placed at the foundation level for the COSO internal control framework. Here, one should similarly think of the ERM control environment as the basis for all other enterprise management components. The internal environment may be thought of as the capstone to the COSO ERM framework. Going back to the ancient era of bridges constructed of bricks, the capstone held the brick arches rising from each side of a span to hold the overall bridge together. This capstone component is also similar to the box at the top of an organization chart that lists the chief executive officer (CEO) as the designated head of a function. This level defines the basis for all other components in an enterprise's ERM model, influencing how strategies and objectives should be established, how risk-related business activities are structured, and how risks are identified and acted upon. While the control environment for COSO internal controls focused on current practices in place, such as human resources polices and procedures, ERM looks at them in a more future-philosophy-oriented approach. The ERM internal environment component consists of the following elements:

- **Risk management philosophy.** This is a set of shared attitudes and beliefs that tend to characterize how the enterprise considers risk in everything it does. More than the CEO letter type of message published with a code of conduct, a risk management philosophy is the kind of attitude that will allow stakeholders at all levels to respond to some high-risk proposal with an answer along the lines of, "No that's not the kind of venture our company will be interested in." Of course, an enterprise with a different philosophy might respond to this same proposal with an answer along the lines of, "Sounds interesting; what's the expected rate of return?" Neither response is really wrong, but an enterprise should try to develop a consistent philosophy and attitude to how it accepts risky ventures. This risk philosophy is particularly important when evaluating SOx internal controls following AS5.

- **Risk appetite.** As discussed, risk appetite is the amount of risk an enterprise is willing to accept in the pursuit of its objectives. This appetite for risk can be measured in either quantitative or qualitative terms, but all levels of management should have a general understanding of this concept as well as the enterprise's overall risk appetite. As mentioned, the word *appetite* had not been often used by internal auditors and other managers prior to COSO ERM, but it is a useful expression that describes an overall philosophy.

- **Board of directors' attitudes.** The board and its committees have a very important role in overseeing and guiding an enterprise's risk environment. The independent, outside directors in particular should closely review management actions, ask appropriate questions, and serve as a check-and-balance control for the enterprise. When a senior enterprise officer has an "it can't happen here" attitude regarding the consideration of possible risks at various levels, members of the board should ask the hard questions about how the enterprise would react if one of those can't-happen events that actually does happen.

- **Integrity and ethical values.** This important ERM internal environment element requires much more than a published code of conduct and also should include a well-thought-out mission statement and integrity standards. These materials help to build a strong corporate culture to guide the enterprise, at all levels, in helping to make risk-based and SOx-compliance decisions. A strong corporate culture, as well as a written code of conduct, is an important element of an enterprise's integrity and ethical values. Stronger positions here might have helped some enterprises to better avoid the accounting scandals in past years that led to the situations at Enron, WorldCom, and others prior to the enactment of SOx. This area should be an essential component in every ERM framework.

- **Commitment to competence.** *Competence* refers to the knowledge and skills necessary to perform assigned tasks. Management decides how these critical tasks will be accomplished through developing appropriate strategies and assigning the proper people to perform them. We have all seen enterprises that do not have this type of commitment. Senior management sometimes makes grand and loud plans to accomplish some goal but then does little to achieve it. The stock market frequently punishes such activities, but with a strong commitment to competence, managers at all levels should take steps to achieve their promised goals.

- **Organization structure.** While an enterprise will develop an organization structure that meets its current needs, that same organizational structure should have clear lines of authority, responsibility, and appropriate lines of reporting. A poorly constructed organization structure makes it difficult to plan, execute, control, and monitor activities. Every professional has seen situations where the organization chart does not allow for appropriate lines of communication. For example, prior to SOx, many internal audit groups had published organization charts showing them reporting to their board of directors' audit committees, but only on paper and with limited day-to-day communications beyond periodic but very brief audit committee meetings. While SOx has changed this, those past environments where the audit committee had only very limited communications with its internal audit function represented a failure in organizational structure. While this situation has been corrected, there will always be many situations where an organization structure needs improvement to achieve effective ERM.

- **Assignments of authority and responsibility.** This ERM component refers to the extent or degree to which authority and responsibility is assigned or delegated. The trend in many enterprises today is to push such matters as approval authority responsibilities down the organization chart, giving lower-level and even first-line employees greater authorization and approval authority. A related trend has been to "flatten" organizations by eliminating middle-management levels.

The benefits from these structures usually include better employee creativity, faster response times, and greater customer satisfaction. This type of customer-facing organization requires strong procedures that outline the rules for all members of the staff, as well as ongoing management monitoring of these actions so that lower-level staff decisions can be overruled if necessary. All individuals should know how their actions interrelate and contribute to the overall objectives of the enterprise. A strong code of conduct is a critical element here. It should be communicated throughout the enterprise with a formal requirement that all stakeholders acknowledge that they have read, understand, and agree to comply with the code.

- **Human resources standards.** Practices in employee hiring, training, compensating, promoting, disciplining, and all other actions send messages to all regarding what is favored, tolerated, or forbidden. When management winks at or ignores some gray-area activities rather than taking a strong stand, that message is often informally but quickly communicated to others. Strong standards are needed so that human resources rules are both communicated to all stakeholders and enforced.

The previously referenced COSO ERM guidance material has other examples of the components necessary to build an effective internal environment. While many refer to the standards and approaches an enterprise should implement to accept and manage various levels of risk, others refer to just good business practices. No matter whether an enterprise has a high or low appetite for risk, it needs to establish control environment practices to manage those risks. For example, the enterprise can give its sales force a rather free rein to do deals without much management supervision and approval. Yet, everyone should know the legal, ethical, and management policy limits of those free-rein practices. Processes should be in place such that if anyone steps over the line regarding the limits of any of those practices, remedial actions are communicated to all who should know and will be swiftly administered. There are many methods for an enterprise to communicate its risk management standards, but a formal statement in the annual report or information on the enterprise's Web home page are often good places. A Web search today for such risk statements will bring many examples, although most are for insurance- and finance-related enterprises. ERM practices have not yet expanded to a broad group of enterprises.

These two internal environment components of COSO ERM, the enterprise's risk management philosophy and its relative appetite for risk, feed other elements of the COSO ERM framework. While risk management philosophy was discussed in terms of board of directors' attitudes and human resources policies, among others, risk appetite is often a softer measure

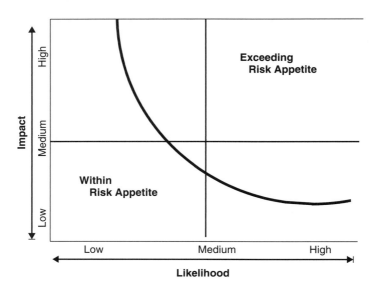

EXHIBIT 9.2 Risk Appetite Map
Source: COSO Enterprise Risk Management: Understanding the New Integrated ERM Framework, Robert R. Moeller, page 61. Copyright © 2007 John Wiley & Sons. Reprinted with permission of John Wiley & Sons, Inc.

where an enterprise has determined that it will accept some risks but reject others in terms of their likelihood and impact. Exhibit 9.2 shows a *risk appetite map* illustrating where an enterprise should recognize the range in which it is willing to accept risks in terms of their likelihood and impact. This map diagram says that an enterprise may be willing to get involved in a high-negative-impact project if there is a low likelihood of an occurrence. There is a third dimension to this chart as well. An enterprise will sometimes have a greater appetite for a more risky endeavor if there is a higher potential return.

Objective Setting Ranked right below the internal environment component in the COSO ERM framework, the *objective setting* component outlines important conditions that must be established before management can create an effective ERM process. In addition to the internal environment outlined above, an enterprise must establish a series of strategic objectives, aligned with its mission or vision, covering operations, reporting and compliance activities.

A *mission statement* often is a crucial element in helping to set objectives; it creates a general, formalized statement of purpose and is a building block for both an overall strategy and the development of more specific functional strategies. Often just a simple, straightforward statement, a mission statement summarizes an enterprise's objectives and its overall attitude toward risks. Properly done, a mission statement should encourage an enterprise to develop high-level strategic objectives to achieve the stated mission objectives and then to select, develop, and implement a series of operations, reporting, and compliance objectives. From the mission statement to strategic objectives, a next step is to develop a series of operational, reporting, and compliance objectives. While *operations* objectives pertain to the effectiveness and efficiency of the enterprise in its goals of achieving profitability and performance, the *reporting* and *compliance* goals cover how the enterprise will report its performance and comply with laws and regulations. COSO ERM also suggests that an enterprise should formally define its goals with a direct linkage to its mission statement, along with measurement criteria to assess whether it is achieving these risk management objectives and it's mission.

The internal environment components of understanding the enterprise's risk management philosophy and recognition of risk appetite call for the objective setting component to more formally define its risk appetite in terms of a tolerance for risk. *Tolerances* are formal guidelines or measures that an enterprise should use—at all levels—to assess whether it will accept risks. Establishing and enforcing risk tolerances can be very difficult, and there often will be problems if these rules are not clearly defined, well understood, and strictly enforced. A good approach is to establish some acceptable form of risk tolerance with a tolerable range of acceptable risks. For example, all products coming off of production lines might have acceptable preestablished error rates of less than some error rate value. An enterprise's production line, for example, may seek to produce goods at an error rate no greater than 0.005%. That is an acceptably low error rate in many areas, and production management here would accept the risk of any product warranty claims or damage to their reputation if there were errors beyond that relatively narrow limit. Of course, today's quality assurance emphasis on Six Sigma programs brings those tolerance limits infinitesimally tighter.[4]

The point here is that an enterprise should define its risk-related strategies and objectives. Within those guidelines, it should decide on its appetite and tolerances for these risks. That is, it should determine the level of risks it is willing to accept, and given those risk tolerance rules, decide how far it is willing to deviate from these preestablished measures. Exhibit 9.3 outlines the relationship of these portions of the objective setting component of COSO ERM with a beginning proposed objective. Starting with an overall mission statement, the approach is to (1) develop strategic objectives to support accomplishment of that mission, (2) establish a strategy to meet

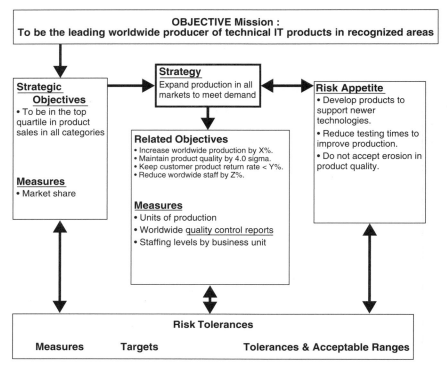

EXHIBIT 9.3   Objective Setting Relationships
Source: Adapted from *Enterprise Risk Management—Integrated Framework: Application Techniques* (New York: COSO, April 2004).

objectives, (3) define any related objectives, and (4) define risk appetites to complete that strategy. This chart was adapted from the previously referenced published COSO ERM guidance material, a good source to gain a more detailed understanding of COSO ERM. In order to manage and control risks at all levels, an enterprise needs to set its objectives and define its tolerances for having to engage in risky practices and for its adherence to these rules. Things will not work if the enterprise establishes risk-related objectives but then proceeds to ignore them.

Event Identification   *Events* are enterprise incidents or occurrences—external or external—that affect the implementation of the ERM strategy and the achievement of its objectives. While the tendency is to think of events in a negative sense—determining what went wrong—they can be positive, negative, or both. There is a strong level of performance monitoring taking place in many enterprises today, but that monitoring process tends to emphasize such matters as costs, budgets, quality assurance, compliance, and the like. The ERM risk objectives, discussed previously, can become lost in this process of monitoring more operational and process-oriented operational objectives. Enterprises usually have strong processes to monitor such events as favorable or particularly unfavorable budget variances, but often do not regularly monitor either the actual events or the influencing factors that are the drivers of such budget variance events.

The COSO ERM Executive Summary Framework documentation, previously referenced, lists the types of influencing factors that should be part of the framework's *event identification* component, including:

- **External economic events.** There is a wide range of external events that need to be monitored in order to help achieve an enterprise's ERM objectives. Ongoing short- and long-term trends may impact an enterprise's strategic objectives and its overall ERM framework. As an external economic event example, in December 2001, after some ongoing currency market turmoil, Argentina declared a major default of its public debt. This external event had a major impact on many different areas, including international credit markets, suppliers of agricultural commodities, and other business dealings in South America. External economic event identification here requires some function in the enterprise to go beyond reported news headlines and raise the flag to suggest that, yes, such a currency default may highlight an enterprise risk-related event.
- **Natural environmental events.** Whether fire, flood, or earthquakes, numerous events can become identified as incidents in ERM risk identification. Impacts here may include loss of access to some key raw material, damage to physical facilities, or unavailability of personnel.
- **Political events.** New laws and regulations as well as the results of elections can have significant risk event–related impacts on enterprises. Many larger enterprises have a *government affairs* function that reviews developments and lobbies for changes. However, such functions may not always be aligned with the enterprise's ERM objectives.
- **Social factors.** While an external event such as an earthquake is sudden and arrives with little warning, most social factors changes are slowly evolving events. These include demographic, social mores, and other event changes that may impact an enterprise and its customers over time. The growth of the Hispanic population in the United States is such an example. As more and more Hispanic people move to a city, for example, the teaching requirements in public schools and the mix of selections in grocery stores will change.

- **Internal infrastructure events.** Enterprises often make benign changes that trigger other risk-related events. For example, a change in customer service arrangements can cause major complaints and a drop in customer satisfaction in a retail unit. Strong customer demand for a new product may cause changes in plant capacity requirements and the need for additional personnel.
- **Internal process-related events.** Similar to infrastructure events, changes in key processes can trigger a wide range of risk identification events. As with many such items, risk identification may not be immediate, and some time may pass before the process-related events signal the need for risk identification.
- **External and internal technological events.** Every enterprise faces a wide assortment of technological events that may trigger the need for formal risk identification. Some may be gradual while others will be more sudden; for example, the Internet has been with us for some time and the shift to a Web environment continues to expand at almost exponential rates. A company might suddenly release a new improvement that causes competitors everywhere to jump into action. Although the idea seems very commonplace today, when Merrill Lynch launched their Cash Management Account (CMA) concept in the mid-1980s, they caused a major stir in the financial services industries. CMA was a service where the customer could have stock brokerage, bank checking accounts, and other financial services all under one roof. In the past, all such accounts were with separate providers with essentially no linkages between them.

An enterprise needs to clearly define what it considers are significant risk events and then have processes in place to monitor those various potentially significant risk events where IT can take appropriate actions. This is really a forward-thinking process that is often difficult to recognize in many enterprises, and the process of looking at these internal and external potential risk events to decide which events require further attention can be a difficult one. Some are immediate needs and others very future directed. The previously referenced COSO ERM *Application Techniques* volume offers some help here. It suggests that an enterprise establish some formal processes to review potentially significant risks and then begin the process of taking action. The COSO ERM guidance material suggests that enterprises consider some of the following approaches:

- **Event inventories.** Management should develop risk-related listings of events common to their enterprise's specific industry and functional area. That is to say, an enterprise should consider establishing some type of a *lessons-learned archive* source. This is the type of data that has historically been supplied by longer-tenure members of an enterprise who can offer "We tried this several years ago, but ..." types of comments.

- **Facilitated workshops.** An enterprise can establish cross-functional workshops to discuss potential risk factors that may evolve from various internal or external events. The result from these would be action plans to correct the potential risks. This type of approach sounds good, but it is often a challenge to allocate sufficient time to meet in cross-functional groups to talk about risks in a what-if format.

- **Interviews, questionnaires, and surveys.** Information regarding potential risk events can come from a wide variety of sources such as customer satisfaction letters or employee exit interview comments. This information should be captured and classified to identify anything that might point to a risk event.

- **Process flow analysis.** The referenced COSO ERM Application Techniques material recommends the use of flow diagrams to review processes and identify potential risk events. These flow diagrams are similar to the internal control documentation prepared as part of SOx Section 404 documentation discussed in Chapter 2. In the absence of COSO ERM, that Section 404 work does not focus on risk event identification, and this ERM analysis can conveniently be combined with the Section 404 work in future update periods.

- **Leading events and escalation triggers.** The idea here is to establish a series of business unit objectives, measurements necessary to meet those objectives, and risk tolerance criteria to promote remedial action. For example, an enterprise's IT group may establish an objective to maintain strong security controls over the risk of a system intrusion. With a measure of the number of identified intrusion attempts identified during a period, a signal of perhaps three intrusion incidents in a given month might trigger further action. Dashboard-type software tools can be used here. These increasingly common software tools operate similarly to the controls on an automobile dashboard, where indicators will flash signals for such conditions as low oil pressure or overheating. The idea is to report on risk status through some simple, easy-to-comprehend graphics monitor, such as red, yellow, and green warning lights.

- **Loss event data tracking.** While the dashboard approach just described monitors risk events as they happen, it is often valuable to put these things more in perspective after the passage of time. Loss event tracking refers to using both internal and public database sources to track activity in areas of interest. These sources can also cover a wide variety of areas ranging from leading economic indicators to internal equipment failure rates. Again, an enterprise should install effective risk identification processes to track both internal and external risk–related events.

The risk identification tools and approaches just discussed can yield some very valuable and useful information to an enterprise that identifies either risks, opportunities, or a combination of both. The key is the need for good analyses of the data as well as initiating plans for action, whether to shield from the risk or to take advantage of potential opportunities.

Risk Assessment   The internal environment component is the cap or cornerstone of the COSO ERM framework. A later section will discuss *monitoring* as a key foundations component to support the framework. *Risk assessment* is in the center of the framework and represents the core of COSO ERM. Risk assessment allows an enterprise to consider the extent to which potential risk-related events may impact an enterprise's achievement of its objectives. These risks should be assessed from two perspectives: the *likelihood* of the risk occurring and its *potential impact*. As a key part of this risk assessment process, management needs to consider both perspectives in terms of *inherent* and *residual* risks, key risk management concepts:

1. **Inherent risk.** Inherent risk are factors that are outside the control of management and usually stem from external factors. Major factors that affect inherent risk within an enterprise may be the size of its budget, strength and sophistication of management, and just the very nature of its activities. For example, the major retailer Wal-Mart is so large and dominant in its markets that it faces a series of inherent risks just due to its sheer size.
2. **Residual risk.** This is the risk that remains after management responses to risk threats and countermeasures have been applied. There will virtually be always some level of residual risk.

These joint concepts of inherent and residual risk imply that an enterprise will always face some risks. After management has addressed the risks that have come out of their risk identification process, they will usually still have some residual risks to remedy. Following this, there will be a variety of inherent risks where they can do little. Wal-Mart, for example, can take some steps to reduce its market dominance–related inherent risks, but can do essentially nothing regarding the inherent risk of a major natural earthquake.

Likelihood and impact are two other key components necessary for performing risk assessments. Likelihood is the probability or possibility that the risk will occur. In many instances, this can be a key management assessment stated in terms of high, medium, or low likelihood of the risk occurring. There are also some good quantitative tools to develop likelihood estimates, but it does little good to estimate the likelihood of a risk occurring unless there is strong supporting data.

Estimating the impact if a risk event occurs is a bit easier. Examples for IT-related risks include the impact of a data server and network center catastrophic loss or failure. An enterprise can develop some relatively accurate estimates such as the costs of replacing facilities and equipment, of restoring systems, and of lost business due to the failure. However, the whole concept behind ERM is not to develop precise, actuarial-level calculations regarding these risks but to gain some measure to provide for an effective risk management framework. Those detailed calculations can be delegated to insurance estimators and others.

An analysis of risk likelihoods and potential impacts can be developed through a series of qualitative and qualitative measures. Resources for more information are the previously referenced COSO ERM Application Techniques material or the Project Management Institute's (PMI's) special-interest group on risk.[5] These sources provide guidance on approaches to determine relative probabilities or other measures regarding risk likelihoods and potential impacts. The basic idea, however, is to assess all of the identified risks—as discussed in the previous section—and to rank them in terms of likelihood and impact in a consistent manner.

Without going through a detailed quantitative analysis, each identified risk can be ranked on an overall relative scale of 1 to 10, with consideration given to the impact and likelihood of each. This can be achieved through a focused management group decision process where each of the identified risks is reviewed and then ranked with respect to this scale. Exhibit 9.4 shows how a series of risks for an enterprise would be evaluated and then assigned relative values. The example shows three risk areas in what would be a much larger and comprehensive list for any enterprise. While scaled only with ordinal values of, 1 to 10 here, results can be plotted with greater granularity. The idea is to identify relative risks and assign some relative rankings. The idea behind this type of analysis and subsequent charting is to identify the upper-right-quadrant high-impact and high-likelihood risks for the enterprise. These are the risks that should receive the most thorough management attention.

The key to this overall process of identifying high-risk events with strong likelihoods and potential impacts is the need for an accurate and balanced review and assessment process. That can be difficult! The most powerful earthquake in recorded U.S. history occurred in the winter of 1811–12 in the central Mississippi Valley near St. Louis, in an area called the New Madrid fault. This earthquake changed the course of the Mississippi River

Risk Name	Risk Definition	Impact	Likelihood	Risk Ranking
1. Accounting risk	Failure to record sales activity accurately and timely may misstate financial reports.	**High:** Accounting errors may have a material impact on financial and operational information.	**Medium:** Despite strong procedures, newer personnel in various locations may make errors.	8
2. Legal risk	Failure to understand current and changing laws and regulations may result in inability to comply with laws in multiple operation jurisdictions.	**Medium:** Even small, technical violations of most regulations should not have a material effect on operations.	**High:** With worldwide operations in multiple jurisdictions, violations—if only technical—can occur.	7
3. Segregation of duties	Inadequately controlled segregation of duties may allow employees to process unauthorized, fraudulent transactions.	**High:** Fraudulent operations could have significant impacts on company operations.	**Low:** Ongoing internal audits and stronger management control practices should prevent such control breakdown events.	5

EXHIBIT 9.4 Risk Ranking Inventory Scoring Example
Source: COSO Enterprise Risk Management: Understanding the New Integrated ERM Framework, Robert R. Moeller, page 75. Copyright © 2007 John Wiley & Sons. Reprinted with permission of John Wiley & Sons, Inc.

with broken glass windows reported in Philadelphia and Washington, DC. That was nearly 200 years ago! If an enterprise has business operations in that part of the world today, should the likelihood and impact of another New Madrid fault event be factored into the analysis? We would argue perhaps not. Unless there were some risk event warnings of active seismic activity in that area, this is an inherent risk that exists but should not be part of the current risk analysis here.

The idea is that an enterprise should use the best data sources available but view risks with a level of perspective. That view of potential risks can be influenced by management overconfidence or pessimism. A team approach is needed, where the enterprise should look at all of these identified risks on a total basis and on a unit-by-unit level. Looking at risks across organizational units represents another dimension of the COSO ERM framework model that will be discussed in the following sections. An example risk here might involve the potential for unfavorable foreign currency fluctuations in several foreign operations, one with a fairly stable national economy and another with an unstable national government. However, the country with the least currency risk might be the operation with the greatest manufacturing plant product quality risk. An enterprise needs to balance these two conflicting national entity higher risks to determine the most effective plan of action.

Overall approaches to reviewing these various likelihood and impact risks need to be considered. As suggested, risk assessment is a key component of the COSO ERM framework. This is where an enterprise evaluates all of the various risks that might impact its various objectives, considers the potential likelihood and impact of each of these risks, considers their interrelationship on a unit-by-unit or total enterprise basis, and then develops strategies for appropriate responses. In some respects, this COSO ERM risk assessment process is not too different from the classic risk assessment techniques that have been used over the years. What is unique is that COSO ERM suggests that an enterprise should take a total approach, across all units and covering all major strategic concerns, to identify its risks in a consistent and thorough manner.

Risk Response Having assessed and identified the more significant risks, a next step is to determine how to respond to these various identified risks. This should be a management responsibility to perform a careful review of estimated risk likelihoods and potential impacts, and with consideration given to associated costs and benefits, to develop appropriate *risk response* strategies. These risk responses can be handled following any one or a combination of four basic approaches:

1. **Avoidance.** This is a strategy of walking away from a risk—such as selling a business unit that gives rise to a risk, exiting from a risky geographical area, or dropping a product line. The difficulty is that enterprises often do not drop a product line or walk away until after the risk event has occurred with its associated costs. Unless an enterprise has a very low appetite for risk, it is difficult to walk away from an otherwise-successful business area or product line just on the basis of

a potential future risk if all seems to be going well at the present. Avoidance can be a potentially costly strategy if investments were made to get into an area, with a subsequent pullout to avoid the risk.

A collective lessons-learned understanding of past activities can often help with this strategy. If the enterprise had been involved in some area in the past with unfavorable consequences, this may be a good way to avoid the risk once again. With the tendency for constant changes and short employment tenures, this collective history is too often lost and forgotten. An enterprise's well-understood and -communicated appetite for risk is perhaps the most important consideration when deciding if a risk avoidance strategy is appropriate.

2. **Reduction.** A wide range of business decisions may be able to reduce certain risks. Product line diversification may reduce the risk of too strong of a reliance on one key product line; or splitting IT operations into two geographically separate locations will reduce the risk of some catastrophic failure. There is a wide range of often-effective strategies to reduce risks at all levels that go down to the obvious and mundane, such as cross-training employees to reduce the risk of someone departing unexpectedly.

3. **Sharing.** Virtually all enterprises as well as individuals regularly share some of their risks by purchasing insurance to help cover those risks. Many other risk-sharing techniques are available as well. For financial transactions, an enterprise can engage in hedging operations to protect from possible price fluctuations such as the use of put or call options to cover price movement fluctuations in securities holdings. An enterprise can also share potential business risks and rewards through joint venture agreements or other corporate structural arrangements. The idea is to arrange to have another party accept some of a potential risk as well as to share in any resultant rewards with the recognition that there will be costs associated with that activity.

4. **Acceptance.** This is the strategy of no action, such as when an enterprise "self-insures" by taking no action to reduce a potential risk and does not even purchase an insurance policy. Essentially, an enterprise should look at a risk's likelihood and impact in light of its established risk tolerance and then decide whether to accept that risk and not allocate resources to the expense of insurance. While foolhardy for some types of risks, for many other risks this acceptance approach is often an appropriate strategy.

An enterprise should develop a general response strategy for each of its more significant risks using an approach built around one or a mixture of the above risk avoidance strategies. In doing so, it should consider the costs versus benefits of each potential risk response as well as strategies that best align with the enterprise's overall risk appetite. For example, an enterprise's recognition that the impact of a given risk is relatively low would be balanced against a low risk tolerance that suggests that insurance should be purchased to provide a potential risk response. For many risks, appropriate responses are obvious and almost universally understood. An IT operation, for example, spends the time and resources to back up its key data files and implements a business continuity plan. There is typically no question of the need for these basic approaches, but various levels of management may question the frequency of backup processes or how often the continuity plan needs to be tested. That is, they may question the extent and cost of planned risk prevention measures.

An enterprise should go back to the several risk objectives that have been established as well as the tolerance ranges for those objectives. Then, it should readdress both the likelihoods and impacts associated with each of the identified risks within those objectives to develop an assessment of those risk categories as well as an overall set of the planned risk responses that align with overall corporate risk tolerances. At this point in the risk assessment process, an enterprise should have assessed the likelihood and potential impact of each of the risks surrounding its objectives as well as some estimates for each. The next step is to develop a set of potential risk responses. This is perhaps the most difficult step in building an effective COSO ERM program. It is comparatively easy to identify a 5% likelihood risk that there will be a fire in the scrap materials bin and then to establish a risk response remedy to install a nearby fire extinguisher. However, the responses to most risks are much more complex and require fairly detailed planning and analysis for an enterprise's risk response strategies.

The enterprise should go through its key high-impact and high-likelihood identified risks and develop a series of risk response plans. This can be a challenging management process! If there is a risk that an enterprise could lose an entire manufacturing operation due to a key but old equipment plant experiencing production failure, potential risk responses might include:

- Acquire backup production equipment to serve as spare parts for cannibalization.
- Shut down the manufacturing production line and plan to move it elsewhere.
- Arrange for a specialized shop to rebuild/reconstruct the old equipment.
- Reengineer the manufactured product along with plans for new product introduction.

Processes of developing risk responses require a significant amount of planning and strategic thinking. The several risk response alternatives involve costs, time, and detailed project planning. In addition to the planning and strategic thinking, this risk response planning process requires management input and approval to recognize alternative risk responses and to have action plans in place to satisfy appropriate responses. For example, one of the old-equipment response strategies outlined above is to acquire a set of backup equipment. If that is to be the approved strategy, action must be taken to acquire the old backup equipment before this activity can be listed as an actual risk response strategy.

An enterprise should always think of potential alternative risk response strategies. The idea is to list all of the identified risks of concern, and for each, management should attempt to estimate their probable inherent risk of occurrence. For example, a management team might estimate the likelihood that a competitor will be the first to market with a product similar to the one being analyzed. This is the type of estimate that might be made through communication with development and marketing personnel. Such an estimate is admittedly sometimes only a best guess, but it should be coupled with an estimate on the impact of the risk occurring. The impact on estimated revenue, or on other factors such as market share, can be used as a measurement. The idea is that all risks listed on such an analysis should be measured against the same impact factors, based on an *accept, avoid, share*, or *reduce risks* strategy. There is no need to list each of these four approaches for each identified risk. For example, an identified risk may have multiple possible avoid strategies but none to reduce risk. For each identified risk, estimates should be developed for the likelihood of that risk event occurring.

COSO ERM calls for risks to be considered and evaluated on an entity- or portfolio-wide basis. This can sometimes be a difficult process in a large, multiunit, multiproduct enterprise, but it provides a starting point in getting these various risks organized for identification of the more significant risks that may impact the enterprise. The idea here is to look at these various potential risks, their probability of occurrence, and the impacts of each. A good analysis here should highlight areas for more detailed attention. This understanding of risks also will help to document SOx Section 404 internal controls for internal controls review and analysis work.

Control Activities   *Control activities* are the policies and procedures necessary to ensure action on identified risk responses. Although some of these activities may only relate to an identified and approved risk response in one area of the enterprise, they often overlap across multiple functions and units. The control activities component of COSO ERM should be tightly linked with the *risk response* strategies and actions previously discussed.

Having selected appropriate risk responses, enterprise management should select control activities necessary to ensure that they are executed in a timely and efficient manner. The process of determining if control activities are performing properly is very similar to completing the SOx Section 404 internal control assessments discussed in Chapter 6. COSO ERM calls for approaches of identifying, documenting, testing, and then validating these risk protection controls. Having gone through the COSO ERM risk event identification, assessment, and response processes, risk monitoring can be executed by the following steps:

Step 1. Develop a strong understanding of the significant risks and establish control procedures to monitor or correct for them.

Step 2. Create fire-drill-type testing procedures to determine if those risk-related control procedures are working effectively.

Step 3. Perform tests of the risk monitoring processes to determine if they are working effectively and as expected.

Step 4. Make adjustments or improvements as necessary to improve risk monitoring processes.

This four-step process is essentially what SOx registered enterprises have been doing to review, test, and then assert that their internal control processes are working adequately. A major difference between COSO internal control procedures under SOx and ERM is that an enterprise *is legally required* to comply with SOx procedures in order to assert the adequacy of its internal controls to their external auditors as part of SEC financial reporting requirements. There are no such legal requirements with COSO ERM at this time. An enterprise should seek to install risk monitoring control activities to monitor the various risks it has identified. Because of the critical nature of many enterprise risks, risk monitoring can be vital to an enterprise's overall health.

Many control activities under COSO internal controls are fairly easy to identify and test due to the accounting nature of many internal controls. They generally include the following internal control areas:

- **Separation of duties.** Essentially, the person who initiates a transaction should not be the same person who authorizes that transaction.
- **Audit trails.** Processes should be organized such that final results can be easily traced back to the transactions that created those results.
- **Security and integrity.** Control processes should have appropriate control procedures such that only authorized persons can review or modify them.
- **Documentation.** Processes should be appropriately documented.

These control procedures, and others, are fairly well recognized and applicable to all internal control processes in an enterprise and also somewhat apply to many risk-related events. Many professionals—whether or not they have an accounting and auditing background—can easily define some of the key controls that are necessary in most business processes. For example, if asked to identify the types of internal controls that should be built into an accounts payable system, most professionals would identify as significant control points that checks issued from the system must be authorized by independent persons, that accounting records must be in place to keep track of the checks issued, and that the check issuing process should be such that only authorized persons can initiate such a financial transaction. These are generally widely understood control procedures. An enterprise often faces a more difficult task in identifying control activities to support its ERM framework.

As was discussed as part of ERM event identification, it is easiest to think of these risk categories in terms of major risk process areas, such as revenue, purchasing, capital spending, and information systems. Specific risk-related control activities can be defined within these categories, whether for the overall enterprise or covering some unit or function. Although there is no generally accepted or standard set of ERM control activities at this time, the COSO ERM documentation suggests several areas as follows:

- **Top-level reviews.** While senior management may be somewhat oblivious to the "do the debits equal the credits?" internal control procedures that are covered by their financial teams and internal auditors, they should be very aware of the identified risk events within organizational units and should perform regular top-level reviews on the status of these identified risks. Regular reviews coupled with appropriate top-level corrective actions are a key ERM control activity.
- **Direct functional or activity management.** In addition to the above top-level reviews, functional and direct unit managers should have a key role in risk control activity monitoring. This is particularly important in a large, diverse enterprise where control activities take place within the separate operating units with the need for communications and risk resolution across enterprise channels.
- **Information processing.** Whether it be hardware-based IT systems processes or paper-based processes, information processing and communication procedures represent a key component in an enterprise's risk-related control activities. Appropriate control procedures should be established with an emphasis on enterprise IT processes and risks.

- **Physical controls.** Many risk-related events involve physical assets such as equipment, inventories, securities, and physical plants. Whether for physical inventories, inspections, or plant security procedures, an enterprise should install appropriate risk-based physical control activity procedures.
- **Performance indicators.** The typical modern enterprise today employs a wide range of financial and operational reporting tools that also can support risk event–related performance reporting. Where necessary, overall performance tools should be modified to support this important control activity component.
- **Segregation of duties.** A classic control activity, the person who initiates certain actions should not be the same person who authorizes or approves them. This key control activity is important whether it be in a smaller business unit where an employee's supervisor would be required to inspect and approve employee actions or with a CEO who should obtain the oversight approval of the board of directors.

While the above are highlighted in the COSO ERM guidance material, these control activities can be expanded to cover other key areas. Some will be specific to individual units within the enterprise, but each of them, singly and collectively, should be important components in support of the enterprise's ERM framework.

Information and Communication   Although described as a separate component in the Exhibit 9.1 ERM framework diagram, the component of *information and communication* is less a separate set of risk-related processes than a set of tools linking other COSO ERM components. This concept, also shown in the COSO Application Techniques material, is illustrated in Exhibit 9.5, showing the information flows across the COSO ERM components. For example, the *risk response* component received residual and inherent risk inputs from the *risk assessment* component as well as *risk tolerance* support from the *objective setting* component. ERM risk response then provided risk response and risk portfolio data to *control activities* as well as risk response feedback to the risk assessment component. Standing alone, the *monitoring* component does not have any direct information connections but has overall responsibility for reviewing all of these functions.

While it is relatively easy to draw such a simple flow diagram of how information should theoretically be communicated from one COSO ERM component to another, in practice, this is often a far more complex process. The process of linking various enterprise systems and information paths together is much more difficult than what is shown in the very

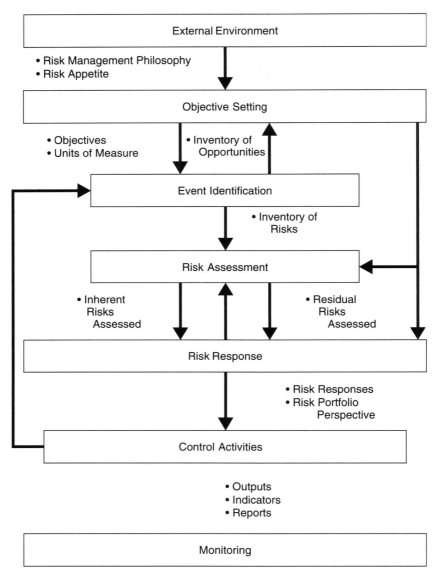

EXHIBIT 9.5   Information and Communication Flows Across ERM Components
Source: COSO Enterprise Risk Management: Understanding the New Integrated ERM Framework, Robert R. Moeller, page 87. Copyright © 2007 John Wiley & Sons. Reprinted with permission of John Wiley & Sons, Inc.

high-level Exhibit 9.5. Many enterprises have a complex web of often not-very-well-linked information systems for their basic operational and financial processes. These linkages become even more complex with attempts to interconnect various ERM processes, given that many basic enterprise applications do not directly lend themselves to risk identification, assessment, and risk response types of processes. Going beyond a comprehensive ERM information application for an enterprise, there is a need to develop risk monitoring and communications systems that link with customers, suppliers, and other stakeholders.

While the *information* half of the information and communication COSO ERM component is normally thought of in terms of IT strategic and operational information systems, ERM *communication*, the second aspect of this component, talks about communication beyond just IT applications, such as the need for mechanisms to assure all stakeholders receive messages regarding the enterprise's interest in managing its risks. A major component of these communication messages should be use of a common risk language throughout the enterprise, such as the definition of the roles and responsibilities of all stakeholders regarding risk management. COSO ERM will be of little value to an enterprise unless the overall message of its importance gets communicated to all stakeholders in a common and consistent manner.

Monitoring   Placed at the base of the stack of horizontal components in the ERM framework model, the *monitoring* component is necessary to determine that all components of an installed ERM continue to work effectively. People in the enterprise change, as do supporting processes and both internal and external conditions, but the monitoring component helps assure that ERM is working effectively on a continuous basis. These include processes to flag exceptions or violations in other components of the overall ERM process. For example, an accounts receivable billing function should identify the overall financial and operational risks if customer bills are not paid on a timely basis. An ongoing, virtually real-time credit collections monitoring tool could provide senior management with day-to-day and trending data on the status of collections. One example is dashboard monitoring tools, discussed previously, that operate like the low oil pressure warning light on an automobile dashboard. These types of ERM monitors should work on a continuous basis.

Going beyond dashboard monitoring tools, enterprise management should take overall responsibility for ERM monitoring. In order to establish an effective ERM framework, monitoring should include ongoing reviews of the overall ERM process ranging from identified objectives to the progress of ongoing ERM control activities. The COSO ERM Application Framework document suggests this monitoring could include the following types of activities:

- Implementation of a strong and ongoing management reporting mechanism, such as cash positions, unit sales, and key financial data. An enterprise should not have to wait until fiscal month-end or worse for these types of status reports, and quick-response "flash reports" should be initiated.
- Periodic reporting processes should monitor key aspects of established risk criteria, including acceptable error rates or items held in suspense Such reporting should emphasize statistical trends and comparisons with prior periods as well as with other industry sectors. This type of reporting would highlight potential risk-related alerts.
- The current and periodic status of risk-related findings and recommendations from internal audit reports. This periodic reporting also should include the status of ERM-related SOx-identified gaps.
- Updated risk-related information from sources such as revised government rules, industry trends, and general economic news. Again, this type of economic and operational reporting should be available for managers at all levels.

Separate or individual evaluation monitoring refers to detailed reviews of individual risk processes by a qualified reviewer such as internal audit. Here the review can either be limited to specific areas or cover the entire ERM process for an enterprise unit; a strong internal audit function may be the best resource to perform such specific ERM reviews. Of course, internal audit is an independent function in an enterprise, and responsible for planning and scheduling its own internal audit reviews. A division controller, for example, cannot just go to internal audit and request that they perform an ERM review of that department's operations. An effective internal audit function will normally have many other review activities on its plate, and any risk-related review would need to be coordinated with other planned internal audit activities. The role of internal audit in the ERM process and in monitoring, in particular, is discussed in following sections.

OTHER DIMENSIONS OF THE COSO ERM FRAMEWORK

Operational Risks

Our previous discussion primarily covered just the *objective setting* dimension of the three-dimensional COSO ERM framework. While objective setting is important for understanding ERM, the two other dimensions of the COSO ERM framework—the *operational* and *organizational* levels—must always be considered as well. Each component of COSO ERM operates in this three-dimensional space where each must be considered in terms of the other related categories. In addition, while the Exhibit 9.1 COSO ERM framework shows each of the objective categories as having the same relative size or width, the category of operations-level risks is often viewed as a much broader and higher-exposure risk category than the others. The objective of operational-level risks refers to the wide number and often differing types of special risks that can impact any area of an enterprise. The ERM framework suggests that an enterprise should develop and document a general set of its operational risks along with related risk likelihood estimates. Following its three-dimensional framework, the ERM operational-level risk objective calls for a set of identified risks for each unit or component of the enterprise.

While it may be relatively easy to understand and document high-level strategic risks through inputs from the board and CEO or to work with either the chief financial officer (CFO) or internal audit for some compliance-level risks, the identification of operational-level risks often requires a fair degree of detailed information gathering and analysis. This is particularly true for a larger enterprise covering multiple geographical areas, product lines, or business processes. The direct managers of these multiple units usually have the best understanding of their unit's operational risks, even though that information can become lost when consolidated for higher-level reporting. In order to gather more detailed background information on potential operational risks, the enterprise's risk management function, or internal audit, should communicate with other enterprise units and develop a set of operational-level risks. While such a list can cover many dimensions, Exhibit 9.6 is a list of the types of operational risks that might be collected for a mid-sized manufacturing company. These risks can take many shapes and forms, but the concept here is that an enterprise should give consideration to the operational-level risks that it may face. The problem with these potential risks is that they are often assembled by members of management, either at a headquarters location or a domestic facility, but may not reflect the true nature of some operational risks at remote units.

More information about operational risks can often be gathered in surveys completed by persons directly impacted by these risks. The idea is to survey direct "on-the-floor" members of the enterprise to better describe the nature of their operational risks. This type of survey, along with follow-up questions, will allow the development of a consistent set of cataloged operational risks across all levels of the enterprise. The questions asked would be similar to the types of detailed questions often used in internal

- **Physical asset protection risks.** Physical facilities, production equipment, and inventory face risks of damage or theft and should be properly secured.
- **Natural hazard preparedness.** Enterprises always face risks of extreme weather conditions, disease outbreaks, and other unexpected events. Risk planning may recognize that probabilities of occurrences are low, but nevertheless should allow for the risk event.
- **Business continuity planning.** While we often consider continuity risks in terms of IT systems, the risk of losing other elements of overall business operations should always be considered.
- **International operations and global political risks.** An enterprise should consider the many risks it may face in a worldwide spectrum and how those risks relate to mainstream operations.
- **Business interruption and interdependency risk analysis.** Beyond just a computer system meltdown or business operation failure, risks should be considered in terms of overall operations. A political conflict elsewhere in the world, for example, may disrupt shipping processes.
- **Industry-specific risks.** Whether a specific product or a business service, product-related and industry-wide risk-related trends should be considered.
- **Information technology security risks.** All enterprises face a wide range of risks to their systems and processes, whether they are Internet-or specific process–related.

EXHIBIT 9.6   Operational Risk Examples

audit internal control assessments, and the results of any available data here could become a basis for developing a better understanding.

Circulated through all levels of an enterprise, with a message encouraging stakeholders to respond in a candid manner, these types of surveys can often gather important information regarding potential risks at a detailed operational level. Enterprise-wide surveys are also similar to the approaches suggested for launching an enterprise-wide ethics function, as discussed in Chapter 12. A manager of a remote operating plant might not have adequately communicated or have had management directly hearing concerns about some plant-level operational risk. A broadly based and confidential survey will allow people to communicate those often local-level operational risks up through the enterprise.

With ERM's portfolio view of risks, an enterprise can face a level of danger if it regularly rolls things up to too much of a summary level, missing or rounding off important lower-level risks. Whatever the level in an organizational hierarchy or the geographical location, managers at all levels should be aware that they are responsible for accepting and managing the risks within their own operational units. Too often, unit managers may gain an impression that risk management is only some senior-level, headquarters type of concern. The importance of COSO ERM and operations risk management, as well as its relationship with SOx Section 404 internal controls, should be communicated to all levels of an enterprise. The operational side of the COSO ERM framework has some specific objectives as summarized below.

Reporting Risks

This operational risk objective covers the reliability of an enterprise's reporting, including the internal and external reporting of financial and nonfinancial data. Accurate reporting is critical to an enterprise's success in many areas or dimensions. While we frequently see news reports regarding the discovery of inaccurate corporate financial reporting and the resultant financial repercussions for the offending entity, that same inaccurate reporting can cause problems in many areas. An example of the risks related to inaccurate reporting can be found with a problem several years ago at the major petroleum company, Royal Dutch Shell. While not an actual financial accounting number, oil and gas exploration companies are required to regularly report their reserves—the amount of oil and gas on their properties that are still in the ground and have not yet been extracted. In January 2004, Royal Dutch announced that due to bad estimates and sloppy recordkeeping, it had been significantly overreporting its estimated petroleum reserves.[6] While this error did not affect its reported financial results and SEC reserve reporting guidelines are not that strong, the market battered its stock upon the announcement, and the CEO, the head of oil exploration operations, and others were forced to resign. The company, under a new chairman, then announced a raft of changes and internal control improvements to repair the damage.

No matter what industry, every enterprise faces major risks with inaccurate reporting at any unit or area. An operating unit must make certain that reported results are correct before they are passed up to the next level in the organization, and consolidated numbers must be accurate, whether in financial reports, tax returns, or in myriad other areas. Systems and processes installed as part of the internal environment should ensure accurate reporting, and be established as components of the event identification and risk assessment components of the ERM framework. The objective of accurate reporting should be a major driver in all ERM activities.

While good internal controls are necessary to ensure accurate reporting, ERM is concerned about the risk of authorizing and releasing inaccurate reports. Strong internal controls should minimize the risk of errors, and an enterprise should always consider the risks associated with inaccurate reporting. While we have not presented all of the details in the matter, Royal Dutch Shell could be an example of this type of risk reporting concern. Reporting reserves requires a management estimate, and the SEC requires three categories of estimates—proved reserves, proved developed reserves, and proved undeveloped reserves. Small errors and discrepancies can be ignored over time until there is a major error that needs to be disclosed. The risk of such inaccurate reporting should be a concern at all levels of the enterprise.

Legal and Regulatory Compliance Risks   Enterprises of any nature operate in environments where they must comply with a wide range of legal risks as well as government-imposed or industry regulations. While compliance rules and risks can be monitored and recognized in many instances, legal risks are sometimes totally unanticipated. In the United States, for example, an aggressive plaintiff legal system can pose a major risk to otherwise well-intentioned enterprises. Asbestos litigation during the 1990s and beyond is an example. A fibrous mineral, asbestos has three extraordinary characteristics: It works as an insulator for heat and electricity; it resists or protects areas from many chemicals; and, when inhaled, it has now been found to cause cancer and other illnesses that can take decades to develop.

A natural insulation material, previously used extensively in building materials and then considered totally benign, it has been subsequently found that too much direct contact with asbestos fibers over time can cause severe lung problems and even death. Miners working underground extracting asbestos have met that fate. Extracted asbestos was used in many other products, such as sealed wrappers to insulate heating pipes or fire protection wall barriers. The risks to persons working or living in a structure with these asbestos-sealed pipes are fairly minimal. Nevertheless, aggressive litigators have brought actions against corporations, claiming that anyone who could have had any contact, no matter how minimal, with a product that used asbestos could be at risk sometime in the future. The result was litigation damage claims against companies that had once manufactured products containing some asbestos, calling for damages for potential human risks in future years. Because of huge damage awards, virtually all major corporations that once used asbestos have gone bankrupt, out of business, or have had to pay huge court-imposed damage losses. This is the type of legal risk that is very difficult to anticipate but that can be disastrous to an enterprise.

COSO ERM recommends that compliance-related risks be considered for each of the risk framework components, whether in the context of the internal environment, objective setting, or risk monitoring, as well as across the enterprise. The COSO ERM guidance material does not offer much additional information on this compliance objective other than to state that IT refers to conformance with applicable laws and regulations. These are important elements of the risk management framework that need to be communicated and understood.

Understanding Regulatory Compliance Risks As enterprises become more interconnected on a worldwide basis and as laws frequently become complex sets of administrative rules, all enterprises face a wide range of regulatory compliance requirements. The number and extent of these is very broad, with some impacting virtually all enterprises and others related to only single business units of an enterprise in a specialized industry sector. The nature of those compliance risks needs to be communicated and understood through all levels of an enterprise. This is also an area where an enterprise may accept a certain level of risk in terms of its concerns regarding legal compliance issues. While an enterprise should not deliberately ignore a major law because of a feeling they never will be caught, they should always take a reasoned approach to these risks in conjunction with their overall philosophy and risk appetites. For example, many regulatory rules specify that all expenditures must be supported by a receipt. While there usually are no reasonableness guidelines, one enterprise could decide that "all expenditures" goes down to employee travel expenses of less than $1, while another might require receipts for anything above $25. The latter enterprise has made a decision that the costs of documenting these small expenditures are greater than any fine it might receive if caught in a regulatory compliance issue. This type of risk-related decision is similar to the new AS5 financial internal control rules for SOx discussed in Chapter 3. When an enterprise establishes such guidelines, they should be communicated to all levels and units.

In order to manage and comply with regulatory risk requirements, an enterprise needs to have an understanding of the nature and extent of all of the regulatory risks it faces as well as the enterprise's overall position on each. This is an area where information is often lacking within an organizational unit. The board of directors and senior management needs to have information on these key regulatory risk areas and actions taken. A regulatory risks status report, as shown in Exhibit 9.7, provides sample information regarding some of the various legal regulatory risks facing a hypothetical enterprise. This sample exhibit shows just a few of the many enterprise-level risks ranging from major to minor, but it might cover a different set of risks for an enterprise in a different industry

Note: This report summarizes examples of some many rules and requirements impacting an enterprise such as our hypothetical Global Computer Products. The organization risks being in violation of many of these example Rules.

1. **Equal Employment Opportunity Commission Employer Information Report (EEO-1) Rules.**
   Rule Summary: The Company must file an employer information report (EEO-1) annually regarding employees and their demographics.
   Current Status: Reports have been filed on schedule, but offshore operations have experienced problems with reporting on occupational categories and this data must be aggregated.
2. **Environmental Protection Agency Export Notification Requirements.**
   Rule Summary: Global Computer Products is required to notify the Environmental Protection Agency (EPA) when exporting substances or products that contain chemicals listed on the Export Notification 12(b) list under the Toxic Substances Control Act (TSCA); 15 U.S.C. s/s 2601 et seq. Since current rules do not have a low-level cutoff, many minor substances or product ingredients trigger large amounts of paperwork.
   Current Status: Rules are difficult to understand, and the company may be out of compliance even though the level of export business here is very low.
3. **EPS Pretreatment Streamlining Rule under Clean Water Act; 33 U.S.C. ss/1251.**
   Rule Summary: A 1999 EPA rule defines pretreatment requirements to remove unnecessary burdens on Publicly Owned Treatment Works (POTWs), industry, and agencies.
   Current Status: May be out of compliance at some facilities. This rule should be finalized because it reduces burdens on POTWs without negatively impacting the environment.
4. **Health Insurance Portability and Accountability Act of 1996 (HIPAA).**
   Rule Summary: HIPAA rules are intended to improve portability and continuity of health insurance coverage for all Global Computer Products employees, and to simplify the administration of health insurance. Implementation of HIPAA has been problematic because of multiple effective dates and the need to reengineer existing processes to eliminate or reduce exposure.
   Current Status: Considerable time and money have been spent trying to comply with these complex requirements, and the company may still be technically out of compliance.

EXHIBIT 9.7 Regulatory Risks Status Report
Source: COSO Enterprise Risk Management: Understanding the New Integrated ERM Framework, Robert R. Moeller, page 105. Copyright © 2007 John Wiley & Sons. Reprinted with permission of John Wiley & Sons, Inc.

such as pharmaceuticals. The problem here is that regulatory risks are never "minor" when an enterprise is found to be in violation of one or another of them. The idea behind this status report is to provide an overall synopsis of compliance with various regulatory risks. This sample report recognizes where there are unit-level SOx internal control deficiencies yet to be corrected.

Enterprise Legal Risks   While the status of regulatory compliance risks is relatively easy to monitor, monitoring legal risks is often a greater challenge. As an example of enterprise legal risks, in 1963, Crown Cork & Seal, an old-line Philadelphia-based packaging company, purchased a cork company, Mundet Cork, which had an insulation business that made one product that, many years prior to its 1963 acquisition, contained the previously discussed asbestos. Crown acquired Mundet in order to take over their metal bottle-cap production division.

On the basis of that acquisition, Crown became the target of thousands of tort claims filed by individuals who claimed to have been "injured" by exposure to the long-obsolete Mundet insulation products containing asbestos. Those suits drove Crown itself to the verge of bankruptcy with cash flow costs as high as $90 million in one year. Crown survived as a much different and smaller enterprise because of all of this. The point here is not to discuss the many problems in the United States associated with asbestos litigation and the many related legal actions, but to mention the types of legal risks that can powerfully impact an enterprise. There are many litigation risks that are unanticipated and difficult to control.

A corporate legal counsel can often play an important role here by circulating legal risk status data to all members of the enterprise and serving as a sounding board for reviewing newer legal risk–related questions. While corporate legal functions are too often involved with day-to-day litigation and advising the board of directors, they should become more of an internal consulting function providing some guidance on the relative legal risks surrounding some proposed new move or venture. This type of background reporting information on legal issues may help managers at all levels to assess any new potential risks when seeking to make a decision.

Legal and regulatory compliance objectives are important elements in any enterprise's COSO ERM framework. The current status of issues as well as any actions to be taken will help to define and shape the enterprise's overall appetite for risk. Whether considering risk event identification, risk control activities on a total enterprise level, or within an individual unit, legal and regulatory actions play a major role in understanding and accepting enterprise risk.

These various enterprise, compliance, and reporting risks form another dimension to the COSO ERM framework. All of the risk elements included here should be evaluated in terms of this COSO ERM framework dimension. For example, no matter what the level of risk or the organizational unit, a manager should consider whether there are any legal or regulatory risks related to the matter.

Entity-Level Risks

The third dimension of the COSO ERM framework calls for risks to be considered on an organization or entity unit level. The Exhibit 9.1 COSO ERM framework shows four divisions or slices in this framework dimension: entity-level, division, business unit, and subsidiary risks. This is not a prescribed company-type division, and ERM suggests that risks should closely follow the official organization chart. Again in consideration of the ERM portfolio view of risk management, risks should be identified and managed within each significant organizational unit, including the consideration of risks on an entity-wide basis and for individual business units.

An example enterprise with four major operating divisions and with multiple business units or subsidiary units under each would have an ERM framework that reflected all of these units. While these risks are important on an overall organizational level, there should be consideration on a unit-by-unit basis to as low a level as necessary to allow the enterprise to understand and manage its risks. COSO ERM does not specify how thinly these unit-level risks should be sliced, and the criticality and materiality of individual business units should be given consideration. For a major fast-food restaurant chain with thousands of units, it almost certainly would not be reasonable to include each individual unit as a separate component in the risk model. Rather, management should define its organizational-level risks at a level of detail that will cover all significant, manageable risks. Reasonableness measures should always be used!

Risks Encompassing the Entire Organization   Multiple-business-unit-level risks should roll up to their entity-level risks. While it is easy for an enterprise to consider some unit-level risks—using the public accounting terminology, discussed in Chapter 3, as being "not material"—an enterprise has to think of all risks as potentially significant. One example is a relatively small subsidiary in a third-world country that is manufacturing fairly low-level casual clothing goods. Often, such a unit would be so small in terms of corporate revenue contributions or its relative size, that it can slip under the radar screen on a senior corporate level. However, there could be issues regarding child labor at the host country that could bring all operations there to the attention of any of several aggressive journalists. As a result of news articles, the enterprise may soon find itself at the center of attention regarding this small subsidiary operation. Such a situation often results in cases where a CEO is asked to publicly comment on policies and procedures at that subsidiary operation when the CEO may have only vague knowledge of its existence.

Our point here is that both major and seemingly small risks can impact an entire enterprise. The delivery of tainted food produced at one small unit of a large fast-food chain can impact the prospects and reputation of the total enterprise. While it is relatively easy to identify high-level entity-wide risks such as compliance with SOx Section 404, and to identify and monitor these as part of the COSO ERM process, care must be taken that smaller potential risks do not slip between the cracks. SOx AS5 auditing standards, as discussed in Chapter 3, suggest a much more risk-oriented approach. However, as risks are identified through established operations objectives or through organization-wide objective setting, they should be considered on an entity-wide basis as well as by individual operating units. Those individual unit risks should be first reviewed and consolidated to identify any key risks that may impact the overall organization. In addition, any organization-wide risks should also be identified.

Business Unit–Level Risks

Risks occur at all levels in a large enterprise, whether a major production division with multiple plants and thousands of employees or a minority ownership position in a foreign country sales company. Risks must be considered in each significant organizational unit. The risks identified in our example minority ownership position in a foreign sales company are risks that are unique to that unit but then should roll up to the operating division and then to the entity. We have cited the example of entity-level risks that might result from failures in manufacturing or human rights standards issues in a small third-world country subsidiary. Risk events here can cause an embarrassment to the overall enterprise, but they should have been controlled all the way down to the small third-world company unit.

Depending on the complexity and number of operating units, enterprise risk responsibility should be divided among appropriate levels of enterprise units. This can often best start as a push-down process where entity- or senior corporate-level management will formally outline their major risk-related concerns and ask responsible management at each of the major divisions to survey risk concerns down through the operating units within that division. In this manner, significant risks can hopefully be identified at all levels of the organization and then managed where they can receive the most direct, local attention.

A major consideration with COSO ERM is the recognition that an enterprise faces a wide range of significant risks at all levels. Some may be significant while others may be just viewed as troubling annoyances. The COSO ERM framework provides a mechanism to consider all of these risks and is an important tool to help assure SOx compliance.

PUTTING IT ALL TOGETHER

The COSO ERM framework has not been with us long enough to point to a series of successful enterprises that have publicly embraced this new model or framework. In addition, the term *risk management framework* has not been used that consistently and often with poor or loose definitions. Sometimes the concept of a risk framework has focused too narrowly on risk management in specific areas rather than the broader ERM focus. Others focus on specific industries or specific types of risk. In addition, many past approaches emphasize reducing—rather than managing—risk. The COSO ERM framework described here addresses an approach applicable to all industries and encompassing all types of risk. With its focus on recognizing an organization's appetite for risk and the need to apply risk management within the context of overall strategy setting, COSO ERM presents some fundamental differences from most risk models that have been used in the past.

COSO ERM is designed to be applied to the total enterprise and to as many smaller supporting units as manageable. This is in contrast to many of the preexisting risk frameworks that stood by themselves, and thus tended to be implemented within silos or specific units of an enterprise. Consequently, earlier approaches to risk management may have been executed very well in one unit with little consideration of how actions of other parts of the enterprise affect specific risks or overall risks. COSO ERM presents an enterprise-wide perspective of risk and standardizes terms and concepts to promote effective implementation across the organization. Internal auditors, in particular, should learn more about COSO ERM and begin to incorporate it into their audit procedures.

COSO ERM arrived after SOx, and is much broader than the current SOx internal control approaches that are built around the COSO internal control framework. Nevertheless, COSO ERM also is an important tool for managing and understanding SOx Section 404 internal controls. It is particularly important with the newer AS5 auditing standards that give more consideration to risk when understanding and evaluating internal controls. External audits will continue to make their decisions on internal control matters when evaluating controls and performing audit tests for their SOx

Section 404 internal control review. However, if enterprise management at all levels can embrace the COSO ERM view of risks, they will have a strong argument for explaining why they have or have not considered risks covering some internal control matter. In addition, COSO ERM is an important tool for understanding the multiple risks an enterprise faces today.

AUDITING COSO ERM PROCESSES

The effective and efficient implementation of COSO ERM is another area where an enterprise can improve its SOx compliance processes as well as where internal audit can help to build more effective internal control procedures. Internal audit's role has been mentioned in prior chapters and will be discussed in more detail in Chapter 11. COSO ERM in a SOx environment is another area where internal audit can help an enterprise to ensure that it is effectively utilizing this risk management framework to achieve SOx compliance.

Of course, to review COSO ERM standards and procedures in this environment, internal auditors need to develop their own strong understanding of ERM controls and processes. To act as either reviewers of controls or consultants to management, internal auditors should gain a good understanding of the COSO ERM framework.

Because COSO ERM does not encourage a financial control type of review, internal auditors should consider documenting the installed COSO ERM processes with an understanding of how they apply to SOx rules. While there are a variety of techniques, individual reviews of an ERM process in a SOx environment might use the following tools:

- **Process flowcharting.** As part of any identified ERM process, flowcharts would have been developed as part of the SOx Section 404 review work. These same process flowcharts can be useful in completing an ERM review of an individual process. This requires looking at documentation prepared for a process, determining if it is correct given current conditions, and updating the process flowcharts as appropriate. These flowcharts should look at risks and their relationship with other ERM procedures.
- **Reviews of risk and control materials.** An ERM process often results in a large volume of guidance material, documented procedures, report formats, and the like. There may often be value to an internal audit review in the risk and control materials from an effectiveness perspective.
- **Benchmarking.** Although an often misused term, benchmarking is the process of looking at another's functions, such as their COSO ERM

procedures, to assess their operations and to develop an approach based on the best practices of others. This is particularly important in a SOx environment. While gathering comparative information is often a difficult task due to the reluctance of competing enterprises, the IIA's "Progress Through Sharing" motto and tradition, discussed in Chapter 11, should help to promote this.

- **Questionnaires.** A good method for gathering information on ERM effectiveness under SOx from a wide range of people, questionnaires can be sent out to designated stakeholders with requests for specific information. This is often a valuable internal audit technique.

The idea for internal audit is to establish some high-level review objectives for the effectiveness of COSO ERM in a SOx environment, gather detailed implementation data as described above, and then assess the effectiveness of COSO ERM in an enterprise and as a tool to support and enhance SOx compliance. Exhibit 9.8 provides COSO ERM audit procedures in a SOx environment.

COSO ERM IN PERSPECTIVE

Because the two framework models look quite similar on first observation, it is very easy to overlook the unique characteristics of COSO ERM. It took many years for COSO internal controls to be recognized as more than an interesting technical study. They had been codified as an auditing standard by the then-important AICPA Auditing Standards Board and this standard received some mention in Institute of Internal Auditors (IIA) publications, but it took the launch of SOx to give it some serious recognition. The initial SOx legislation talked about an internal accounting standard "to be established," but the PCAOB's mandate that COSO internal controls should be the standard came later. Arriving after SOx, COSO ERM does not yet have that same level of recognition. The IIA was an important early proponent and elements of ERM can be seen in the new version of the CobiT framework, as discussed in Chapter 7, but it still is not at the same level of importance and significance today for an enterprise as COSO internal controls.

This recognition may take some time! That the two frameworks sort of look alike and both have COSO in their names has caused some confusion. However, the risk-related emphasis of the new AS5 auditing standards as well as an increasing recognition of risk issues in professional literature has somewhat increased our professional interest and attention for enterprise risk management, particularly when attempting to achieve SOx internal control compliance. The three-dimensional ERM framework helps to place

A. Has the enterprise adopted a formal enterprise risk management program following COSO ERM?
   a. Has the risk management program been approved by senior management, including the audit committee or a risk management committee?
   b. Has a *chief risk officer* (CRO) been assigned to manage the program?
   c. If no formal ERM program is in place, is there evidence of plans to establish such a program?
B. Is there a formal program in place to identify all significant risks facing the enterprise?
   a. Does risk identification cover all significant risk areas: financial, operational, regulatory, and other risks?
   b. Is there evidence of the enterprise defining a "risk appetite" that is used and communicated for all ERM activities?
   c. Is there a formal process to rank identified risks by their potential significance and likelihood?
   d. Are cost impacts or other appropriate methods used in risk response planning?
   e. Is there a process in place to review and update identified risks on a periodic basis?
C. Is there an ongoing monitoring process to review identified risks?
   a. Is there formal documentation to record risk monitoring activities?
   b. When a risk event is identified through the monitoring process, is there a formal process to identify severity and take appropriate next steps?
   c. Is there a formal reporting process to describe ongoing risk management activities?
D. Does the ERM process cover all significant areas of risk: strategic, operational, reporting, and compliance risks?
   a. Are ERM activities regularly coordinated with SOx internal control reviews and investigations?
   b. Are ERM activities planned and coordinated with internal audit?
   c. Are enterprise corporate governance and oversight activities closely linked with ERM activities?
E. Are ERM activities installed in all significant business units ranging from corporate level to individual business units?
   a. Are ERM processes effectively linked with IT service support and delivery processes?
   b. Is there close communication/coordination between ERM activities and facility security processes?
F. Has the enterprise published and distributed effective policies and standards to describe its ERM activities?

EXHIBIT 9.8 COSO ERM Internal Audit Procedures in a SOx Environment

risk and internal control issues in a better perspective when evaluating SOx compliance.

The overall theme of this book has been the changes to SOx processes since its enactment after the 2002 fall of Enron. While the basic legislation has not really changed, both PCAOB rule-setting regulators and enterprises are beginning to take a much more risk-based compliance approach rather than following strictly detailed rules. A concept behind SOx is to improve enterprise internal controls and to create an atmosphere where these controls can be assessed and measured. Given the new AS5 rules, the application of the COSO ERM framework to SOx compliance issues should ease things. COSO ERM should be an important tool in our understanding of and compliance with SOx rules.

ENDNOTES

1. "COSO Enterprise Risk Management Integrated Framework," COSO.
2. "COSO Releases a New Risk Management Framework," *Accounting Today*, 10/25/2004.
3. The reader is encouraged to access the entire description of COSO ERM. A full copy of COSO ERM and supporting summary material can be either downloaded or purchased through the AICPA or the COSO Web site at //www.coso.org. The reader is also encouraged to explore Robert Moeller's *COSO Enterprise Risk Management: Understanding the New Integrated ERM Framework* (New York: Wiley, 2007).
4. Six Sigma is a disciplined methodology for eliminating defects (driving toward six standard deviations between the mean and the nearest specification limit) in any process—from manufacturing to transactional and from product to service.
5. www.risksig.com.
6. "Reporting Problems at Shell," *The Guardian*, London, www.ruesges.com, March 24, 2004.

CHAPTER 10

International Standards: ISO, Quality Auditing, and SOx

In the years following World War II, the United States became the world-wide economic and political leader. This dominance now has been so great for so long that many in the United Sates have all but ignored standards set elsewhere in our increasingly globally connected worldwide economy. However, the best standards and processes are often collaborative efforts that take into account worldwide national needs and requirements. The International Standards Organization's (ISO's)[1] international standards cover a wide range of areas, ranging from defining fastener screw threads in an automobile engine to the thickness of a personal credit card. The standards also have been expanded to cover areas that are important for governance and enterprise quality.

This chapter will provide an overview and introduction to several of these important ISO standards, with a focus on ISO 9001 quality standards and how they relate to the Sarbanes-Oxley Act (SOx) Section 404 requirements. That is, if an enterprise can attest that it has an effective quality management system, following ISO guidance; can it also attest that it has effective SOx internal controls? The chapter will also provide an introduction to several other ISO standards, including ISO's international standards for information technology (IT) management systems and for information security management.

The management and implementation of many ISO standards usually brings us out of the corporate office, visited by internal and sometimes external auditors, and into enterprise production areas. Quality auditors, often quite different in background and approach from the Institute of Internal Auditors (IIA) internal audit teams, play an important role here. The chapter will discuss the quality audit function, the role of its American Society for Quality (ASQ) professional organization in establishing standards, and how quality auditing is related to our more familiar IIA-background internal auditors.

We will conclude this chapter with an introduction to another area of international standards that is becoming increasingly important for effective corporate governance—international accounting standards. While the United States has been using accounting procedures following the generally accepted accounting principles (GAAP) that have evolved over the years, almost all of the rest of the world has been using accounting standards following International Accounting Standards Board (IASB) procedures. These international accounting standards are just about the same as GAAP but differ in some small but important areas. Although the United States and its Securities and Exchange Commission (SEC) financial reporting rules are not quite there yet, there are efforts to achieve convergence and we should soon see one set of consistent accounting standards. This chapter will look at the current status of these international accounting standards.

IMPORTANCE OF ISO STANDARDS IN TODAY'S GLOBAL WORLD

The ISO, based in Geneva, Switzerland,[2] is responsible for developing and publishing a wide range of international standards in many business and process areas. Some of these standards are very broad, such as ISO 14001, covering effective environmental control systems, while others are very detailed and precise, such as a standard covering the size and thickness of a plastic credit card. The broad ISO standards are important because they enable all worldwide enterprises to speak the same language when they assert that they have, for example, an effective ISO 14001 environmental control system; the detailed ones are also very critical—to allow, for example, an ATM machine anywhere in the world to expect to receive the same size and thickness of a credit card.

ISO standards are developed through the collaborative efforts of many national standards-setting organizations such as the American National Standards Institute (ANSI) and other similar groups throughout the world. This process gets itself started with a generally recognized need for a standard in some area. An example would be ISO 27001 on information security management system requirements. This standard outlines the high-level requirements for an effective information security management system. The ISO 27001 standard was developed through the efforts of international technical committees sponsored by ISO in cooperation with the International Electrotechnical Commission (IEC) international standards-setting group. The standard is not specific in its detailed requirements but contains many high-level statements along the lines of "the organization shall . . . ."

Because numerous international governmental authorities, professional groups, and individual experts are involved in such a standards-setting groups, the process of building any ISO document typically is a long and slow one. An expert committee develops an initial draft standard covering some area, the draft is sent out for review and comment with a specified comments due date, and the committee then goes back to review draft comments before either issuing the new standard or sending a revised draft out for another round of reviews and suggested changes. After many drafts and comment periods, the standard will be published. Enterprises can then take the necessary steps to comply with the standard, but to certify their compliance they must contract with a certified outside auditor, with skills in that standard, to attest to their compliance.

Many enterprises in the United States first got involved with these international standards through the ISO 9000 quality management system standard in the 1980s. They were faced with the high-quality design standards and systems of many non-U.S. products, such as Japanese automobiles. Compliance with this ISO 9000 standard allowed worldwide enterprises to design their operations in accordance with a single, consistent standard and then to assert that they have a quality management system in place in accordance with the international standard.

ISO standards are much more than the Information Technology Infrastructure Library (ITIL) best practices guidelines discussed in Chapter 8. The standards are published and controlled by the ISO organization in Geneva following strict copyright rules. They are not the kinds of materials that can be downloaded through a casual Goggle search but must be purchased. Many of the actual ISO standards are just very detailed outlines of practices to be followed. While certainly out of context, Exhibit 10.1 is an example of an actual extract from a section of the ISO 27001 information security management systems standard describing the control of documents for an information security management system (ISMS). With some references to other sections of this standard, the guidance is clear and unambiguous and often points to other areas for follow-up. For example, line 5.1.b in this very brief extract states that management should define the roles and responsibilities for information security. This is very much of a prompt or reminder for appropriate levels of action as well as a checklist of questions for internal auditor reviews.

An enterprise can just follow and rely on ISO standards similar to the ITIL best practices discussed in Chapter 8, but ISO standards usually represent much more than just best practices. They represent a performance measure for an enterprise and its peers. These are worldwide standards that will allow an enterprise to hold itself out and qualify that it is operating in accordance with a consistent international standard. Although there are many different standards to select, another example can be found in ISO 13485 on quality management regulatory requirements for medical devices. This standard covers the quality standards covering human health-care devices.

5   Management Responsibility
5.1 Management Commitment
Management shall provide evidence of its commitment to the establishment, implementation, operation, monitoring, review, maintenance and improvement of the ISMS by:

   a. establishing an ISMS policy;
   b. establishing roles and responsibilities for information security;
   c. ensuring roles and responsibilities for information security;
   d. communicating to the organization the importance of meeting information security objectives and conforming to the information security policy, its responsibilities under the law and the need for continual improvement;
   e. providing sufficient resources to establish, implement, operate, monitor, review, maintain and improve the ISMA (see 5.2.1);
   f. deciding the criteria for accepting risks and the acceptable levels of risk;
   g. ensuring that internal ISMS audits are conducted (see 6); and
   h. conducting management reviews of the ISMS (see 7).

Note: The terms and definitions taken from ISO/IEC 27001:2005 Information technology security techniques—Information security management systems— Requirements clause 5.1 a through h, are reproduced with permission of the International Organization for Standardization (ISO). This Technical Report can be obtained from any ISO member and from the Web site of the ISO Central Secretariat at the following address: www.iso.org. Copyright remains with ISO.

EXHIBIT 10.1   ISO Standards Example: 27001 on Management Commitment
Source: Reproduced with the permission of the International Organization for Standardization (ISO). Copyright ISO.

For example, the standard calls for an enterprise manufacturing such devices to establish appropriate calibration controls. Because of the diversity of different calibration approaches, a standard cannot specify one approach, but the enterprise should hold out only that it has appropriate mechanisms in place.

In order to attest to its compliance to an ISO standard, an enterprise must contract with an authorized outside reviewer to assess its adherence to that standard. This ISO certification is a process similar to an external audit of financial records performed by certified public accountants (CPAs). Financial statement audits require a licensed CPA external auditor to assess whether an enterprise's financial reports are "fairly stated" following good internal controls. These are high-level words, but when either an investor or the SEC finds such a signed external audit report along with the final reported results, there is a level of assurance that these financial reports are indeed fairly stated and based on good internal control procedures.

For ISO certifications, this process is similar to CPA-led financial auditing that is based on generally accepted auditing standards (GAAS) performed by a major public accounting firm. While we do not have a "Big Four" set of major ISO auditing firms here, national standards-setting organizations qualify outside reviewers to perform external audits of various ISO standards. There is no ISO GAAS, but a wide degree of diversity in audit objectives since a reviewer for ISO 27001 on IT security management systems will be looking for different control procedures than would an ISO auditor for 13485 medical device quality management systems. In all cases, however, the qualified ISO outside auditor may identify areas for corrective actions and publish a report to management similar to an internal audit process. Once the ISO auditor's recommendations are corrected, the outside reviewer will certify that the enterprise is in compliance with that standard.

Once certified, the enterprise can advertise to the outside world that it does have an effective process in place that meets a specific ISO standard. For example, a customer for a medical diagnostic device would want to know if a potential supplier of such a medical device product is in compliance with ISO 13485. That same medical device manufacturer would also want to gain assurance that its prime component suppliers are similarly ISO qualified.

ISO STANDARDS OVERVIEW

Compliance with appropriate ISO standards is not at the same level of requirement as the need for an audited financial statement. Because of SEC financial reporting rules, the lack of an audited financial report or a report with an unfavorable auditor's opinion can be very damaging for publicly traded enterprise. While virtually all publicly traded enterprises are expected to have audited financial statements, the rules are not the same regarding compliance with ISO standards. In many instances, compliance with an ISO standard is only voluntary but nevertheless essential. We have cited the ISO standard covering the thickness and size of a personal credit card. An enterprise that issued cards or readers that were not in compliance with such a standard would soon fail in the marketplace.

ISO standards covering quality management systems are a bit different. An enterprise can all but ignore a standard such as ISO 9000 calling for quality management and still succeed within a national marketplace. For example, in the United States, some senior managers have looked at this ISO standard as "too much paperwork" and have made no efforts to achieve compliance. However, as we move to a more worldwide business trading environment, many more will request such certification. What was once just nice to have has become almost mandatory. Although there are a wide range of ISO standards, the following sections will discuss several ISO standards areas that are important in today's world of heightened internal controls and governance.

ISO 9001 Quality Management Systems and SOx

ISO 9000 has a heritage dating back to World War II, when both sides of the conflict required strong product uniformity while operating at extremely high levels of production volume. Even if the products produced were bullets and bombs, there was a need for strict product quality control. The results on the Western Allies side were some strong quality assurance standard procedures and the emergence of *industrial engineers*—production quality assurance and quality control specialists. After the war, ISO was established as part of the General Agreement on Trade and Tariffs (GATT), one of the international agreements to bring the world into more of a peacetime environment. ISO 9000 on quality management systems was one of the earlier ISO standards. This international standard first received most of its attention in the newly recovering European countries.

Japan was another rebuilding and recovering postwar country that had strongly embraced quality management systems in the 1950s and 1960s. They really got started by inviting a series of U.S.-based quality systems experts including W. Edwards Deming and others to help establish quality processes at many plants in Japan. Many of these quality systems experts were people whose ideas were all but ignored in the United States. However, their philosophies and techniques were heavily embraced by Japanese industry, and by the mid-1970s, Japanese electronic and automobile manufacturers began to make deep inroads into U.S. markets due to the quality and value of their products. Despite their then-dominant product offerings and market advantages, many in the United States began to recognize that these Japanese-manufactured products were superior in many respects to their own. ISO 9000 quality standards became an increasingly important factor in measuring and assessing the quality of products.

ISO 9000 is an important family of standards for quality management systems. Maintained by ISO, these standards include requirements for such matters as:

- Monitoring processes to ensure they are effective
- Keeping adequate records
- Checking output for defects, with appropriate corrective action where necessary
- Regularly reviewing individual processes and the quality system itself for effectiveness
- Facilitating continual improvement

Each of the above refers to processes, not specific actions. However, in asserting that it is in compliance with ISO 9000 (actually 9001), the enterprise is affirming, for example, that it is monitoring its key processes to be effective. This requires significant changes to management procedures and supporting documentation. It creates a required level of expectation. Any enterprise, on a worldwide scope, that holds itself out as adhering to such standards is stating that it has effective quality systems in place. A company or organization that has been independently audited and certified to be in conformance with ISO 9001, for example, may publicly state that it is "ISO 9001 certified" or "ISO 9001 registered." Certification to an ISO 9000 standard does not guarantee the compliance (and therefore the quality) of end products and services; rather, it certifies that consistent business and production processes are being applied.

The actual certification is achieved through a review by a registered audit expert certified for the particular ISO standard. This process is similar to the CPA's review of an enterprise's financial statements. Regulated by national standards organizations, these auditors are authorized to register an enterprise's compliance with an ISO standard.

ISO 9000 Documentation Processes   ISO 9000, as well as other ISO standards, imposes heavy documentation requirements on an enterprise. It is not sufficient for an enterprise to just claim some process has been once documented, and there must be an ongoing process to keep that documentation current over time. In past years and before ISO standards, many went through one-time efforts to create documentation and then never kept it current. This is the kind of situation that many internal auditors have often faced. Internal auditors would frequently ask if some system or process they were reviewing was documented. As they were often met with an admission that the documentation was out of date or nonexistent, this lack of documentation would become an internal audit finding but with little definitive corrective action. ISO 9000 compliance raises documentation requirements to a whole new level. An outside reviewer must certify that the enterprise is in compliance, and it can then certify to the outside world that it is in compliance with the standard.

As a clarification, ISO 9000 is not just one standard but really a series of *certifiable* standards and guidelines:

- ISO 9001: Certifiable standard dealing with design
- ISO 9002: Certifiable standard dealing with manufacturing
- ISO 9003: Certifiable standard dealing with manufacturing and assembly
- ISO 9004: Guideline defining a quality system

These standards are periodically updated with the current version known as ISO 9001:2000. To add to the complexity of things, an enterprise can claim that it is only in compliance with an earlier version, ISO 9000:1994; there is also the QS 9000 series of standards that are similar but pertain to just the automotive industry. A certifiable standard means it is subject to review by an outside auditor, as discussed previously. These standards are periodically updated with the current year appended to the standard. The current version of this quality standard is ISO 9001:2000. For purposes of this discussion, we will just use the more generic term of ISO 9000 to reference these quality management system standards.

ISO 9000 is a set of standards for a continual improvement–driven quality system, no matter whether for a manufactured component or a service process. Exhibit 10.2 shows this quality management system process, which is driven by internal procedures for continual improvements as well as customer requests. This is a continual process where existing processes should be monitored, actions planned, and improvements implemented for subsequent monitoring and assessment. For many, the continual improvement quality process is nothing new. Internal auditors and systems development professionals have used essentially the same set of general processes going back to the early days of IT systems development, in what was and still is called the *Systems Development Life Cycle* (SDLC),[3] a process to develop new IT information systems. However, those SDLC-developed

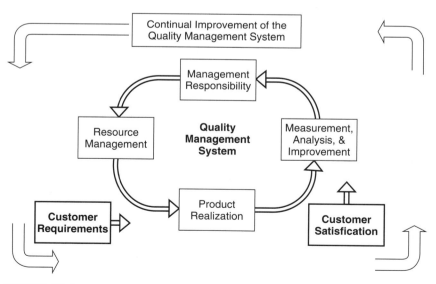

EXHIBIT 10.2   The Quality Management System Process

applications called for a major amount of documentation that was often ignored or not updated. The missing documentation was often shrugged off by many managers or IT developers with the claim that there were too many changes happening and they were too busy. As a result, many IT applications today are developed through more informal, iterative rapid application development processes.

Solid and accurate documentation is extremely important for an enterprise seeking to claim ISO registration. The issue here is that ISO registration covers a worldwide global span. When ISO 9001:2000 Section 4.2.3 states, among other provisions, that "A documented procedure should be established to define the controls needed" along with "a) to approve documents for adequacy of issue," a documentation control system is needed to demonstrate compliance with that standard. ISO best practices in any area call for a hierarchy of documentation starting with top-level manuals to explain the *whys* and then down to instructions describing the *hows* of the practice. Exhibit 10.3 shows this documentation hierarchy with documentation and forms providing proof at the base of this matter. This documentation is essential to support a quality management system and certainly will be required by external ISO certification auditors.

These paragraphs have provided only a very high-level description of the ISO 9000 quality management process. This is important for all types of enterprises to assert to their own internal management and to the outside world that they represent a quality-focused enterprise. Just to represent

EXHIBIT 10.3 ISO Documentation Hierarchy

the breadth of ISO 9000 certification, in 1995, the American Institute of Certified Public Accountants (AICPA) became the first major worldwide professional organization to become ISO 9001 certified.[4] Organizations of all types should consider adopting ISO 9000 processes.

ISO 9000 and SOx: Common Threads   Many financial managers or internal auditors argue that they are busy enough with their SOx compliance and they may question why they should get involved with ISO standards. They might further argue that ISO quality management standards belong on the production floor, and they are or should be more interested in SOx issues. Author William A. Stimson, a quality audit specialist, has compared SOx and ISO 9000 requirements and has found many common threads.[5] Chapter 2 of this book provided an overview of the SOx legislation; some of the requirements common to major sections of both the SOx legislation and ISO 9000 include:

- SOx Title II on auditor independence is very similar to guidance in ISO 9001.
- SOx Title III on corporate responsibility for financial reporting (Section 302) is similar to the ISO 9001 requirements that the enterprise's executive committee must certify certain reports as true and also attest to their compliance with the report contents.
- SOx Title IV on financial disclosures (the often-dreaded Section 404!) is similar to ISO 9001 on management's responsibility for the quality management system; both call for standards to certify that internal controls are effective and that there is a code of conduct in place.
- SOx Title VIII on corporate and criminal fraud accountability has similar requirements to the ISO 9001 rules on management's responsibility for records and documents.

Our point here is not to attempt to do a point-by-point match of SOx and ISO 9000 rules but to highlight areas where these two very different standards have some similar requirements. Perhaps a major difference is that SOx comes with criminal penalties for noncompliance while the failure to achieve ISO standards will primarily merely reduce an enterprise's competitive edge.

As with many ISO standards, ISO 9000 outlines requirements for the continuous improvement of an enterprise's quality management system. The idea is that there is not just one set of attributes but the need for an enterprise to accept inputs from its customers in order to initiate continuous improvement processes. Exhibit 10.4 lists the high-level key elements or contents of ISO 9000. Each of these sections is supported by more detailed

0	Introduction
1.0	Scope
2.0	Normative References
3.0	Definitions
4.0	Quality Management System
4.1	General Requirements
4.2	Documentation Requirements
5.0	Structure and Responsibility
5.1	Management Commitment
5.2	Customer Focus
5.3	Quality Policy
5.4	Planning
5.5	Responsibility, Authority, and Communication
5.6	Management Review
6.0	Resource Management
6.1	Provision of Resources
6.2	Human Resources
6.3	Infrastructure
6.4	Work Environment
7.0	Product Realization
7.1	Planning of Product Realization
7.2	Customer-Related Processes
7.3	Design and Development
7.4	Purchasing
7.5	Production and Service Provision
7.6	Control of Monitoring and Measuring Devices
8.0	Measurement, Analysis, and Improvement
8.1	General
8.2	Monitoring and Measurement
8.3	Control of Nonconforming Product
8.4	Analysis of Data
8.5	Improvement

EXHIBIT 10.4 ISO 9001: 2000 Key Elements

requirements. For example, Section 4.0 on quality management system requirements has a 4.1 and 4.2 on general and documentation requirements followed by more detailed items such as 4.2.3 not shown in this exhibit, on the control of records. It is not the intention of this chapter to reproduce these ISO standards; they can be secured through the previously referenced ISO Web site. However, Exhibit 10.5, Section 8.2.2 on internal auditing, shows the nature and content of these ISO standards. There are a lot of requirements built into a single paragraph!

An enterprise organization must conduct periodic internal audits to determine if the QMS conforms to ISO 9001, and has been effectively implemented and maintained. Audit program planning must take into consideration the status and importance of activities and areas to be audited, and the results of previous audits. The audit procedure, scope, frequency, and methodologies must be defined. These audits must be performed by personnel other than those who performed the activity being audited. Timely corrective action must be taken on deficiencies found during these audits, with follow-up actions including verification of corrective action implementation and reporting verification results.

EXHIBIT 10.5   ISO 9000 Standards Example: Section 8.2.2 on Internal Auditing

IT Security Standards: ISO 17799

There are two related information security management systems standards, ISO 17799 and ISO 27001, discussed in the following section. The first of these, ISO 17799, was first published in the United Kingdom (UK) as BS7799 in 1995; the standard has been updated over the years and is now known as ISO 17799 2005, and it is scheduled to be renumbered as ISO 27002. Today, ISO 17799 represents an important IT-related security standard designed to help any enterprise that needs to establish a comprehensive information security management program or improve its current information security practices.

ISO 17799 is a standard about *information* and information security in a very broad sense. Since such information can exist in many forms, the standard takes a very broad approach and includes a wide range of security standards covering security regarding:

- Data and software electronic files
- All formats of paper documents including printed materials, handwritten notes, and even photographs
- Video and audio recordings
- Telephone conversations as well as e-mail, fax, video, and other forms of messages

The concept here is that all forms of information have value and need to be protected just like any other corporate asset. Many enterprises today do not even consider security standards in many of these broad areas, but the ISO standard suggests they should be covered when appropriate. In addition, the infrastructure that supports this information, including networks, systems, and functions, must also be protected from a wide range of threats including everything from human error and equipment failure to theft, fraud, vandalism, sabotage, fire, flood, and even terrorism.

Similar to all other ISO standards, this published standard does not really prescribe *what* is specifically required but outlines areas where there are requirements for security-related standards. Exhibit 10.6 is an outline of some of these high-level standards areas taken directly from ISO 17799. The standard does not contain detailed requirements for each of these areas—to be a thorough and consistent international standard would require a huge, extensive text that certainly would not be all-inclusive and would soon be out of date. Rather, line 4.2 in this outline calls for security standards covering third-party access policies. ISO does not outline the details of such a standard but calls for the enterprise to have a documented and approved policy covering third-party access policies. This is somewhat of a heads-up type of checklist; an enterprise should develop its own appropriate sets of more detailed standards and procedures in this area. Their type and extent can depend on many factors, but the ISO 17799–compliant enterprise should certainly address this issue along with the other topic areas in the standard.

As a first step to implementing ISO 17799, an enterprise should identify its own information security needs and requirements. This requires performing an information security risk assessment along the lines of the Committee of Sponsoring Organizations' enterprise risk management (COSO ERM) processes discussed in Chapter 9. Such an assessment should focus on the identification of major security threats and vulnerabilities as well as how likely it is that each will cause a security incident. This process should help to pinpoint an enterprise's unique information security needs and requirements.

Too often missed in this getting-ready-for-ISO-17799-information-security-standards-setting process, an enterprise should identify and understand all of the legal, statutory, regulatory, and contractual requirements that the organization, its trading partners, contractors, and service providers must meet. This requires an understanding and identification of an enterprise's unique legal information security needs and requirements.

ISO 17799—soon to become ISO 27002—is the first of a series of international standards meant for any organization that uses internal or external computer systems, possesses confidential data, depends on IT to carry out its business activities, or simply wishes to adopt a higher level of security by complying with a standard. Although a relatively new standard and not in common application, at least in the United States at present, compliance with the ISO 17799 standard constitutes a mark of confidence in an enterprise's overall security, in a manner just as ISO 9000 has become a guarantee of quality. Compliance should promote an increased level of mutual confidence between partners, where each can attest that it has established security standards in compliance with a recognized guideline for those standards. In addition, as ISO 17799 compliance becomes more common, it may result in potentially lower premiums for computer risk insurance but certainly will

1. Scope: A high-level description of the application of this standard.
2. Terms and definitions: Consistent with other ISO standards, all major terms are defined (e.g., definition of what is meant by "confidentiality").
3. The standards or need for a high-level information security policy.
4. Requirements for an enterprise security organization:
   4.1 Information security infrastructure
   4.2 Security and third-party access policies
   4.3 Outsourcing considerations
5. Asset classification and control standards:
   5.1 Accountability for assets
   5.2 Information classifications
6. Personnel security:
   6.1 Security considerations in job definitions and resources
   6.2 User training for personnel security
   6.3 Standards for responding to security incidents and malfunctions
7. Physical and environmental security including requirements for:
   7.1 Secure areas
   7.2 Equipment security
   7.3 General controls
8. Communications and operations management:
   8.1 Operational procedures and responsibility
   8.2 System planning and acceptance
   8.3 Protections against malicious software
   8.4 Housekeeping
   8.5 Network management requirements
   8.6 Media handling and security
   8.7 Exchanges of information and software
9. Access control:
   9.1 Business requirements for access control
   9.2 User access management
   9.3 User responsibilities for security standards
   9.4 Network access control
   9.5 Operating system access control
   9.6 Application access management
   9.7 Monitoring standards for systems access and use
   9.8 Mobile computing and related networking
10. System development and maintenance standards:
   10.1 Security requirements hardware and software systems
   10.2 Application systems security
   10.3 Cryptographic controls
   10.4 Security of system files
   10.5 Security in development and support processes
11. Business continuity management standards.

EXHIBIT 10.6   ISO 17799 Standards Topic Area

---

12. Security standards covering compliance issues:
    12.1 Compliance with legal requirements
    12.2 Reviews of security policy and technical compliance
    12.3 Systems audit considerations

EXHIBIT 10.6 (*Continued*)

yield better protection of confidential data and improved privacy practices and compliance with privacy laws. ISO 17799 is a structured and internationally recognized methodology that should help an enterprise to develop better management of information security on a continuing basis. It is a code of practice that supports the information security management systems requirements of the related security standard, ISO 27001.

IT Security Technique Requirements: ISO 27001

While ISO 17799 is a high-level code of practice covering security controls, ISO 27001 is what ISO defines as the "specification" for an information security management system (ISMS). That is, this standard is designed to measure, monitor, and control security management from a top-down perspective. The standard essentially explains how to apply ISO 17799, and it defines the implementation of this standard as a six-part process as follows:

1. **Define a security policy.** A fundamental component of any standard is the need for a formal, senior management–approved policy statement. All other compliance aspects of the standard will be measured against this policy statement.
2. **Define the scope of the ISMS.** ISO 17799 defines security in rather broad terms that may not be appropriate or needed for all enterprises. Having defined a high-level security policy, an enterprise needs to define the scope of its ISMS that will be implemented. For example, ISO 17799 defines an additional element of its security requirements as video and audio recordings. This may not be necessary for a given organization and then would be specifically excluded from its ISMS scope.
3. **Undertake a risk assessment.** The enterprise should identify a risk assessment methodology that is suited to its ISMS environment and then both develop criteria for accepting risks and define what constitutes acceptable levels of risk.
4. **Manage the risk.** This is a major process that includes formal risk identification, risk analysis, and options for the treatment of those risks. The latter can include applying appropriate risk avoidance controls,

accepting risks, taking other steps to avoid them, or transferring the risks to other parties such as insurers or suppliers.

5. **Select control objectives and controls to be implemented.** This is the same audit and control process discussed elsewhere in this book. For each defined control objective, the enterprise should define an appropriate controls procedure.

6. **Prepare a statement of applicability.** This is the formal documentation that is necessary to wrap up the ISMS documentation process. Such documentation matches up control objectives with procedures to manage and implement the ISMS.

As can be seen from these six outlined steps, risk analysis and security policies are fundamental to this standard.

Because of strict ISO copyright rules, we have not supplied any extracts of the ISO 27001 text beyond the brief example excerpt in Exhibit 10.5. However, that example shows the standard as a set of tight and unambiguous text. There is little specific detail but enough to allow an enterprise to implement its ISMS. The formal standard concludes with an appendix section listing control procedures for each of the objective details in the standard. However, ISO 27001 should really not be considered as a comprehensive set of control procedures that will change as technology changes, but rather as an outline for the framework of an ISMS that should be continually implemented, monitored, and maintained.

ISO 17799 (soon to be renamed ISO 27002) and ISO 27001 are already global standards, with established compliance and certification schemes in place—particularly in the United Kingdom and the overall European Union. Both of these standards will continue to evolve to track technology, and will expand with even wider changes. We can see them being more closely tied with control frameworks such as CobiT[6] (discussed in Chapter 5) in future periods. As such, therefore, there can be little doubt that these ISO standards will continue to grow in their influence and adoption will continue to expand. The astute compliance manager should monitor ongoing progress and begin to build an appropriate ISMS.

Service Quality Management: ISO 20000

Many professionals will agree that we live in a world with too many standards—many of which are similar to others with like objectives but that are not connected to each other. ISO 2000 on service quality management introduces some much-needed standards convergence. This is an international standard for IT service management, and it introduces or summarizes many of the ITIL service management best practices that were discussed in Chapter 8. The standard consists of two parts, Part 1 on implementing service management and the following Part 2 section describing best practices for service management. The Part 1 standard specifies the need for a series of service management documented processes, such as defining requirements for implementing such a management system, new or changed service requirements, and documented relationship, control, resolution, and release processes. Quite correctly, the standard takes the best practices approach of ITIL and calls for formal documented processes to support them.

ISO 2000 calls for an enterprise to adopt and be certified that it has adopted the ITIL best practices discussed in Chapter 8. Formally, this standard "promotes the adoption of an integrated process approach to effectively deliver managed services to meet the business and customer requirements." ISO 2000 is the first global standard for IT service management and is fully compatible with and supportive of the ITIL framework. It will undoubtedly have a significant impact upon the use and acceptance of ITIL best practices and the whole IT service management landscape.

In future years, we should see an increasing level of recognition of the importance of ISO service-related standards. In our increasingly global economy, no matter what national restrictions may be imposed across borders from time to time, internal standards are needed to define common practices and to better facilitate communication. When an enterprise or service organization—anywhere in the world—has achieved ISO 9000 quality management certification, customers and users can expect a certain minimum level of documentation and process standards. The ISO 27001 IT security standards should soon reach a similar level of importance and recognition. With our comments on ISO 2000, on ITIL, and ISO 9000's similarities with SOx, we should see increasing convergence trends between ISO and standards in other areas. The interested professional should understand and embrace these important ISO standards.

QUALITY AUDIT PROCESS

While many think of only the CPA-type external or the Institute of Internal Auditors (IIA) internal professionals as *auditors*, there are other professionals who also call themselves auditors. Examples here might be federal government contract auditors or the audit reviewers of health-care or hospital standards. These other auditors typically do not work in the corporate offices that are the domain of the CPA-type external or IIA-associated internal auditors. While the IIA-member internal audit professional, discussed in Chapter 11 as well as in other chapters of this book, often has little contact with them, *quality auditors* are another group of audit professionals who play an important role in many enterprises. Administered through the American Society for Quality (ASQ) professional organization, they are a unique internal audit–like professional group that has its own standards, codes of ethics, and professional certification designations. Traditionally known as quality auditors rather than just internal auditors, these professionals have responsibilities to review a wide range of ISO standards-compliance, work-simplification, and quality-related processes in the enterprise. Quality auditors have historically operated "on the shop floor" in primarily manufacturing enterprises and often have had little contact with the IIA-type internal auditors, who are more often based in headquarters operations.

Although they have historically been separate from the IIA type of internal auditors, quality auditors are being brought closer to the IIA internal auditor than they have been in the past. More accurately, each of these internal audit professional groups is changing in terms of objectives and approaches in ways that bring them closer together. The classic IIA internal audit professional should have an understanding of the activities of quality auditors and how their work fits in the overall environment of corporate governance.

Terminology can also be a bit confusing here. Although the expression *quality auditor* traditionally described this professional, many in this ASQ-sponsored professional group now call themselves just internal auditors. While some of these quality auditors may belong to the IIA as well, they have their own separate professional organization, the Quality Audit Division (QAD) of the American Society for Quality (ASQ). That enterprise is the leading proponent of the quality movement in the United States with a wide range of publications, professional certifications, and separate divisions covering industries such as aerospace or pharmaceuticals as well as professional practices, such as the QAD. ASQ is very involved with the ISO worldwide quality standards and its QAD is responsible for compliance audits against those ISO standards.

The QAD's stated mission is "To support auditors and other stakeholders by defining and promoting auditing as a management tool to achieve continuous improvement, effective communication, and increased customer satisfaction." Their use of just the designation "auditor" often causes some confusion regarding the roles of these quality auditors. In addition, the profession recognizes several other levels of auditing:

- **Self-audit.** This is a quality audit performed within the enterprise to review compliance with ISO standards and the like.
- **Second-party audit.** Quality auditors must often perform reviews to assess whether their suppliers are operating in compliance with standards. A second-party audit occurs when an enterprise's own quality auditors visit a supplier to test its compliance with standards.
- **Third-party audit.** This is an audit performed at the enterprise by an independent organization, such as an ISO registrar, a government

agency such as the Department of Labor's Occupational Safety and Health Administration (OSHA) or the Federal Drug Administration (FDA).

Although historically called quality auditors, these professionals often call themselves just auditors today.

Things can be even more confusing because the ASQ designates their professionals as either internal or external auditors. An ASQ internal auditor reviews controls and standards within the enterprise while an external auditor, in this context, performs third-party reviews at other enterprises to establish such matters as ISO certifications as discussed above. While a quality auditor may be a member of the IIA in addition to the ASQ, the external quality auditor has no regular relationship with the AICPA and its CPA designation. We will generally use the term *quality auditor* for all of our references here to these ASQ-background auditors throughout this chapter to make a distinction between IIA-sponsored internal auditors and CPA-certified external auditors.

While the IIA has its Certified Internal Auditor (CIA) professional designation and the Information Systems Audit and Control Association (ISACA) has its Certified Information Systems Auditor (CISA), the ASQ has the Certified Quality Auditor (CQA) professional certification. Within the CQA are specialty designations such as for hazardous analysis or biomedical auditing. These certifications require designated levels of work experience and successfully passing an examination. ASQ quality auditors are involved in similar professional activities and have standards similar to IIA internal auditors, and the ASQ has a series of specialized national meetings and conferences for ASQ quality auditors.

Role of the Quality Auditor

ASQ procedures, standards, and their quality auditing guidance materials are similar to the standards used by IIA internal auditors. Quality auditors follow many of the same general internal audit steps as IIA-sponsored internal auditors in their procedures for developing programs, reporting findings, and the like. ASQ quality audits have their own professional certification, the examination and professional experience–based Certified Quality Auditor (CQA) designation. Quality auditors usually are not involved with financial issues that come with reviews of financial internal controls or financial statement integrity, but they often follow published standards such as ISO 9000, and their audits often tend to be more quantitative and metrics-oriented than the work of the typical internal auditor. The work of quality auditors is often closely aligned with the classic tools used by quality assurance specialists.

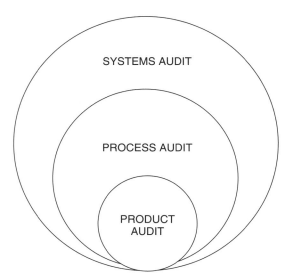

EXHIBIT 10.7   Types of Quality Audits

Quality audit standards introduce a set of terminologies that may be unfamiliar to many IIA-background internal auditors as well as the managers accustomed to working with them. For example, as shown in Exhibit 10.7, quality audits can be structured as part of their scope and objectives as product, process, and systems audits:

- A *product audit* is an assessment of a final product or service and its "fitness for use" against stated requirements or specifications. In a manufacturing sense, a product audit would be performed on some item that has just passed its final inspection and is ready for delivery to the customer.
- A *process audit* is the major type of audit performed by quality auditors. This is a review to verify conformance to standards, methods, procedures, or other requirements.
- A *systems audit* is not an IT-related review but an audit that covers all aspects of a control system. This type of review is conducted to verify, through objective evidence, that all aspects of management systems and organizational plans are implemented to adequately meet identified requirements.

Another aspect of quality audits is that they are typically more analytical than the usual IIA type of internal audit. Because of their traditional background as engineering technicians rather than accountants, quality auditors

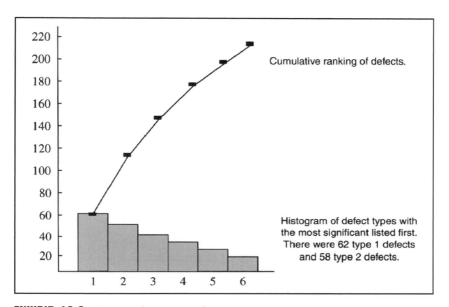

EXHIBIT 10.8 Pareto Chart Example
Source: Brink's Modern Internal Auditing, Sixth Edition, Robert Moeller, Page 651.
Copyright © 2005 John Wiley & Sons. Reprinted with permission of John Wiley & Sons, Inc.

tend to make greater use of analytical tools and techniques in their workpaper analyses and audit reports. An example might help explain such a typical quality auditor approach. Exhibit 10.8 shows a Pareto chart, a common diagram used in quality-related audit analyses. The idea of this common quality audit chart is to rank the types of errors or problems found by the auditor on the vertical axis with the most severe problems listed first. In this example, there were 62 cases of defect 1 during the period reviewed. Similarly, there were 58 cases of defect 2 with increasingly fewer cases for the other defects. The numbers of cumulative defects are plotted on the vertical axis. The line goes from 62 to (62 + 58 = 120) for the second point and continues. The idea behind a Pareto chart is to see which defects require the most attention. The less than 10 instances of defect 6 shown here should require less management attention.

While quality auditors have traditionally used tools such as Pareto charts to review quality defects and make recommendations, in recent years the worldwide movement to the ISO 9000 family of quality management standards and other ISO quality management systems standards has very much changed their role.

Internal audit requirements are common in most ISO standards. For example, Section 8.2.2 of ISO 9001:2000, shown in Exhibit 10.5, describes requirements for internal audits of ISO standards. It calls for management to conduct internal audits at planned intervals to determine whether the quality management system conforms to requirements of the standard and is effectively implemented and maintained. These standards also contain requirements for audit programs, management's responsibility, and other matters. Similar audit requirements exist for other quality management system ISO standards. Section 6 of ISO 27001:2000, for example, is titled *Internal ISMS Audits* and states, among other matters,

> *The organization shall conduct internal ISMS audits at planned intervals to determine whether the control objectives, controls, processes and procedures of its ISMS:*
>
> a. *conform to the requirements of this International Standard and relevant legislation or regulations;*
> b. *conform to the identified information security requirements;*
> c. *are effectively implemented and maintained; and*
> d. *perform as expected.*

Again, this section of the standard has more substance, but the extracts are presented to illustrate the requirements of audits for ISO standards. Any enterprise that is launching and seeking standards certification must establish a quality audit function. Although this ISO standard calls for "internal audits," the typical IIA-oriented corporate internal audit function, might give this requirement a "not my job" type of response today.

Quality audit functions are often organized more informally than IIA-trained internal auditors with their board of directors' audit committee reporting relationships. The following sections will discuss this quality audit process. There is somewhat of a disconnect between quality auditors, following ASQ standards, and the IIA internal auditors, following their professional standards, as discussed in Chapter 11. Over time, however, we should see a greater level of convergence between these auditing processes.

Quality auditors are often involved with tests for improvement based on their findings from an earlier review. To accomplish this continuous improvement process, the data in a new review must be analyzed for trends and identification of weaknesses. The quality auditor then compares results to goals and objectives, and analyzes process data to identify risks, inefficiencies, opportunities for improvement, and negative trends. The results may be recommendations for changes in procedures, or in other elements of the process, such as improvements in acceptance criteria or methods of monitoring. Changes in equipment or technology may also be among the quality auditor's recommendations for continual improvement. In many respects, quality auditors recommend more significant changes to the improvement cycle than has been the case with internal auditors.

Performing Quality Audits

Traditional IIA-issued internal auditing standards are well recognized among many professionals. The IIA's Standards for the Professional Practice of Internal Auditing, discussed in Chapter 11, provides a good overview of those standards and discusses the overall profession of internal auditing. What we are describing as the ASQ-sponsored practice of quality auditing brings a somewhat different perspective to auditing. Although it has its roots in earlier quality assurance and industrial engineering processes, quality auditing is particularly important for measuring compliance to ISO standards, and there are both internal and external components to this auditing practice.

ASQ-driven audits—quality audits—are somewhat different. They are reviews performed to assess regulatory compliance rules or to meet requirements for ISO standards registration or certification. They are also important because they are a key feedback loop in an enterprise's quality system to keep management informed about compliance with their documented systems procedures. As discussed, quality audits are further characterized as either internal or self-audits or second- or third-party audits. Under these rules, a quality audit may be performed as a *self-audit* by persons very close to the actual process operations. Quality audits are typically not performed by a separate internal audit department but by persons in the enterprise who can demonstrate a level of objectivity.

In addition to the internal or self-audit, second- or third-party audits may occur. Quality audits take place in the ISO standards environment where an enterprise must check that its suppliers and others are in compliance with certain standards. *Second-party audits* occur when an enterprise performs a quality audit on one of its suppliers. A *third-party audit* occurs when an outside registrar or a regulatory agency, such as OSHA or the FDA, performs an independent review. The concept is that an enterprise must determine that its suppliers are in compliance with some standard through a second-party review. However, in order to hold itself out to others as being in compliance with a standard such as ISO 90001, it must contract with a certified independent registrar to certify that compliance. This classification of different types of quality audits is shown in Exhibit 10.9.

Internal quality or self-audits are generally much more extensive than second- or third-party reviews. As part of a self-audit, an enterprise's

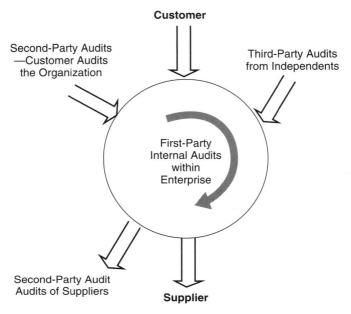

EXHIBIT 10.9 Classifications of Quality Audits

auditors should be interested in compliance with applicable standards with these objectives:

- To verify that the implemented system is working
- To verify that supporting training programs are cost effective
- To identify people or groups not following procedures
- To provide evidence to management and others that processes are working as documented

The quality audit process follows steps that are similar to many other types of internal and external audits, except that there may not be a high level of detailed audit standards here. In contrast, Chapter 3 introduced the AS5 auditing standards for audits of financial statement internal controls under SOx. Quality audits do not have the same level of standards for performing the reviews. However, the audit steps are similar, starting with the audit plan, then the development of audit procedures, and finally the concluding audit report and steps to achieve corrective actions. Exhibit 10.10 outlines typical quality audit process steps.

- Pre-Audit Activities
  1. Preparation for audit— establish audit objectives.
  2. Planning for all audit activities.
- The On-Site Audit
  1. Opening meeting— meet with auditee and outline planned procedures.
  2. The audit— activities will depend on the nature of the review.
  3. Closing meeting— discuss findings and present draft report at end of field-work review.
- Post-Audit Activities
  1. The audit report— report on findings and recommendations.
  2. Management review— discuss audit results with all levels of management.
  3. Corrective actions— negotiate plan to correct audit findings.
  4. Follow-up/corrective action audits.

EXHIBIT 10.10 Quality Audit Process Steps

These steps may appear very similar to many familiar with IIA internal audit or generally accepted auditing standards (GAAS) financial audit standards. Perhaps a major difference is that quality auditors are much more involved with correcting audit findings and launching corrective actions initiatives. When compared with the IIA professional standards discussed in Chapter 11 that define separate duties as internal auditors and internal consultants, the roles of the quality auditor as the assessor of control weaknesses and as consultant in helping with corrective actions are much closer to each other than the IIA standards. In addition, quality audit procedures and findings are often more detailed and analytical than would be expected in typical internal and external financial audits. For example, CPA external auditors use statistical sampling theory to develop audit conclusions based on very small sample sizes compared to large populations of data they are assessing. Quality auditors sometimes sin on the other side of things by pulling very large samples of materials to support their audit work.

As the importance of compliance with a growing number of ISO standards becomes greater, we will almost certainly see the role of the quality auditor moving more to an enterprise's "front office" and audit committees and their management better understanding that there are many common needs for both ASQ-trained quality auditors and IIA-trained internal auditors. We will almost certainly see their two professional organizations move closer together in future years.

IFAC INTERNATIONAL ACCOUNTING STANDARDS

An ongoing topic of this book has been a discussion of some of the new or evolving Sarbanes-Oxley and other internal control standards that are impacting enterprises today. Some of these may have a direct and immediate impact, such as the just-enacted AS5 rules discussed in Chapter 3. We have also discussed emerging trends, such as the increased acceptance of the ITIL best practices discussed in Chapter 8 or the increased importance of and reliance on ISO standards discussed earlier in this chapter. International accounting standards have not yet been adopted in the United States, but may become an issue going forward.

Even more important than the need for consistent auditing standards is the even greater need for consistent accounting practices. That is, basic transactions should be accounted for and tracked in a consistent manner. For example, there are many worldwide interpretations of what constitutes a sale—do we need to have an actual cash purchase or just a promise to pay—and all enterprises should be accounting for and recording these accounting transactions in a consistent manner. In the United States, basic accounting rules fall under what is known as generally accepted accounting principles (GAAP). Other, more detailed and very specific accounting rules are prescribed by the Financial Accounting Standards Board (FASB), an independent accounting rules-setting authority whose rules are recognized by the SEC. These U.S. accounting principles and rules are not the same throughout the world.

While many accounting standards, such as double-entry bookkeeping, are accepted and recognized throughout the world, others may have the same intent or may be different as part of various national practices. The practice of driving on the right- or left-hand side of the road is such an example of a different sort of national practice. No matter which standard is followed, automobile drivers can still easily get from point A to B as long as all drivers follow the same rule. The same is somewhat true for accounting practices as well. If everyone in that country treats a sale in the same manner, sales results across various companies will be comparable within that country. This becomes a bit more complex because we are an increasingly global economy. Accounting as well as auditing practices in Belgium, for example, need to be comparable to nearby neighbor France. In addition, there is a need for some consistency between Germany or the United States and both of those countries. As enterprises become increasingly global, there is a need to have at least a general understanding of the differences and consistencies in accounting standards across international borders.

Accounting and auditing standards had been established over the years on a country-by-country basis by professional or governmental boards as well as by some international standards-setting bodies. Individual countries may fully or only generally accept these international standards. The United States is an example of the latter. With strong established practices in many areas, the United States often takes the lead for some or goes its own way regarding other standards.

As we move into the world of international organizations, we run into a gaggle of initials to describe these various standards-setting groups. One can just think of the United Nations (UN) with its UNESCO, FAO, UNICEF, UNCTAD, and many more. International accounting and auditing standards also use often-confusing sets of initials. There are International Standards of Auditing (ISA), as well as International Accounting Standards (IAS). The ISA auditing standards are established by the International Federation of Accountants (IFAC) through its International Auditing and Assurance Standards Board (IAASB), which issues these ISAs as well as International Auditing Practice Statements (IAPS). To further complicate the picture, there is also the International Organization of Supreme Audit Institutions (INTOSAI) whose Auditing Standards Committee contributes to the work of IAASB.

Acronyms again, the International Accounting Standards Board (IASB) publishes its accounting standards as International Accounting Standards (IAS) as well as in a series of pronouncements called International Financial Reporting Standards (IFRS). They somewhat provide a foundation for most counties worldwide and have been adopted by the E.U. member countries.

In a step toward eliminating the existing differences between U.S. GAAP and IFRS standards, FASB and IASB have identified a series of financial accounting differences. Some of these are very basic where some accounting practice is allowed under one and not the other. Others represent sometimes complex differences in tax reporting treatments and other matters. Exhibit 10.11 is an example of just a few of these identified differences. In many instances, resolution of these differences is not like switching between English or metric units of measurement. It requires a give and take on each side, and to resolve any matter, the supporting accounting standards must change.

The need for consistent auditing standards really became obvious with the passage of SOx. The legislation was framed with the mindset that the SEC could review the accounting records of nonregistrant foreign firms. However, as most non-U.S. companies were using IFRS standards, it would be impertinent to expect them to convert to U.S. GAAP and to keep two sets of books to reflect the different standard. Developing and implementing a consistent set of accounting principles will be a long, slow process, but one that is essential. We should soon see the two sets of accounting standards—IFRS and U.S. GAAP—converge.

The following are a few examples of what has been identified as a fairly lengthy list of differences between IFRS and GAAP accounting standards. Some of these have been resolved or are in the process of resolution.

Issue 1: **Comparative prior-year financial statements**
IFRS: One-year comparative financial information is required.
U.S.: GAAP states that comparatives are "desirable." SEC regulations generally require three years of comparative financial information (balance sheet two years).

Issue 2: **Extraordinary items**
IFRS: *Originally* prohibited, but rules have been changed to permit reporting.
U.S.: Extraordinary items are permitted but restricted to infrequent, unusual, and rare items that affect profit and loss.

Issue 3: **Method for determining inventory cost**
IFRS: *Last-in-first-out* (LIFO) accounting is prohibited.
U.S.: LIFO is permitted.

Issue 4: **Inclusion of overdrafts in cash**
IFRS: Included if they form an integral part of an entity's cash management.
U.S.: Excluded.

Issue 5: **Classification of deferred tax assets and liabilities**
IFRS: Always noncurrent.
U.S.: Classification is split between the current and noncurrent components based on the classification of the underlying asset or liability.

Issue 6: **Basis of property, plant, and equipment**
IFRS: May use either revalued amount or historical cost. Revalued amount is fair value at date of revaluation less subsequent accumulated depreciation and impairment losses.
U.S.: Generally required to use historical cost.

EXHIBIT 10.11   Sample Differences Between IFRS and U.S. GAAP

ENDNOTES

1. International Organization for Standardization (ISO), Geneva Switzerland.
2. www.iso.org.
3. There are numerous published references to the SDLC process. A Google search on SDLC system development will get the reader started.
4. http://www.qualitydigest.com/june99/html/body_iso_9000.html.

5. William A. Stimson, *ISO 9001 & Sarbanes-Oxley: A System of Governance* (Chica, CA: Paton Press, 2006).
6. CobiT stands for *C*ontrol *O*bjectives for *I*nformation *T*echnology, a framework for managing IT and general internal controls. The CobiT framework is discussed in Chapter 5.

CHAPTER 11

Internal Audit in a Sarbanes-Oxley Environment

Even though the internal audit function has historically been a key resource over the years in helping enterprises to build effective internal controls, it was given somewhat of a short shrift in the initial days of Sarbanes-Oxley (SOx). Internal audit was barely mentioned in the SOx legislation, and some advisory consulting firms argued then that internal auditors should have little if any role in helping their enterprises to define and document SOx internal controls. Their argument then was that internal auditors were not truly independent. That is, if internal auditors helped their enterprise to develop that first round of SOx Section 404 internal control documentation, they could not come back later and objectively audit the internal controls they had helped to design. Because of these concerns, some internal audit functions effectively sat on the sidelines in the first years of SOx Section 404 reviews as enterprise financial management, in many cases, brought in outside consultants to document and assess internal controls for their external auditor attestations.

With the ongoing enterprise needs for people with internal auditor–like skills, however, this environment certainly has changed, and internal auditors today have been enjoying a SOx-inspired renaissance. Several factors have been drivers here. First, the external auditor rules for SOx assessments of internal controls have changed. The new Auditing Standard No. 5 (AS5) rules discussed in Chapter 3 strongly emphasize the importance of internal audit in SOx internal control assessment work. In addition, SOx has very much tightened the relationship of internal audit to an enterprise's audit committee. SOx has strengthened the corporate governance responsibilities of audit committees and their relationships with internal audit. This chapter will look at the role of internal auditors in achieving SOx compliance and their audit committee relationship as it exists today.

Internal audit standards are maintained by their professional organization, the Institute of Internal Auditors (IIA). It publishes the *International Standards for the Professional Practice of Internal Auditing*,[1] which each IIA member is expected to know, understand, and follow. These standards were updated, about the same time SOx became effective, to better define the dual roles of internal control implementer and reviewer that internal auditors often play in their enterprises. The first is the traditional internal audit role as an independent reviewer of internal controls, and the second better defines internal auditors' frequent role as internal consultant to their enterprises. These revised IIA standards rules better define the very important roles of internal auditors today in helping an enterprise achieve SOx compliance. This chapter will look at IIA standards rules and more recent changes to them up through the IIA's January 2007 standards modifications.

Another potentially significant definitional change to the practice of internal auditing occurred in mid-2007, when the IIA published what they described as an updated *common body of knowledge* (CBOK)[2] for the profession. Internal auditors are involved with many different areas of an enterprise and use a wide variety of tools and techniques, but there never had been an IIA-sponsored attempt to define those shared knowledge and practice areas that support the profession of internal auditing. While not a practice standard such as the Project Management Institute's (PMI's) well-regarded "Project Management Book of Knowledge (PMBOK),"[3] the IIA's recently released CBOK membership survey to describe a wide variety of internal audit common practices. The following sections provide a summary of the IIA's new CBOK survey and how it can best be used by internal auditors to assess their SOx, audit assurance, and corporate governance practices and review activities.

PROFESSION OF INTERNAL AUDITING

People in all types of businesses often talk about "the auditors" without a good understanding of whom these people really are and their roles and responsibilities. This might be because today we have a variety of people in the modern enterprise who call themselves "auditors," including the quality auditors from a process improvement group, ISO certification registrants, external auditors from the CPA firm, auditors from various branches of government, and internal auditors. The term *internal auditing* can sometimes raise even more questions in terms of their specific role, meaning, and function. The focus of this chapter is on the profession of internal auditing, as defined by the IIA, and understanding the role of internal auditing in reference to the standards established by their professional organization. The IIA was founded in the United States after World War II and has defined the profession and developed evolving standards for it over the years. The IIA defines the practice of internal auditing as follows:

> *Internal auditing is an independent, objective assurance and consulting activity designed to add value and improve the organization's operations. It helps an organization to evaluate and improve the effectiveness of risk management, control, and governance processes*

This statement becomes more meaningful when one focuses on its key terms. First, *auditing* suggests a variety of ideas that can be viewed very narrowly, such as the checking of arithmetical accuracy or physical existence of accounting and other process records. More broadly, auditing is described as a thoughtful review and appraisal at the highest organizational level. We use the term *auditing* here to include this total range of levels of service, from detailed checking—verifying that a procedure is working correctly—to higher-level consulting types of appraisals.

Internal defines work carried on within the enterprise by its own resources—normally employees. Internal auditing work is distinguished from audit-related work carried on by outside public accountants or other parties (such as government regulators) who are not directly a part of the particular enterprise. The remainder of the IIA's definition of internal auditing describes a number of other important terms, on almost a word-by-word basis, that apply to the profession:

- **Independent.** Auditing that is free of restrictions that could significantly limit the scope and effectiveness of the review or the later reporting of resultant findings and conclusions.
- **Objective assurance.** This reference refers to the appraisal function of internal auditing. At the request of their audit committee, management, and others, internal auditors perform objective and independent reviews to assess internal controls and other compliance and governance processes.
- **Consulting activity.** Internal auditors have always served as internal consultants to enterprise management. However, a recent redefinition of internal audit emphasizes this important internal consulting role.
- **Add value and improve effectiveness.** Internal audit's role is not just to find "what is wrong" in an enterprise but to bring in some value through their recommendations.
- **Emphasis on risk management, control, and governance processes.** This definition emphasizes three important areas of internal audit activity. Whether an assurance-based review or serving as an internal consultant, all internal audit activities should focus on one or more of these three areas risk management, control and governance.

Internal auditing should be recognized as an internal control process that functions by assessing risks and then measuring and evaluating the effectiveness of multiple levels of other enterprise controls. When an enterprise establishes plans on many levels, and then proceeds to implement them in terms of its operations, it must do something to monitor those operations to assure the achievement of its established objectives. These further efforts can be thought of as *controls*. While the internal audit function is itself one of the types of controls used, there is a wide range of other controls. The special role of internal audit is to help measure and evaluate those other controls. Thus, internal auditors must understand their own role as a control function in relation to the nature and scope of other types of controls in the enterprise.

Internal auditors who do their job effectively become experts in what makes for the best possible design and implementation of all types of internal controls. This expertise includes understanding the interrelationships of various controls, their relative risks, and their best possible integration in the total system of internal controls. It is thus through the control door that internal auditors come to examine and evaluate all organizational activities and to provide service to the enterprise. Internal auditors cannot be expected to equal—let alone exceed—the technical and operational expertise pertaining to the various activities of the enterprise they may review. However, internal auditors can help their responsible business units achieve more effective results by appraising existing controls and providing a basis for helping to improve those controls. Working under the direction of their audit committees, they are important resources for establishing effective corporate governance processes.

Internal Auditing History and Background

It is normal for any activity—including a self-assessment activity such as internal auditing—to develop as a result of emerging needs. At its most primitive level, self-assessment or internal auditing functions get started when individuals are asked to sit back and survey something their peer employees have done. At that point, the individual assessor asks himself how well a particular task has been accomplished and, perhaps, how it might be done better if it were to be repeated through improved processes. If a second person is involved in this activity, the assessment function would be expanded to include an evaluation of her participation in the endeavor. In a small business, the owner or manager may be doing this review—to some extent—for all enterprise employees. In all of these situations, the assessment or internal audit function is being carried out directly as part of a basic management role. However, as the operations of an enterprise become more voluminous and complex, it is no longer practicable for an enterprise owner or top manager to have enough contact with all operations to satisfactorily review the effectiveness of performance. These responsibilities need to be delegated.

Although this hypothetical senior manager could build a supervisory system to try to provide a personal overview of operations, that same manager will find it increasingly difficult to know whether the interests of the enterprise are being properly served as the enterprise grows larger and more complex. Are established procedures being complied with? Are assets being properly safeguarded? Are the various employees functioning efficiently? Are current approaches still effective in the light of changing conditions?

The ultimate response to these types of questions is that the manager must obtain further help by assigning one or more individuals to be directly responsible for reviewing activities and reporting on the above mentioned types of questions. It is here that the internal auditing activity comes into being in a formal and explicit sense. The first internal auditing assignments were usually originated to satisfy very basic and sharply defined operational needs. The earliest special concern of management was whether the assets of the enterprise were being properly protected, whether organizational procedures and policies were being complied with, and whether financial records were being accurately maintained. There was also considerable emphasis on maintenance of the status quo. To a great extent and certainly many years prior to SOx, this internal auditing effort was once viewed by members of management and others as a closely related extension of the work of external auditors.

The result of this earlier lack of understanding of their responsibilities was that internal auditors were once viewed as playing a relatively narrow role in their enterprises, with relatively limited responsibility in the total managerial spectrum. An internal auditor in those earlier days of the profession often was viewed as a financially oriented checker of records and more of a police officer than a co-worker. In some enterprises in the distant past, internal auditors had major responsibilities for reconciling canceled payroll checks with bank statements or checking the mathematics in regular business documents. In retail enterprises, internal auditors were once responsible for reconciling daily cash sales to recorded sales receipts.

Understanding the history of internal auditing is important because this old image still exists, to some extent, for internal auditors today. This is so even though internal auditing functions today are now very different. Over a period of time, the operations of various enterprises increased in volume and complexity, creating managerial problems and new pressures on senior management. In response to these pressures, management recognized the possibilities for better utilization of their internal auditors. Here were individuals already set up in an audit function, and there seemed to be every good reason for getting greater value from these individuals with relatively little increase in cost.

At the same time, internal auditors perceived these opportunities and initiated new types of services themselves. Thus, internal auditors gradually took on broader and more management-oriented responsibilities in their work efforts. Because internal auditing had its roots initially in accounting-oriented processes, this upward trend was felt first in the accounting and financial control areas. Rather than just reporting the same accounting-related internal control exceptions—such as some documentation lacking a supervisor's initials—internal auditors began to question the overall control process they were reviewing. Subsequently, internal audit valuation work began to be extended to include many nonfinancial, operational areas in the enterprise.

Although people with the title of "auditor" were in place in many larger organizations going back at least to the turn of the twentieth century, they really did not follow consistent approaches, as there was no real information sharing across these new professionals. This was corrected when the IIA was launched in 1942. Its first membership chapter was started in New York City, with a Chicago chapter soon to follow. The IIA was formed by people who had been given the title "internal auditor" by their enterprises and who wanted to both share experiences and gain knowledge from others in this new field. A profession was born that has undergone many changes over subsequent years.

New business initiatives, such as the Committee of Sponsoring Organizations (COSO) internal control framework discussed in Chapter 4, or the requirements of SOx discussed in Chapter 2, have caused a continuing increase in the need for the services of internal auditors. The IIA has grown from its first, 25-member charter chapter in 1942, to an international association with over 140,000 members and hundreds of local chapters worldwide. The internal audit profession has reached a major level of maturity and is well positioned for continuing dynamic growth.

Internal auditing today involves a broad spectrum of operational activities and levels of coverage. In some enterprises today, internal auditing has moved beyond being a staff activity roughly tied to the controller's department, and has a role that is constantly being redefined. SOx has been a more recent but major driver of change for internal auditors. While they once had only nominal reporting relationship to their board audit committee, SOx has strengthened and formalized that relationship. However, in other enterprises, internal audit still continues to function at a routine compliance level. In still other situations, internal audit suffers from being integrated too closely with regular accounting activities, which limits virtually all of its audit work to strictly financial areas. These are all exceptions that do not reflect the potential capabilities of internal auditors.

Today's internal auditor is formally and actively serving the board of directors' audit committee. While many internal audit functions once had an almost nonexistent, strictly dotted-line reporting relationship to their audit committee—with little direct communication—the chief audit executive (CAE) today has a direct and active level of communication with that same audit committee. This overall situation reflects major progress in the scope of internal audit's coverage and level of service to all areas of the enterprise. The internal auditing profession itself, through its own self-development and dedication, has contributed to this progress and has set the stage for a continuing trend toward greater recognition and responsibility.

Relationships of Operational, Financial, and Information Systems Auditing

During the 1960s, there was a trend toward using the term *operational auditing* in place of the traditional *internal auditing*. The rationale was that *internal auditing* was a term tied too closely with basic financial auditing, including the review of both financial control activities and financial statements. Internal auditors began to call themselves *operational auditors* because of their desire to focus more of their efforts on the other operational processes in the enterprise that could potentially point to areas for increased profit and overall management service. In its most extreme form, the so-called operational auditing function would disassociate itself entirely from the so-called financial areas. Internal auditors would claim, for example, to have no expertise on the financial controls surrounding an accounts receivable operation. Rather, they might look at process controls and ignore the issue of whether the cash received was properly recorded and tied to financial accounts including the general ledger. Management often became confused if not dismayed when their internal auditors all but ignored important accounting or financial-related issues. This separation of responsibilities created issues of both substance and self-interest for the *operational audit*–oriented internal auditors.

This concept of a strict operational auditor has somewhat gone away. If anything, the role has been assumed by the quality auditors discussed later here and in Chapter 10. Today's IIA-affiliated internal auditors are concerned with accounting and financial processes, and some expertise in these areas is generally considered to be essential. Coverage of accounting and financial controls and processes has also provided an opportunity for expanding the range of internal audit services into the broader operational areas. Since accounting or financial records directly or indirectly reflect all operational activities, financially oriented internal audit reviews often open doors to the other activities. A strong example is the pervasive influence of IT in all aspects of enterprise operations. This combination of operational and financial internal audit practices as well as information systems or information technology (IT) auditing is essential for evaluating and assessing SOx internal controls today.

Internal audit needs to have an adequate coverage of key accounting and financial areas, and the responsibilities of those who do that will inevitably spill over into an overview of broader operational areas. This perceived failure to cover key financial areas was one of the arguments external audit firms made to senior management, starting in the early 1990s, when they offered to take a greater role in these processes by providing internal audit outsourcing services. That is, the reporting responsibilities of many internal functions were transferred to an external audit firm that managed the function. For the years leading up to the enactment of SOx, it almost appeared that the major public accounting firms were all but taking over internal auditing through these outsourcing arrangements. Now, because of questions about the oversight of these outsourced internal auditors prior to the collapse of Enron, SOx has prohibited independent, external auditors from also performing internal audits for the same enterprise. These rules are discussed in Chapter 2 as part of the general overview of key SOx rules today.

In the wake of SOx and the internal control assessment requirements of the Act's Section 404 and 302 requirements, internal audits' roles and responsibilities are changing again as we move through the first decade of the twenty-first century. Internal auditors today are a far more important element in an enterprise's overall internal control framework than they have been in the past.

INTERNAL AUDIT PROFESSIONAL STANDARDS

Every profession requires a set of standards to govern its practices, general procedures, and ethics. These standards allow specialists performing similar work to call themselves professionals because they are following a recognized and consistent set of best practices or standards. The key standards for internal auditors are the previously referenced IIA's *International Standards for the Professional Practice of Internal Auditing*, a set of guidance material that once was known as "The Red Book" by many internal auditors, before the Internet. Those older IIA standards, last published in 1995, were lengthy and sometimes difficult to embrace. The IIA made major revisions to their standards in 2004, with ongoing changes and updates since. This section will summarize the IIA standards as well as some more recent changes.

We will also revisit the IIA Code of Ethics for internal auditors, an important supporting foundation for internal auditors in today's world of frequent open questions regarding professional ethics. The IIA's standards represent a *must-know* set of information for internal auditors today. While any standards are an evolving set of rules that may not exactly reflect all industry practices at a given point in time, these recognize a set of guidelines for internal auditors worldwide to follow in their service to management. The internal audit standards, summarized here and available from the IIA,[4] represent important guidance for today's internal auditor.

Internal Auditing's Professional Practice Standards Background

Internal auditors work in a large variety of environments and are asked to perform internal audit reviews in a diverse number of operational and financial areas. Because of this diversity, internal audit is faced with a wide spectrum of professional challenges, including that management expects their internal auditors to perform reviews in a competent and consistent manner. The IIA is the key internal audit professional organization here, and through its Internal Auditing Standards Board, develops and issues standards that define the basic practice of internal auditing. Known as the *International Standards for the Professional Practice of Internal Auditing*, these standards are designed to:

- Delineate basic principles that represent the practice of internal auditing as it should be.
- Provide a framework for performing and promoting a broad range of value-added internal audit activities.
- Establish the basis for the measurement of internal audit performance.
- Foster improved organizational processes and operations.

The Standards aid in this process; and they provide a guideline for management to measure their internal auditors as well as for internal auditors to measure themselves. The Standards also set some constraints upon internal audit activity.

As stated in its materials, the IIA first issued their Standards in 1978 "to serve the entire profession in all types of business, in various levels of government, and in all other organizations where internal auditors are found . . . to represent the practice of internal auditing as it should be. . . ." Prior to their approval, the most authoritative document was the Statement of Responsibilities of internal audit, originally issued by the IIA in 1947 and subsequently revised over the years until their published Standards.

The foreword to the first, 1978 IIA Standards describes them as "the criteria by which the operations of an internal auditing department are evaluated and measured." This foreword goes on to state, "Compliance with the concepts enunciated by the Standards is essential before the responsibilities of the internal auditor can be met."

The Standards are developed by the IIA's Professional Standards Committee based on their own professional expertise as well as comments from IIA members and other interested parties. Because of the diverse group of participants who have developed the earlier Standards, the final language sometimes had some overlaps, compromises, and incompleteness in some areas.

All internal auditors today are expected to follow these standards. It would be a rare internal audit function today that did not have an internal audit charter, and those charters will strongly affirm adherence to the IIA's Standards. Internal auditors may have also come from some other professional area, such as banking, corporate accounting, or an external audit firm. In addition, the profession of internal auditing is worldwide, with IIA members sometimes following different national internal auditing standards and in many languages. Many such disciplines have professional organizations and standards that, generally, will not be in conflict with the IIA Standards. They may use slightly different terminology, but should follow audit practices that fit under the IIA Standards. As a matter of practice, the IIA's Standards take precedence over any conflicting professional standards.

The IIA Standards set the rules for all internal auditors as well as their overall internal audit departments. These standards do not yet have the same legal authority as the public accounting auditing standards that were previously issued by the American Institute of Certified Public Accountants' (AICPA's) Auditing Standards Board or by today's Public Company Accounting Oversight Board (PCAOB), but the IIA Standards represent the only widely recognized set of performance standards for internal auditors. Organization management will judge the professional adequacy of their internal audit function by its compliance with IIA Standards, and board audit committees should insist that the internal audit department *formally* adopt the IIA Standards as part of its charter.

All internal auditors must develop a strong understanding of these standards. While they will not tell an internal auditor how, for example, to review the internal controls surrounding an invoicing system, they provide some good requirements on how to perform effective internal audits. While differences may affect the practice of internal auditing in various business or national environments, compliance with the IIA Standards is required if the responsibilities of internal auditors are to be met. If internal auditors are prohibited by laws or regulations from complying with certain parts of the Standards, they should comply with all other parts of the Standards and make appropriate disclosures.

Structure of the IIA Standards

The IIA Standards are spread between what are called *Attribute, Performance*, and *Implementation* Standards. The Attribute Standards address the characteristics of organizations and parties performing internal audit activities. Performance Standards describe the nature of internal audit activities and provide quality criteria against which the performance of these services can be evaluated. While the Attribute and Performance Standards apply to all internal audit services, the Implementation Standards apply to specific types of engagements and are further divided between standards for assurance and consulting activities for those specific engagement types. This split reflects that internal auditors sometimes do strictly audit assurance–type projects, such as reviewing internal control performance in some area, and sometimes audit consulting–related work.

The Attribute Standards are numbered in sections as the 1000 Series of Standards, while Performance Standards are classified in the 2000 Series. Implementation standards, further designated as *A* for assurance or *C* for consulting, are organized under each of these Attribute and Performance Standards. The following sections describe the Attribute and Performance Standards in some detail as well as some of the descriptive Implementation Standards. Recognizing that internal auditors may be asked to just review internal controls or to act more as internal consultants, there may be multiple sets of Implementation Standards with sections for each of the major types of internal audit activity. Implementation Standards established for internal audit assurance activities are coded with an *A* following the Standard number (e.g., 1130.A1), and those covering internal audit consulting activities are noted by a *C* following the Standard number (e.g., nnnn.C1).

Our objective here is not, however, to just reproduce these IIA published standards but to highlight some key areas of their contents. All internal auditors as well as other interested professional should develop an understanding of these standards. The IIA Web site (www.theiia.org) is an official source for these IIA internal audit standards, and the reader is advised to consult that source, whether or not an IIA member today.

Internal Audit Attribute Standards   Attribute Standards address the characteristics of organizations and individuals performing internal audit activities.

Currently numbered from paragraph 1000 to 13000, they cover broad areas that define the attributes of today's modern internal auditor. Here, as well as with the Performance Standards listed below, we have listed and described these standards at a high level by their paragraph numbers:

1000: Purpose, Authority, and Responsibility. The purpose, authority, and responsibility of the internal audit activity must be formally defined in a charter, consistent with the Standards, and approved by the board of directors. Separate Implementation Standards state that internal auditing assurance and consulting services must be defined in a formal internal audit charter.

1100: Independence and Objectivity. The internal audit activity must be independent, and internal auditors must be objective in performing their work. Subsections under this discuss the importance of both individual and organizational objectivity as well as the need to disclose any impairment to internal audit independence or objectivity.

1110: Organizational Independence. While the IIA Standards do not specify that internal audit should report to their audit committee, that reporting relationship must be free from any interference in determining the scope of internal auditing, performing work, and communicating results. While we often think of internal audit in today's SOx world with its board audit committees, internal audit can operate in many international locations or for many different types of organizations. Whether serving a not-for-profit organization in the United States or a governmental enterprise in a developing country, internal audit nevertheless must exhibit organizational independence.

1120: Individual Objectivity. This really repeats the basic principle of internal auditing: Internal auditors should have an impartial, unbiased attitude and avoid conflicts of interest.

1130: Impairments to Independence or Objectivity. If internal audit's independence or objectivity can be impaired either in fact or in appearance, the details of any impairment must be disclosed as part of the audit work. This could be a management-imposed impairment or one due to the background or other circumstances surrounding an individual internal auditor. There are several Assurance and Consulting attribute standards here, but one summarizes this standard:

1130.A1: Internal auditors must refrain from assessing specific operations for which they were previously responsible. Objectivity is presumed to be impaired if an *internal* auditor provides services (assurance here, but consulting in a similar paragraph) for an activity for which the *internal* auditor had responsibility within the previous year.

This independence standard is important! Because of their specialized knowledge, internal auditors are sometimes asked to go back to the group where they once worked to audit it. No matter how hard they may try to act to the contrary, they will not be viewed as objective by others.

1200: Proficiency and Due Professional Care. Engagements must be performed with proficiency and due professional care. There is an important proposed new implementation standard here:

1210.A1: The CAE must obtain competent advice and assistance if the internal audit staff lacks the knowledge, skills, or other competencies needed to perform all or part of and internal audit engagement.

1210.A2: Internal auditors must have sufficient knowledge to evaluate the risk of fraud and the manner in which it is managed by the organization, but are not expected to have the expertise of a person whose primary responsibility is detecting and investigating fraud.

This section 1210.A2 of fraud-related guidance is somewhat weak. External audit standards, under the pre-PCAOB auditing standard SAS No. 99, require external auditors to aggressively think about "red flag" indicators that might include the possibility of fraud and to look for potential fraud in the course of their audits. Internal auditors should maintain a greater awareness about the possibility of fraud in the course of their internal audits. Internal auditors are often the best investigators to find these circumstances.

1210.A3: Internal auditors must have general knowledge of key information technology risks and controls available in technology-based audit techniques. However, not all internal auditors are expected to have the expertise of an internal auditor whose primary responsibility is information technology.

This is a *very important* internal auditing standard! Recognizing that there always is a need for IT audit specialists, the Standard states that *all* internal auditors must have an understanding of information systems risks and controls.

1220: Due Professional Care. Internal auditors must apply the care and skill expected of a reasonably prudent and competent internal auditor. Due professional care does not imply infallibility. Another section of these standards goes on to state that in exercising due professional care, an internal audit must consider:

- Extent of work needed to achieve the engagement's objectives
- Relative complexity, materiality, or significance of matters to which assurance procedures are applied
- Adequacy and effectiveness of risk management, control, and governance processes
- Probability of significant errors, irregularities, or noncompliance
- Cost of assurance in relation to potential benefits

This internal audit standard really says that an internal auditor must be cautious in beginning and performing an internal audit. The first of these bullet points, the extent of work, says that an internal auditor, for example, must perform an adequate level of investigation and testing before just coming to a final audit recommendation.

1220.A2: In exercising due professional care, an internal auditor must consider the use of technology-based audit tools and other data analysis techniques.

1220.A3: The internal auditor must be alert to the significant risks that might affect objectives, operations, or resources. However, assurance procedures alone, even when performed with due professional care, do not guarantee that all significant risks will be identified.

1230: Continuing Professional Development. A standard on the need for continuing professional education or development. Internal auditors must enhance their knowledge, skills, and other competencies through continuing professional development.

1300: Quality Assurance and Improvement Program. The CAE must develop and maintain a quality assurance and improvement program that covers all aspects of internal audit activity.

1310: Requirements of the Quality Assurance and Improvement Program. The quality assurance and improvement program must include both internal and external assessments.

1311: Internal Assessments. These should include ongoing internal audit performance reviews through self-assessment or by other persons within the organization, with knowledge of internal auditing practices and the Standards.

1312: External Assessments. External assessments must be conducted at least once every five years by a qualified, independent reviewer or review team from outside the organization. The cheif audit executive must discuss with the board:

- The need for more frequent external assessments and
- The qualifications and independence of the external reviewer or review team, including any potential conflicts of interest.

Internal Audit Performance Standards   Performance standards describe the nature of internal audit activities and provide quality criteria against which the performance of these services can be measured. There are six Performance Standards, along with sub-standards and Implementation Standards that apply separately to compliance audits, fraud investigations, or control self-assessment projects. While we are summarizing these standards here, the interested professional should contact the IIA (www.theiia.org) to obtain them in either computer-downloaded or printed format:

2000: **Managing the Internal Audit Activity.**   The CAE must effectively manage the internal audit activity to ensure it adds value to the enterprise. This Standard covers six substandards on Planning, Communication and Approval, Resource Management, Policies and Procedures, Coordination, and Reporting to the Board and Senior Management. These sub-standards generally describe such good internal audit management practices as 2040 on Policies and Procedures, stating that the CAE must establish such guides.

Standard 2060 on Reporting to the Board and Senior Management contains guidance applicable to today's SOx rules: "The chief audit executive must report periodically to the board and senior management on the internal audit activity's purpose, authority, responsibility, and performance relative to its plan. Reporting must also include significant risk exposures and control issues, corporate governance issues, and other matters needed or requested by the board and senior management."

2100: **Nature of Work.**   The internal audit activity must evaluate and contribute to the improvement of governance, risk management, and control processes using a systematic and disciplined approach.

2110: **Governance.**   The internal audit activity must assess and make appropriate recommendations for improving the governance process in its accomplishment of the following objectives:

- promoting appropriate ethics and values within the organization;
- Ensuring effective organizational performance management and accountablity;

- Communicating risk and control information to appropriate areas of the organization;
- Coordinating the activities of and communicating information among the board, external and internal auditors, and management.

2120: Risk Management. The internal audit activity must évaluate the effectiveness and contribute to the improvement of risk management processes.

2120.A1: The internal audit activity must evaluate risk exposures relating to the organization's governance, operations, and information systems regarding the:

- Reliability and integrity of financial and operational information;
- Effectiveness and efficiency of operations;
- Safeguarding of assets; and
- Compliance with laws, regulations, and contracts.

2120.A2: The internal audit activity must evaluate the potential for the occurence of fraud and how the organization manages fraud risk.

2120.C1: During consulting engagements, internal auditors must address risk consistent with the engagement's objectives and be alert to other significant risks.

2120.C2: Internal auditors must incorporate knowledge of risks gained from consulting engagements into their evaluation of the organization's risk management processes.

2120.C3: When assisting management in establishing or improving risk management processes, internal auditors must refrain from assuming any management responsibility by actually managing risks.

2130: Governance. The internal audit activity, consistent with the organization's structure, should contribute to the governance process by proactively assisting management and the board in fulfilling their responsibilities by:

- Assessing and promoting strong ethics and values within the enterprise
- Assessing and improving the process by which accountability is ensured
- Assessing the adequacy of communications about significant residual risks within the organization
- Helping to improve the board's interaction with management and the external and internal auditors
- Serving as an educational resource regarding changes and trends in the business and regulatory environment

These IIA Standards are very consistent with SOx requirements, and internal auditors should be able to follow the SOx principles of good corporate governance through adherence to these standards.

2200: Engagement Planning. Internal auditors must develop and record a plan for each engagement, including the scope, objectives, timing, and resource allocations.

2201: Planning Considerations. In planning an audit engagement, internal auditors must consider:

- The objectives of the activity being reviewed and the means by which the activity controls its performance
- Significant risks to the activity, its objectives, resources, and operations and the means by which the potential impact of risk is kept to an acceptable level
- The adequacy and effectiveness of the activity's risk management and control systems compared to a relevant control framework or model
- The opportunities for making significant improvements to the activity's risk management and control systems

2201.A1: When planning an internal audit engagement for parties outside the enterprise, internal auditors must establish a written understanding with them regarding the objectives, scope, respective responsibilities, and other expectations, including restrictions on distribution of the results of the engagement and access to engagement records.

2201.C1: Internal auditors must establish, an understanding with consulting engagement clients about objectives, scope, respective responsibilities, and other client expectations.

2210: Objectives must be established for each internal audit engagement.

2210.A1: Internal auditors must conduct a preliminary assessment of the risks relevant to the activity under review, and engagement objectives should reflect the results of this assessment.

2210.A2: An internal auditor must consider the probability of significant errors, fraud, noncompliance, and other exposures when developing the engagement objectives. This is related to the risk assessment considerations discussed previously.

2210.C1: Consulting engagement objectives must address risks, controls, and governance processes to the extent agreed upon with the client.

2220: Engagement Scope. The established scope of an internal audit must be sufficient to satisfy the objectives of the engagement.

2220.A1: The scope of the engagement must include consideration of relevant systems, records, personnel, and physical properties, including those under the control of third parties.

2220.A2: If significant consulting opportunities arise during an assurance engagement, a specific written understanding as to the objectives, scope, respective responsibilities, and other expectations should be reached and the results of the consulting engagement communicated in accordance with these consulting standards. This says that an internal auditor can begin an audit at a strictly assurance level, but may expand it to a consulting-level audit if there is a need or a management request.

2220.C1: In performing consulting engagements, internal auditors must ensure that the scope of the engagement is sufficient to address the agreed-on objectives. If internal auditors develop reservations about the scope during the engagement, these reservations must be discussed with the audit client to determine whether to continue with the engagement.

2230: Engagement Resource Allocation. Internal auditors must determine the appropriate and sufficient resources necessary to achieve the audit engagement's objectives based on an evaluation of the nature and complexity of each engagement, time constraints, and available resources.

2240: Engagement Work Program. Internal auditors must develop and document work programs that achieve the engagement objectives. These work programs should establish procedures for identifying, analyzing, evaluating, and recording information during the engagement. They also should be approved prior to their implementation, with any adjustments approved promptly.

2300: Performing the Engagement. Internal auditors must identify, analyze, evaluate, and record sufficient information to achieve the engagement's objectives.

2330: Recording Information. Internal auditors must record relevant information to support the conclusions and engagement results.

2330.A1: The CAE must control access to engagement records, and must obtain the approval of senior management and/or legal counsel prior to releasing such records to external parties, as appropriate.

2330.A2: The CAE must develop retention requirements for engagement records that are consistent with the organization's guidelines and any pertinent regulatory or other requirements.

2330.C1: The CAE must develop policies governing the custody and retention of engagement records, as well as their release to internal and external parties. These policies must be consistent with the enterprise's guidelines and any pertinent regulatory or other requirements.

2340: Engagement Supervision. Engagements must be properly supervised to ensure objectives are achieved, quality is assured, and staff is developed.

2400 and 2410: Communicating Results. Internal auditors must communicate their engagement results, including the audit's objectives and scope, as well as applicable conclusions, recommendations, and action plans including the internal auditor's overall opinion and or conclusions.

> **2410.A1:** Final communication of engagement results must, where appropriate, contain the internal auditor's overall opinion and/or conclusions.

> **2410.A2:** Internal auditors are encouraged to acknowledge satisfactory performance in engagement communications.

> **2410.A3:** When releasing engagement results to parties outside the organization, the communication must include limitations on distribution and use of the results.

2420: Quality of Communications. Communications must be accurate, objective, clear, concise, constructive, complete, and timely.

2421: Errors and Omissions. If a final communication contains a significant error or omission, the CAE must communicate corrected information to all *parties* who received that original communication.

2430: Use of "*Conducted in conformance with the International Standards for the Professional Practice of Internal Auditing*". Internal auditors are encouraged to report that their engagements are "conducted in conformance with the *International Standards for the Professional Practice of Internal Auditing*". However, internal auditors may use the statement only if the results of the quality assurance and improvement program demonstrate that the internal audit activity conforms with the *Standards*.

2431: Engagement Disclosure of Noncompliance with IIA Standards. When noncompliance with the Standards impacts a specific engagement, communication of the results should disclose the:
- Standard(s) with which full compliance was not achieved
- Reason(s) for noncompliance
- Impact of noncompliance on the engagement

2440: Disseminating Results. The CAE must communicate the final results of audit work to appropriate persons who can ensure that the results are given due consideration.

2440.A2: If not otherwise mandated by legal, statutory or regulatory requirements, prior to releasing results to parties outside the organization, the CAE must:

- ○ Assess the potential risk to the organization.
- ○ Consult with senior management and/or legal counsel as appropriate.
- ○ Control dissemination by restricting the use of the results.

2440.C1 and C2: The CAE is responsible for communicating the final results of consulting engagements to clients. During consulting engagements, risk management, control, and governance issues may be identified. Whenever these issues are significant to the organization, they should be communicated to senior management and the board.

2500: Monitoring Progress. The CAE must establish and maintain a system to monitor the disposition of results communicated to management as well as a follow-up process to monitor and ensure that management actions have been effectively implemented or that senior management has accepted the risk of not taking action.

2600: Resolution of Management's Acceptance of Risks. When the CAE believes that senior management has accepted a level of residual risk that *may be* unacceptable to the organization, the matter must be discussed with senior management. If the decision regarding residual risk is not resolved, the CAE and senior management must report the matter to the board for resolution.

These current IIA Standards represent a significant improvement over the older and very lengthy standards that were in place up until the late 1990s. Significantly, recent 2008 changes, change the standards by specifying "must" to "should" in the directions. The Standards conclude with a glossary of terms to better define the roles and responsibilities of internal auditors. Another important point for internal auditors is the definition of *independence*. The word frequently appears in internal auditing literature, but here is the official definition of internal auditor independence:

> *Independence is the freedom from significant conflicts of interest that threaten objectivity. Such threats to objectivity must be managed at the individual auditor level, the engagement level, and the organizational level.*

These are important concepts for today. We again emphasize that *the previously listed paragraphs are not the verbatim IIA Standards but an edited and annotated version.* We have eliminated some of the more minor standards statements, changed a few words in some cases, and added our descriptive comments. As stated before, internal auditors should obtain the official version of these standard through the Institute of Internal Auditors (www.theiia.org).

Recent IIA Standards Changes: External Assessments

Following the IIA's motto, "Progress Through Sharing," IIA members on a worldwide basis are encouraged to identify new practices or areas of concern as well as areas of perceived shortcomings in their existing published standards. After a lengthy process of review and analysis, formal changes to the Standards are released from time to time. This is not a trivial process, as all IIA members are expected to know and comply with changes to these standards. As this book goes to press, the most recent change to the IIA Standards was released in January 2007, where an additional section was added to the 13000 Quality Assurance standards with a Section 1312, on External Assessments:

> **1312: External Assessments.** External assessments must be conducted at least once every five years by a qualified, independent reviewer or review team from outside the organization. The cheif audit executive must discuss with the board:
> - The need for more frequent external assessments and
> - The qualifications and independence of the external reviewer or review team, including any potential conflicts of interest.

This is a major change! The concept of a *quality assurance review* (QAR) was first introduced through some new but general quality standards with the 2002 release of revised standards. When first issued, they were considered to be particularly important, reflecting the enhanced role played by internal audit departments in the risk, control, and governance activities of many major corporations today. However, there was no time or compliance requirement in those initial standards. Some internal audit functions in larger enterprises and certainly many governmental internal audit departments developed their own QAR processes, but many only put QARs on their "to-do" lists for some future action. This new once-every-five-years requirement for a QAR, starting in 2007, means the clock is ticking for many internal audit functions. The following discussion of the CBOK survey results shows that too many internal audit functions are still not addressing this quality assurance standard. At present, a significant number of internal audit functions, worldwide, are not following these quality assurance standards today.

The whole concept of an internal audit QAR, performed by external reviewers, is to ensure consistent quality in internal audits and the audit organization. The objective of such an external review QAR is to provide evidence to the board audit committee, management, and the internal audit staff itself that their internal audit activity is complying with IIA Standards and the Code of Ethics. In addition, internal audit activities should be concerned about the success of the enterprise's internal controls, ethics, governance, and risk management processes. The scope of a QAR review should include:

- Assess the efficiency and effectiveness of the department based on established IIA, departmental, and other applicable standards.
- Review internal audit's applicable audit candidates and their methods for annual risk assessment leading to an audit plan.
- Evaluate organizational structure, staffing, and internal audit approach of the department.
- Determine how internal auditing is perceived through interviews and surveys with customers, including governance personnel.
- Examine techniques and methodology for testing controls. Identify ways to enhance the department's policies and practices.

The above is not an all-inclusive set of requirements, but it outlines some of the quality elements any QAR should be considering. If an internal audit function has built in its own quality assurance standards, per the previously discussed quality assurance standards, many of these practices should already have been in place. The challenge here is the requirement for an *external* quality assurance reviewer, and this raises concerns on three major levels:

1. Any external reviewer must understand the overall process of operational and compliance-based internal auditing as well as IIA Standards and such formats as COSO and the Control Objectives for IT framework (CobiT).
2. This is a quality assurance review and not a "do the debits equal the credits" financial audit type of exercise. American Society for Quality (ASQ) quality auditor skills, introduced in Chapter 10, could provide some key guidance for such an external reviewer.
3. Enterprise confidentiality can be critical. The QAR reviewer is being asked to gather some information by reviews of internal audit workpapers. However, audit workpaper documentation may contain considerable amounts of sensitive data. Enterprise senior management might not want an external QAR reviewer, no matter how independent, to be examining such potentially confidential data.

Beyond these three concerns, an enterprise may face a challenge finding the appropriate external persons to perform these QARs. Although there certainly are other providers, as this book goes to press, a Web search for "Internal Audit Quality Assessment" does not provide many potential candidates. With the clock starting on this once-every-five-years requirement, the number of qualified external review candidates can be expected to grow.

What happens if a CAE and the internal audit department do not meet this five-year requirement? It is certainly not a legal requirement or as serious as an external auditor failing to issue an audited 10K financial report. However, the CAE should share this QAR requirement with his or her audit committee and provide reasons why internal audit is not in compliance with internal audit professional standards. In our risk-averse environment today, this can be an issue and no one wants to be on record as being out of compliance.

We have discussed the every-five-years requirement for external QARs as an example not only of how internal audit standards are changing over time, but also of how such changes can have major impacts on internal audit functions in an enterprise. The CAE and enterprise management should monitor such standards changes on a continuous basis and should take all necessary corrective actions as required.

IIA and ISACA's Codes of Ethics

Although our discussion on codes of ethics here appears after the introduction of the IIA Standards and even recent revisions to those standards, the placement of our discussion does not mean that ethics are just an after-the-fact consideration. They are an important element in defining an effective internal audit function. The purpose of the IIA's Code of Ethics, displayed in Exhibit 11.1, is to promote an ethical culture in the profession of internal auditing. This idea of an ethical culture is necessary and appropriate when users of internal audit services rely on their objective assessments on risk management, internal control, and governance. The IIA's Code of Ethics is based on the principles of internal auditor integrity, objectivity, confidentiality, and competency. These are the behavior norms expected of internal auditors and they are intended to guide the ethical conduct of internal auditors.

The current IIA Code of Ethics replaces an earlier and much lengthier 1988 version that had 11 specific articles defining preferred practices; that version in turn replaced a 1968 version with eight articles. The current 2000 version, with its highlighted emphasis on integrity, objectivity, confidentiality, and competency, becomes much easier to understand and recognize than the rather detailed articles in the prior version. Any person

1. **Integrity**

   Internal auditors:

   1.1 Shall perform their work with honesty, diligence, and responsibility.

   1.2 Shall observe the law and make disclosures expected by the law and the profession.

   1.3 Shall not knowingly be a party to any illegal activity, or engage in acts that are discreditable to the profession of internal auditing or to the organization.

   1.4 Shall respect and contribute to the legitimate and ethical objectives of the organization.

2. **Objectivity**

   Internal auditors:

   2.1 Shall not participate in any activity or relationship that may impair or be presumed to impair their unbiased assessment. This participation includes those activities or relationships that may be in conflict with the interests of the organization.

   2.2 Shall not accept anything that may impair or be presumed to impair their professional judgment.

   2.3 Shall disclose all material facts known to them that, if not disclosed, may distort the reporting of activities under review.

3. **Confidentiality**

   Internal auditors:

   3.1 Shall be prudent in the use and protection of information acquired in the course of their duties.

   3.2 Shall not use information for any personal gain or in any manner that would be contrary to the law or detrimental to the legitimate and ethical objectives of the organization.

4. **Competency**

   Internal auditors:

   4.1 Shall engage only in those services for which they have the necessary knowledge, skills, and experience.

   4.2 Shall perform internal auditing services in accordance with the *Standards for the Professional Practice of Internal Auditing.*

   4.3 Shall continually improve their proficiency and the effectiveness and quality of their services.

EXHIBIT 11.1 IIA Code of Ethics

Source: IIA Code of Ethics, Copyright © 2004 by The Institute of Internal Auditors, Inc., 247 Maitland Avenue, Altamonte Sprints, Florida 32710-4201 USA. Reprinted with permission.

performing internal audit services, whether or not a member of the IIA, should understand and follow this code of ethics.

The IIA Code of Ethics applies to both individuals and entities that provide internal auditing services. For IIA members and recipients of or candidates for IIA professional certifications, breaches of the Code of Ethics will be evaluated and administered according to the IIA Bylaws and Administrative Guidelines. The IIA goes on to state that even if a particular element of internal audit conduct is not mentioned in this Code, this does not prevent the conduct or practice from being unacceptable or

---

The Information Systems Audit and Control Association, Inc. (ISACA) sets forth this Code of Professional Ethics to guide the professional and personal conduct of members of the association and/or its certification holders.

Members and ISACA certification holders shall:

1. Support the implementation of, and encourage compliance with, appropriate standards, procedures and controls for information systems.
2. Perform their duties with objectivity, due diligence and professional care, in accordance with professional standards and best practices.
3. Serve in the interest of stakeholders in a lawful and honest manner, while maintaining high standards of conduct and character, and not engage in acts discreditable to the profession.
4. Maintain the privacy and confidentiality of information obtained in the course of their duties unless disclosure is required by legal authority. Such information shall not be used for personal benefit or released to inappropriate parties.
5. Maintain competency in their respective fields and agree to undertake only those activities which they can reasonably expect to complete with professional competence.
6. Inform appropriate parties of the results of work performed; revealing all significant facts known to them.
7. Support the professional education of stakeholders in enhancing their understanding of information systems security and control.

Failure to comply with this Code of Professional Ethics can result in an investigation into a member's, and/or certification holder's conduct and, ultimately, in disciplinary measures.

EXHIBIT 11.2 ISACA Code of Ethics
Source: Control Objectives for Information and Related Technology (CobiT®), 3rd Edition, Copyright © 1996, 1998, 2000, the IT Governance Institute (ITGI), http://Isaca.org and http://itgi.org, Rolling Meadows, IL 60008 USA. Reprinted with permission.

discreditable. Violators of the Code, whether a member, certification holder (such as a Certified Internal Auditor (CIA)), or candidate, can be held liable for disciplinary action.

The Information Systems Audit and Control Association (ISACA), as well as its affiliated research arm, the IT Governance Institute, are a professional audit organization that historically represents or speaks primarily for information systems auditors. ISACA is also the professional enterprise that administers the CISA (Certified Information Systems Auditor) examination and program and is responsible for the CobiT internal control framework discussed in Chapter 5. With its information systems audit and IT governance orientation, ISACA represents a somewhat different group of auditors. Historically, ISACA drew a large number of members from the public accounting, external audit firms and it has had a very strong international membership in some areas. However, many IIA members belong to ISACA as well, and while the two groups do not have many joint meetings or other endeavors, each represents an important segment of the audit community.

While ISACA—fortuitously—does not have its own set of professional standards beyond its CobiT framework guidelines, it does have a code of ethics as shown in Exhibit 11.2. Based on its IT heritage, the ISACA code is more oriented to technology-related issues. It is a set of professional standards that applies to and should be followed by information systems audit professionals. Although the wording is different, there is nothing in the ISACA code that is contrary to the IIA Code. Internal auditors, whether working primarily in information systems areas or with a more general internal control orientation, should exercise strong ethical practice in their work.

Importance and Relevance of the IIA Standards

The IIA *Standards for the Professional Practice of Internal Auditing* are an important set of guidance materials for any internal auditor. Because of the many different environments where internal auditors will work, the many different types of audits performed, and the varying demands for internal audit services, the typical internal auditor will perform many different day-to-day functions. However, whenever there are questions or uncertainties, the professional internal auditor should consult these standards for guidance.

The previous sections have provided a somewhat summarized, edited, and annotated version of these standards. Our editing changes to these materials are minor and include such things as using *CAE* for *chief audit executive* and combining a pair of *A* and *C* advisories in the IIA standards when they both essentially say the same thing. Compliance with these standards is an effective way to assess the quality of any internal audit function.

CBOK: INTERNAL AUDIT'S COMMON BODY OF KNOWLEDGE

Our beginning discussion in this chapter on some of the origins of internal auditing has highlighted how the profession has evolved from accounting and mathematical-accuracy checkers to today's internal control evaluation specialists. The Internal audit profession has come a long way. Following the high-level IIA Standards just summarized, internal auditors are using them while working in corporate, non-for-profit, and governmental agencies worldwide. In addition, internal auditors are working in all sizes of enterprises, in all industry areas, and under many different conditions. Despite all of these variations, however, there is a wide range of both similarities as well as differences in internal audit practices.

Going beyond the IIA Standards, the AS5 standards in Chapter 3, pertinent law, and some other areas, there are not very many rights or wrongs in internal audit practices. Rather, there should be a whole range of best practices under the overall guidance of the IIA Standards. Beyond these formal standards, many internal audit best practices have been communicated from one internal auditor to another through IIA publications and activities, following their "Progress Through Sharing" motto. However, many internal audit professionals, over the years, have expressed a need to better formalize things and develop an internal audit *common body of knowledge* (CBOK). Although there had been several limited attempts to develop such a body of knowledge, the IIA Research Foundation (IIARF) launched a major effort in 2006 to develop such a CBOK for the internal audit profession. The result was published in mid-2007 in their *A Global Summary of the Common Body of Knowledge.*[5] The following sections will discuss the research approach used to develop CBOK as well as some high-level results from the study.

What Is a Common Body of Knowledge?

Business and professional terms and acronyms often get used and reused so often that we really miss their true meanings. The expression *common body of knowledge* falls in that category. A Web search for CBOK on Google or one of the other better search engines gives a long list of professional organizations that have developed their own CBOKs. For example, the Bank

Administration Institute (BAI) has released a CBOK for risk professionals and the Institute for the Certification of Computer Professionals (ICCP) has its own IT-oriented CBOK. Even more common, some professional organizations have tacked the *BOK* suffix to a set of practices common to their profession. For example, the Project Management Institute (PMI) has published its set of best practices as The Project Management Book of knowledge or *PMBOK*. The concept here is that specialized professional organizations have tried to capture all of the terms or concepts that a professional operating in that field should know. Even the U.S. Department of Homeland Security is developing an IT-based security standard that it calls the *Essential Body of Knowledge* (EBOK).[6]

The formats of these various published BOK documents differ. Some are little more than outlines—sometimes not too detailed—while others are fairly detailed descriptions of the knowledge areas where a professional will be expected to have some skills or to operate. The PMI's *PMBOK*[7] is a good example of what a professional should expect in a book-of-knowledge compendium. The guide breaks down all elements of the project management process, describing inputs, tools and techniques, and then outputs for each element. The elements are then linked to other activities in the project management process. The *PMBOK* must be considered or linked with general management knowledge and practice as well as application knowledge areas, as shown in Exhibit 11.3. This same concept must be considered for all published bodies of knowledge.

IIARF's CBOK Approach

The Institute of Internal Auditors Research Foundation (IIARF) launched its CBOK effort in 2005. Its stated objective was to prepare a comprehensive survey that captures the state of the internal auditing profession throughout the world including:

- The knowledge and skills that internal auditors possess
- The skill and organizational levels used for the practice of internal auditing work
- The actual duties performed by internal auditors
- The structure of internal audit organizations
- The types of industries that practice internal audit
- The regulatory environment of various countries

CBOK had an objective to document the understanding of the unique value-added role that internal auditing has in enterprises throughout the world. Based on this understanding, a CBOK objective was to better define

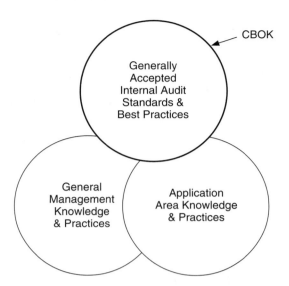

EXHIBIT 11.3 Relationship of CBOK to Other Internal Control Disciplines

the future of internal auditing and ensure that it remains a vibrant and relevant contribution to enterprises. The IIA plans to use the results of its CBOK study to improve standards, procedures, and other offerings in future years in areas including:

- Internal audit certifications and examinations
- Revised standards
- Published practice advisories
- Educational programs and products
- Other internal audit publications.

The objectives of the IIA's CBOK survey to date were not to develop some high-level standards for performing internal audits, such as the approach used in the PMI's *PMBOK* or ITIL best practices that can be found in Chapter 8. Rather, the IIARF had an objective of gaining a better knowledge of the current duties and activities of internal auditors in various chapter units worldwide and of individuals operating as CAEs, audit managers, internal audit seniors/supervisors, staff members, and others affiliated with internal audit.

The IIARF's approach was not to define any internal audit best practices but to find out what internal auditors are doing today in their practice of internal auditing. A team of contractors was engaged, detailed surveys forms developed, and some 9,000 surveys were sent to individual internal auditors and audit functions. The summarized results provide a thorough view of what internal audit departments—what the CBOK document calls Internal Audit Activities (IIAAs, another acronym!)—are doing as part of their internal audit work. Although the IIARF reports that all results have been captured in a detailed database, the initial published results provide only a high-level look at survey responses. Significantly, there is no split between CBOK's defined IIAA's at larger enterprises, such as those in the United States and the United Kingdom, and those in the many smaller enterprise internal audit functions worldwide.

CBOK's Findings: Some Concerns

The CBOK surveys were assembled similar to a consumer-type survey where respondents were asked to answer to questions based on a rating score ranging from 1 to 5 for each question. That is, a response of 5 meant the respondent Strongly Agreed to the question, 4 was just Agreed, and a score of 1 indicated Strongly Disagreed. The results were published as a single mean value but with no standard deviation values to show the variances or ranges of those responses. For example, the CBOK contained the evaluation statement, "Your internal audit activity brings a systematic approach to evaluate the effectiveness of internal controls." A reported 2,374 CAEs responded to this question with mean value of 4.35.

A problem with this type of reported result is that we really do not have any further information to support these types of responses or variances in the reported scores. While the CAE for an effective internal audit function would be expected to respond to such a question with a score of 5, the published CBOK begs the question, *Why did a certain portion of CAEs report that their internal audit function did not have a Strongly Agree score of 5 in place to evaluate internal controls?* Is it because a certain portion of groups are not that effective or because of a natural tendency—shared sometimes by this author—to not rate such survey scores on the extreme high or low end of the range? This is a problem with many of CBOK's reported responses. From CAEs to audit staff member, almost everything is reported with scores greater than 4.0 but less than 5.0.

Three CBOK evaluation statements were ranked under 4.0 but above 3.5:

1. Your internal audit activity brings a systematic approach to evaluate the effectiveness of governance processes.
2. The way our internal audit activity adds value to the governance process is through direct access to the audit committee.

3. Compliance with the IIA's *International Standards for the Professional Practice of Internal Auditing* is a key factor for your internal audit activity to add value to governance processes.

With all levels of internal auditors reporting lower scores to these three questions, there would appear to be some internal audit management concerns here. Of course, decoding things is always a concern. Regarding the second point above, does this say that a larger number of respondents do not feel internal audit activities add value to their enterprise's governance activities; or that they do not have sufficient access to their audit committees; or both?

The CBOK study is filled with tables showing—based on these survey responses—what internal audit functions are doing across the world. If nothing else, this type of reported information will allow a CAE to assess whether his or her internal audit function is performing activities in line with other internal audit functions worldwide. We have extracted the results from two of CBOK's published table results, but the interested reader should contact the IIARF to receive a copy of the recently published CBOK results.

Exhibit 11.4 shows internal audit activity use, by rank, of various common internal audit tools and techniques. CBOK selected 16 internal audit tools and techniques and ranked them by their utilization. While the tabled results were by various staff levels in internal audit, we are just reporting a summary list here. Not unexpectedly, the Internet and related e-mail processes are the most important of these tools and techniques. Process-modeling software was ranked lowest here, but this also is not surprising as this type of software and the supporting notations for its use are difficult for many and somewhat complex. The next lowest response here, total quality management techniques, was surprising to at least this author. The IIA has strongly emphasized quality management processes over recent years and built it into their Standards; Chapter 10 discusses the importance of quality management procedures.

Exhibit 11.5 contains a series of CBOK survey statements that were directed to CAEs and internal audit managers, asking whether the statement currently applied to their internal audit function, whether likely in the future, or whether not applicable or planned. While certain survey questions certainly would not apply to some not-for-profit and other internal audit groups, some of the results here are surprising. For example, to the statement, "The organization has implemented an internal control framework," only about 70% of internal audit managers responded that they have such an internal control evaluation process currently in place, with the bulk of the others planning to do something within the next three years. With IIA Standards calling for such activities to be in place in order to be an effective

Rank	Internal Audit Tool or Technique
1	Internet or e-mail communication
2	Risk-based audit planning
3	Analytical review
4	Electronic workpapers
5	Statistical sampling
6	Computer-assisted audit techniques
7	Flowchart software
8	Benchmarking
9	Process mapping application
10	Control self-assessment
11	Data mining
12	Continuous/real-time auditing
13	IIA quality assessment review tools
14	Balanced scorecards
15	Total quality management techniques
16	Process-modeling software

Note: These rankings were adapted from Table 2-6 in the IIARF's 2006 CBOK study.

EXHIBIT 11.4   Internal Audit Ranked Use of Key Tools and Techniques

and compliant internal audit function, it appears that much more work is needed! Beyond the tables, extracted here, CBOK is filled with other interesting and sometimes perhaps disturbing observations:

- **Compliance with internal auditing standards.** Although not directly summarized in a table, some CBOK responses should be disturbing to several levels of the profession. For example, some 82% of all CBOK respondents state that they use IIA Standards in whole or in part. These are the ground rules for internal auditing, and one really wonders about the nearly 20% who say they do not use these standards, even in part!
- **Quality assurance and improvement programs.** A shortcoming that is highlighted in Exhibit 11.4, IIA Standard 1300 requires the CAE to "develop and maintain a quality assurance and improvement program that covers all aspects of the internal audit activity and continuously monitors its effectiveness." The Standard goes on to specify that internal audit functions should develop a program to monitor and assess the effectiveness of their own quality programs and should arrange for an external quality review assessment at least once every five years by

Statement	Number of Respondents	Currently Applied	Likely to Apply within the Next 3 Years	Will Not Apply in the Foreseeable Future	Not Applicable
Internal audit is required by law or regulation where the enterprise is based.	3464	61.2	43.1	12.9	12.8
Internal auditors have an advisory role in enterprise strategy development.	3445	28.9	32.7	30.3	8.0
Internal audit complies with a corporate governance code.	3447	67.7	22.7	4.3	5.3
Internal audit has implemented an internal control framework.	3443	70.5	24.3	3.5	1.7
Internal audit has implemented a knowledge management system.	3423	25.6	43.9	20.6	9.9
The internal audit function has provided training to audit committee members.	3424	34.0	32.3	18.5	15.1
Internal audit assumes an important role in the integrity of financial reporting.	3437	55.7	25.6	13.7	4.9
Internal audit educates enterprise personnel regarding internal controls, corporate governance, and compliance issues.	3437	64.3	25.3	7.3	3.1
Internal audit places more emphasis on assurance activities than on consulting services.	3448	71.5	15.2	844.0	4.9

Note: These findings were extracted from Table 2-14 from the IIARF's 2006 CBOK study.

EXHIBIT 11.5 CBOK Survey Results from Internal Audit Managers

a qualified independent review facility from outside the organization. Compliance here is dismal, with over 50% of internal audit functions not in compliance with this standard.

- **Relationship with the audit/oversight committee.** Given that governmental internal audit functions as well as some not-for-for-profits do not have audit committees, CBOK found that over 90% of CAEs with audit committee reporting relationships feel they have appropriate access to their audit committee. However, only 63% of those with audit committee reporting relationships meet with their audit committee chairperson in addition to formally scheduled meetings. This implies that many CAEs do not have easy, ad-hoc reporting relationships with their audit committee.

- **Internal auditor continuing professional education.** IIA Standards require 40 hours per year of continuing professional education over a three-year period, or a total of 120 hours. Recognizing that attainment of this standard may be difficult in some parts of the world due to the small population of internal auditors in those places, the CBOK found that internal auditors were generally deficient in the requirement. Only 22% of CAEs met this 120-hour target, while another 35% were close but not meeting requirements, at 90 to 119 hours.

The CBOK report contains many other areas where internal auditors were found to be missing key standards or requirements. As stated, CBOK is not a benchmark of existing best practices but a measure of the current state and activities of the internal audit profession worldwide. The IIA now plans to revise and enhance this CBOK study on an ongoing basis. There appear to be many areas for improvement.

Using CBOK to Improve Internal Audit Practices

As discussed earlier, the IIA's CBOK is not a guide to internal auditor best practices. Rather, it describes a wide range of internal audit current activities and how they are practiced. For the CAE as well as the audit committee and management responsible for internal audit within an enterprise, this recently published CBOK should be viewed as somewhat of a wakeup call regarding how individual internal audit groups are performing in relationship to survey results and to IIA Standards. In general, CBOK points out many areas where an internal audit function should improve.

An individual CAE should not use the IIA's CBOK as a justification for no action, saying that some practice is not being followed because only a less-than-majority percentage of others are doing it. Rather, such matters should highlight possible areas for improvement in the Standards. For example, if over 50% of internal audit functions were found to be not in compliance with a requirement for a periodic external third-party review, perhaps the Standard needs some rethinking or revision. As all internal auditors should know, when reviewing compliance in some area, a finding that "everybody does it" is not an excuse for an internal control or other failure. Rather than the PCAOB's approach of issuing SOx auditing rules with little chance for review or comment, the IIA's Standards are established through a volunteer committee effort. Through their local IIA chapters, internal auditors should get more involved with this standards-development process. More important, the Standards do effectively define the body of knowledge or sets of best practices for internal auditing.

Internal audit always has had a key role in the corporate governance process, but SOx and the AS5 standards discussed in Chapter 3 make that role even more important in the audit process. Audit functions and enterprise corporate management should monitor the published IIA Standards, viewing them as both requirements and minimum standards for best practices. They should point to areas of continual improvement for internal audit functions.

ENDNOTES

1. *Standards for the Professional Practice of Internal Auditing* (Altamonte Springs, FL: The Institute of Internal Auditors).
2. *A Global Summary of the Common Body of Knowledge* (Altamonte Springs, FL: Institute of Internal Auditors Research Foundation, 2006).
3. Project Management Institute, www.pmi.org
4. *Standards for the Professional Practice of Internal Auditing* (Altamonte Springs, FL: Institute of Internal Auditors, 2004).
5. The Institute of Internal Auditors Research Foundation, Altamonte Springs, FL, 2007.
6. *Information Technology (IT) Security Essential Body of Knowledge (EBK)* (U.S. Department of Homeland Security, October 2007).
7. *Project Management Body of Knowledge* (Project Management Institute, Upper Darby, PA:).

CHAPTER 12

Importance of Effective Corporate Governance

Compliance with Sarbanes-Oxley (SOx) presents a real challenge for most if not all enterprises today. Things have become a little easier since SOx was first enacted in 2002, with changes such as the new AS5 rules, discussed in Chapter 3, and our better understanding of control frameworks to define and understand internal Controls, such as Chapter 5's discussion on the importance of the control objectives for IT (CobiT) framework. However, the real key to compliance with legislation, such as SOx, is a strong system of governance within an enterprise. A concept that was seldom even discussed some years ago, corporate governance refers to the rules and procedures that an enterprise will establish to manage itself. A strong system of governance requires that all stakeholders—employees, vendors, and others—understand those rules and follow them. Even more important, all levels of management must actively support and communicate those governance rules and practices.

This concluding chapter looks at SOx and corporate governance from several perspectives. Chapter 7 discussed the current status of some important SOx requirements beyond Section 404, including rules for whistle-blowers that allow persons observing any form of internal accounting control improper practices to blow the whistle and report the matter for resolution. These SOx-based federal rules supporting whistleblower actions lay out a fairly formal process whereby the concerned whistleblower can report the matter through appropriate channels within the enterprise or through federal administrative and legal procedures. There are strong advantages for an enterprise to encourage stakeholders to report any such concerns through internal enterprise channels rather than to outside administrative or legal sources. This chapter will discuss establishing processes within the enterprise that will allow any stakeholder to feel open to report their concerns.

More important than having an anonymous facility to report whistle-blower concerns, an enterprise should take steps to encourage an atmosphere and culture that will encourage stakeholders at all levels to consistently act in a proper and ethical manner. A key element of strong corporate governance policies is the need for a strong ethics program in an enterprise. While there can be many elements of what we call *ethics* in the enterprise, two key factors are well-understood stakeholder rules—that is, codes of conduct and consistent messages from senior management endorsing these practices. This chapter will discuss approaches to establish an ethics program in an enterprise—a strong component in establishing effective governance programs. We will also emphasize the increased importance of the audit committee of the board of directors in this environment.

This chapter and the overall book will conclude with a discussion on monitoring compliance with the regulations and best practices. Many of the topics discussed throughout this book require an effective internal audit function in the enterprise to monitor and review compliance. With increasing governance and compliance rules impacting all enterprises today, some have established the function of *chief compliance officer* (CCO) with their enterprises. The chapter will explore the roles, responsibilities, and reporting relationships of this new corporate officer position. The chapter will conclude with reassertions of good compliance review procedures in today's environment along with the importance of internal audit and new roles such as a CCO.

REPORTING WHISTLEBLOWER INCIDENTS: ESTABLISHING A HOTLINE FACILITY

Under SOx, any employee or other stakeholder can become a whistleblower by reporting what that person feels is an illegal or improper activity covering accounting, internal control, and auditing. The drafters of SOx probably envisioned that the typical whistleblower would be a member of the corporate accounting staff who hears of plans for some fraudulent transactions, or a concerned employee at a remote unit that is not frequently visited by corporate staff, such as internal audit. As discussed in Chapter 7, whistleblower rules are designed to encourage stakeholders to report on any suspected fraudulent or illegal acts in an anonymous and protected manner. Reporting these concerns is often a challenge in many enterprises. Although a senior manager may proclaim, "My door is always open," administrative assistants and others often prevent this easy access. In addition, concerned employees may fear retribution or worse by reporting some matter.

Many enterprises today have established *hotline functions* to report potential ethics violations or concerns. In many cases, these facilities were established beginning in the mid-1990s, prior to SOx, when there were other types of ethics concerns, and when we had a series of the concerns that led to the COSO internal control framework. Most of these facilities include confidential telephone line facilities administered through the ethics department, Human Resources, or an independent provider. These are often 800toll-free telephone operations that operate on a 24-hours-a-day, 7-days-a-week basis, allowing any employee or stakeholder to call anonymously and either ask a question, report a concern, or blow the whistle on some matter. Often known as a *hotline facility*, the idea is to provide an independent facility where all stakeholders can ask questions, seek advice, or report possible wrongdoings at any level. These are not legally required functions. The items reported may range from allegations of theft of company property, to human resources complaints, to just asking troubling questions. In most cases, the hotline operator will take all of the necessary information, asking questions when needed, and then pass the reported incident to an appropriate authority for investigation and resolution. The hotline operator will typically assign the reported incident a case number so the caller can later check on resolution.

Hotlines are often staffed with knowledgeable human resources veterans; the operators are often particularly skilled at answering human resources issues, such as treatment in the workplace. Where there have been any allegations of wrongdoing, the recorded case is shifted to others for investigation, such as to the legal department. In some instances, these hotlines have turned into little more than corporate "snitch" lines where many minor gripes or infractions are reported. While many established ethics hotlines were set up to be "friendly" in answering employee questions and giving some advice in addition to investigating reported incidents, using this same, already-established facility for the SOx whistleblower program places some new controls and responsibilities on such a hotline function. While the more friendly help aspects of an ethics hotline can still apply, federal whistleblower rules require that the function have much more formalized processes. This is particularly true in areas such as confidentiality, documentation requirements for all records, and efficient processing of any investigations. In addition, the employee calling in a SOx whistleblower allegation is legally protected from any future recrimination. In some respects, a bubble has to encapsulate the whistleblower such that there can be no actions of any sort directed at that employee by the employer until the whistleblower action is resolved. There is no legal requirement to establish separate ethics help and SOx whistleblower lines. Callers would be confused about which to call in any event. However, with the SOx whistleblower requirement, control procedures need to be enhanced in any established ethics hotline facility. Exhibit 12.1 contains some guidelines for setting up a whistleblower hotline program for a SOx whistleblower facility.

- Establish independent — preferably toll-free — telephone lines for facility. The lines must not go through other company switchboards.
- Train all operators for the facility with the basic provisions of federal whistleblower rules. Also, establish scripts such that callers can ask the same general questions.
- Advertise and promote the facility throughout the enterprise with an emphasis that for all items reported, the caller will be able to check status, all callers will be treated anonymously, and there will be no recriminations for caller actions.
- Implement a logging form to record all calls. Maintain the date and time of the call, the caller name or identification, and the details reported.
- Establish a routing and disposition process such that the status of who has the call information and the status of any investigation can be determined.
- Establish a secure database for all whistleblower data with appropriate password protection.
- Working with human resources, develop procedures to fully but anonymously protect any whistleblower from recriminations of any sort.
- Develop a process for closing out all whistleblower calls, documenting all actions, if any.

EXHIBIT 12.1 Guidelines for Setting Up a SOx Whistleblower Hotline

The existence of any ethics hotline or whistleblower facility will be of little value unless it is communicated and sold to all members of the enterprise. Even if such a hotline has already been launched, the fact that the line can be used for any potential SOx whistleblowers needs to be communicated. The goal should be to investigate and promptly resolve all calls—and especially whistleblower calls—internally to avoid outside investigators and lawyers.

The provisions of SOx apply to all SEC-registered corporations, whether large or small, and all registrants need to take steps to demonstrate compliance. While there are consulting firms that offer SOx compliance help, an enterprise can often establish effective SOx hotline compliance through a dedicated team effort led by internal audit, human resources, and legal counsel resources.

A hotline program can be an effective vehicle to gather advance information on employee observations and concerns that could lead to even bigger enterprise problems. Where implemented, these have been effective mechanisms to learn about such matters as sexual harassment concerns, employees and supervisors violating rules, and a wide range of other matters. These concerns go beyond SOx internal accounting control rules and cover the wide range of employee issues and concerns regarding corporate procedures or even human resources handbooks.

This author had a major role in developing and implementing a hotline function for a major retail organization in the middle 1990s. Called a "help line," the unit was staffed with some long-term employees who were trained on such matters as a new code of conduct but also understood many other rules and policies. Many of the telephone calls to this facility covered Topics that could have been easily found in the employee human resources manuals, but the operation did identify issues that were passed off to the corporate legal department. Some matters were little more than personal jealousies, but the facility did reveal such issues as "sweetheart" deals with vendors that were illegal and costing the corporation major money.

Whether in large or small enterprises, the implementation of a hotline function can aid in one aspect of SOx compliance but will improve overall governance. Key success factors that make such a hotline function work include:

- **Have trained, knowledgeable people staffing the telephones.** Whoever answers the telephone must know enough about the enterprise to recognize local acronyms, jargon, and location names. Long-term in-house employees are a plus but are expensive. There are outside services that can be contracted to provide this type of service, but every effort must be made to provide these people with a level of enterprise training.
- **Publicize the existence of the hotline facility.** This may take Web notices, company newsletter announcements and the like, but all stakeholders should be aware of its purpose, hours, and procedures. It is important to publicize that all reported information and anonymity will be protected. Because many do not understand the many nuances of SOx, the hotline might be advertised as a vehicle to report violations of the enterprise code of conduct.
- **Preserve and protect the confidentiality of callers.** The use and value of a hotline will be reduced quickly if word gets out on the street that people know that "Sally called to report about Harry." This author's hotline facility back in the middle 1990s avoided the use of personal names and assigned case numbers to each caller and documented concern. While there were situations where it was necessary to obtain the caller's name, care was taken that the caller voluntarily allowed the use of his or her name.
- **Document, document, and document.** Although hotline concerns can be reported through e-mail or other vehicles, most will often come via telephone calls. It is essential that call operators accurately transcribe

these matters, including what was initially called in, what was asked, and the responses.

- **Establish a process for call disposition.** While some calls will be merely to report some concern, in many cases the caller will want to know the disposition of that call. Although names and details do not need to be revealed, the hotline should allow callers to find out the disposition or handling of calls. Provide a facility where the original caller can get back to the help desk and retrieve some status information based on the assigned case number. Of course, the hotline operator should respond with something more than "It has been reported and resolved."
- **Keep the legal department in the loop.** Since they may get involved in prosecutions or other matters based on hotline calls, the enterprise's legal department should be kept very aware of hotline activities; they might be managing investigations or actions for others. They should be a strong supporter and ally for any enterprise hotline function.

An enterprise hotline function should be more than just something to support SOx whistleblower rules. If such a facility has already been installed and is in operation, an enterprise might want to expand its scope to ensure that the operators are aware of and can respond to and follow-up on SOx-related calls. When launching such a facility to assist with SOx compliance, the scope of the hotline should be promoted and expanded to cover the many human resources, code of conduct violations, and other issues that are often individual stakeholder concerns.

BUILDING AN ENTERPRISE-WIDE ETHICAL CULTURE

While many SOx issues, such as having an audit committee "financial expert" or implementing Committee of Sponsoring Organizations (COSO) internal controls, should be fairly easily managed regardless of enterprise size, the SOx whistleblower requirements discussed in Chapter 7 and the hotline whistleblower call-resolution processes discussed in this chapter could present a challenge for many enterprises. Effective compliance here requires sending a message throughout the enterprise that interested persons have a right to ask questions and to raise issues on what they think they have observed as improper actions. Implementing these matters means more than sets of published corporate directives; it requires refreshing the overall corporate culture based on an understanding of ethics and best practices.

Implementation of any enterprise-wide initiative requires leadership. While the CEO and other senior managers can deliver the message of the importance of initiatives here, there must be some direct leadership to implement things. Often, internal audit can play a lead role here, and this certainly would be a responsibility of the somewhat-new chief compliance officer (CCO) function discussed in the chapter. The level of compliance—especially for a hotline whistleblower program—depends on how much time and cost the enterprise wants to devote to this area, ranging from minimal compliance to a well-designed program. For many enterprises that have not yet designated a CCO function, the *chief audit executive* (CAE) coupled, perhaps, with the head of human resources might be the key resources to launch a SOx ethics and whistleblower compliance program with an emphasis on the following areas:

- Corporate mission statement and code of conduct
- Ethics and whistleblower training
- Implementing the whistleblower program
- Keeping SOx programs current and active

Corporate Mission Statement and Code of Conduct

Every enterprise, no matter how big or small, needs a mission statement to describe its overall objectives and values. It should be a source of direction—a compass—to let employees, customers, stockholders, and other stakeholders know what the enterprise stands for and what it does not. Once little more than a nice but tired-sounding slogan, an effective mission statement today is very important in our current era of SOx compliance and good corporate governance. An effective mission statement can be a great asset to an enterprise, enabling it to better achieve its overall goals and purposes.

A good mission statement should make a positive statement about an enterprise; it should inspire stakeholders to harness their energy and passion and increase their commitment to achieving goals and objectives. The idea is to create a sense of purpose and direction that will be shared throughout the enterprise. Going back some years ago, perhaps one of the better examples of a mission statement was expressed by U.S. president John F. Kennedy in the early 1960s:

> *This nation should dedicate itself to achieving the goal, before this decade is out, of landing a man on the moon and returning him safely to Earth.*

Those simple words describe a mission and vision much better than an extensive document of many pages. Sometimes called *values statements* or *credos*, examples of these statements can be found in the annual reports of many enterprises. Some are lengthy while others seem to be little more than fluff. The best are closer to the above moon-landing statement in their style.

Once an enterprise has developed a new mission statement or has revised an existing one, it should be rolled out to all enterprise stakeholders with a good level of publicity. Using a tone-at-the-top approach, senior managers should explain the reasons for the new mission statement and why it will be important for the enterprise. The mission statement should be posted prominently on facility billboards, in the annual report, as standard clicks on Internet home pages, and in other places to encourage all stakeholders to understand and accept it. That mission statement should not just stand by itself. A series of other key steps are needed to build an effective ethics and compliance function, starting with surveys and other mechanisms to build an effective ethics and compliance function.

While a mission statement is a keystone to hold together the overall structure of corporate governance, the code of conduct provides the supporting rules for enterprise stakeholders. Although these codes have been in place at major enterprises for many years, SOx requires that enterprises must develop a "code of ethics" for their senior financial officers to promote the honest and ethical handling of any conflicts of interest and their compliance with applicable governmental rules and regulations. The issuance of this code of ethics is to be disclosed in the enterprise's periodic financial reports, and a financial officer's willful violation of that signed code could result in personal criminal penalties. While the SOx financial officer–level code is mandated, an enterprise's code should cover all stakeholders. While SOx uses the expression *code of ethics*, we refer to it here by a common name, the *enterprise code of conduct*.

The effective enterprise today should develop and enforce a code of conduct that covers appropriate ethical, business, and legal rules for all enterprise stakeholders, including the financial officers highlighted in SOx. Also discussed in Chapter 2 as well, a code of conduct should be a clear, unambiguous set of rules or guidance that outlines what is expected of all members of the enterprise, whether officers, employees, contractors, vendors, or any other stakeholders. The code should be based on both the values and legal issues surrounding an enterprise. That is, while all enterprises can expect to have code-of-conduct prohibitions against sexual and racial discrimination, a contractor with many defense contract–related rules or issues would have a somewhat different code of conduct than a large fast-food multi-restaurant operation. However, any such code should apply to all members of the respective enterprise from the most senior level to the part-time clerical employee. A code-of-conduct rule prohibiting erroneous financial reporting should be the same whether directed at the chief financial officer (CFO) for incorrect financial reporting or at the part-timer for an incorrect or fraudulent weekly timecard.

Codes of conduct should be kept current and relevant, with ensuring SOx compliance being an appropriate time to revisit that code. All too often in the past, these codes were originally drafted as rules for the lower-level employees with little attention given to the more senior members of an enterprise. While SOx code-of-conduct rules are more focused on senior enterprise officers, they really should apply to all enterprise stakeholders. Working with senior members of management and the audit committee, an enterprise should examine its existing code of conduct to determine if its rules still fit in our post-SOx era of today. Of course, if an enterprise has never really drafted and implanted a code of conduct or has some long-forgotten and meaningless document, this is the time to develop and implement a code of conduct that applies to all levels of stakeholders and broadcasts a strong message to them.

As discussed, SOx requires that all enterprises have a code of conduct for their senior financial officers. No matter the enterprise size, such a code should be developed, communicated, and accepted by all members of the enterprise. Beyond the SOx accounting and internal control financial fraud issues, a general code of conduct will outline the rules to all stakeholders. There are consultants available to help draft such materials, but the key managers for most enterprises should be able to develop their own code based on their business, its issues, and what they feel should be right or wrong. The idea is to lay out a set of guidance rules outlining rights and wrongs for the enterprise.

No matter how small the enterprise, once the code has been released, all stakeholders should be asked to formally acknowledge their knowledge, understanding, and acceptance of the code. This affirms to them the rules of right and wrong in business dealings. These code topics will also be the basis of the matters that may be reported through the previously discussed hotline function. A code of conduct is an important overall management tool that should help enhance overall SOx compliance.

Ethics and Whistleblower Training

Managers responsible for SOx's accounting, internal control, and auditing process areas should have the goal to promote good ethical behavior such that most SOx whistleblower issues are reported only for true accounting and internal control matters, and that they are reported to the corporation's whistleblower hotline or help facility rather than to regulators or outside lawyers. A key strategy to promote this behavior is stakeholder training, and a series of formal training programs should be launched to promote ethics-related behavior and the availability of the enterprise's whistleblower program. Key things to consider for this ethics and whistleblower training include:

- The training should be more than a management-level speech about the "new rules" and the need to follow them.

- There should be a strong statement that senior management has endorsed and expects all employees to follow the ethics program. This is the tone-at-the-top message we have mentioned several times.
- Specific whistleblower rules should be outlined, including how to report matters and how they will be resolved. In addition, it must be emphasized that there will be no retribution to whistleblowers.
- The training should focus on ethical-dilemma types of issues, where there is no easy right or wrong answer, but where the employee is expected to do the right thing. *Doing the right thing* should be an ongoing program message.
- While larger enterprises will often launch multiple levels of training sessions for various groups of employees, the smaller enterprise can be just as successful with a single session that covers the entire enterprise from executive levels to the shop floor.

Ethics and whistleblower training is an effective way to launch these SOx-related initiatives. It should not be treated as a one-time endeavor but presented periodically, perhaps once a year, to keep the ethics program familiar with all members of the enterprise.

Implementing the Whistleblower Program

An employee training program, just discussed, is needed to launch an ethics and whistleblower program in an enterprise. However, an even greater requirement should be to establish a resource for the receipt and disposition of any whistleblower calls. The hotline function discussed previously is appropriate for a larger organization but may be too much for the smaller enterprise. Whistleblowers need a facility to anonymously report any such concerns, and for some it may be appropriate to outsource this facility, with a variety of service functions that provide telephone banks for reporting such matters. These providers, easily located through a Web search for "Sarbanes-Oxley whistleblower," will assign a requesting enterprise a toll-free hotline number supported by round-the-clock trained agents to answer whistleblower calls. Their services should provide regular reports to a designated contact person in the subscribing company for investigation and resolution.

Whether performed by an in-house function or outside provider, investigation, resolution, and whistleblower confidentiality are key factors in the success of this process. That designated hotline contact person mentioned above must be someone who can totally preserve the whistleblower's confidentiality with no hint of retribution. The whole idea here is to have an inside function that stakeholders will trust. Such a facility may discourage some from lodging whistleblower issues with outside regulatory or legal authorities.

Keeping SOx Programs Current and Active

Once launched, enterprises of any size need to keep their ethics and whistleblower programs current and active. This can be an even greater problem for the smaller enterprise that does not have sufficient resources to assign to the program or to even one individual. The team that originally launched this program should review the program on an annual basis by revisiting and updating the code of conduct and assessing the progress or problems with the hotline whistleblower program.

We have suggested some action steps to launch an ethics and SOx whistleblower program. A formal compliance function or internal audit often can be key resources in making these things happen as either of these resources typically has exposure to all levels of the enterprise. Also, internal audit will have regular contact with the audit committee, through frequent reports and meetings, as well as with key financial management.

CHIEF COMPLIANCE OFFICER ROLES AND RESPONSIBILITIES

The 2002 SOx legislation does not specify or suggest who in a registrant enterprise should implement and monitor compliance with the many new SOx rules and procedures. In the first years of establishing compliance, some enterprises established special groups as part of their financial management function; some used internal audit to provide this help, while still others hired outside consultants to perform much of the work. Each of these help resources have tended to be one-time approaches, and an enterprise needs some type of ongoing facility to maintain compliance going forward. SOx is just not going away any time soon. Some things have been simplified, such as the new AS5 rules discussed in Chapter 3, and we have developed better approaches to document and understand SOx internal controls, such as the use of the CobiT framework discussed in Chapter 5. However, an enterprise needs some type of resource—a point person—to monitor and manage SOx compliance as well as compliance with the many other rules impacting enterprises today.

Enterprises today are increasingly establishing the position of chief compliance officier (CCO) as a resource and function to review and manage compliance with SOx and the many other rules impacting an enterprise. This is or should be a *C-level position* in an enterprise. This expression refers to the CFO, a corporate officer, and other chiefs or heads of major corporate functions, such as the CAE. The head of internal audit position is often not a corporate officer, but someone who has a reporting relationship with senior corporate officers. The CAE, for example, will have a very close reporting relationship with the chair of the audit committee and may report to the CFO for administrative purposes.

A CCO oversees the overall enterprise *compliance program*, which functions as an independent and objective body that reviews and evaluates compliance issues/concerns within the organization. The position has an objective of ensuring that the board of directors, senior management, and all stakeholders are in compliance with the rules and regulations of appropriate regulatory agencies, that enterprise policies and procedures are being followed, and that behavior in the organization meets the enterprise's code of conduct. The CCO and its supporting Compliance Office exists:

- As a channel of communication to receive and direct compliance issues to appropriate resources for investigation and resolution
- As a final internal resource with which concerned parties may communicate after other formal channels and resources have been exhausted

A typical CCO acts as staff to the CEO with a strong relationship to board and its audit committee. A CCO should monitor and report on the results of the compliance/ethics efforts in the enterprise and provide guidance for the board and the senior management team on all matters relating to compliance, whether SOx or other regulatory issues. The CCO, together with a supporting Corporate Compliance Committee, would be authorized to implement all necessary actions to ensure achievement of the objectives of an effective compliance program.

Still a new position for many enterprises, the CCO typically develops, initiates, maintains, and revises policies and procedures for the general operation of an enterprise compliance program and its related activities to prevent illegal, unethical, or improper conduct. A CCO manages day-to-day operations of many compliance programs, with an emphasis on SOx, and develops, periodically reviews, and updates the enterprise's code of conduct to ensure continuing currency and relevance in providing guidance to management and all stakeholders.

A CCO collaborates with other enterprise functions including risk management, internal audit, and human resources to direct compliance issues to appropriate existing channels for investigation and resolution. In addition, a CCO should consult with the enterprise legal staff as needed to resolve difficult legal compliance issues. The CCO should respond to alleged violations of rules, regulations, policies, procedures, and code-of-conduct issues, often highlighted by the hotline function's reported calls, by evaluating or recommending the initiation of investigative procedures. In addition, a CCO should develop and oversee a system for uniform handling of such violations.

Properly organized and structured, the staff of the CCO should act as an independent review and evaluation body to ensure that compliance issues and concerns within the enterprise are being appropriately evaluated, investigated, and resolved. As part of this, a CCO should monitor, and as necessary, coordinate compliance activities of other enterprise departments to remain abreast of the status of all compliance activities and to identify trends. The CCO should identify potential areas of compliance vulnerability and risk, should develop and implement corrective action plans for the resolution of problematic issues, and should provide general guidance on how to avoid or deal with similar situations in future periods.

A CCO should provide reports on a regular basis, and as directed or requested, keep the Corporate Compliance Committee of the board and senior management informed of the operation and progress of compliance efforts. We have referenced a board Corporate Compliance Committee here, but if a Compliance Committee has not been established this would be the audit committee. Just as we should be seeing more CCO functions in enterprises in the future, we may also see a growing number of board Corporate Compliance Committees.

Other responsibilities of a CCO should be to ensure the proper reporting of violations or potential violations to duly authorized enforcement agencies as appropriate or required, and to establish and provide direction and management of the compliance hotline. A CCO should institute and maintain an effective compliance communication program for the enterprise, including promoting use of the compliance hotline and heightened awareness of the enterprise's code of conduct, and understanding new and existing compliance issues and related policies and procedures.

In addition, a CCO should work with human resources and others as appropriate to develop an effective compliance training program, including introductory training for new employees as well as ongoing training for all employees and managers. The CCO would monitor the performance of the enterprise's overall compliance program and relate these activities on a continuing basis, taking appropriate steps to improve its effectiveness.

The CCO is a new responsibility in today's enterprises. We currently see this position most frequently in enterprises with high regulatory responsibilities beyond just SOx. For example, banking and financial services enterprises are all facing a wide range of regulatory and compliance requirements. The role of a CCO along with a dedicated staff to monitor and help with compliance implementations can be very valuable. We shall almost certainly see more CCOs in years to come.

BOARD OF DIRECTORS AND THE AUDIT COMMITTEE

The board of directors is the ultimate manager of all stockholder/investor-owned enterprises as well as for most large private organizations. Directors may be either elected stockholders, known as outside or nonemployee directors, or very senior members of management, called inside or employee directors. With their overall tenures in office and general responsibilities based on established corporate charter documents, boards of directors are charged with independently reviewing and approving all major decisions for the enterprises they manage. They are the independent managing representatives for the stockholders, with a responsibility to make major decisions for the corporation based on their assessment of the risks and potential benefits presented to them.

Board responsibilities and actions are further divided into a series of specialized board member committees. For example, there will be a nominations committee to select new board candidates for upcoming shareholder elections and a compensation committee to look after the needs of senior management. Perhaps the most significant of these committees for SOx and corporate governance purposes is the audit committee—independent directors whose responsibilities include but are not limited to:

- Selecting and coordinating the work of the independent accountants
- Managing and reviewing the work of internal auditors
- Reviewing and approving the financial results of the enterprise
- Taking overall responsibility for internal accounting controls

SOx introduced a large number of changes to boards and their audit committees. As another example and not mandated by SOx, our prior discussion of the CCO position suggested the need for a board-level compliance committee.

Because of their oversight responsibilities, audit committee members must be independent directors with no connection to organization management. There are no size restrictions, but a full board with perhaps 12 to 16 members will often have a five- or six-member audit committee. An audit committee may invite members of management or others to attend audit committee meetings and even to join in on the committee's deliberations. However, any such invited outside guests cannot be full voting members. An organization's board of directors is a formal entity given the responsibility for the overall governance of that organization for its investors or lenders. Because all members of the board can be held legally liable through their actions on any issue, a board and its committees enact most of its formal business through resolutions, which become matters of organization record.

The board of directors and its individual members are a level above organization senior management and somewhat beyond the organization charts and procedures that most employees encounter. New members of a typical board are recruited through existing board members or major investors and are officially elected by the stockholders at an annual meeting. While major investors, bankers, and the CEO often have a role in recruiting board members, the board and a majority of the stockholders make essentially all major decisions. The board can make all major decisions for the enterprise, including even terminating the CEO. Public corporation board governance procedures and other operating procedures are essential for assessing and dealing with risks. Beyond senior corporate officers, most corporation employees—with the exception of internal audit—have little contact with their boards of directors beyond seeing a face in the annual report. It is valuable for all employees and managers to understand how their boards operate and how they manage operations and risks.

Boards and Audit Committees in Today's SOx World

When the SOx legislation was being drafted, there were major attempts to find out what or who had been wrong or was "not minding the store" to cause then-major corporations, such as Enron and WorldCom, to fail in a sea of accounting misdeeds. One prominent casualty was the American Institute of Certified Public Accountants' (AICPA's) role in setting auditing standards and reviewing the public accounting auditing process. The failure of their self-governing auditing governance processes resulted in the Public Company Accounting Oversight Board (PCAOB), the auditing regulatory authority introduced in Chapter 2. There were strong feelings then that board governance processes needed to be fixed as well, and SOx is filled with new rules and requirements covering boards and their audit committees.

Another major criticism that was raised after the fall of Enron was that many board audit committee members did not appear to understand the financial and internal control issues that they were overseeing. People were elected to board audit committees because of their business or professional backgrounds but often did not understand complex or even basic financial accounting or internal control issues. SOx attempted to fix this. As was summarized in Chapter 2, SOx requires that at least one audit committee independent director be what SOx called a "financial expert" with some specific knowledge requirements for that role. These new rules have really heightened the responsibilities and activities of corporate boards and their audit committees.

SOx has introduced some major changes to board governance practices and has certainly made the typical board member very busy. Serving on a board of directors now requires a major personal and professional commitment for a board member. This is an area where SOx has brought major improvements to corporate governance.

ASSESSING SOX INTERNAL CONTROLS

SOx was introduced to major business enterprises in the United States, and its provisions have gradually begun to encompass entities worldwide and of all sizes. In addition to some tough new rules introduced by SOx, its passage has led to massive new compliance requirements and changes in the way we conduct business operations. As we wrap up this book, it may be an appropriate time for an enterprise to assess how it is doing with its level of compliance in this new environment.

These past chapters have discussed changes to many of the initial SOx-era compliance rules, such as AS5 discussed in Chapter 3, making our evaluation of internal controls more risk-based, and evolving new standards, such as the information technology infrastructure library (ITIL) framework and ISO 17799 (in Chapters 8 and 10, respectively) that make internal control procedures more measurable and easy to track. Because there is a mass of other new compliance guidelines that do not apply for everyone, we have all but ignored many of these other compliance requirements. An enterprise needs to know which regulations impact it, where it stands in compliance with these rules, and what procedures are in place to monitor current and ongoing compliance. This reference to compliance with the rules has two dimensions. Some of these are effectively legal requirements, such as SOx Section 404 rules, where an enterprise needs to establish effective internal accounting controls in order to receive audited financial statements for SEC reporting and the investing public. Other compliance rules are voluntary and are based on a business decision. For example, an enterprise does not have to follow ITIL best practices or the CobiT control framework, but our discussions of these areas hopefully point to their multiple advantages.

Business compliance today requires a lot more than a CEO passing out a directive that all units of an enterprise must be in compliance with all applicable laws and regulations by some designated target date. A good first step is to establish a CCO function, as discussed previously, or to form a high-level compliance committee composed of representatives from finance, legal, internal audit, and key operating units. Either should have a strong dotted-line reporting relationship to the audit committee. Starting with an organizing round of sessions and then with ongoing periodic reviews, the compliance committee should address the following:

- What are the key legal requirements impacting the enterprise and what is the current level of compliance?
- For those requirements where compliance is less than adequate, what processes are in place to achieve compliance and what are the risks of noncompliance?
- Beyond legal requirements, what procedures should the enterprise be following and what are the compliance or noncompliance trade-offs with these?
- What are the evolving legal compliance and best practice standards trends that might impact the enterprise, and what steps are being taken to monitor and take any required actions?

These questions are very high level, but they emphasize that an enterprise today must monitor and accept these evolving new compliance rules and best practices procedures. An effective internal audit function might be the best resource to play a leadership role in performing periodic compliance audits regarding these standards.

In addition to just monitoring compliance, the CCO function, the compliance committee, or an effective internal audit function should make every effort to embrace these newer, evolving standards in their ongoing reviews and communications with management. This means developing a strong understanding of the three topic areas that make up part of the title of this book: AS5, CobiT, and ITIL. AS5 is important to the external auditors who will be reviewing internal accounting controls, but its risk-based rules should provide a framework for much of our ongoing evaluations of internal accounting controls. While certainly not a required framework methodology, CobiT provides a useful tool to measure and understand internal controls. Finally, ITIL should be considered as something more than just procedures within the traditional "computer room"; it is a set of very important service management best practices that will help an enterprise today to meet and even exceed these compliance requirements in a cost-effective manner.